The Limits *of*
PROTECTIONISM

Building Coalitions for Free Trade

M I C H A E L   L U S Z T I G

U N I V E R S I T Y   O F   P I T T S B U R G H   P R E S S

Published by the University of Pittsburgh Press, Pittsburgh, Pa., 15260
Copyright © 2004, University of Pittsburgh Press
All rights reserved
Manufactured in the United States of America
Printed on acid-free paper
10 9 8 7 6 5 4 3 2 1
ISBN 0-8229-5843-0

Library of Congress Cataloging-in-Publication Data
Lusztig, Michael, 1962–
    The limits of protectionism : building coalitions for free trade /
Michael Lusztig
    p. cm.
Includes bibliographical references and index.
    ISBN 0-8229-5843-0 (pbk. : alk. paper)
    1. Protectionism. 2. Free trade. 3. Free trade—Government policy.
4. Free trade—Political aspects. I. Title.
    HF1713.L868 2004
    382'.71—dc22   2003027099

To Anika, Chrissy, Madison, Mitchell, Owen, Ryder, and Simon

Contents

Tables and Figures

Acknowledgments

Oftentimes books get started long before the metaphorical pen is set to paper. Such was the case with this one, which came out of a heated debate with a professor in graduate school many years ago. A good deal of time and money were needed to see the idea through to print. Money was the more important. This book could not have been written without the generous financial assistance of the Social Sciences and Humanities Research Council of Canada, which funded this project under the auspices of grant number 410-96-0257. In addition, the University of Western Ontario contributed to this project, both through its federal work-study program and a Vice-President's Grant. Finally, I am grateful to the John G. Tower Center for Political Studies at Southern Methodist University for its financial support. All this monetary support was put to excellent use: the book could not have been completed without first-rate research assistance. My thanks go to Miriam Desjardins, Erin Eckols, Mike Edwards, Lauren Johnson, Laura Stephenson, Nicole Vaz, and Steve Whiting. A special debt of gratitude is owed to Laura Stephenson, who, in addition to putting hundreds of hours into research assistance, coordinated the activities of many of the other RAs. An entire filing cabinet full of photocopies stands as testament to Laura's incredible dedication.

In addition to time and money, this project relied on the brains of others. Countless friends and colleagues took the time to read all or parts of this manuscript and to make important intellectual contributions. For their assistance I am grateful to Paul Brace, James Brander, Mark Brawley, Ian Brodie, Christine Carberry, Peter Dombrowski, Jeffrey Frieden, Patrick James, Douglas Lemke, Nathan MacBrien, Barbi McClennen, Hudson Meadwell, Philip Oxhorn, James Lee Ray, Laura Stephenson, and two anonymous reviewers at the University of Pittsburgh Press. In addition to making a helpful intellectual contribution to the manuscript, Nathan MacBrien and Deborah Meade at the University of Pittsburgh Press rendered the review and publication process incredibly fast and hassle free. Christine Carberry and

Trish Weisman spent hours proofing the manuscript and suggesting innumerable changes. The book could not have been completed without the selfless support of any of them. An early version of the idea contained in this book was published as "The Limits of Rent-Seeking: Why Protectionists Become Free Traders," *Review of International Political Economy* 5 (1998). I am grateful to Taylor and Francis (www.tandf.co.uk) for their very liberal permissions policy.

The final ingredients that went into this book were patience and forbearance. I supplied neither. I extend a huge debt of gratitude to my wife, Chrissy, who, in addition to the intellectual and logistical support noted earlier, provided all the requisite residual support as well. I am deeply grateful to her for this and so many other things.

Acronyms

AAA	Agricultural Adjustment Act (U.S.)
ABM	Asociación de Banqueros de México (Association of Mexican Bankers)
ACM	Australian Chamber of Manufacturers
ACMA	Associated Chambers of Manufacturers of Australia
ALP	Australian Labour Party
AMC	Australian Manufacturing Council
AMIB	Asociación Mexicana de Intermediarios Bursátiles (Mexican Securities Industry Association)
AMIS	Asociación Mexicana de Instituciones de Seguros (Association of Mexican Insurance Institutions)
ANZCERTA	Australia–New Zealand Closer Economic Relations Trade Agreement (see also CER)
APEC	Asia-Pacific Economic Cooperation
ARENA	Aliança Renovadora Nacional (National Alliance for Renewal; Brazil)
ATFNZ	Apparel and Textile Federation of New Zealand
BCNI	Business Council on National Issues (Canada)
BNDE	Banco Nacional de Desenvolvimento Econômico (Bank for National Economic Development; Brazil)
CACEX	Carteira de Comércio Exterior (Foreign Trade Agency, Bank of Brazil)
CAI	Confederation of Australian Industry
CANACINTRA	Cámara Nacional de la Industria de Transformación (National Chamber of Manufacturing Industry; Mexico)
CCE	Consejo Coordinador Empresarial (Business Coordinating Council; Mexico)
CER	Closer Economic Relations (see also ANZCERTA)
CET	Common External Tariff

CFIB	Canadian Federation of Independent Business
CIBA	Council for International Business Affairs (Australia)
CMA	Canadian Manufacturers' Association
CMNH	Consejo Mexicano de Hombres de Negocios (Mexican Businessmen's Council)
CNA	Consejo Nacional Agropecuario (National Agriculture and Livestock Council; Mexico)
CNI	Confederação Nacional de Indústrial (National Industrial Confederation; Brazil)
COECE	Coordinadora de Organismos Empresariales de Comercio Exterior (Coordinating Body of Foreign Trade Business Associations; Mexico)
CONCAMIN	Confederación de Cámaras Industriales (National Confederation of Industrial Chambers; Mexico)
CONCANACO	Confederación de Cámaras Nacionales de Comercio (National Confederation of Chambers of Commerce; Mexico)
CONMIA	Confederation of Manufacturing Industry Associations (Australia)
COPARMEX	Confederación Patronal de la República Mexicana (Employers' Confederation of the Republic of Mexico)
CORFO	Corporacíon de Fomento de la Produccíon (Chilean Development Corporation)
COSB	Canadian Association of Small Business
CPC	Confederación de la Producción y Comercio (Confederation for Production and Commerce; Chile)
CRI	Committee for Reciprocity Information (U.S.)
CUFTA	Canada–U.S. Free Trade Agreement
DECEX	Departmento de Comércio Exterior (Foreign Trade Department, Bank of Brazil)
DFAT	Department of Foreign Affairs and Trade (Australia)
DUP	Directly unproductive profit seeking
EEC	European Economic Community
EPTI	Export Performance Taxation Incentive (New Zealand)
FTAA	Free Trade Area of the Americas
GATT	General Agreement on Tariffs and Trade
GDP	Gross domestic product
GNP	Gross national product
IAC	Industries Assistance Commission (Australia)

IC	Industries Commission (Australia)
IMF	International Monetary Fund
ISI	Import-Substituting Industrialization
ISIC	International Standard Industrial Classification
Manfed	Manufacturers' Federation (New Zealand)
MDB	Movimento Democrático Brasileiro (Movement for a Democratic Brazil)
MERCOSUR	Mercado Común del Sur (Common Market of the South)
MP	Member of Parliament
MTIA	Metal Trades Industry Association (Australia)
MTN	Multilateral Trade Negotiation (also called Tokyo Round of the GATT)
NAFTA	New Zealand–Australia Free Trade Agreement
NAFTA	North American Free Trade Agreement
NAM	National Association of Manufacturers (U.S.)
NEP	National Energy Programme (Canada)
NIRA	National Industrial Recovery Act (U.S.)
NTB	Nontariff barrier
OECD	Organisation for Economic Co-operation and Development
OPEC	Organization of Petroleum Exporting Countries
PAN	Partido Acción Nacional (National Action Party; Mexico)
PDC	Partido Demócrata Cristiano (Christian Democratic Party; Chile)
PDS	Partido Democrático Social (Social Democratic Party; Brazil)
PECE	Pacto para la Estabilidad y el Crecimiento Economico (Pact for Economic Growth and Stability; Mexico)
PICE	Programa de Integración y Cooperación Económica (Program of Integration and Cooperation; Brazil and Argentina)
PMV	Passenger motor vehicle
PND II	Plano Nacional de Desenvolvimento II (Second National Development Plan; Brazil)
PQ	Parti Québécois (Canada)
PRD	Partido de la Revolución Democrática (Party of the Democratic Revolution; Mexico)
PRI	Partido Revolucionario Institucional (Institutional Revolutionary Party; Mexico)

PRONAFICE	Programa Nacional de Fomento Industrial y Comercio Exterior (Program to Promote Industrialization and Foreign Commerce; Mexico)
PRONASOL	Programa Nacional de Solidaridad (Program of National Solidarity; Mexico)
PSE	Pacto de Solidaridad Económica (Economic Solidarity Pact; Mexico)
RTAA	Reciprocal Trade Agreements Act (U.S.)
SAA	Special Advisory Authority (Australia)
SECOFI	Secretaria de Comercio y Fomento Industrial (Secretariat of Trade and Industrial Development; Mexico)
SITC	Standard Industrial Trade Classification
TAA	Temporary Assistance Authority (Australia)
TAC	Trade Agreements Committee (U.S.)
TCF	Textiles, clothing, and footwear
TCS	Tariff Concessions System (Australia)
TMA	Tripartite Monetary Agreement (U.S.)
TPA	Trade Promotion Authority (U.S.)
WTO	World Trade Organization

1

The Limits of Rent Seeking
A Prescriptive Model

> People of the same trade seldom meet together, even
> for merriment and diversion, but the conversation
> ends in a conspiracy against the public, or in some
> contrivance to raise prices.
>
> ADAM SMITH, *The Wealth of Nations*

It has become a cliché in these troubling times to note that freedom does not
come for free. The logic extends into the realm of trade. The price for free
global markets is sometimes paid by politicians whose enthusiasm for the
economic benefits leads them to underestimate the political costs. More
often, risk-averse politicians eschew the benefits of trade, fearing electoral
sanction. This risk aversion, however, imposes opportunity costs of its own.
There is little debate among economists that free trade is, in the aggregate,
economically beneficial. It expands firms' productive capacities, encourages
specialization and efficiency in the productive sector, and broadens consumer choice while subjugating prices to the rigor of market competition. It
provides incentives for innovation and stimulates foreign investment. It creates jobs and, with time, raises wages. Free trade fosters economic interdependence between nations and hence creates disincentives for trading states
to escalate conflicts. Economically speaking at least, under most conditions
free trade represents a dominant strategy for states seeking to maximize aggregate wealth.

    A significant problem, however, is that the economic benefits of free trade are not well understood by the general (and voting) public. Free trade might be generally advantageous, but it is not a vote getter; often, in fact, it is a vote loser. Free traders have a much harder time getting out their message than do protectionists. One reason is that there are obvious dislocation costs associated with free trade. Plants close, workers lose jobs, local economies are badly hurt. These are the sorts of human-event stories that are tailor-made for the evening news. Less interesting to viewers, and hence the media, are stories about the economic advantages inherent in Ricardo's theory of comparative advantage (1960), prospects for more favorable economies of scale, and the altered incentive structures for direct and portfolio foreign investment. Al Gore may have out-debated Ross Perot on CNN's *Larry King Live*,[1] but the most memorable event was Perot's earlier reference to the "giant sucking sound" that would be created as U.S. companies pulled up stakes and departed for Mexico to take advantage of labor-cost savings. Gore's own rhetorical stunt, presenting Perot with a framed photograph of the sponsors of the disastrous Smoot-Hawley Tariff of 1930, was not as effective. Nor, manifestly, was the logic that the North American Free Trade Agreement (NAFTA) did not create the low-wage economy and therefore was not terribly likely to have an overwhelming impact on plant closings in the United States. The point that stuck was that NAFTA would create a giant sucking sound.

More problematic for free trade is the fact that protectionist coalitions form far more readily than do advocacy groups. As students of international political economy and public choice theory have long maintained, free trade represents an asymmetric public good (Tullock 1967; Peltzman 1976; Becker 1983; Rowley and Tollison 1988; Lake 1988a; Baldwin 1989). While the aggregate benefits may outweigh the costs, the effects are unevenly distributed. The benefits of free trade are broad but latent. The costs, concentrated and manifest, are borne by a comparatively small number of producers who had enjoyed "rents" derived from the insulation of the domestic market. (Economists define a rent as the return on a factor of production in excess of its opportunity cost. For example, a rent may be thought of as the difference between a professional baseball player's salary and the optimal salary he could earn if not playing ball.) Consumers, often uninspired by (or unaware of) the link between free trade and marginal reductions in retail prices typically fail to man the metaphorical barricades in support of free trade. Protectionist producers—rent seekers—react differently; given the stakes involved, they can be relied on to mobilize for retention of such state-supplied rents as direct subsidies, tax breaks, or impediments to imports such as tariffs or nontariff barriers.[2] For their part, elected governments faced with the choice of appeasing indifferent consumers or belligerent producers have an obvious incentive to gratify the latter (see Lavergne 1983; Frey 1984; Lake 1988a; Tullock 1988; Baldwin 1989; Williamson 1994a).[3]

Governments generally are not indifferent to the economic benefits of free trade. A strong economy typically rewards incumbent officeholders. While the palliative effects of free trade are sufficiently delayed that only the most optimistic incumbents would plan to reap direct benefits, the negative economic effects of protectionism can weigh heavily on a country's economic performance. Even if trade liberalization is not directly politically rewarding, in other words, it may have powerful indirect political benefits. Voters do not necessarily have to know why the economy is performing well; it is enough that they recognize that it is. Finally, government leaders can be expected to look out for the best interests of the countries they govern. Provided that the price is not too high (such as sacrificing a political career), it must be assumed that many government leaders (1) have an interest in national aggregate wealth maximization and (2) recognize that free trade is an efficient means to this objective.[4]

Given that government leaders have an incentive to liberalize trade, it is of fundamental importance to determine circumstances under which trade can be liberalized without incurring excessive political cost. I believe that governments can minimize the political risks associated with significant liberalization of trade. I argue here that under certain conditions, rent-seeking opponents of trade liberalization actually may turn into critically important allies of governments attempting major policy shifts from protectionism to free trade. Where domestic rent seekers are persuaded that the government cannot or will not provide sufficient rents, rent seekers may pursue a second-most-preferred strategy that entails attempting to secure access to cheaper factor inputs and to foreign markets by actively supporting trade liberalization. This transformation of behavior on the part of rent seekers is a condition that can be exploited by adroit government actors, and a menu of options is presented here for governments that seek to reduce rents without suffering severe political backlash.

Free trade should not be presented as an optimal policy choice under all circumstances. I merely assume that, all things being equal, free trade is economically beneficial. This is not a heroic assumption, and countless others, from Ricardo onward, have justified it. That said, in assessing the rationality of any course of action, one must be cognizant of the desired ends. Free trade is sound policy if governments' objectives are to maximize aggregate levels of wealth. Of course, it is easy to imagine circumstances where governments have other first-order objectives. For example, where governments are more concerned with national security than wealth maximization, free trade becomes less attractive. Ricardian theory proves that the United States would be better served economically to import some of its strategic munitions from low-wage economies rather than produce them itself. For obvious reasons, however, this is unlikely to be a preferred choice. Similarly, as recent protests in Seattle, Genoa, and Quebec City have suggested, many believe (rightly or wrongly) that trade liberalization undermines other important objectives, including environmental protection and sovereignty of less-developed nations.

In addition, I do not assume that free trade will distribute wealth equitably. However, since free trade forces governments to stop redistributing wealth to the productive sector, there is an assumed progressive element to trade liberalization. Indeed, this is why free trade is so intimately tied to early liberal thought. But there is no guarantee that increasing aggregate wealth will benefit all equally or equitably. The worker whose job is sacrificed for the long-term health of his former employer's company or the economy at large takes cold comfort in economic theory. And it is not just workers who suffer real, human costs. Dislocation associated with free trade forces many businesses from the marketplace. A lifetime's work of building a business can be wiped out in a tidal surge of competition unleashed by free trade. Thus, I aim not to lose sight of the fact that the overall objective of freer trade is to maximize wealth, not to maximize justice.

The Costs of Rent Seeking

Economists have long been concerned with two related phenomena: monopoly (or collusive oligopoly) costs and activity that dissipates resources without productive benefit. The latter falls under the broad rubric of directly unproductive profit seeking (DUP),[5] a subset of which is rent seeking. The costs of monopoly are familiar to all students of elementary economics. The supply curve under monopoly conditions is artificially restricted, leading to less output and higher commodity prices than would have occurred under conditions of free competition. However, the literature on rent seeking, developed initially by Tullock (1967), suggests that the societal deadweight cost of monopolies is much higher. Indeed, the competition for monopoly rents, which includes lobbying and advertising as well as attendant personnel costs, constitutes a dissipation of resources that could otherwise have gone into more productive activity. As Brooks and Heijdra (1988, 32) suggest, "The basic explanation of why wealth-seeking behavior here generates waste is that individuals withdraw resources from some sector of the economy, and spend these resources on rent-seeking activities without at the same time expanding the output of the sector they wish to enter."[6]

In the aggregate, those in competition for monopoly rents often will allocate resources in excess of the total amount of the rents they seek to capture. (Here we can think of a lottery. The total money spent on tickets is greater than the total prize payout.) The opportunity costs for this competition are lost to society as a whole. Finally, as Krueger points out, rent seeking alters societal incentive structures, providing, for example, resource-diverting competition among those who seek personal utility by virtue of being in a position to supply monopoly rents.[7] Rent seeking in the trade policy arena involves largely the pursuit of monopoly or oligopoly rents in the form of barriers to import penetration and/or direct subsidies (see Lavergne 1983).

In sum, protectionist rent seeking tends to be inefficient. Devices such as tariffs, import licenses, quotas, and voluntary export restrictions impose deadweight costs onto society at large. Because it skews incentive structures within the marketplace, import protection diverts resources from sectors enjoying comparative advantage toward those that operate less efficiently (Ricardo 1960; Tullock 1967; Krueger 1974). An important qualification, however, concerns infant industries. Industries in newly developed countries, potentially competitive in world markets save for catch-up costs associated with late entry into the game, might efficiently be protected in the early years of their development. Such protection represents an investment in the prospect for long-term competitiveness of the new industry. Most industrializing countries, therefore, have allowed their nascent manufacturing sectors to develop behind tariff walls.[8]

Nevertheless, such a strategy has the potential to generate negative byproducts. Domestic protectionism provides incentives for producers to emerge in sectors that suffer comparative disadvantage. In many cases, such producers can exist only as long as the state provides sufficient import protection. Even for industries in other, potentially more competitive sectors, import protection may discourage innovation, quality control, efficiency, and international competitiveness. As long as production for the domestic market is profitable, there may be no incentive to assume the risks and costs of restructuring operations to compete in world markets. Indeed, inertia may prolong protectionist policies even after they become suboptimal. Goldstein (1993a, 226) points to postwar opposition by American farmers to agricultural trade liberalization under the General Agreement on Tariffs and Trade (GATT) as an example. Insofar as American farmers were internationally competitive in the 1940s, the failure to liberalize agricultural trade under the GATT meant that foreign markets, potentially receptive to American agricultural exports, were rendered less accessible. In short, protectionist strategies designed to provide temporary shelter for infant industries become institutionalized, and governments seeking to reduce tariff rates face opposition from powerful domestic rent seekers.[9] It is for this reason that departure from the tradition of protectionism is so difficult politically. As Anderson and Garnaut (1986, 171) put it, "Producer groups in each industry can be viewed as the demanders of protection for their industry, and political leaders as the suppliers. It seems reasonable to assume . . . that political leaders tend to adopt policies so as to maximize their chances of remaining in office, while groups who expect to gain (lose) from a particular policy seek (oppose) its adoption by investing in lobbying and propagandising up to the point where they perceive that expected net benefits from further expenditure are zero."

Conversely, because radical shifts toward trade liberalization do occur, it is clear that the policy is not wholly intractable. Moreover, experience shows that countries that open their economies to external competition often are able to maintain free trade while fighting only limited rearguard battles with domestic rent seekers. Indeed, under such circumstances, former protectionists often tend to be in the forefront of the fight for further liberalization of trade, and at the very least offer little resistance to freer trade.

I have two objectives here: (1) to explain the conditions under which formerly protectionist interests become free traders and (2) to identify a prescriptive means by which risk-averse governments can engage in difficult trade policy decisions, while assuming a minimum of political cost and risk. I offer the limits of rent seeking model to explain behavioral changes—both individual and aggregate—among rent seekers and the rent-seeker population. Case studies illustrate the process by which governments are able to induce and predict certain behavioral characteristics on the part of rent seekers.

The Limits of Rent Seeking

The limits of rent seeking argument can be made most clearly in ideal-typical terms (see also Lusztig 1998). Imagine a world in which producers have two means of creating profits. They can dedicate resources to competition in world markets (call this adjustment); alternatively, they can seek rents in the pursuit of a protected domestic market in which they are well placed to secure a pertinent market share (call this rent seeking).[10] Given this profit-making dichotomy, it is possible to construct for each producer an indifference curve between expected utility from adjustment and from rent seeking. Each producer implicitly selects a production strategy that entails a degree of adjustment and a degree of rent seeking. Some firms, of course, will adopt an asymptotic position, eschewing in any meaningful sense one strategy or the other.

Points selected by individual producers on the indifference curve will largely be a function of circumstances such as past history, relations with the state, changes in technology and market opportunities, risk acceptance, and even inertia. Of course, a producer's decision in selecting the optimum production point also is influenced by the cost of adjustment relative to the cost of rent seeking. Where protection is relatively cheap, more producers will prefer production points that involve limited adjustment; by the same logic, where protection is relatively expensive (that is, where governments are less inclined to grant rents), a larger share of the producer population will opt for production points involving a greater degree of adjustment.

Producers who select production points involving a good deal of adjustment can be expected, broadly speaking, to support trade liberalization initiatives. Adjustment typically entails increased reliance on low-cost factor inputs (e.g., labor and unfinished goods), many of which may be imported, as well as reciprocal access to export markets. Those more reliant on state-supplied rents are classified as protectionist rent seekers and are of more immediate interest.

Within the rent-seeker population, and again imposing ideal-typical classifications, we can suppose a further dichotomy. One category of rent seeker consists of domestic producers whose capital is immobile and who have invested in sectors that, due to competitive and comparative disadvantages, could not possibly compete internationally. These producers, in other words, select a production point heavily skewed in favor of rent seeking. For them, should there be a dramatic increase in cost or decrease in availability of state-supplied rents, the results would be disastrous, the degree of requisite adjustment prohibitive. A mythical and extreme example would be olive farmers in Finland. Theoretically (given large and expensive greenhouses), such producers could survive, but they would require enormous state-supplied rents. Should these rents be significantly reduced, such producers would be unable to survive import competition and would be forced to exit the market. These producers are styled inflexible rent seekers. For them, state-supplied rents are necessary for survival.

The second ideal-typical category of rent seeker also prefers rent seeking to adjustment but conceivably could restructure operations to compete internationally. Although there are costs involved, such producers, by virtue of enjoying fairly mobile capital and relatively cheap access to critical factor inputs, could substitute profits from adjustment for profits from rent seeking should the costs of protection rise significantly or the environment in which they find themselves change dramatically. These are flexible rent seekers. Akin to the idle adolescent who prefers a parental allowance to getting the metaphorical haircut and job, flexible rent seekers are those who will not starve if forced to survive by earning their living in the free market. Of course, upon choosing to adjust to increased import penetration, flexible rent seekers actually prejudice their own chances to receive state-supplied rents in the future. As Hathaway (1998) notes, strong market performance in the face of import competition demonstrates to governments that state-supplied rents are no longer vital to industry performance. In other words, as flexible rent seekers adjust to new conditions, they undermine their ability to convince governments of the need to supply rents.

This distinction between flexible and inflexible rent seekers is of interest because the two groups will respond differently to significant reductions in state-supplied rents. The distinction between flexible and inflexible rent seekers is important for governments attempting to determine the downside political risk of comprehensive free-trade policies. A rent-seeking population that is predominantly flexible responds differently to the policies enacted by a liberalizing government than does a predominantly inflexible population. Flexible rent seekers ultimately will dedicate fewer resources to punishing governments that liberalize trade. (Such punishment manifests as a range of behavior from temporarily withdrawing political support for the government all the way to actively campaigning to defeat and replace it.) Instead, the preponderance of resources will be dedicated to restructuring operations to withstand import competition. Such restructuring includes product and service innovation, rationalization of product lines and personnel, and perhaps most important, exploration of new markets to replace market shares lost at home.[11] Moreover, as firms and industries become more export oriented, they seek a general reduction in domestic tariffs and other import barriers, both to generate reciprocal concessions abroad (Finger 1991, 126) and to reduce the costs of imported factor inputs and hence make their own products more competitive internationally. A related point is that more liberal domestic trade policy increases the foreign-exchange earning capacity of other countries, thus potentially expanding demand for the exports of the liberalizing country (Pugel and Walter 1985, 468).

Flexible rent seekers will rely on governments to create market opportunities abroad and will seek to foster influence with them. They are predicted to shift from protectionists to free traders when state-supplied rents drop below a critical level—that is, the level below which it no longer pays flexible rent seekers to produce predominantly for the domestic market. Note that this critical level is not a universal threshold; it will vary from industry to industry and firm to firm. Consequently, reducing rents below the critical level actually turns flexible rent seekers into (long-term) allies of governments that have a preference for freer trade (see also Hathaway 1998). Former protectionists become integral to an emerging free-trade coalition; what we witness is actually a reversal of rent seeking on the part of flexible rent seekers.

Inflexible rent seekers, on the other hand, may be expected to do one of two things. The more politically benign reaction is to exit the marketplace voluntarily (see Staiger 1995). The less benign is to retaliate against governments that reduce rents. There are few opportunity costs for inflexible rent seekers who seek to punish governments that reduce rents below the critical level;[12] such rent reduction is a death sentence. The result is a "short shadow of the future" (Axelrod 1984) for relations between the government and inflexible rent seekers. Of course, governments that survive the wrath of inflexible rent seekers typically find themselves in a stronger position. The least efficient strata of the producer population are culled—either through voluntary exit or inevitable attrition—providing greater flexibility with respect to trade policy in the future.

Flexible and inflexible rent seeker are ideal-typical classifications, and most rent seekers ultimately conform to the characteristics of one category or the other, but some rent seekers demonstrate traits associated with both. Thus, some firms and industries, even as they adapt to increased import competition, continue to lobby the government for a return to increased protectionism. Similarly, as certain industries decline, they may shift from being flexible rent seekers to having mixed characteristics and begin pressing for increased protectionism.[13]

Also, while examination of each sector or firm's capital mobility and international competitiveness may provide some predictive insights, these axiomatically will be imprecise. Some industries will not be sufficiently introspective and risk accepting, nor enjoy the prescience, to predict ahead of time to which category of rent seeker they conform. Faced with a choice between the certainty of the status quo and uncertainty associated with change, many firms will eschew risk even where the potential for reward is greater. Such risk aversion does not constitute a serious problem for this analysis. It merely indicates that there may be a time lag between the elimination of state-supplied rents and the predicted behavior of domestic rent seekers. Over the short term, rent seekers unable to gauge their international competitiveness may be expected to conform to the predicted behavior of both flexible and inflexible rent seekers. That is, they will seek to force restoration of state-supplied rents *and* restructure operations to compete in world markets. Eventually, the grim force of the market will force inflexible rent seekers to come to terms with their economic mortality. By contrast, flexible rent seekers, recognizing that they can compete, will modify their behavior; rather than attempting to force restoration of rents, newly aware flexible rent seekers will switch tactics and lobby for greater access to foreign markets.

Finally, reliance on broad ideal-typical classifications presents certain empirical challenges. I provide no a priori means to establish what sort of producer profile will generate what behavioral response in any given firm, nor do I attempt to predict the ultimate behavior of government actors. Many of the same factors that influence firms' decisions about the optimal trade-off between rent seeking and adjustment (especially historical development and state-society relations) also influence the behavior of government actors. Therefore I do not attempt to establish a set of causal sequences that generate specific policy outcomes. Rather, I rely on the logic of the limits of rent seeking model to articulate a menu of policy options. Part of what makes the analysis in the case studies so interesting is the variation across cases in selections from the policy menu.

It is with respect to policy outcomes that the current analysis differs most markedly from studies that rely on factor-based models (see Rogowski 1989 and especially Hiscox 2002).[14] I do not set up my argument as an alternative to factor-based analysis per se, and there is a good deal of logical overlap between my study and Hiscox's; many of the cases are common to both analyses. My argument, however, is more sensitive to the idea that government actors play a proactive role in the formation of trade policy. Indeed, because governments can manipulate the levels of available rents, they can also alter the incentive structures for those within the producer population. While the limits of rent seeking model suggests that coalitions are critical to the realization of trade policy objectives, this model is based on the premise that it is not possible to make predictions about what sorts of coalitions will form.

Rather, the characteristics of emerging coalitions will be determined in large part by the strategies adopted by governments seeking to liberalize trade.

Avoiding the Blame

Given the basic logic of the distinction between flexible and inflexible rent seekers, three variables emerge to determine the extent to which governments will be punished for reducing rents. From these, prescriptions can be gleaned for future governments seeking to reduce state-supplied rents.

Catalysts for Rent Reduction

The first relevant variable turns on why rents are reduced in the first place. There are three processes that may trigger rent reductions: crisis, mandated change, or shifting government objectives. These vary in the extent that they expose liberalizing governments to risk.

The first trigger mechanism is economic crisis. As the term is used here, crisis describes depressions, severe and sustained recessions, or discrete events that have the effect of disrupting commerce in a particular sector or industry for a sustained period. Crises are widely recognized as catalysts for policy change because they lower, for both governments and society as a whole, the utility derived from the status quo (see Skowronek 1982; Krasner 1984; Gourevitch 1986; Goldstein 1988; Putnam 1988; Grindle and Thomas 1991; Keeler 1993; Williamson 1994a; Rodrik 1996). In addition, crises generate increased and more widespread demands on governments to distribute public resources. At the same time, however, governments find that during times of crisis, there are fewer resources available for distribution. The result tends to be a decline in each rent seeker's share of state-supplied subsidies, or, put differently, an increase in the cost of rent seeking.

In addition, for at least two reasons, crises create incentives for governments to reduce barriers to import protection. First, because crises often are a function of unsustainable trade deficits (usually combined with insufficient foreign funding for these deficits), they force countries to rely on strategies of export-led growth. In turn, by the logic of reciprocity, export-led growth exerts downward pressure on import barriers. Second, crises narrow the utility gap for governments between the status quo and policy reform. In normal times, governments are loath to lower import barriers, because the trade policy status quo is supported by the rent-seeker population, and any attempt to reduce rents will be met with political resistance. However, crises decrease the marginal political costs of orthodox economic reform vis-à-vis the status quo (which axiomatically produces negative utility). The short-term adjustment costs associated with trade liberalization are masked some-what by the crisis. Thus, crises serve to increase the benefits and lower the risk of trade liberalization.

The second potential catalyst for rent reduction is mandated change. Most world governments are members of at least one, and typically several, international regimes. Each of these regimes—the most prominent are the GATT (now the World Trade Organization, WTO), the International Mone-tary Fund (IMF), and the International Bank for Reconstruction and Devel-opment (World Bank)—enjoys at least some ability to compel member states to comply with its rules. On occasion, a regime may put pressure on a state to liberalize trade. After each round of the GATT, for example, member states are expected to live up to agreed-upon reforms. Similarly, states that avail themselves of loans from the IMF or World Bank may find those regimes imposing structural adjustments as a condition of continued access to credit. When international regimes mandate a reduction in state-supplied rents, governments must choose whether or not to comply.

I put qualified emphasis on the fact that governments have a choice under such circumstances. I do not mean to imply that mandates from in-ternational regimes are wholly exogenous factors, outside of the control of governments that are themselves parties to international organizations. On the other hand, the costs of noncompliance are generally perceived to be high, a perception shared by state actors and their domestic constituents. Countries often are dissatisfied with the decisions taken by international regimes; typically, however, they operate within the constraints imposed on them by the regime. Excellent examples are Canada's capitulation to the tar-iff reductions mandated by the Tokyo Round of the GATT (chapter 5) and Mexico's adherence to the neo-orthodoxy prescribed by the IMF, World Bank, and GATT during the 1980s (chapter 4). In other words, there are meaningful examples of regime-mandated rent reductions that, while tech-nically endogenous to a government's decision to reduce rents, are opera-tionally exogenous. Moreover, the apparently exogenous nature of such rent reductions is manifest; governments may make credible claims to their do-mestic constituents, including rent seekers, that they had no option but to re-duce state-supplied rents in the face of a mandate from an international regime.[15]

In this way governments can insulate themselves from some of the harshest criticisms (and penalties) generated by the reform process. A good example of this is the Canadian government's insistence in the aftermath of the Uruguay Round of the GATT that it had fought valiantly, but unsuccessfully, to prevent the elimination of agricultural supply management devices and import quotas. Canadian farmers accepted the government's decision to replace these nontariff barriers with much more visible and temporary (albeit high) tariff barriers and did not mobilize to punish the government or to lobby for noncompliance with the GATT (see Finger 1991; Reguly 1993).

Mandated change alters governments' incentive structures regarding trade liberalization. As with crises, mandated change lowers the utility of maintaining the status quo, while mitigating, at least somewhat, the risks involved in liberalizing trade. Both crises and mandated change can be thought of as structurally imposed rent reductions. What they have in common is that both provide governments with "plausible deniability" that they had an option in the decision to reduce rents. Similarly, both create circumstances in which the status quo no longer yields positive utility. The third trigger mechanism, however, affords no such protection.

The third catalyst is reduction in rents based on strategic considerations.[16] Under such circumstances, the decision to reduce rents is unambiguously endogenous. Although this is a risky course of action, under some circumstances the strategic reduction of rents may serve the government's interest, even at the expense of alienating rent seekers. For example, governments with a first-order preference for freer trade might seek to reduce rents by gambling that initial opposition to free trade will be offset by long-term support for the policy by flexible rent seekers. The risks to such a strategy may be mitigated by reducing rents incrementally.

Another strategic consideration is what I have called the high-risk model of trade liberalization. Political entrepreneurs may enact free trade as a means of realizing other objectives that provide sufficiently generous payoffs to offset the political costs involved in alienating rent seekers. This argument is spelled out comprehensively elsewhere (Lusztig 1996); however, in its briefest form, it is as follows. Typically, governments pursue their objectives in the legislative arena, a task that involves the construction of a coalition of interests in support of these objectives. On occasion, however, governments seek more ambitious goals, such as significant transformation of the polity. These transformations might be called alignment games, and they constitute attempts to affect electoral realignments. Realignments are sharp, durable transformations in party identification created when parties are able to attract the support of groups not previously aligned with that party (see especially Key 1955; Burnham 1970). A catalyst for realignment occurs when political entrepreneurs attempt to alter the regime-defining (or institutional) structure of the polity. The creation (or elimination) of institutions can have an abiding impact on the bases of a party's political support. An oft-cited example is President Lincoln's abolition of slavery, which saw the Republican Party capture the preponderance of the African American vote in the decades following emancipation. It was not until another major institutional innovation—the New Deal—that the African American vote switched overwhelmingly to the Democrats.

Where the realization of institutional reform dedicated to electoral realignment is the primary objective of the political entrepreneur, the conditions may be right for the enactment of radical policy innovation, such as the reduction of state-supplied rents. To reach desired institutional objectives, the political entrepreneur must construct a facilitating coalition consisting of all actors with the ability to block the institutional initiative. Where such actors are indifferent, or even hostile, to the political entrepreneur's overarching objective, they must be enticed into the coalition through the use of direct incentives. These incentives may take many forms. The one of greatest interest is policy innovation. Specifically, on occasion political entrepreneurs are obliged to offer trade liberalization, even at the cost of alienating rent seekers, as a means of buying support for their institutional objective.[17] Strategic rent reductions may offer high political payoffs but do not offer much in the way of protective camouflage for liberalizing governments.

Distribution of Rent Seekers

The second variable regulating the punishment absorbed by governments is the distribution of rent seekers, specifically, the proportion of rent seekers who are flexible versus inflexible. Where populations are largely flexible, governments that reduce rents below the critical threshold for most producers can expect relatively little resistance. By contrast, where the rent-seeker population is largely inflexible, the punishment to which government will be exposed will be greater. Indeed, while retaliation by inflexible rent seekers axiomatically will be temporary, by their nature democratically elected governments are more sensitive to short-term than to long-term considerations.

In part governments can make objective assessments about the ability of their producer populations to survive increased import competition. However, these assessments often are of limited utility. Even if such studies could predict accurately the abilities of firm and industry managers to make the correct decisions in restructuring operations to meet increased import competition, these analyses could not be expected to capture more nebulous issues. Risk acceptance is an excellent case in point. Few producers know ahead of time, with absolute certainty, the extent of their competitiveness in global markets. That is, not all rent seekers will be immediately certain as to their status as flexible or inflexible. Over the long term, of course, this is not a problem. Flexible rent seekers come to recognize their global competitiveness; inflexible ones exit the market. But in the short term, risk-averse flexible rent seekers may be slow to recognize the economic reality and may seek to exact political punishment. The unfortunate political fate of Sir Robert Peel in the aftermath of Corn Law repeal illustrates this point (see chapter 2). Indeed, it is the danger of catching risk-averse, flexible rent seekers off guard that tells against the use of the so-called big bang strategy for rent reductions.

Even the best economic analyses, then, are expected to be weak predictors of political behavior. The issue is further confused by the fact that all rent seekers have an incentive to portray themselves as inflexible and as operating close to the threshold necessary for survival. Producer groups rarely admit that high tariff or subsidy levels are necessary to ensure high profits. Rather, state-supplied rents tend to be portrayed as necessary for firm or industry survival. Because flexible rent seekers have an incentive to mimic inflexible rent seekers, governments find themselves having to play games with incomplete information (see Lusztig, James, and Kim 2003).

The propensity to mimic creates incentives for governments unable to gauge the makeup of the rent-seeking population to eschew the risk of reducing the supply of rents. The logic is simple. Trade liberalization provides marginal political benefits to government. In fact, free trade typically is politically unpopular, and the political benefits are derived over the medium and long terms (when the government may be out of office) through improved performance of the national economy. On the other hand, where governments are unable to gauge the makeup of the rent-seeker population, the risks of trade liberalization are high. A large rent reduction in a rent-seeker population that is predominantly inflexible can have disastrous political consequences. Indeed, the high-risk to low-direct-benefit ratio of trade liberalization policies explains the historic reluctance of governments to engage in such action.

Other issues are raised by the facility with which flexible rent seekers can portray themselves as inflexible. While both flexible and inflexible rent seekers use the same tactics in seeking rents, other actions provide contrast. Differences between flexible and inflexible rent seekers leave historical traces. It is relatively easy, therefore, to distinguish flexible from inflexible rent seekers ex post facto, when rent-seeking activity is unsuccessful. When state-supplied rents are reduced below the level necessary for survival, inflexible rent seekers will continue to try to force the government to restore rents. Ultimately, of course, inflexible rent seekers will be notable for their failure to survive. Under the same circumstances, flexible rent seekers will pursue a second-most-preferred strategy: restructuring for international competition and seeking access to a greater range of export markets.

The issue of distinction becomes more problematic before the fact, however, when governments must decide on a course of action in the absence of much knowledge regarding the portion of flexible rent seekers in the rent-seeker population. (The same problem exists for analysts attempting to offer prescriptive solutions.) If the rent-seeker population consists of too great a share of inflexible rent seekers, governments can expect to be punished severely. As well, the resulting negative economic climate will affect the government's popularity. Opposition parties can be expected to capitalize on the government's unpopularity and to reverse (or at least promise to reverse) the reduction in rents upon coming to power.

Of course, discussing the fact that the distribution of rent seekers affects the extent to which governments will be punished provides few prescriptive clues. What is needed is a mechanism by which governments can identify the distribution of flexible and inflexible rent seekers within the producer population. A clue to the nature of this identification mechanism is found in the literature on international crisis bargaining. One of the problems facing negotiators in a crisis is that those who are irrevocably committed to their position often cannot distinguish themselves from those less committed but with an incentive to mimic committed negotiators. As Wagner (1989, 189) suggests, "Because there is nothing a nonbluffer can do that a bluffer would not have the ability and incentive to imitate, the recipient of a threat can never be completely convinced that the threatener is not bluffing."

In such a circumstance both the nonbluffer and the recipient have an incentive to deter the bluffer. One method that nonbluffers use to distinguish themselves from bluffers is to send signals that are costly to communicate as a means of demonstrating commitment to their position.[18] By this logic, bluffers can be distinguished from nonbluffers because they are unlikely to be willing to bear the price of costly signals. Wagner suggests, for example, that the U.S. blockade of Cuba during the missile crisis was a costly signal, because it risked a military confrontation with the Soviet Union but served to signal U.S. resolve over Cuba (Wagner 1989).

Another means of separating bluffers from nonbluffers is for the recipient of the threat to create conditions under which the former are forced to take actions that distinguish themselves from the latter. In such circumstances, recipients may be said to force signals. Flexible rent seekers represent bluffers (they mimic inflexible rent seekers when lobbying for retention of state-supplied rents), while governments interested in liberalizing trade—the recipient of the bluffs—must find a way to force a signal (see Lusztig, James, and Kim 2003).

One means by which the government can force signals is to reduce rents, observe the behavior of the rent-seeking population, and then make its calculations accordingly. Provided that rents are reduced below the critical-level threshold for some proportion of the rent-seeking population, the reduction of rents forces a separation in the behavior of flexible and inflexible rent seekers.[19] The obvious flaw, of course, is that while this constitutes an effective identification mechanism, it is no better (and indeed, no different) than the government's original objective. What is required is a means of reducing rents in a relatively costless way as a prelude to a more significant reduction that might be undertaken after the government has had an opportunity to evaluate the costs by observing the behavior of the rent-seeking population. This is where the third relevant variable comes into play.

Size and Sequence of Rent Reductions

The third and final relevant variable is the size and sequence of rent reductions. At one level, the point that the size of rent reduction is related to the punishment governments may absorb is entirely intuitive. There is a certain linearity implied. Rent seekers will be angry about a rent reduction of q and roughly twice as angry about a rent reduction of 2q. On the other hand, given the logic of the limits of rent seeking model, the larger the rent reduction, the greater the likelihood that producers will be obliged to abandon their current production points. Generally speaking, the smallest rent reductions will motivate only a few rent seekers to abandon their equilibrium production point, because only a few will find that the marginal reduction is sufficient either to force them into a nonviable position (for inflexible rent seekers) or to induce them to seek their profits in more market-oriented ways (for flexible ones). By contrast, larger reductions have the potential to affect a larger number of producers at the margin—that is, trigger the conversion of flexible rent seekers into free traders and inflexible ones into market casualties. Ironically, then, larger rent reductions may be less politically costly than smaller ones. On the other hand, it can be very difficult to estimate the optimal size of rent reductions. Where governments guess wrong, large rent reductions can lead to large political costs.

Where rent reductions are structurally imposed, the size of the rent reduction may be less relevant. However, when governments reduce rents for strategic considerations (and governments may well seek to follow structurally imposed reductions with strategic ones), issues of size and sequence become more important. Generally speaking there are four ideal-typical strategies for rent reductions from which governments can choose.

The first strategy is the big bang approach. This is a swift, bold reduction in rents whereby the government engages in large-scale rent reductions and then tries to weather the storm the best it can. The trick is to ensure that the rent reduction is sufficiently large to ensure behavior modification on the part of the rent-seeker population. The advantage of this approach is that the pain—for both government and rent seeker—is over quickly. The disadvantage is that, at least over the short term, the government assumes a large and cohesive mass of opposition. Indeed, not only will inflexible rent seekers have plenty of allies with whom they can mobilize, but flexible rent seekers, caught off guard and perhaps unaware of their abilities to compete internationally, may also retaliate. Indeed, as Roger Douglas, the architect of the successful reform of the New Zealand economy, notes (1993, 223), "Vested interests continuously underestimate their own ability to adjust successfully in an environment where the government is rapidly removing privilege across a wide front." Governments that choose this strategy, especially in the absence of some protective camouflage (in the form of a concurrent crisis or regime mandate to reform) are extremely risk acceptant. The big bang strategy was employed without such protective camouflage in three cases discussed here. In Britain and Australia, more than a century apart, Sir Robert Peel and Gough Whitlam, respectively, used the strategy with politically disastrous results. Only in Chile, under the brutal dictatorship of Augusto Pinochet, did such a tactic have the desired effect of altering the production profile of rent seekers without generating a backlash sufficient to bring down the government.

More effective are circumstances when the big bang approach is used in conjunction with, or in the aftermath of, a rent reduction generated by crisis or regime-mandated change. In such cases—Canada and Mexico are good examples—the big bang approach did not lead to political backlash, either because rent seekers were convinced of the inevitability of trade policy reform or because the structurally imposed rent reduction had already forced the behavior modification predicted by the limits of rent seeking model.

A second strategy is divide and conquer. Here, a government faced with rent-seeking interests from a number of broad sectors within the economy uses a modified form of the big bang strategy but does not subject all sectors of the economy to it simultaneously. Instead, relevant sectors are treated to large and swift rent reductions seriatim. For example, if agriculture gets its dose first, the government is faced with only one angry constituency. By the time that constituency has restructured and rationalized, it is at least as eager as, or more eager than, the government that the liberalization process be extended—both on the grounds of fairness and to reduce, as quickly as possible, the costs of factor inputs. New Zealand used the divide-and-conquer approach successfully in the 1980s and 1990s. Indeed, starting with the far more competitive agricultural sector, the New Zealand government forced inflexible rent seekers from the marketplace and obliged flexible rent seekers to become more competitive. As a result, it was the farmers who served as standard bearers in the assault against the long-standing policy of industrial import protection.

The third strategy that governments may employ is iteration. As with the divide-and-conquer approach, the government seeks to build its free-trade coalition over time. However, while divide and conquer takes on one broad sector at a time, culling the inflexible rent seekers and making allies out of the flexible, iteration reduces rents across a wide range of industries, albeit gradually, using a series of incremental rent reductions. The effect is the same. With each reduction, a new stratum of rent seekers is affected. Inflexible ones die off; flexible ones join the pro–free-trade coalition. Like the divide-and-conquer approach, iteration has the advantage both of demonstrating the government's resolve and of signaling its intent. While this may cause groups to mobilize in opposition to these strategies preemptively, opposition may be muted by concomitant reduction of factor input costs that facilitate the restructuring process. Alternatively, soon-to-be-affected groups may also see the handwriting on the wall and either exit the market or adjust preemptively. The United States in the 1930s is an excellent illustration of the success of the iteration strategy.

The advantage of both divide and conquer and iteration is that they are far safer than the big bang technique. The pace of reform can always be modified in response to the reactions of rent seekers. Thus, governments are able to update their assessments of the extent to which the rent-seeker population is flexible, as well as to determine the optimal size of rent reductions to force behavioral changes on the part of rent seekers. There are disadvantages, however. These strategies take longer than the big bang approach, which serves to extend the length of time that governments are exposed to risk. Moreover, over time governments can lose the initiative, and the process can bog down.

Indeed, America's use of iteration under President Franklin D. Roosevelt took years to generate significant change in the policy demands of many important business groups. Similarly, the New Zealand government's divide-and-conquer strategy was forced to survive a change in government in 1990. While this change did not affect the reform process, there was fear and speculation that it might.

The final strategy is the path of least resistance. The government pursues rent reductions in the absence of a comprehensive game plan. Here government, recognizing the need to liberalize, and perhaps even responding to structurally imposed imperatives to do so, reforms in an ad hoc fashion. Rent reductions follow the path of least resistance. Protection is granted to groups strong enough to put pressure on the government, and the toughest decisions are put off until the future. A hallmark of the path of least resistance is that governments make progress in lowering aggregate levels of rents but continue to concentrate assistance in the least efficient sectors of the economy—that is, the ones in most dire need of the discipline imposed by exposure to global competition. The advantage is that this technique is safe. The least committed rent seekers are encouraged to join the free-trade coalition, while the government is insulated from severe retaliation—those who fight back are granted compensatory rents. Thus, the government is able to build a pro–free-trade coalition at little risk.

The disadvantages are that the technique thwarts the logic of the limits of rent seeking model. The least efficient strata of the rent-seeking population are not culled. Rather, they form a powerful, rival coalition to the free traders. Indeed, the path of least resistance approach creates an incentive for flexible rent seekers to redouble lobbying costs in the face of painful cuts rather than attempt to adjust. (In other words, the cost of rent seeking relative to adjustment is low.) Indeed, endogenous tariff studies have demonstrated that protection-seeking behavior intensifies according to the size of the rents available as well as the likelihood of achieving them (Brock and Magee 1978; Pugel and Walter 1985). Australia's inability to convert to a free-trading nation, despite apparently significant reforms dating to the early 1980s is testimony to the inefficacy of such a strategy. Similarly, Brazil has used the strategy to ill effect.

In sum, the logic of forced signaling and incremental rent reductions provides governments that have a first-order preference for trade liberalization a means of strategic rent reduction that entails limited political risk. Critical to the success of such an initiative, however, independent of patience and the ability to estimate optimal rent reductions, is political determination. Indeed, at the same time that government attempts to force behavioral changes from the rent-seeker population, it must maintain a firm whip hand. Where government falters and reverses policy on rent reduction, it risks creating the incentive for flexible rent seekers to delay restructuring in the hopes of convincing government to backtrack. As de la Cuadra and Hachette (1991, 276) caution, "Lack of faith in the permanence of reforms is self-fulfilling; it retards any major adjustment and further fuels pressure on the authorities to reverse the policy."

The Model

The full form of the limits of rent seeking model is as follows. It begins with a reduction in rents that pushes rents below the critical threshold for at least some of the rent-seeker population. This reduction may be structural in nature—that is, necessitated by crisis or by the dictates of an international regime—or it may be strategic. In either case, it leads to some form of separation in behavior among some portion of the rent-seeker population. This initial reduction increases the government's information about the proportion of flexible rent seekers within the producer population. (The greater the initial reduction of rents, the greater the information received.) Depending on the signals the government receives, and its risk propensity, the government may then seek an additional reduction in rents (or multiple reductions). Ultimately, when rents are reduced below the critical threshold for the preponderance of the rent-seeker population, a major source of protectionism is removed. Flexible rent seekers actively support, or at least acquiesce to, free trade, whereas inflexible rent seekers are culled from the producer population. The argument is illustrated schematically in figure 1.1.

It should be borne in mind that the dependent variable is the behavior of rent seekers, not the policy outcome. Thus, while the two tend to be highly correlated, they are not identical; the transformation of flexible rent-seeker behavior will not axiomatically translate into policies of freer trade. Producer groups exercise considerable influence over government, but their voices are not decisive. Other sources of domestic opposition—labor and cultural organizations are important examples—may dissuade governments from pursuing greater trade liberalization, even if rent-seeking producer groups alter their trade policy strategies.

Domestic economies also feature sources of dynamism other than that stimulated by the reduction of state-supplied rents. Factors such as technological development, reduced transport costs, major wars, and shifting access

Figure 1.1: Rent seekers and the reduction of state-supplied rents

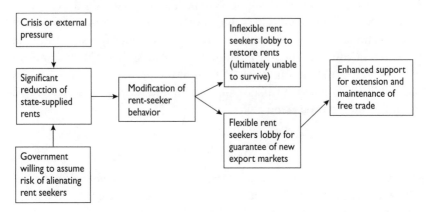

to markets abroad may stimulate flexible rent seekers to operate more efficiently to increase exports and no longer seek protection at home (Ferguson
1984; Gourevitch 1986; James and Lake 1989; Rogowski 1989; Uslaner 1994).
These groups will lobby for free trade independently of state reduction of
rents.

On the other hand, none of these domestic factors is able to account for
the creation and maintenance of support for free-trade policies in the cases
examined here. In Canada, Chile, Mexico, New Zealand, and, to a lesser extent, Australia and Brazil, long traditions of business support for protectionism were reversed extremely quickly. Similarly, in Britain the agricultural
sector abandoned the commitment to protection rapidly. While factors such
as technological change and reduced transport costs affected business attitudes, it is not clear what specific developments could have triggered so rapid
a reversal in the policy demands of the business communities. Indeed, the
twentieth century was replete with examples of significant technological
change, which, while undoubtedly responsible for changing trade policy demands among some within the business communities studied here, did not
trigger rapid, widespread reversals in policy demands.[20] The U.S. case is
slightly different, given that a world war and concomitant technological
change intervened between the start of the rent-reduction process and the
full conversion of flexible rent seekers. However, there is strong evidence that
the limits of rent seeking model is a persuasive explanation of shifting trade
policy preferences among American industrial producers.

The model is not a perfect predictor. For Australia and Brazil, the model
simply does not work. In spite of large and significant rent reductions in

both countries, a significant, seemingly immutable coalition of protectionists persists, acting as a drag on the extension of the liberalization process. This failure in predictive capacity is both good and bad for the model: it provides demonstrable falsifiability but also needs to be explained.

It is possible that the apparent failure of the Australian and Brazilian cases is simply an artifact of insufficient historical perspective. After all, Chile during the first half of the 1980s could have been judged a failure by the criteria employed here. I suspect, though, that neither Australia nor Brazil is misclassified via the illusion of perspective. Unlike Chile, both Australia and Brazil chose poorly from the prescriptive menu explained here. I predict that in the absence of another round of rent reductions, which will entail abandonment of the path of least resistance strategy, neither Australia nor Brazil will benefit from the logic spelled out in the limits of rent seeking model.

A final objection that might be raised is that trade policy preferences among flexible rent seekers changed in all countries as the result of market closure abroad. While intuitively sound, this hypothesis stands up poorly to closer inspection. The British free-trade experiment, for example, came during a period in which world markets were opening. In the United States, market closure in Europe occurred in direct response to the Smoot-Hawley Tariff. Yet, as late as 1939 (nine years after world markets closed), a strong majority of small and medium-sized businesses in the United States preferred higher tariffs to lower ones. Trade liberalization occurred in Chile and began in Australia prior to the rise of the "new protectionism." In Canada, while rising U.S. protectionism in the early 1980s constituted a threat, it is important not to overemphasize this point.[21] Even in 1982, when congressional action against foreign imports reached its height, only a fraction of cases targeted Canada, with even fewer of these being successful (Watson 1987, 340). In Mexico, NAFTA was initiated in 1990, well after the deepest wave of U.S. protectionism had passed. Moreover, prior to the opening of the Mexican economy in the middle of the 1980s, the bulk of Mexican exports were in minerals and crude oil, products not threatened by U.S. protectionism (Ramirez 1993, 183–84). Finally, New Zealand was forced to alter its export profile in the early 1970s with Britain's entry into the European Common Market but did not embrace free trade for at least a decade thereafter.

Trade politics is an excellent illustration of risk-benefit analysis on the part of governments. Most political leaders (and the vast preponderance of their economic advisors) accept Ricardo's virtual truism that under almost all circumstances free trade (even if unilateral) works to the aggregate economic benefit of the liberalizing nation. However, because there is imbalance in the distribution of costs and benefits (with the former highly concentrated, and hence significant, and the latter widespread and, at the individual level, marginal), there are high political risks and low political benefits involved in trade liberalization. Thus, the typical equilibrium outcome is the maintenance of significant barriers to import penetration and other forms of state-supplied rents.

Reduction in these rents, it follows, occurs when the risk-benefit ratio is altered. What I have characterized as structural causes of rent reduction—crisis and mandated change—serve to lessen the risks involved in trade liberalization. Strategic reductions, by contrast, take place under conditions when political leaders sense the potential for heightened political benefits from the liberalization of trade.

The limits of rent seeking model builds on this logic, suggesting that dynamics inherent in the liberalization process can help leaders mitigate cost and help assess risk. Trade policy need not be structurally determined by the preferences of societal forces (Ikenberry, Lake, and Mastanduno 1988). In a prescriptive sense, this implies that democratically elected governments may have a good deal more flexibility in the making of trade policy than the prevailing literature suggests. In this context my analysis also contributes to an emerging literature about the conditions under which states are able to enact policies with broad-based (but shallow) social appeal, yet which offend concentrated (but deeply committed) interests (see Bhagwati 1989; Arnold 1990; Rodrik 1992; Bates and Krueger 1993; Douglas 1993; Williamson 1994b; Lusztig 1996; Kingstone 1999). In other words, it challenges the dominant (demand-driven) theory that small, concentrated, and homogenous groups consistently will subvert the national interest in the framing of public policy (Olson 1965, 1982; Lavergne 1983; Frey 1984; Lake 1988a).

The model also complements and extends existing theories within international political economy.[22] Indeed, the emphasis on the demise of inflexible rent seekers reinforces Milner's position (1988, 1993) that the business sector is an important force resisting protectionism in the United States. The model builds on Milner's argument in a number of ways. First, it provides antecedent explanations about how free-trade policies come to be passed. Second, the model explains why business shifts its preferences from protectionism to free trade.[23] Third, the present argument strengthens Milner's theory by suggesting that because protectionist businesses tend to be culled from the population, business is more likely to support free-trade policies well into the future.

Finally, the model also is consistent with Olson's argument (1982) that traditionally stable systems encourage the proliferation of rent seekers. The shocks provided by exogenous forces (such as crisis), or by governments seeking to reduce deadweight costs, prove fatal to inflexible rent seekers previously sheltered in the rarefied atmosphere of the protected economy.

Countries included in this study range from modern liberal democracies to hegemonic and prehegemonic powers, and to underdeveloped proto-democracies on the path to democratic transition. They span four continents, while the period under study extends from the present back to the middle of the nineteenth century. These countries were selected to illustrate the applicability of the arguments over a wide variety of times and locations.

2

Britain and the Golden Age
of Free Trade

In 1846, Great Britain repealed its historic and elaborate system of agricultural protection known as the Corn Laws. Repeal is celebrated as the event that ushered in the era of British global hegemony, which lasted through the nineteenth century. It also is widely recognized as Britain's point of transition from an agricultural economy to an industrial one. While it is difficult to quibble with these characterizations, the implicit corollary is that British agriculture went into a steep decline after 1846. Certainly such a decline was the dire prediction of the fierce cadre of Corn Law supporters. Indeed, so controversial was repeal that the sponsoring Conservative government of Sir Robert Peel was turned out of power on the strength of a revolt by its own parliamentary party in the House of Commons.

In reality, while there were certainly severe transition costs to a free-trading economy, much of the British agricultural sector flourished in the aftermath of repeal, and the 1850s and 1860s are generally regarded as the golden age of British farming. Even with the onset of a global depression after 1873,[1] Britain did not follow the example of many of its trading partners and close its agricultural markets. Instead, and generally with the blessing of the farming community, Britain retained its commitment to free trade throughout the long economic slump that colored the fourth quarter of the nineteenth century.

British farmers underwent a dramatic shift in orientation during this period. Even during the golden age, British cereal producers did not enjoy competitive advantage in world markets. Given the depressed and globally protectionist climate of the 1870s, it is curious that Britain, a country in which the landed aristocracy still held considerable political power, did not reimpose agricultural protection and that protectionists within the agricultural sector were largely unsuccessful in mobilizing support for protectionism from British farmers.

The limits of rent seeking model can help to explain this phenomenon and to show that the prime minister, Sir Robert Peel, might have avoided much of the political cost associated with Corn Law repeal had he employed an iterative strategy for reducing agricultural rents. Indeed, evidence suggests that the potential existed for agricultural allies in the quest for freer trade. The potential for an alternative political outcome of Corn Law repeal is of some historical interest. Ironically, it is doubtful that Peel himself would have cared a great deal. Peel was less concerned about his own political fate than about the survival of the regime. While it may seem strange to us today, the still-recent French Revolution clearly suggested to Peel the fragility with which the landed elites retained their prerogative to rule in the face of a shift toward industrialization as the dominant mode of production. In the fall of 1845, fearful that the impending Irish potato crop failure could foment wide-scale rebellion, Peel employed the big bang strategy with personally disastrous political results.

The limits of rent seeking model is applicable to this important and broadly analyzed historical case: agricultural support for protectionism was greatly undermined by the repeal of the Corn Laws. There were three direct effects. First, many marginal, or at least risk-averse, farmers, presumably the ones most wedded to subsidization of the agricultural sector, abandoned their farms, thereby depriving the agricultural protectionist movement of its most committed constituents.

Second, hardier farmers adopted new farming techniques—known as high farming—which allowed them to compete effectively with increased imports or to shift production into areas where they enjoyed competitive advantage. High farming entailed scientific improvements to the land through mechanization, better drainage of surface water, new and more abundant fertilizers, optimal crop rotation, and diversification between arable crops and livestock, known as mixed farming. In short, high farming is what More (1989, 131) describes as "high inputs of capital to achieve high output" (see also Prothero 1912; Moore 1965; Chambers and Mingay 1966; Thompson 1981).

Third, the increased general prosperity that followed Corn Law repeal deepened agricultural commitment to free trade. This commitment, while possibly partially psychological,[2] had tangible roots as well. Not only was a richer society capable of consuming a greater quantity and range of agricultural products, but factor inputs critical to high-farming techniques also became less expensive. The overall result was a shift in the profile of British agriculture. The weakest stratum was rationalized out of the market, while much of the remainder became committed to free-market principles and resistant to the reimposition of tariffs.

The Historical Context

For much of their long existence, the English Corn Laws constituted a mechanism for regulation of cereal prices, including wheat, oats, and barley.[3] By the start of the eighteenth century, largely for reasons of national security, the focus of the Corn Laws had shifted from protection of consumers to safeguarding producer interests. Cereal prices were kept high through severe restrictions on imports, although these were relaxed upon the realization of a predetermined high-water mark, or pivot price. In addition, as Britain settled into the mercantilist age, export bounties were granted to producers. Because farmers received subsidies to send their surplus products to foreign markets, cereal prices were not depressed by good harvests at home.

The Corn Laws were relevant to more than mere price regulation, however. The threat of blockade during war, for example, made agricultural self-sufficiency a paramount objective. Also notable was the fact that Britain's social structure rested on the agrarian mode of production. As the Industrial Revolution swept Britain and the preeminence of agricultural production was threatened, the Corn Laws became important as a symbolic indicator of the continued sociopolitical superiority of the landed classes. But by the end of the Napoleonic War, the stage was set for conflict between the established agrarian elites and industrial parvenus who sought to recast the rules—both political and economic—in their own favor.

The first metaphorical shot fired in the nineteenth-century dispute over the Corn Laws was from the agricultural protectionists, who feared that war's end could spell financial peril. They succeeded in securing the highly controversial Corn Law of 1815. Under the new law, cereals could be imported and warehoused duty free, but they could not be brought to market in Great Britain until the realization of a very generous pivot price, variable by commodity.[4] A break from tradition, the 1815 pivot price was dichotomous. Below the pivot, imports were prohibited; above it, importation was duty free. For the most important cereal, wheat, the pivot price was 80 shillings a quarter, a departure from the market price of over 126s. 6d. in 1812 but well above the prewar mean of about 50s.

The Corn Law of 1815 provided unprecedented import protection to the landed gentry and their tenant farmers. The predictable effect was to shift marginal land into cereal production. Chambers and Mingay (1966, 127) estimate that the average domestic yield of wheat rose by as much as one-third between 1815 and 1846 (see also May 1987, ch. 4). On the other hand, while the postwar Corn Law was generous, it was not sufficient to overcome structural disadvantages suffered by cereal farmers and their landlords. Bad harvests from 1809 to 1812 had kept cereal prices extremely high by historical standards. By 1813, farmers and landlords alike had undertaken investment decisions predicated on the assumption that war and high cereal prices would continue. They were wrong on both counts. As a result, not only did agrarian living standards fall, but high rents charged to tenant farmers and expensive land improvements could not be recouped by postwar cereal prices (Prothero 1912, ch. 15).[5] The problem was that high tariffs did not guarantee high prices. Strong domestic harvests and increased cultivated acreage were just as destructive as a flood of foreign corn.[6]

In the end, the Corn Law of 1815 was an awkward compromise between the interests of agricultural producers and consumers. A subsidization of poor wartime investments, the act failed adequately to restore agricultural rents; however, it did increase, or at least increase the perception of, wage-based inflation. It created, in other words, an unstable equilibrium contested and detested by both town and country (see Wordie 2000). In 1828, the Conservative government took steps to depoliticize the Corn Law issue through the reintroduction of a sliding scale of import protection. The polar points on the scale were a prohibitive duty of 34s. 8d. on a quarter of wheat when the domestic price fell to 52s. and a nominal 1s. duty once wheat reached 73s. per quarter.[7] The law's great virtue was that it removed the dichotomous pivot. Unfortunately, under the sliding scale, duties did not vary in lock step with prices. Most problematic was the fact that import duties fell off extremely quickly upon the realization of a domestic price of 70s. Thus, a duty of 10s. 8d. was to be paid at the home price of 70s., but that tariff fell to 2s. 8d. when the price of wheat rose to 72s. (Barnes 1965, 200). The predictable result, of course, was a booming market in grain speculation. While an improvement on the 1815 law, the 1828 act also failed to satisfy either protectionists or free traders.

The Corn Laws did not play an enormous role in the politics of the 1830s. In part, this is because the Great Reform Act (1832) eclipsed the issue. The Reform Act represented an extension of the franchise, albeit modest, to the industrial elites and to a wider base of tenant farmers. The battle over reform had drawn sharp distinctions between the Conservative and Whig parties. The latter, which managed to secure passage of the law, became seen as champions of the middle class. By contrast, the Conservatives resisted reform. In the end, a parliamentary standoff between the parties was broken in the face of rioting on the part of middle- and working-class activists and the threat of the creation of new peers if the House of Lords attempted to block the bill (Brock 1973).

Substantively, the Reform Act did little. Certainly it did not greatly change the social composition of Parliament. Procedurally and symbolically, however, it represented a changing of the guard. Concessions had been made, not in a reasoned and dispassionate manner, but in the face of potential rebellion. Many Conservatives, including Peel, felt that a dangerous precedent had been set. Peel's letter to Lord Harrowby on February 5, 1832, illustrates the point:

> Why have we been struggling against the Reform Bill in the House of Commons? Not in the hope of resisting its final success in that House, but because we look beyond the Bill, because we know the nature of popular concessions, their tendency to propagate the necessity for further and more extensive compliances. We want to make the 'descensus' as 'difficilis' as we can—to teach young inexperienced men charged with the trust of government that, though they may be backed by popular clamour, they shall not override on the first springtide of excitement every barrier and breakwater raised against popular impulses; that the carrying of extensive changes in the Constitution without previous deliberation shall not be a holiday task. . . . Suppose that we had given way, that we had acquiesced in the Bill, and given no trouble to the Ministers. My firm belief is that the country, so far from being satisfied with our concessions, would have lost all reverence and care for remaining institutions, and would have had their appetites whetted for a further feast at the expense of the Church, or the monarchy (Peel 1970, 201–2).[8]

Peel might have been too optimistic with respect to the success of his mandate. As the middle class acquired greater political standing, some of its members sought a stronger voice in the economics of the day. It was for this reason that, in 1839, the Anti–Corn Law League was founded in the industrial city of Manchester; it was to play a significant role in Sir Robert Peel's decision to repeal the Corn Laws.

Trade Liberalization in the 1840s

The Catalyst

Peel came to power in 1841, ironically due to the parliamentary defeat of the previous Whig administration over its proposed reduction of agricultural import duties. Peel's great strength was his ability to recognize the changing spirit of his times. A true conservative, Peel's guiding principle was the desire to preserve the essential social structure of Britain; his tactics were to enact preemptive reforms against obvious symbols of social discontent as a means of heading off more comprehensive change. Pertinently, by the 1840s, Peel had come to believe that while aristocratic rule might be preserved, aristocratic privilege could not—at least as it pertained to agricultural protectionism.[9] Ultimately, his motive for repeal of the Corn Laws in 1846 was the realization that any attempt to retard industrial economic hegemony was destined to end in failure, and possibly revolution.[10]

Peel's great weakness was his inability to recognize that others were not equally sensitive to the winds of change. He believed, correctly as it turned out, that rural Britain could survive Corn Law repeal. He advocated the introduction of new high-farming techniques that would allow farmers to engage in land improvement and/or crop substitution as a means of overcoming the negative effects of import competition. He believed, in short, that the rigor of the market was a far more potent palliative for what ailed the countryside than was economic paternalism. Much of rural Britain ultimately came to accept this conclusion—but not until long after Peel had been relegated to the sidelines of British politics.

On the surface, the England of the early 1840s was politically placid. There were extraparliamentary pressure groups seeking social change: the Irish Repealers, who wished to sever the union between Britain and Ireland; the Chartists, who sought amelioration of economic and political conditions for the working classes; and the Anti–Corn Law League, which demanded repeal of the Corn Laws. However, none seemed sufficiently powerful to threaten the security of the realm. Within the Tory Party itself, however, the faintest outlines of destabilizing division were present. Much of the controversy centered on Peel, whose popularity was manifest in the early 1840s but who had long been distrusted in the "Ultra-Tory" wing of the party.

The fault lines dated to the Catholic emancipation crisis of 1829. Emancipation eliminated the Catholic disabilities—policies that discriminated against British Catholics—and concomitantly weakened the symbolic ties between the Anglican Church and the state. Specifically, emancipation abrogated vows repugnant to Catholics, such as the Oath of Supremacy and the Declaration Against Transubstantiation and the Worship of the Virgin Mary, as a condition of sitting in Parliament or holding corporate office under the Crown. Although he had been personally opposed to elimination of Catholic disabilities, Peel had been instrumental in securing passage of emancipation legislation. The potential political costs of continuing the Catholic disabilities in Ireland, measured in regime instability, were too great. The episode represented the first example of Peel's willingness to trade off policy concessions for the overall stability of the regime (see Peel 1857, 1:105; Doubleday 1856, 464–75; Kitson Clark 1964).[11]

Early in the new Peel administration, the prime minister appeared to confirm the worst fears of the Ultra-Tories; in 1842, he reduced agricultural protection.[12] The legislation, which covered roughly 750 commodities, retained the 1828 sliding scale but reduced duties downward. Whereas the 1828 scale had been designed to keep the domestic price of wheat at close to 64s., the 1842 duty sought an equilibrium price near 56s. (Trumbull 1892, ch. 4; Trevelyan 1913, 72).[13] The reduction, Peel believed, not only would discourage speculation in the grain market, but also would lower bread prices and wages.[14] Ultimately, he hoped that the 1842 Corn Law would undercut popular agitation and preserve the sociopolitical status quo. As he wrote to John Wilson Croker on October 30, 1842, "Rest assured of this, that landed property would not be safe during this next winter with the prices of the last four years, and even if it were safe it would not be profitable very long. Poor rates, rates in aid, diminished consumption, would soon reduce the temporary gain of a nominal high price" (Peel 1970, 530–31).

The 1842 Corn Law was not well received in the countryside, especially when it was followed up a few months later with a repeal of the import prohibition on livestock (Crosby 1977, 122–29; see also Broughton 1911). But for the more progressive members of the cabinet, the 1842 legislation represented an effective first step along the path to the conversion of flexible agrarian rent seekers. Home secretary Sir James Graham wrote to Peel on December 30, 1842, "It is a question of *time*. The next change in the Corn Laws must be to an open trade; and if our population increase for two or three years at the rate of 300,000 per annum, you may throw open the ports, and British agriculture will not suffer. But the next change must be the last;

it is prudent not to hurry it; next Session is too soon; and as you cannot make a decisive alteration, it is far wiser to make none" (Peel 1970, 551; emphasis in original).

Whatever the accuracy of Graham's prediction, the political advice given to his prime minister was faulty. The 1842 reduction, while unpopular, did not trigger the kind of reaction that the government had desired. The Anti–Corn Law League continued to grow in popularity, wealth, and importance. Similarly, there was little appreciable change in the behavior of farmers. Few farms failed, and few farmers adopted new, scientific farming techniques (Prothero 1912, ch. 17). Peel's 1842 legislation did not reach the critical threshold of rent reduction necessary to trigger behavioral change for the preponderance of British agricultural rent seekers.[15] By the time Peel did make a "decisive alteration" to the Corn Laws, he faced a large and mobilized coalition of rent seekers.

That decisive alteration came in 1846. The final chapter in the life of the Corn Laws opened in the late summer of 1845, with rumors coming out of Ireland that the staple potato crop would fail, creating the prospect of famine. From that point onward, Peel lost control of the pace of the repeal process. On November 22, Whig leader Lord John Russell announced his commitment to full repeal of the Corn Laws. With that announcement, the fate of agricultural protection was doomed. Peel had long been convinced that the Corn Laws were anachronistic. With Russell's November 22 missive, they had become dangerous.

Russell's conversion to free trade was problematic for two reasons. As with the Whigs' conversion to support for the Reform Act two decades previously, Peel recognized that Russell's very public action would raise expectations. To the minds of many, Russell's conversion would link repeal to amelioration of the Irish crisis; failure to act could lead to the sort of violence that had occurred during the stalemate over the Reform Bill. Also, and equally problematic, Peel knew that even if Russell could take control of the House of Commons, the latter would have virtually no chance of steering a repeal bill through the House of Lords.[16] Again, the result was likely to be public agitation and, worse, concession in the face of violence.[17]

Peel spent the month of December attempting to secure the support of his cabinet for total repeal of the Corn Laws. On January 27, 1846, he unveiled repeal legislation in Parliament, putatively as a means of alleviating the suffering in Ireland. Certainly the crisis explains the timing of repeal; it is unlikely, however, that Peel's stated rationale for repeal convinced any of his cabinet colleagues save for the Duke of Wellington, who decried that "[r]otten potatoes have done it all; they put Peel in his damned fright" (Gre-ville 1885, 82). A more typical reaction was that of Croker (1884, 268), who wrote to Graham in February 1846 "that Ireland has had anything to do with the grand convulsion . . . I cannot concede. Ireland has no more to do with it than Kamschatka."

The rotten potato theory may have provided some popular justification for repeal, but Peel can scarcely have hoped to deceive any but the most gullible of the political elite. Repealing the Corn Laws smacked of locking the barn after the horse had been stolen. As Henry Goulburn pointed out in a letter to Peel, elimination of the Corn Laws would neither increase the exist-ing store of grains nor likely increase supply in the near future (Peel 1857, 2:202). Moreover, it is not clear how changes to the marginal price of wheat would have ameliorated the plight of largely subsistence farmers whose sta-ple crop had failed.

The answer to why Peel fabricated the myth of repeal as a response to cri-sis lies in his larger strategic considerations. By casting repeal as a response to the Irish crisis, Peel eliminated an economic anachronism, while at the same time signaling to extraparliamentary agitators such as the Chartists and Irish Repealers (as well as other would-be reform activists) that social agitation had not been a factor in the decision. The Corn Laws were doomed with the Russell letter of November 22. It remained only to ensure that repeal be ef-fected in a way that would not create an incentive for other agitators to press for broader and deeper reforms that could affect the foundational character-istics of the regime.

Peel was a conservative, but one who took great stock in Thomas Macauley's famous maxim, "Reform that you may preserve." Part of the preservation process, however, depended on ensuring that reform serve as a final settlement to the matter at hand, and not merely as a prelude to more meaningful changes. Enacted properly, as Peel believed Catholic emancipa-tion had been, reform was the political equivalent of amputation—ghastly and unpleasant, but a sacrifice designed to preserve the larger organism. Ef-fective reform mandated that the ruling elites be perceived as holding the whip hand, controlling the agenda as well as the pace and breadth of change (see Kemp 1962; Adelman 1989, ch. 5). If elites were seen as merely reacting to social pressures, such unprincipled concessions would merely create new grievances, often without satiating the old. The ultimate cost would be steady erosion of faith in the existing order.

For Peel, the quintessential case of unprincipled concession to extra-parliamentary agitation had been the Great Reform Act of 1832. That precedent had been reckless and potentially revolutionary. Indeed, Chartism and even agitation over the Corn Laws could be traced to unrealized expectations that had been born of the reactive Whigs' handling of the Reform Act. He was adamant that this precedent must not be repeated with the Corn Laws. The problem was that without some exogenous justification (the Irish crisis, for example), it would be difficult to spin repeal as anything other than a concession to the great engine of agitation for repeal, the Anti–Corn Law League.

Although superbly funded and organized, the league's efforts to effect a meaningful and permanent change to the Corn Laws had borne little fruit during the first six years of its existence.[18] Partly, the league had been defied by circumstance: bumper crops and low food costs in 1842, 1843, and 1844 had undermined much of its relevance. Equally, the league had engaged in rather suspect strategies—an urban registration drive met with tepid enthusiasm and an attempt to elect proleague members to Parliament in by-elections was largely unsuccessful (Fay 1932, ch. 6; Barnes 1965, ch. 11; McCord 1968, ch. 8, epilogue). But in 1845, fate presented the league with a golden opportunity. It is often the case in politics that crises, even if beyond the immediate control of the government, serve to rally opponents of the regime by providing a common cause for heretofore discrete grievances. Crises, in other words, become the mortar to bind disparate disaffected groups. To Peel, Ireland was about more than rotten potatoes in 1845. It represented the potential for a revolutionary coalition of minorities, led by the superbly organized Anti–Corn Law League (see Greville 1885, 94). The Duke of Wellington had it almost right. It was not potatoes, but rather uncontrollable reform, that "put Peel in his damned fright."

The league's ultimate success was tied to the fact that it recognized the strength of its own hand in 1845. The leader of the league, Richard Cobden, clearly understood Peel's ultimate objectives regarding reform and preservation of the existing order. Cobden was convinced as early as the spring of 1845 that Peel was merely in search of a pretext for repeal.[19] The Irish crisis provided Peel with his excuse and Cobden with his weapon. That Peel understood his predicament in late 1845 and early 1846 is clear from his rather desperate actions.[20] That Cobden wished to reinforce Peel's fears is clear from the former's speech to the House of Commons on February 27, 1846, in which he threatened to redouble efforts to mobilize and expand the electorate, concluding with the threat, "You may think there is something repulsive to your notions of supremacy in all this" (Cobden 1870, 1:376). Cobden later wrote of the speech, "Even in the Commons, it is quite necessary to shake the rod of democracy in their faces" (McCord 1968, 203). Similarly, he wrote to Henry Ashworth on February 19, "It is the League, and it only, that frightens Peel. It is the League alone which enables Peel to repeal the law" (Morley 1905, 377). The ever-perceptive Croker shared the sentiment, writing to Wellington on April 5 that Peel's conversion to free trade was "nothing but the result of *fright* of the League" (Croker 1884, 65; emphasis in original).[21]

Corn Law repeal received Royal Assent on June 26, 1846. Three days later, Peel, abandoned by the bulk of his party and supported only by his loyal "Peelite" rump, became the second prime minister in five years to lose office over the issue of reduction in agricultural rents.

The Big Bang Strategy

History, quite justly, has judged Peel kindly. He was a politician who placed his convictions over his electoral fortunes. It is clear from his memoirs that Peel eliminated the Corn Laws in full cognizance of the political dangers but in keeping with his desire to protect the integrity of the realm. He employed the dangerous (and disastrous) big bang strategy not because he was a political ingenue, but because he felt compelled to do so by extant circumstances in 1845 and 1846. The big bang approach is politically dangerous; Peel's fate proves it. The limits of rent seeking model indicates that Peel misplayed the repeal issue during the critical years 1842–1844. Peel made two related mistakes. In seeking to paper over divisions within his own party, he failed to signal clearly his private intention to repeal, and, flowing from this, he failed to employ a strategy of iteration. Circumstantial evidence suggests that such a strategy could have succeeded.

Peel's first mistake was to play his cards too close to the vest in the aftermath of the 1842 Corn Law. His public stance, designed to appease the Ultra-Tories, was that the 1842 legislation had settled the matter of urban distress and that he would not repeal the Corn Laws unless compelled to do so in the national interest (Stewart 1971, 15). Privately, however, he was far from certain that the Corn Laws should be preserved (Morley 1909, 260). Beyond fear of rebellion, or (almost as distressing) concession in the face of extraparliamentary agitation, Peel was convinced that the plight of the landed interests was exacerbated by consumers who were too poor to consume and who therefore had to be supported by the poor rates. In other words, British agriculture in general, and the landed classes in particular, were actually harmed by agricultural protection. As was to prove to be the case, Peel believed that free trade would increase the general prosperity to the benefit of town and country alike.

But what was so clear to his sharp mind was less obvious to others. To some extent, Peel recognized this fact. In October 1842, he wrote to Charles Arbuthnot, "The true friend to the 'astounded' and complaining Ultra is the man who would avert the consequences which would inevitably follow if some of them could have their way" (Peel 1970, 533). Still, Peel appears to have been convinced that time would prove his views correct. This was also the gist of Graham's advice to Peel in the letter of December 30, 1842, quoted earlier.

In retrospect, Peel would have done better not to trust his fellow conservatives to see the wisdom of his Ricardian economic arguments. Indeed, while Peel was no doubt correct that the "astounded and complaining" Ultras would have been better served as a whole in the long run by free trade, he failed to consider that the aggregate benefits would mask large discrepancies among winners and losers. Many potential losers were quite rational in their opposition to repeal. Moreover, as public choice theorists have long understood, the benefits of free trade are tougher to sell politically than are the obvious fruits of protection. Maintaining public support for the Corn Laws while trusting to the good sense of the landed classes ultimately to see the economic light was not good politics.

The distinction between the private and public Peels caught both his party and its core agrarian constituency off guard in the fall of 1845. The sudden public shift in Peel's support for the Corn Laws generated distrust and resentment, even among those who ultimately came to benefit from free trade. As Stewart (1971, 15) puts it, "Clearer symptoms of discontent in 1842 might have forced Peel's private reservations into the open, thereby starting a fruitful debate on the subject of the Corn Laws within the party." As it was, the sudden policy shift left the Peelite coalition in the Conservative party on the policy defensive and in a numerical minority. By contrast, an iterative strategy would almost certainly have precluded the rapid and massive defection of Peel supporters to the Ultra faction of the party.

Of course, it would be erroneous to suggest that Peel did not attempt to play an iterative strategy. He did, of course, most manifestly with the 1842 Corn Law. But the attempt was half-hearted and abortive. Certainly William Gladstone suggested that Peel could have cut deeper in 1842 without harming the landed interest. Peel, concerned about the prospect of cabinet resignations and defeat in the House of Lords, maintained the cautious approach (Morley 1909, 253–54). This was wise because the logic of iteration suggests that conservative estimations of rent reductions are preferable. However, iteration relies on the government's willingness to signal its resolve. Peel failed to do so. Thus, while Peel followed up the 1842 legislation with repeal of livestock import prohibition and with legislation to lower the import duty on Canadian wheat to one shilling, he failed to make clear his commitment to repeal. In other words, he gave hope to those who preferred resistance to acquiescence.

Obviously iteration would not have been a costless strategy. Each rent reduction would have created controversy and put enormous pressure on Peel's government. On the other hand, the constituency within his own party that Peel would have alienated, the Ultras, were already opposed to him. Had iterative rent reductions been coupled with more aggressive programs designed to subsidize farmers and landlords for the costs of land improvement (as were contained in the 1846 repeal legislation) it is possible to envision a less catastrophic outcome. Peel could well have used iteration to expand the size of the free-trade coalition, which itself could have served as a counterweight to the influence of the Ultra wing. This argument is made more compelling by the fact that there existed the potential for an agrarian free-trade coalition in the early 1840s (Musson 1972).

The picture painted by most historians is that the issue of repeal was contested by a protectionist agrarian class and a victorious rising middle class committed to free trade. In reality, as Aydelotte (1967) shows, the politics of protection in early Victorian Britain was more complex. Aydelotte examines the class background of members of Parliament (MPs) who voted on Third Reading of the Corn Laws Repeal Bill in May 1846. Since the Conservatives were the only party to divide meaningfully over Corn Law repeal, Aydelotte looks at that party only. Among Conservative MPs, members of the landed class and businessmen divided in almost identical proportions (31 percent of Tory landed elites supported repeal, as compared to 32 percent of businessmen).[22] Of course, this does not mean that MPs were perfect proxies for their respective social classes. More meaningful differences appear if the geographic division between urban and county seats is taken into account. Forty-eight percent of borough MPs voted in favor of repeal, compared to 17 percent of rural MPs (Aydelotte 1967, 54).

While these data lead to the intuitive conclusion that repeal was less popular in the countryside than in the towns, they also suggest that agrarian interests (or at least their proxies in Parliament) were not monolithically protectionist. Schonhardt-Bailey (1991) explores the question of whether such agrarian divisions existed outside of Parliament as well. Her findings mirror those of Aydelotte—there was significant division over agricultural protection in the British countryside. She notes that by the mid-1830s, stimulated by the railway boom and the development of a capital market, a substantial number of agriculturalists had begun to expand their nonagricultural holdings. Indeed, the railway boom, and concomitant increased exports in heavy industry and mining, generated greater returns on diversified holdings. The result, Schonhardt-Bailey notes (1991, 556), was that "diversification into potentially (and in some regions of the country, predominantly) nonagricultural ventures allowed landowners to spread their investment risks among various sectors of the economy not directly benefiting from the expansion (or maintenance) of British agricultural production. . . . [I]n the extreme, landowner interests began to resemble those of industrialists favoring free trade, or more moderately, their interests simply became less sharply defined, perhaps bordering on indifference." Schonhardt-Bailey suggests that the extent to which constituents had engaged in portfolio diversification may well have influenced how MPs voted on the issue of agricultural protection. Examining death duty registers and income tax returns from 1830 to 1850, Schonhardt-Bailey constructed indexes of diversification. She finds that MPs from more diversified agricultural regions were more likely to support free trade than were those from less diversified constituencies. Again, if we assume that MPs serve to some extent as proxies for their constituency preferences, there is evidence of agrarian sympathy for trade liberalization in the 1840s.

A final significant and often-overlooked point showing that there existed at least some agrarian support for (or at least willingness to go along with) repeal was that the ultimate Corn Law bill of 1846 was passed through the House of Lords. In fact, only 22 peers voted against the bill on Third Reading in that chamber (Christie 1928, 51–52). While it took some statesmanship on the part of the Duke of Wellington to navigate the bill's passage, the fact remains that the highest strata of the agrarian class were in a position to kill the repeal initiative and chose not to do so (Barnes 1965, 278; Greville 1885, 47).[23]

Ample evidence exists to support the counterfactual argument that Peel could have survived repeal had he adopted an iterative strategy in 1842. It is hardly conclusive, of course. What is clear is that Peel's economic analysis was on target. Repeal would stimulate rapid economic expansion; the agricultural class as a whole could survive repeal. Finally, at least in his own mind, Peel was convinced that his actions had preserved the integrity of the realm. His memoirs illustrate this point most vividly in the aftermath of the

1848 Revolution in France.

> Many of the men who had been the loudest in the condemnation of the
> measures of 1846, and the least scrupulous in imputing dishonesty and
> treachery to the advisers of them, openly rejoiced on the 10th of April,
> 1848 that provision had been made (by a lucky accident, of course) for
> the total repeal of the Corn Laws. . . . On the removal of all danger from
> popular disaffection, or, I should rather say, on the signal proof of gen-
> eral contentment and devotion to the cause of order, the admissions
> made as to the causal good-fortune of the measures referred to were
> speedily retracted. They were retracted without due reflection on the
> causes which had conspired in the hour of danger to promote loyalty to
> the Throne and confidence in the justice of Parliament (Peel 1857,
> 2:312–13).[24]

The ultimate proof of the soundness of Peel's economic reasoning can be
seen in the near-universal support that free trade enjoyed through the half
century following repeal. From a politically marginal policy in the late 1830s,
free trade became all but universally supported in the 1850s and beyond. By
the fourth quarter of the nineteenth century, despite a fierce depression that
lasted more than twenty years, Britain remained a free-trading economy.
Even the dominant protectionist movement of the time—the fair-trade
lobby—sought not a return to prohibitive import barriers but rather merely
an end to the perceived injustice of Britain's policy of unilateral free trade in
the face of market closure abroad. The explanation for this sea change in attitudes toward free trade in Britain was understood intuitively by Peel and is
clear from the logic of the limits of rent seeking model.

Fate of the Rent Seekers

In the aftermath of repeal, the British government broadened its commitment to free trade. In 1853, import duties were removed from 120 additional items, and after the 1860 Cobden-Chevalier Treaty with France, only
48 categories of imports were subjected to any duties whatsoever (Eichengreen 1992, 162–63).[25] There was very little immediate protectionist backlash, although James Caird, a tenant farmer, expressed the sentiments of his
class, "Anyone who had been long accustomed to lean upon a crutch would
feel very uncomfortable if it were suddenly knocked away from him. If he
were a real cripple, that would be a very cruel act. If he only fancied himself
one, it might be the kindest thing in the world; but whether a true cripple or

a hypochondriac, he would be very angry in the first place. The cripple would fall down from weakness, the hypochondriac would throw himself down in bewilderment and despair. Both would be disposed to cry—'Give me back my crutch!'"[26] The principal debate surrounding trade policy during the 1860s turned on whether to maintain the status quo or to liberalize further by repealing the revenue duties (Brown 1943, 4). Free trade, in Britain and elsewhere, came to be associated with prosperity and good economic times.

In part, the transition to what is generally known as the golden age of free trade was facilitated by fortuitous circumstances. During the 1850s, for example, the Crimean War precluded the importation of Russian wheat at around the same time that gold discoveries in Australia and California raised commodity prices, increased opportunities for trade, and provided a general economic stimulus. A decade later, wars in the United States and continental Europe again disrupted the flow of imports and coincided with bountiful domestic harvests. In all, while wheat imports increased during the 1850s, the predicted catastrophic fall in grain prices in the immediate aftermath of repeal failed to materialize.[27]

The good times were not destined to continue. With the depression of 1873–1896, Britain was the only major industrialized country that did not reimpose tariffs on agricultural and/or industrial goods.[28] The living standards of British farmers declined during the depression. The result, somewhat predictably, was a mild resurgence of protectionist sentiment. What was surprising was how weak the protectionist backlash was. For most of the 1870s, economic decline in agriculture was generally blamed not on free trade, but rather on poor weather and bad harvests (Thompson 1981, 108). Certainly this was the conclusion of the 1879 Royal Commission on the Depressed State of the Agricultural Interest.[29] However, bad harvests at home coincided with a flood of imported grains from abroad. These imports, stimulated by peace and the railroad boom, were made more difficult to take by virtue of market closure abroad. Much of the protectionist clamor, however, focused merely on the one-sidedness of Britain's free-trade policy (Brown 1943, ch. 1).[30]

In the end, free trade remained firmly entrenched, and widely acclaimed, for the remainder of the century (see esp. Imlah 1958, ch. 6). As late as 1890, almost twenty years into the depression, Brown suggests that to criticize the efficacy of free trade in Britain was a "very hazardous enterprise" (Brown 1943, 3). This was underscored in the early twentieth century. Joseph Chamberlain's 1903 campaign for tariff reform was soundly rejected by British voters three years later. It was not until the Great Depression of the 1930s that Britain's commitment to free trade ultimately faltered.

Inflexible Rent Seekers

Typically, charting the progress of inflexible rent seekers in the aftermath of a rent reduction is difficult. Enterprises fail for a number of reasons. Recessions and depressions—themselves often catalysts for rent reductions—may well be the cause of enterprise failure, making direct causal links difficult to establish. Indeed, the nineteenth-century depression certainly forced many farmers from their farms (Imlah 1958, 184–85).

Repeal did not generate the rural upheaval that many had feared. Some even have suggested that economically, repeal was a largely spurious event (Clapham 1930, 476; Chambers and Mingay 1966, 125). However, behavior typically is predicated on perceptions about the future, and in the late 1840s and early 1850s, that future appeared bleak for the agricultural community (Hansen 1961, 265–66). While obviously we do not have the benefit of opinion polls to capture in any systematic way the attitudes of the least efficient and/or most risk-averse farmers, British emigration records provide a rough proxy. Emigration, in other words, constitutes the triumph of exit over voice—the prerogative of the inflexible rent seeker.

For present purposes, Van Vugt (1988) conducted the most effective study of British emigration (see also Hansen 1961). He examined passenger lists of ships carrying British emigrants to the United States in 1851. Comparing data from passenger lists to the 1851 British census, Van Vugt found that emigrant farmers were strongly overrepresented: they consisted of 6.5 percent of the census, but 21.4 percent of the passenger sample.[31] For purposes of comparison over time, Van Vugt also constructed an "index of representation." This rough measure is derived by dividing the percentage of emigrants whose occupation involved agriculture into a like percentage on the census and multiplying by 100. For 1851, the index of representation was 84. By contrast, studies conducted by C. J. Erickson for 1831, 1841, and the late 1880s generated scores of 76, 73, and 61 respectively (Van Vugt 1988, 415–517). The contrast is clear. Not only were British farmers overrepresented by occupation among 1851 emigrants, but the proportion of emigrant farmers in the immediate aftermath of repeal was greater than it had been previously and would be subsequently. The obvious implication is that repeal spurred out-migration of British farmers who, correctly or otherwise, predicted that the demise of agricultural protection would doom their farms.

Certainly there was reason for many farmers to fear for their future prosperity. Van Vugt cites a number of newspapers, both liberal and conservative, that emphasized the dire plight of farmers at the time. Such widespread reporting could not *but* have a negative psychological effect on risk-averse farmers. Moreover, there was a viable economic basis for concern. By 1851, imports of wheat, barley, and oats had more than doubled from their 1840–1845 averages; prices of these commodities had slipped as well, albeit within the bounds of normal fluctuation (Van Vugt 1988, 420; Vamplew 1980, 391).

Many British farmers adopted new forms of agriculture—either through improvements to the land or through a shift in production to more profitable means of farming, usually raising of livestock. Both options required a significant investment of capital. For many small grain farmers, such adaptation was not a viable choice.

If inflexible rent seekers consisted mainly of farmers who could not afford to adapt to the new agricultural status quo, we would expect to see a disproportionately large share of undercapitalized farmers emigrating in the immediate postrepeal era. Available data do not allow us to confirm this hypothesis. However, passenger lists do indicate, in some cases, emigrants' county of residence. These may be compared to Caird's (1967) authoritative 1850–1851 survey of agriculture in English counties—which classifies counties on a four-point scale from "severely distressed" to "prosperous"—to provide another rough proxy.[32] Once again, I rely on Van Vugt. Of emigrating farmers who articulated a county of residence, 60 percent came from severely distressed counties; 33.2 percent were from "moderately distressed" or "minimally distressed" counties. None hailed from prosperous counties.[33]

While the available data allow for only crude measurement, they do seem to support the idea that repeal sparked a brief exodus of English farmers from the most distressed counties. These farmers, the least likely to have access to the capital necessary to shift production to means more compatible with global competition, represent inflexible rent seekers. They also represent a small portion of the farming population. Indeed, most farmers, consistent with behavior predicted for flexible rent seekers, altered production techniques to accommodate market conditions thrust on them by repeal.

Flexible Rent Seekers

Survival by flexible rent seekers in Britain can be attributed to a combination of serendipity and high farming. Fortune smiled, at least at first, on those who farmed the choicest land. For these farmers, life continued largely as before; the imperative to reform did not arrive until grain prices fell sharply with the depression of 1873–1896. But for many, repeal served as a harbinger for the cold winds of change. By the mid-1850s, the transition to high farming was well under way.

While drainage of surface water and other land improvements were not unheard of in the far mists of British history, high-farming techniques were a nineteenth-century phenomenon. Moore dates the high-farming movement to the aftermath of the Napoleonic War. Specifically, he notes two distinct and familiar reactions to the postwar agricultural distress. The political response was to cry for relief; the economic was to improve the land (Moore 1965; see also Prothero 1912, ch. 1; Adams 1932; Orwin and Whetham 1964).

An early key to improvement was drainage. Britain's wet climate played havoc with the heavier, clay soils that potentially were the most fertile. Undrained land, heavy and slow under the plough, was less productive than was better drained soil. In wet seasons, crops were forced to compete with hydrophilic weeds. Early- and late-season rain arrested the growth of grass, negatively affecting livestock; similarly, the effects of early or late frosts told more severely. Finally, undrained land required more bare fallow than did properly drained soil.

Traditional surface drainage methods consisted of raised ridges and intervening drainage furrows, which carried rainwater away from crops. The problem, however, was that nutrients and fertilizers were carried away with the rainwater. Subsurface draining techniques, the most effective of which involved cutting trenches into the land, filling them with stones or tree boughs, and before re-covering them, were far more preferable, allowing nutrients to percolate into the soil. With the invention of the more durable clay pipe in 1843, manufactured to standard sizes, subterranean drainage became cheaper, although still prohibitive to many farmers (Prothero 1912, ch. 17; Sturgess 1966; Chambers and Mingay 1966, 174–77; Orwin and Whetham 1964, 100–1; Grigg 1989, ch. 4).

There were additional benefits associated with high farming. As productivity increased, high farmers took to supplementing the effects of improved drainage with ever-larger doses of fertilizer. To increase fertilizer supply, many began to enlarge their livestock holdings, thus moving into the mixed farming that, through the logic of diversification (and later, changing consumption patterns on the part of newly affluent British consumers) allowed them to prosper even as wheat prices declined in the 1870s (Moore 1965, 546; May 1987, 104).

Mechanization was another important innovation. Mechanized threshers and reapers, which had been invented in the United States, slowly found favor in Britain. Uneven terrain and smaller fields forced British farmers to adapt and tinker with new equipment. Between 1851 and 1870, for example, British inventors applied for nearly three hundred patents for reapers alone. By 1874, almost half of the cereal harvest was realized by machine (May 1987, 104).

Even so, high farming was controversial in early Victorian England. It met with strong resistance in some quarters from tenants and landlords alike. Land improvement was expensive, and as the boom years of the 1810s had shown, the volatility of commodity prices made it a risky proposition. Drainage costs came to roughly £5 per acre—the equivalent of perhaps four years' gross rental income (Murphy 1973, 605). Land improvement mortgages were difficult to obtain. Thus, if landlords sought to make improvements, they were often obliged to finance the enterprise themselves. Tenants, moreover, even if they could secure capital, often did not enjoy sufficient security of tenure to make land improvements a viable option. Finally, as with any innovation, there was a great deal of resistance to high farming. For example, even where landlords provided incentives for their tenants to adopt new farming techniques, these were often resisted by farmers wedded to more traditional means of agriculture. As late as 1850, W. E. Aytoun wrote in *Blackwood's*, "If high farming could be shown to be productive, high farming would be the rule and not the exception" (Moore 1965, 553; see also Prothero 1912, 374; Fletcher 1961, 424; Chambers and Mingay 1966, 160–62).

Others, however, were less encumbered by traditional thinking. Peel, a founding member of the English Agricultural Society,[34] had long been an advocate of scientific farming techniques. It is telling that in his "repeal speech" (January 27, 1846), Peel spent a great deal of time articulating a concomitant plan to assist British farmers in adapting to a more competitive environment. To this end, a large number of rural burdens—including highway taxes, prosecution costs, maintenance of prisoners, policing costs, medical relief, and teachers' salaries—were eliminated or reduced. In addition, Peel sought to lower factor inputs necessary for effective high farming. Specifically, he recommended free importation of maize and buckwheat (principally for fattening cattle and generating richer manure), as well as a reduction in seed duties. Most important was the commitment to provide low-interest loans to farmers for the purpose of land improvements, most importantly drainage (Peel 1853, 595–600; see also Peel 1857, 2:195; Moore 1965, 553–56; Read 1987, 168–71).[35] Indeed, the three-year phase-out of the Corn Laws, so difficult to reconcile with immediate relief for Ireland, becomes far more comprehensible in the context of the Drainage Act. Obviously, given Peel's political fate, compensatory legislation was deemed inadequate; high farming did not catch on with the majority of flexible rent seekers until the 1850s.

Compensation ultimately became at least a small factor in the shift to high farming on the part of flexible rent seekers.[36] Equally importantly though, as Peel had foreseen, high farming and free trade had a symbiotic effect. This symbiosis was both direct and indirect. The direct relationship is obvious: the prospect of foreign competition obligated farmers to become more productive. Indirectly, free trade contributed to a steady increase in aggregate wealth in Great Britain. As a result, consumption patterns changed with respect to both durable goods and foodstuffs. As ever, Caird put it most clearly, writing in the late 1870s.

> Thirty years ago probably not more than one-third of the people of this country consumed animal food more than once a week. Now, nearly all of them eat it, in meat or cheese or butter, once a day. This has more than doubled the average consumption of animal food in this country.... The leap which the consumption of meat took in consequence of the general rise of wages in all branches of trade and employment, could not have been secured except by such a rise in prices as fully paid the risk and cost of transport. The additional price on the home-produce was all profit to the landed interests of this country (Caird 1878, 289; see also Armitage-Smith 1898, ch. 9).

In the aftermath of repeal, champions of high farming had advocated that farmers actively pursue mixed farming—that is, to diversify their holdings by shifting a greater portion of production to livestock. While such dual production was hardly a novelty, the integration of crop and livestock production was a postrepeal innovation. Caird (1967, 488–89) articulated the logic clearly: "The safe course for the English agriculturalist is to endeavour, by increasing his livestock, to render himself less dependent on corn, while he at the same time enriches his farm by their manure, and is enabled to grow heavier crops at less comparative cost." This was advice that farmers could take to heart. Cereal acreage peaked in 1855 in Britain; after that time, it declined steadily (Chambers and Mingay 1966, 183; Thompson 1981, 110).[37] The shift in production profiles is most stark in the years leading up to, and including, the nineteenth-century depression. Table 2.1 examines two representative commodities—wheat and cattle production—from 1866 through 1896. During this period, when import competition was steepest, and the

Table 2.1
Production of wheat and cattle in Great Britain, 1866–96

YEAR	ACRES OF WHEAT (Millions)	CATTLE (Millions)
1866	3.350	4.786
1867	3.368	4.993
1868	3.652	5.424
1869	3.688	5.313
1870	3.501	5.403
1871	3.572	5.338
1872	3.599	5.625
1873	3.490	5.965
1874	3.630	6.125
1875	3.342	6.013
1876	2.996	5.844
1877	3.169	5.698
1878	3.218	5.738
1879	2.890	5.856
1880	2.909	5.912
1881	2.806	5.912
1882	3.004	5.807
1883	2.613	5.963
1884	2.677	6.269
1885	2.478	6.598
1886	2.286	6.647
1887	2.317	6.441
1888	2.564	6.129
1889	2.449	6.140
1890	2.386	6.509
1891	2.307	6.853
1892	2.220	6.945
1893	1.898	6.701
1894	1.928	6.347
1895	1.417	6.354
1896	1.694	6.494
Change, 1866–96	*−97.8%*	*35.7%*

Source: Great Britain (1968, 98, 122).

greatest premium, therefore, was on productive farming, wheat acreage declined by almost 100 percent; cattle husbandry increased by more than one-third.

Mixed farming ultimately is what saved the British farmer in the latter half of the nineteenth century, even in the teeth of the depression. After repeal, high farming also consisted of what Pusey (1842) called high feeding. When grain prices were low, many clayland farmers eschewed the cereal market, opting instead to use their produce to fatten their livestock and make their profits through the sale of "fatstocks." This strategy was greatly enhanced through new technology such as artificial fertilizers and mechanized threshing machines. With increased demand for milk and meat on the part of newly affluent Britons,[38] cereal crops often became factor inputs to more lucrative enterprises. Indeed, well-drained soils permitted the optimal production of root crops, livestock, manure, and cereals (Chambers and Mingay 1966, 184; Fletcher 1961, 422; Thompson 1981, 105–6; Murphy 1973, 609–12).

Table 2.2
Gross agricultural output in the United Kingdom, 1867–1903
(in £ million)

	1867–69	1870–76	1894–1903
Wheat	35.38	27.56	7.72
Barley	16.78	17.56	9.43
Oats	10.54	9.07	8.07
Potatoes	14.02	13.82	11.34
Hay/straw/fruit/vegetables	20.11	19.40	21.75
Other crops	7.34	7.58	3.64
Total arable	*104.17*	*94.99*	*61.95*
Beef	34.90	45.67	42.05
Mutton	25.92	30.51	25.20
Pig meat	18.60	22.95	19.13
Horses	1.50	2.00	3.00
Milk	33.78	38.51	43.56
Wool	7.49	8.27	3.24
Poultry/eggs	4.57	6.96	10.00
Total livestock	*126.76*	*154.87*	*146.18*

Source: Fletcher (1961, 432).

As table 2.2 suggests, the depression had widely differential effects on farmers. Many of those whose livelihood centered wholly on cereals and other arable production suffered (see Jones 1968, 17–25; Perren 1973). As Thompson (1981, 113) puts it, not every farmer who entered the depression was there at the end, "purring with satisfaction at the size of his bank balance." Some farmers, risk averse or uncertain about the future of the cereal market, were slow to adapt; some were simply unwilling (Armitage-Smith 1898, 181). Jones (1974, 202–3) points out that "[m]any farmers regarded the wheat crop with an almost mystical reverence" and quotes one farmer as suggesting that "none [sic] of us have been able sufficiently to throw off the trammels of custom and association, which led him to look for profit first to the stack rather than to the stall." Jones's farmer was not alone. Brown (1987, 35–36) cites the *Agricultural Gazette* and the *Retford News* circa 1880 admonishing farmers for admitting to failure by eschewing the "less profitable, though more professional pursuit of corn-growing." Finally, adaptation was made more difficult by the structure of many agricultural leases, which, at least until the 1890s, restricted tenants' abilities to use the land most profitably (Kindleberger 1964, 246–47; compare Ó Gráda 1994, 156–59). For these less-adaptable farmers, as figure 2.1 illustrates clearly for wheat, the tough times of the depression were magnified by increased competition from foreign producers.

But misfortune was not universal. Declining grain prices had two beneficial effects for mixed and livestock farmers. First, it lowered feed (i.e., production) costs. Thus, to the extent that cereal farmers may have wished to stem the flow of imported cereals during the tough years, livestock farmers had the opposite preference. Mixed farmers grew increasingly reliant on purchased factor inputs, principally feeds and fertilizers, and much of it imported. This was especially true of guano, which was widely used and imported from Peru, and oilcakes used as livestock feed (More 1989, 131; Murphy 1973, 609–12; May 1987, 109–10). During the 1850s, British farmers purchased roughly £10 million of inputs per year. By the 1870s, this had risen to £17 million (Perren 1995, 2).

Second, as the value of wheat fell, declining bread prices, combined with higher working-class wages, stimulated demand for higher-quality foodstuffs, such as meat, eggs, and dairy products. Meat prices held up much better to import competition. Although chilled beef from the United States began to be imported after 1875, and frozen meat arrived from Australia beginning in 1880, consumers were willing to pay a premium for higher-quality British meat. Dairy products also enjoyed competitive advantages over

Figure 2.1: Imports of wheat and flour, 1820–1909

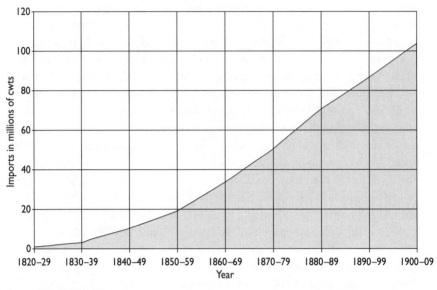

Source: May (1987, 107).

imports. The expansive network of railways allowed dairy farmers to get their product to market quickly (Armitage-Smith 1898, 177–79; Fletcher 1961, 423–24; More 1989, ch. 14). Divergent production profiles on the part of British farmers help to explain why the agricultural protection movement was so weak in Britain, even in the face of market closure abroad. Thus, while the depression had the entirely intuitive effect of harming most forms of agricultural production, high and mixed farming allowed farmers to ride out the storm. Importantly for our purposes, these flexible rent seekers appear to have retained their commitment to free trade and open markets.

The case of Britain in the nineteenth century provides an interesting illustration of the limits of rent seeking model: while rent seekers behaved as expected in the face of a significant rent reduction, Sir Robert Peel was unable to escape political sanction. Repeal was not the wrong move, but Peel probably selected a suboptimal strategy to achieve it.

The big bang strategy did not work; there is no guarantee that iteration would have either. On the other hand, the evidence suggests that a coalition of free-trading, or at least ambivalent, interests could have been constructed in the countryside. The strategy would not have been costless, of course. However, it would have served to spread the political backlash over time and should have provided the benefit of a larger, mobilized set of allies within the landed classes.

Another reason to question whether Peel selected poorly is that the assumption is that Peel's optimal preference was to undercut democratic agitation while preserving his political career. However, it is not clear that he valued both objectives equally. Rather, it seems likely from his selfless actions of 1845–1846 that he valued the first far more highly than he did the second. Insofar as repeal appears to have served Peel's overarching objectives, it is difficult to criticize the means by which he achieved them.

Most politicians are more concerned, however, about the political fates that accompany their decisions. As an illustration of the means by which trade liberalization can be undertaken in a way that imposes few political costs, Peel's use of the big bang strategy was a failure. However, as a demonstration of the logic of the limits of rent seeking model, the British case must rate as a success. As expected, a significant rent reduction appears to have forced inflexible rent seekers from the marketplace. Emigration records appear to show that farmers were, as Van Vugt puts it, "running from ruin," or at least ruin as they perceived it. Flexible rent seekers, by contrast, became strong adherents of high farming, especially after 1855. As a result, even in the face of a long and bitter depression, British agriculture did not roll back the clock. Instead, it remained free trading and prosperous.

3

Pressure Groups and the Basis of American Hegemony

In the years between the passage of the Smoot-Hawley Tariff in 1930 and the end of the Second World War, the United States was transformed from a protectionist, inward-looking economy to a world hegemon, establishing and underwriting a global free-market economy under the auspices of the GATT, the IMF, and the World Bank. During the same period, the U.S. business community also largely altered its production profile and trade policy preferences. The fundamental shift in U.S. trade policy, undertaken without serious political backlash, provides both illustration of the limits of rent seeking model and prescriptive lessons for other countries seeking to liberalize trade.

The transformation of flexible rent-seeker behavior in the United States is more complex than in most of the other cases presented here. The intervention of World War II between the initial, gradual reduction in rents under the Reciprocal Trade Agreements Act (RTAA) in the mid-1930s and the subsequent full transformation of most of the industrial rent-seeker population leaves the causality of the process somewhat ambiguous. Undoubtedly the war and its concomitant technological advances had some impact on the trade policy preferences of U.S. businesses in the postwar era. The devastation of foreign producers not only lessened the threat of import penetration but created opportunities for export expansion in rapidly rebuilding economies in Europe and elsewhere.

On the other hand, the transformation of flexible rent-seeker behavior in the United States was not determined solely, or even principally, by war. Between 1934, when the reduction in rents began, and the end of that decade, the majority of big businesses in the United States appear to have altered their orientation toward trade, a trend that was later mirrored by small and medium-sized firms (see Bauer, de la Sola Pool, and Dexter 1972, esp. 113–16). In addition, past experience suggests that the devastation of foreign competitors in war is not a sufficient condition for the transformation of flexible rent-seeker behavior. After World War I, for example, despite conditions equally advantageous to U.S. business as the post–World War II era, most American businessmen advocated protectionism under the Fordney-Mc-Cumber and Smoot-Hawley acts (see Schattschneider 1935; Ferguson 1984; Gourevitch 1986; Frieden 1988; Goldstein 1993b). Moreover, the intervention of war does not explain why American farmers, who were internationally competitive and traditionally free trading (but who continued to derive significant state-supplied rents in the postwar era even as industrial rents were slashed), were and remained vocal opponents of the extension of the GATT to the agricultural sector (Goldstein 1993a). Finally, war cannot explain the proclivity of most American industrialists to maintain support for free trade long after competitors in Europe and Japan had recovered and begun to challenge American dominance in manufacturing. Indeed, the majority of U.S. businesses remained free traders even after the decline of American hegemony in the early 1970s, pushing for the extension of free trade under the GATT, NAFTA with Canada and Mexico, and the proposed Free Trade Area of the Americas (FTAA; see Milner 1988; Pew Research Center 1997).

Although set against the backdrop of the Great Depression, and hence at least partly stimulated by crisis, the American case is largely a story of strategic rent reductions. The administration of Franklin D. Roosevelt, anxious to recast its electoral alliance to include farmers, labor, the urban poor, and international business and finance (Gourevitch 1986, 176–78), used the iteration strategy to transform U.S. foreign economic policy in the 1930s and 1940s. Under the auspices of the RTAA, a broad pro–free-trade coalition was continually strengthened until it had largely vanquished advocates of protectionism. While the process was slow—small and medium-sized enterprises remained less supportive of trade liberalization through the 1930s—the transformation was effected without much political backlash. So complete was the transformation, moreover, that even the Republican Party, the traditional party of import protection, was converted to support for free trade throughout the remainder of the twentieth century.

The Historical Context

Historically, free trade did not have particularly strong roots in the United States. The first tariff, of 1789, was fairly modest, reflecting the need for revenue, the quest for national security (that is, less reliance on Great Britain),[1] and to a limited extent the influence of vested interests. The Napoleonic War (including the blockade of Europe) created great opportunities for American agricultural and shipping interests and tended to dampen pressure for a more restrictive industrial tariff. The War of 1812, by contrast, underscored the need for revenue generation through a protective tariff and saw a sharp rise in import protection (Taussig 1923, pt. I, ch. 1, sec. II).

As is so often the case with war, technological changes and increased industrial activity brought with them a demand for continued and even increased import protection. Where there is a constituency, political market forces dictate there will emerge a faction or party to supply the good (Downs 1957; Grossman and Helpman 1994). In the case of the early United States, this constituency found voice through Henry Clay and his American System, a policy of protection for manufacturing that, in turn, would not only allow for the further development of infant industries but would continue to generate national revenue and stimulate the demand for primary production in the vast tracts of western land. The results were the protectionist tariff of 1816 (which, although a reduction in the tariff rate, kept tariffs above their antebellum levels) and the even more generous tariff of 1824 (Pincus 1977, 21, 36–46; Curtiss 1896, 577–82).[2]

The high-water mark for protectionism in this era was reached with the 1828 Tariff of Abominations.[3] Like most politics of the day, the tariff issue was largely regional, with northern industrialists and, on occasion, western farmers aligned against an antitariff South.[4] Western farmers tended to vacillate on the tariff issue. Generally, prior to the 1840s, western farmers were persuaded by the advantages of a home market for their goods (which were effectively kept out of the lucrative British market until the repeal of the Corn Laws in 1846). However, periodic South-West alliances in the early 1830s and mid-1840s,[5] aided by a healthy budget surplus, declining popularity of the tariff, and the perceived imperative to relieve the South of further abominations, led to pressures for tariff reduction for most of this period. Indeed, tariff rates fell with both the Compromise Tariff of 1833 and the 1846 Walker Tariff. On the other hand, the 1837 crisis and the prevailing North-West alliance were the driving forces behind the protectionist Black

Tariff of 1842 (James and Lake 1989, 9–14; see also Curtiss 1896, 587–601; Stanwood 1903, 2:ch. 11; Taussig 1923, chs. 2–3; Pincus 1977, 10–11).

Of course, the tariff issue was not solely hostage to regional politics. In large part, tariff rates were set in accordance with national finances.[6] When the budget was in surplus, there was downward pressure on the tariff; when in deficit, the reverse was true. Moreover, regional preferences were distorted by political actors seeking to create and maintain broad electoral alliances in a period of growing polarization.

In the 1840s and 1850s, protectionism largely was kept at bay. Corn Law repeal and, to a lesser extent, the Walker Tariff were harbingers of the golden age of free trade. In Europe, free trade was institutionalized through the 1860s with the Cobden-Chevalier Treaty of 1860 between Britain and France (see, for example, Durham 1930). In the United States, financial crisis after 1857 and ultimately war brought the golden age of free trade to a sudden halt, first with the (prewar) 1861 Morrill Tariff and more importantly with the 1862 and 1864 Tariff Acts.[7]

The tariff of 1864 was enacted partly in compensation for the massive internal revenue acts of the same year. Tariffs were necessary both to offset the tax burden on domestic producers and to mitigate any advantages that might accrue to foreign producers as a result of the increased internal revenue obligations (Stanwood 1903, 2:128). On the other hand, it seems fairly clear that the internal revenue issue also served as a stalking horse for the gratification of protectionist demands that would prove intractable and highly successful long after the end of the war.[8]

By the time of the next major tariff revision in 1883, protectionism was firmly entrenched. Regional tensions were still prevalent in tariff debates, with the agricultural regions, the South and West, by now united against the tariff. Moreover, tariff rates continued to fluctuate according to the demand for national revenue. However, rent-seeking industrial interests, with increasingly institutionalized influence in Congress, tended to dominate. While the 1883 act featured some tariff reductions, these were largely cosmetic. The main thrust of the legislation was to build on the protectionist benchmark established with the 1864 tariff.

The 1883 Tariff Act was followed with the protectionist McKinley Tariff of 1890 and Dingley Tariff of 1897.[9] Collectively these constituted an exercise in maintaining protectionism while seeking to expand foreign markets, particularly in Latin America, through the use of reciprocal trade agreements. True reciprocity, however, was undermined by two factors. First, unlike most European countries, the United States was unwilling to generalize preferences granted under specific treaties. Whereas most other countries operated according to the principle of unconditionality—where a concession to one most-favored nation is a concession to all—the United States maintained its tradition of conditional (country-specific) concessions that were available only to countries that provided discrete reciprocal benefits. The effect, of course, was that a concession to one served as a penalty to all others who, in the absence of their own specific concessions, were placed at a disadvantage vis-à-vis access to the U.S. market.[10] Second, the provisions for reciprocity under the McKinley and Dingley tariffs were not as generous as they might have appeared on paper. Congress placed a number of "tropical" (and hence non-import-competing) goods such as sugar, molasses, coffee, tea, and hides on the duty-free list. However, the president was given the power to assess penalties to countries that exported such goods if reciprocal concessions were not made. In short, the reciprocity provision was a means of persuading foreign governments to extend import concessions to the United States in exchange for concessions on goods that the United States required anyway (see Ashley 1926, 226–27; United States Tariff Commission 1919, 145–49; Wilson 1971, 68–70; Brenner 1978, ch. 1; Rhodes 1993, ch. 2).

The overall effect of the McKinley Tariff was to liberalize trade slightly. The list of products on the duty-free list was expanded from about one-third of imports to roughly one-half. Moreover, the average nominal tariff rate fell. In import-competing sectors, however, the tariff on dutiable imports actually rose from 45.1 to 48.4 percent (Lake 1988a, 100). The effect was to provide greater rents to core manufacturing constituents of the Republican Party. As Stern (1971, 38–39) notes, "With the passage of that legislation the Republicans had given hitherto unequaled legislative expression to the view that the national interest required little more than supplying the manufacturers with a profusion of protectionist favors."

The Dingley Tariff, which restored tariffs reduced under the short-lived 1894 Wilson-Gorman Tariff, represented the culmination of the partisan divide that characterized the Reconstruction era. That cleavage, emerging out of the Civil War, increasingly pitted tight-money/high-tariff Republicans against free-silver/free-trading Democrats. The cleavage was institutionalized with the realigning election of 1896, the Dingley Tariff, and the so-called System of '96 that generally informed the parties' economic positions through the first three decades of the next century.[11]

With the System of '96, however, came new pressures from progressives within the Republican Party, who demanded a more scientific and nonpartisan application of the tariff. Such demands had been voiced periodically since the Civil War, as the increasing complexity of the tariff made it difficult for Congress to do more than sort out competing interest-group demands. It is no surprise that this had resulted in an inflationary trend in the tariff rate.

The 1909 Payne-Aldrich Tariff made concessions to a scientific tariff, chiefly through introduction of the so-called cost-equalization principle as the ostensible basis for U.S. tariff rates. Under this principle, U.S. tariffs would be used to offset production cost differentials between foreign and U.S.-made goods. This more scientific approach was designed to limit the rents afforded by the tariff. While it undermined the ability of rent seekers to extract exorbitant rents, an obvious side effect was to compensate for comparative disadvantage and (by virtue of increasing the costs of some intermediate goods) penalize sectors that enjoyed comparative advantage. In essence, the cost-equalization principle obviated the benefits of international trade.

Democratic control of Congress and the presidency following the 1912 elections contributed to a liberalizing trend with the Underwood Tariff of 1913.[12] The Underwood Tariff saw the nominal tariff rate fall to its lowest level since the Civil War. The dutiable import rate fell from 41.0 percent under Payne-Aldrich to 26.8 percent, while the percentage of goods on the duty-free list rose from 51.3 to 67.5 (Lake 1988a, 154–55). The tariff was based on a modification of the cost-equalization principle known as the competitive tariff, under which import duties were to reflect the level necessary for the maintenance of "legitimate" domestic industries without necessarily being based on the equalization of foreign and domestic production costs. The effect was to allow a certain amount of import competition for domestic producers. However, since there was no definition of either legitimacy or necessary level of protection, the process of tariff making under the competitive tariff principle was largely arbitrary.[13]

With the passage of the Underwood Tariff, Republicans accused the Democrats of producing an unscientific tariff. Under the provisions of the competitive tariff, congressional judgment was substituted for dispassionate scientific investigation of the optimal tariff rate. Progressive Republicans pressed for the creation of an independent investigative commission that could provide the information necessary to generate a truly scientific application of the tariff. The motive was what might be called progressive protectionism—import protection that was not overly preferential to rent-seeking special interests. As a consequence, in 1916 a permanent, nonpartisan Tariff Commission was established as a body responsible to Congress, to serve as a counterweight to rent seekers while still maintaining the cost-equalization principle (see Bernhardt 1922, ch. 1; Becker 1982, 86–89).

The Underwood Tariff remained in place for nine years, a fairly impressive tenure given that it bucked a steady trend of high levels of import protection. Its longevity may be explained in part by the fact that while the Democratic Party remained far less committed to protection than did the Republicans, neither party was keen to articulate its position terribly strongly. Democrats tempered their free-trade position for fear of alienating rent-seeking producers in critical districts. Republicans had to contend with a powerful Progressive sentiment within their ranks. In addition, the producer sector itself was far from cohesive on the tariff issue. While most industrialists sought high levels of import protection, some business groups also advocated expansion into foreign markets, especially following World War I. It was for this reason that broad-based business organizations such as the U.S. Chamber of Commerce, for example, were in favor of more generous reciprocity provisions even as they advocated import protection (Wilson 1971, ch. 1; Becker 1982, ch. 4). Finally, war in Europe had the effect of providing sufficient protection to U.S. producers that the tariff ceased to be an issue until the early 1920s.

The return to peace and the subsequent economic downturn, especially in the agricultural sector, brought new pressures for protectionism. The proliferation of wartime industries created increased demand for a protective tariff upon the resumption of normal economic relations between the United States and its European trading partners. Moreover, the war had created a new stimulus for nationalism and isolationism, a sentiment reflected in the Republican dominance of the 1920 elections. In the countryside, the urbanization of America combined with falling commodity prices to create a sense of serious concern. Farmers, once the backbone of free trade, began to seek the security of protected markets for their goods (Kelly 1963).

This shifting attitude on the part of farmers removed a moderating influence on the tariff. Rather than serving as a counterweight to rent-seeker demands for excessive industrial tariffs, agricultural interests began to logroll their protectionist demands with those of industrial rent seekers, beginning with the Emergency Tariff of 1921. The effect of this logrolling was not as pernicious as it would become with the 1930 Smoot-Hawley Tariff, but it served to raise tariff rates significantly.

Against this strengthening protectionist coalition, however, came the aforementioned growing divisions within the business community. The Janus-faced commitment both to domestic protection and international expansion created tensions that could not be reconciled in the 1920s and 1930s. By the early postwar era, an internationalist wing of the business community, featuring capital-intensive manufacturers, found itself in opposition to a much larger nationalist wing composed of manufacturers in more labor-intensive sectors (see Wilson 1971, chs. 1, 3; Ferguson 1984; Frieden 1988).

The 1922 Fordney-McCumber Tariff recognized the growing dichotomy within the business sector and constituted a compromise between nationalist and internationalist aspirations. On the one hand, at the urging of rent seekers, import duties were raised substantially over those provided by the Underwood Tariff (Wilson 1971, 82). On the other, Fordney-McCumber strengthened the United States' commitment to reciprocity by jettisoning conditionality in favor of the unconditional most-favored-nation principle. Moreover, the 1922 tariff introduced the so-called flexible-tariff provision whereby presidential discretion in the tariff rate was expanded to allow for downward revision of import duties. Finally, the Tariff Commission was expected to continue as a counterweight to rent-seeker demands in Congress by providing an alternative source of advice on the tariff to Congress and (as a consequence of the flexible tariff) the president.

As the 1930 Smoot-Hawley Tariff attests, the Tariff Commission failed to provide much of a bulwark against the rising tide of protectionist rent seeking. The reasons were partially logistical and mostly political. Logistically, the Tariff Commission was hamstrung by the ubiquitous cost-equalization principle. Generating accurate information on comparative production costs for even a single commodity proved to be extremely complicated. Politically, the dominance of the protectionist alliance of farmers and (nationalist) industrialists created a great incentive for Congress to placate voting constituents by logrolling rent-seeker demands rather than to rely on recommendations of the Tariff Commission.

By one measure, Smoot-Hawley was the most protectionist tariff since 1828, raising the average dutiable tariff rate from 38.2 percent to a staggering 55.3 percent.[14] As domestic manufacturers already enjoyed 96 percent of the U.S. market share, Smoot-Hawley was largely redundant regarding international trade, serving instead to provide rents to domestic producers through greater oligopolistic profits (Kelly 1963, 12–13). Certainly it is impossible to ignore Smoot-Hawley as one of the factors leading to the severity of the global depression of the 1930s.

Trade Liberalization in the 1930s

In retrospect, the timing of the Smoot-Hawley Tariff could not have been more unfortunate. As Kindleberger (1973) has argued, the 1920s witnessed the dying gasps of Britain's ability to lead the world economy. As the heir apparent to the mantle of world hegemon, the United States was uniquely situated to promote the international economic unity and cooperation that might have mitigated the most severe effects of the Great Depression. Instead, the United States retreated into isolationism.

Smoot-Hawley is vilified as the pinnacle of successful rent-seeking activity in the United States. Future secretary of state Cordell Hull described the marriage of congressional logrolling and pressure group self-interest as "a continuous round of political and legislative debauches with graft aforethought" (quoted in Allen 1953, 115). The problem, however, was not so much graft as an institutionally determined outcome. It would have been a brave legislator indeed who resisted the temptation to provide his own constituents with protectionist favors, given the horse trading that surrounded the eighteen-month Smoot-Hawley bargaining process.[15]

The economic effects of the 1930 tariff were devastating to the U.S. economy. Between 1929 and 1932, gross national product (GNP) fell from $104 billion to $58 billion, corporate profits went from $10 billion to $3 billion, durable manufactures declined by 70 percent, and unemployment skyrocketed from four hundred thousand to approximately twelve million (Brady 1988, 85). U.S. exports in 1933 were just over half of the volume of 1929 and under a third of the value (United States Tariff Commission 1948, 2). President Herbert Hoover's response was to stay the course of monetary orthodoxy and trade protectionism that had underscored his party's economic policy throughout the century. The ineffectiveness of this strategy opened the door to Franklin D. Roosevelt, who easily won the 1932 presidential election.

All this is not to suggest, however, that Smoot-Hawley was the only policy blunder leading and contributing to the Depression. U.S. insistence on repayment of war debts owed by European allies, for example, as well as an end to generous lending practices by U.S. banks had conspired, by the late 1920s, to squeeze America's former military allies in Europe into a severe liquidity crisis. The stock market crash of 1929 only made a bad situation worse. The prevailing increase in interest rates limited the options of indebted European countries. Unable to secure new loans, the only avenue open to them was to expand their export sectors as a means of growing out from under their financial burdens (see Jones 1934, esp. 256–57). Smoot-Hawley effectively closed this course of action.[16] Equally problematic was the American decision to go off the gold standard in April 1933, thereby exacerbating the existing menace of widespread predatory currency devaluation (Kindleberger 1973).

The Catalyst

Trade liberalization during the 1930s in the United States served the strategic objectives of Franklin Roosevelt. While the ambient crisis of the Depression served his interests, it did not provide a structural imperative for liberalization. As in the case of Peel in Great Britain, trade liberalization was not Roosevelt's overarching objective. Manifestly, he was more interested in extricating the United States from the clutches of the Great Depression. Moreover, and unlike Peel, Roosevelt did not harbor a private belief that free trade was inevitable or even desirable. His First New Deal, in fact, retained the economic nationalism that had characterized the Hoover administration. For Roosevelt, free trade, manifested in the RTAA, was a purely instrumental policy. It was inimical to his First New Deal coalition; it was critical to his second. While an extraordinary leader serving at an extraordinary time, Roosevelt was far more the prototypical politician than was Peel. For Peel, politics could be sacrificed to principle; for Roosevelt, as he showed in the remarkably agile shift from his First New Deal coalition to his second, politics and principle did not need to be incompatible.

Roosevelt's First New Deal coalition was a quasi-corporatist alliance between the administration, the agricultural sector, and the nationalist industrial sector. Agriculture was enticed into the coalition through a series of farm supports (which were reinforced and extended throughout the Depression and most of the postwar era) under the auspices of the Agricultural Adjustment Act (AAA).[17] To ensure the support of the nationalist business sector, the administration sponsored the National Industrial Recovery Act (NIRA), by which industrial prices were supported through a network of industrial "codes"—essentially a process of government-sanctioned sectoral collusion designed to keep business profitable.[18] Like the farmers, the nationalist business community was attracted by the administration's commitment to the retention of the Smoot-Hawley tariffs, the abandonment of the gold standard, and periodic devaluations of the currency.

The weakest part of the coalition was the business sector. The 1920s had witnessed growing fissures in the solidarity of the business community's support of the System of '96. By the early 1930s, the cleavage was even deeper, as most of the financial sector, as well as the more dynamic new industries, rejected the economic nationalism inherent in both the System of '96 and the First New Deal (Ferguson 1984; Gourevitch 1986; Frieden 1988). At the same time, while a strong majority of U.S. businesses were still protectionist,[19] it was an uneasy ally of the Roosevelt administration. The nationalist business sector, represented most prominently by the U.S. Chamber of Commerce and the National Association of Manufacturers (NAM; Berkowitz and McQuaid 1980, 89–90; Finegold and Skocpol 1984, 182),[20] began to chafe under what it considered to be the economic paternalism of the New Deal. Indeed, these protectionist forces were hostile to state intervention in any area outside of their own narrow interests.[21] In time, nationalist business leaders, especially the American Liberty League, founded in the summer of 1934, would emerge as among Roosevelt's fiercest and most aggressive critics.[22]

As the nationalist business sector became ever more belligerent throughout 1934, Roosevelt equivocated over whether to abandon protectionist business interests in favor of new coalition partners (see esp. Roosevelt 1967, 210–13), pertinently the more dynamic internationalist elements within the business and financial community. Representing new and dynamic industries that had grown up largely after World War I, the internationalists differed from their nationalist counterparts in that they tended to be more capital intensive and innovative and hence more cosmopolitan in orientation. The internationalists, many of whom would be widely recognizable as today's multinational behemoths, did not favor the antagonistic relationship with organized labor that was so prominent with the labor-intensive, nationalist business sector. Indeed, it was the willingness to accommodate the demands of organized labor that would make the internationalists an ideal coalition partner for Roosevelt's Second New Deal.[23] Ultimately, it was the desire to curry favor with the internationalists that motivated Roosevelt to send the Reciprocal Trade Agreements bill to Congress, even before the ultimate disintegration of the First New Deal coalition. Ferguson (1984, 86) describes Roosevelt's motives: "With the pressure [from erstwhile supporters] beginning to tell on Roosevelt, he looked around for new allies. . . . As the First New Deal coalition disintegrated under the impact of interindustrial and class conflicts, Roosevelt turned more definitively toward free trade. He pushed through Congress a new bill (opposed by steel, chemicals, and other industries) giving [Cordell] Hull the authority to negotiate lower tariffs and then let him build support for the trade treaties."

The RTAA represented a significant shift in administration trade policy. Most importantly, the legislation shifted tariff-making authority from Congress to the executive branch, by allowing the administration to negotiate reciprocal trade agreements without the necessity of congressional oversight. The act was to expire, barring renewal, within three years. Under the terms of the act, the president was authorized to enter into bilateral accords that reduced (or increased) U.S. tariffs by as much as 50 percent from their baseline

(Smoot-Hawley) levels.[24] In this way, Congress—cognizant of its own culpability in the Smoot-Hawley Tariff—was able to bind its own hands and insulate the trade policy process from rent-seeking pressures. While the RTAA retained the flexible-tariff provision of 1922, it abrogated the cost-equalization principle, thereby allowing for meaningful liberalization of trade under Ricardian principles. Finally, the RTAA created an important counterweight to self-serving testimony by producers before Congress. A Trade Agreements Committee (TAC) was convened to study the impact of potential trade agreements on each sector. While such studies could be, at best, rather imprecise, they were more impartial, compiled as they were by unelected bureaucrats with little incentive to yield to pressure from rent-seeking producers.[25]

Politically, the RTAA was a central component of the reorientation of Roosevelt's bases of political support. The eighteen months that followed the passage of the act witnessed the progressive breakdown of Roosevelt's First New Deal coalition. By 1935 the transition from First New Deal to second was complete. Out was conservative, inward-looking, and nationalist business. In were organized labor, the urban underclasses, and the cadre of internationalist industry and finance that had been excluded from the First New Deal coalition. Significantly, the agricultural sector remained part of the Second New Deal coalition (see Gourevitch 1986, ch. 4; Lusztig 1996, ch. 3).

The Second New Deal was characterized by internationalism and institutional innovation. The internationalist dimension was manifested in a number of ways. For example, in 1935, Roosevelt determined that the RTAA was to operate according to the unconditional most-favored-nation principle.[26] The next year Roosevelt further committed the United States toward internationalism by entering into the Tripartite Monetary Agreement (TMA) with Britain and France to stabilize the currencies of all three nations, thereby depriving each of the means to limit imports through manipulation of the money supply. The TMA restored the currencies of all three nations to gold convertibility and committed each to mutual consultations prior to currency devaluation. Moreover, it built on the 1934 Gold Reserve Act, which, after the large U.S. currency devaluation of that year, set up a fund to stabilize all major currencies that were subjected to severe pressures to devalue. The agreement was soon joined by Belgium, the Netherlands, and Switzerland, laying the foundations for the monetary regime founded at Bretton Woods in 1944.[27]

As in the First New Deal, institutional innovation was at the heart of the second. Specifically, labor and the urban poor were enticed into the Democratic fold by the National Labor Relations (Wagner) Act and the Social Security Act, respectively. The Wagner Act greatly expanded the rights of organized labor. It enforced the right of workers to unionize (by majority vote) and strike, while prohibiting company-run unions. It also created an active voice for the government in labor negotiations, most prominently in the form of mediation through institutions such as the National Labor Relations Board. As a consequence, trade unionism doubled between 1935 and 1939. This was no mean feat during an economic climate in which high unemployment levels militated against the power of labor.[28]

The Social Security Act was omnibus legislation designed to appeal to a broad range of constituents. It underwrote a nationwide scheme of unemployment insurance; provided for the transfer of federal funds to the states for the purpose of welfare spending on the needy; and created a matching funds regimen with the states to launch a range of programs including vocational retraining, infant and maternal health aid, and assistance to disabled children. Finally, it introduced a comprehensive old-age security system.[29]

The political logic of such institutional innovation was clear to reformers within the Democratic Party. As a party staffer reported to one of Roosevelt's closest advisers, Raymond Moley (1966, 526), in anticipation of the 1936 election,

> There are two or three million more dedicated Republicans in the United States than there are Democrats. The population, however, is drifting into the urban areas. The election of 1932 was not normal. To remain in power we must attract some millions, perhaps seven, who are hostile or indifferent to both parties. They believe the Republican Party to be controlled by big business and the Democratic Party by the conservative South. These millions are mostly in the cities. They include racial and religious minorities and labor people. We must attract them by radical programs of social and economic reform.

As in any coalition, the objectives of the core Second New Deal groups differed, but in the main the coalition was remarkably cohesive (Gourevitch 1986, 147–53). Indeed, the Second New Deal coalition continues to form the foundation of Democratic Party electoral support. (The most prominent exception is the business sector, which, with the shift toward internationalism on the part of the Republicans, has largely supported that party since the late 1960s [Uslaner 1992].) However, while the political fit among the Second New Deal coalition partners made it a natural choice for Roosevelt, the movement toward internationalism was fraught with risk. Roosevelt could ill afford to swim too obviously against the prevailing isolationist tide that still characterized mid-1930s America. His strategic objectives in liberalizing trade required careful procedural orchestration.

The Iteration Strategy

Equally as important as the motivation behind the RTAA was the imperative to spin the act in such a way as to preclude concerted action by a mobilized coalition of nationalists. Instead, the RTAA would rely on iteration to effect a slow shift in the overall orientation of American trade policy. The administration orchestrated its trade strategy carefully. For example, it ensured that the legislation was presented not as a change in government policy (which it was), but rather as a response to prevailing and impending crisis. Thus, Roosevelt declared in the spring of 1934 that the RTAA was "part of an emergency program necessitated by the economic crisis through which we are passing" (quoted in United States Tariff Commission 1948, 2). Similarly, in his press conference of March 2, 1934, when the president was pressed to announce whether the new trade legislation constituted a permanent tariff policy or if it would be terminated after three years, he responded, "You will see the word 'emergency' very distinctly in the message" (Nixon 1969, 2:5). Hull also was insistent in his testimony before the Senate Finance Committee that congressional support for the RTAA was "only urged as an emergency measure to deal with a dangerous and threatening emergency" (United States 1934b, 5). Belying the emergency-related mandate of the legislation, of course, was the fact that its effects were to be gradual.

The government also was careful to emphasize, again somewhat disingenuously, the limited scope and domestic costs of the new trade bill. Hull's memoirs provide clues to the administration's strategy. He notes that "while advocating international cooperation at all times, we were faced with the extremely difficult task of being careful not to present and urge measures in such numbers as to alarm people and precipitate isolation as an acute political issue in the nation. Had we done so, the Roosevelt Administration would have been thrown out of power bodily" (Hull 1948, 177). Similarly, Hull (1948, 359) pointed out that although the president had the authority to lower the Smoot-Hawley rates by as much as 50 percent, "We had made it clear that we did not for a moment contemplate such a drastic, horizontal action." Gardner applauds the strategy: "No sensible policy maker . . . could advocate anything like free trade or even a general tariff reduction. Hull and his aides reached for the next best thing (in truth in some ways it was the *best*)—

reciprocal trade agreements with the unconditional most-favored-nation principle" (Gardner 1964, 140; emphasis in original).

The language of the legislation also underscored the sensitivity of the task of effecting meaningful trade liberalization. The wording of an early draft of the bill, written in the State Department, advanced the objective of the "lowering of tariffs and trade barriers in the United States and the world over" (Eckes 1995, 142). By contrast, the version of the bill sent to Congress did not mention tariff reduction. Instead, H.R. 8687 was motivated by the objective of "expanding foreign markets for the products of the United States ... by regulating the admission of foreign goods into the United States in accordance with the characteristics and needs of various branches of American production" (Eckes 1995, 141–42).[30]

Politics also demanded caution in the operation of the RTAA. The unconditional most-favored-nations principle was fraught with two attendant dangers (Hody 1996, 126–27). First, it created an incentive for third parties to free ride on U.S. tariff concessions. Third-party nations that already benefited from existing reciprocal trade agreements might have little incentive to provide fresh concessions to the United States. Second, concessions granted in a reciprocal trade agreement with one country could generate harmful externalities. For example, a country might be granted tariff reductions on a particular commodity that, when generalized to all most-favored nations, would inflict unacceptable harm on domestic industries.

Against these dangers, the United States implemented safeguards. The most important was the chief-supplier principle, whereby negotiators sought reciprocal trade deals with countries that were the chief suppliers of a particular commodity. In this way generalized concessions would be more likely to be marginal to third-party free riders. Moreover, negotiators would be more focused on the potentially injurious effects of tariff reductions and therefore would be more likely to avoid negative externalities.[31]

The need to avoid negative externalities was critical, so the administration sold the RTAA under the no-injury concept. While this was somewhat specious (for free trade to be effective, inefficient industries would have to be forced to restructure or fold), Roosevelt insisted that injury could be avoided through iterative reductions in the tariff and through vigilance on the part of negotiators to avoid causing undue harm to domestic producers. As he noted in his speech to Congress in March 1934, "The successful building up of trade without injury to American producers depends upon a cautious and gradual evolution of plans. . . . No sound and important American interest will be injuriously disturbed" (quoted in Eckes 1995, 142).[32]

The no-injury concept, like the justification of the RTAA as an emergency measure, appears to have been little more than political rhetoric in 1934. Reminiscent of the cost-equalization principle, its putative objective was to secure the benefits of trade without sustaining the costs (although Roosevelt's proclamation of the no-injury concept was qualified in that it extended only to "sound" and "important" interests). Insofar as such gain without pain constituted an economic illusion, it seems clear that the no-injury concept merely served the prerequisite of providing political camouflage to what was to become an assault on the tariff orchestrated within the Department of State.[33]

Finally, the most important aspect of the Roosevelt-Hull strategy was to exploit the logic of "a cautious and gradual evolution of plans." The objective was to rely on the logic of iteration, whereby trade policy would be perceived as a struggle among competing interests rather than a policy imposed on producers by the government. Where possible the RTAA was defended on a case-by-case basis, rather than as a general principle. While the objective of expanding foreign markets was universally accepted, Roosevelt and Hull saw no percentage in seeking to educate voters on the economic theory that underlay trade liberalization. Where domestic producers were hurt as an inevitable result of securing foreign markets through reciprocal access, the iterative approach that underscored the RTAA program provided a fairly easy defense. A good case in point is Roosevelt's response to manganese producers' criticism of the RTAA. After disputing their claim that jobs would be lost in the manganese sector, he explained that cheap manganese imports would facilitate the production of domestic steel. The result would be a tenfold increase in jobs, and hence vastly expanded production, in other sectors.[34]

On the other hand, the cumulative effect of numerous iterative rent reductions was significant. As one study noted of the period 1930–1939, "Never before in world history had the direction of global trade relations moved so broadly and deeply toward reduced trade barriers" (Cohen, Paul, and Blecker 1996, 33). Between 1934 and 1947—that is, prior to the Geneva Round of the GATT—the United States entered into reciprocal trade deals with 27 countries (see table 3.1).

By 1947, in the absence of agreements signed under the RTAA, the average U.S. ad valorem tariff rate would have been 48.2 percent for all dutiable imports. With the agreements in place, the average ad valorem duty, though still formidable, was roughly one-third less. The effects are more dramatic for commodities covered by trade agreements. For these goods, in the period

Table 3.1
Pre-GATT reciprocal trade agreements signed, 1934–47

Year taking effect	Country
1934	Cuba
1935	Belgium and Luxembourg
	Haiti
	Sweden
1936	Brazil
	Canada
	Colombia
	Finland
	France
	Guatemala
	Honduras
	Netherlands
	Nicaragua
	Switzerland
1937	Costa Rica
	El Salvador
1938	Czechoslovakia
	Ecuador
1939	Canada (supplemental)
	Cuba (supplemental)
	Turkey
	Venezuela
	United Kingdom
1940	Argentina
	Canada (second supplemental)
	Canada (third supplemental)
1942	Cuba (second supplemental)
	Peru
1943	Iceland
	Mexico
	Uruguay
1944	Iran
Total	*32*

Source: United States Tariff Commission (1955).

1934–1947, average ad valorem duties fell by roughly 44 percent, or almost the maximum amount permitted under the terms of the RTAA prior to 1945 (United States Tariff Commission 1948, 3: tab. 2).[35] It is also instructive to note that the lion's share of these reductions occurred prior to the start of World War II. In 1947, 89 percent of U.S. total and dutiable imports came from countries with which the United States had trade agreements in place by 1940 (Brenner 1978, 157).

The effects on state-supplied rents suggested by these data, of course, are imprecise. Ad valorem rates do not take into account alternative means of import protection. Therefore, these data are not as useful as effective rates of import protection. On the other hand, it would be foolish to discount the effects of these tariffs. Tariffs were the principal import barrier during this era. Moreover, they were in place for a reason. As Brenner (1978, 158) suggests, "*Someone* had wanted the duties at their preagreement level and, given the influence protection-seeking interests had on the tariff bills, it seems fair to infer that many of the duties were reduced from levels preferred by these interests" (emphasis mine). Indeed, Hull (1948, 370) recounts that even before the trade agreements program was in place, the administration was bombarded by "an avalanche of protests" from "the special interests which thought that higher tariffs helped them."

It is also clear that the RTAA had an impact on trade volume in the United States. Comparing 1934–1935 with fiscal 1938–1939 reveals an increase in total trade of dutiable nonagricultural imports of 17.3 percent. Significantly, for countries with which a trade agreement was in place, total dutiable nonagricultural imports rose by almost one-third (30.7 percent). For nonagreement countries, imports of such goods actually shrank by 0.3 percent. Nonagricultural exports also rose sharply during this same time, by 64.1 percent. Once again, the difference between agreement and nonagreement countries is stark, with nonagricultural exports rising by 68.4 percent to the former, and 39.7 percent to the latter (Letiche 1948, 30).

Fate of the Rent Seekers

Inflexible Rent Seekers

By definition, the fate of inflexible rent seekers in the United States was economic demise. Whether this was due to the iterative reductions in state-supplied rents associated with the Reciprocal Trade Agreements program or was simply the cumulative effect of the long years of depression is not clear. Certainly the Depression played a large role. As table 3.2 suggests, the number of manufacturing establishments in the United States declined by more than 30 percent between 1929 and 1933. Whether the short-term trend line toward recovery later in the decade would have been steeper without the RTAA rent reductions is a counterfactual argument that cannot be demonstrated. However, whatever the cause—crisis or strategic rent reduction—it is clear that the weakest strata of the U.S. manufacturing sector were culled in the early 1930s.

Equally clear is the fact that rent seekers experienced far less access to government decision makers in the post-1934 era. The distress calls of inflexible rent seekers, therefore, were less likely to be heard, or to be heeded, than would have been the case earlier. Prior to the RTAA, congressional hearings on the tariff provided ample opportunity for rent seekers to influence trade legislation. In the aftermath of the RTAA, rent seekers were limited to two avenues of trade policy influence. The first was congressional hearings on triennial renewal of the reciprocity legislation. The second was a body constructed under the auspices of the RTAA called the Committee for Reciprocity Information (CRI).

The CRI allowed societal interests to voice their positions on each reciprocal trade deal. Before the formal negotiation of any trade agreement (although, pertinently, after the conclusion of preliminary negotiations), a notice of hearings was posted by the CRI. The committee, consisting of high-ranking officials, many of whom sat on the TAC, prepared a report for the TAC that reflected the concerns and interests of affected societal interests. On the other hand, because public hearings were not conducted until after

Table 3.2
Manufacturing establishments in the United States, 1929–39

YEAR	NUMBER OF MANUFACTURING ESTABLISHMENTS
1927	187,629
1929	206,663
1931	171,450
1933	139,325
1935	167,916
1937	166,794
1939	173,802

Source: U.S. Bureau of the Census (1975, 666).
Note: Data are not available for 1940–47.

preliminary negotiations were concluded, the TAC already had undertaken comprehensive research on concessions to be granted and sought. Thus, testimony from societal interests could be evaluated in the light of existing information and knowledge. As Haggard (1988, 117) suggests, the process was designed to increase the "costs of protectionist lobbying while decreasing the likelihood of success" (see also Brenner 1978, chs. 4–5). It is reasonable to conclude, therefore, that the CRI muffled the dying demands of many inflexible rent seekers.

Inflexible rent seekers were not completely routed by the transformation of American trade policy, however. Even today, industrial protectionists still constitute an active, albeit minority, component of the producer population (see, for example, Hufbauer, Berliner, and Elliott 1986; Schiller 2000). In large part, this is a function of the robust quality of the no-injury concept. That concept, so helpful in selling the RTAA, proved to be a double-edged sword for those seeking to administer trade liberalization. On the one hand, as the example of the CRI suggests, during the early years of the RTAA an industry seeking relief was forced into "a maze of administrative procedures" that was often sufficient to deter all but the most committed rent seekers (Finger 1991, 131). On the other hand, the so-called escape clause has emerged as a means to shelter strategic industries in decline.

The escape clause first was used in the 1943 agreement with Mexico. It provided the U.S. government the right to modify or withdraw concessions negotiated in a reciprocal trade deal if doing so would remedy serious injury to a domestic producer.[36] After 1945, the clause was included in all future trade agreements. Protectionists have met with varying degrees of success in applying for escape-clause relief. Between 1948 and 1952, for example, of 113 petitions for tariff increases under the escape clause, only 15 were granted (Destler 1995, 141). Escape-clause relief was made more difficult under the 1962 Trade Expansion Act, with domestic producers obligated to demonstrate both serious injury and that the major (that is, greater than all other factors combined) cause of injury was U.S. tariff concessions. As a result, there were fewer petitions over the next dozen years, and these met with an equally dismal success rate. However, the Trade Act of 1974 served to liberalize the escape-clause process. Henceforth, relief could be sought if tariffs were a "substantial" (i.e., not less than any other) cause of injury, or threat thereof. Petitions increased, although rates of relief increased only slightly (Destler 1995, 140–45).

The escape clause was not the only instrument of postwar protectionism. The short-lived "peril point" was an attempt to reinstitute the cost-of-production equalization principle in the 1950s. In addition, U.S. trade law has long provided for relief against predatory trade practices abroad. Finally, politically important protectionist sectors, most prominently textiles, steel, and, of course, agriculture, were bought off with "special case" legislation. Special cases were exempted from the liberalization process as a means of precluding them from joining a "protectionist coalition [to] overthrow the liberal order, [or] impede an administration's trade-expanding initiatives" (Destler 1995, 24).[37]

The variety of remedies available under the rubric of the no-injury concept should not distract attention from the fact that both the volume and tenor of protectionism changed in the aftermath of the RTAA. Hody (1996, 138) notes that by the late 1940s, protectionists had ceased in the attempt to resurrect the old system of congressional tariff making and were operating within the bounds set by administrative tariff making. Similarly, Bauer, de la Sola Pool, and Dexter (1972, 37) argue that Congress, the great facilitator of rent-seeking activity, found that the "power to dole out favors to industry [was] not worth the price of having to beat off and placate the insistent pleas of petitioners." Furthermore, because the RTAA institutionalized the importance of export markets, it also "changed the trade policy preferences of key congressional representatives" (Bailey, Goldstein, and Weingast 1997, 327). In large part this explains the Republican shift toward trade liberalization beginning in the 1940s.

Flexible Rent Seekers

As always, the fate of the flexible rent seekers is easier to track. However, as would be expected by the iterative nature of the rent-reduction process, the conversion of flexible rent seekers from protectionists to free traders took place over a number of years. Specifically, it appears that by 1940, one section of the flexible rent-seeker population, consisting disproportionately of larger firms, had embraced trade liberalization. Most of the remainder of the flexible rent seekers seem to have become free traders over the next decade.

The fact that exports rose sharply in the wake of the passage of the RTAA, and did so even to countries with which the United States did not have agreements in place, is suggestive of a new, more export-oriented ethos of production on the part of U.S. industrialists. It appears that even as ad valorem rates remained fairly generous in the late 1930s, flexible rent seekers had taken measures to compensate abroad for market shares lost, or expected to be lost, at home.[38]

Other data reinforce this conclusion. For example, submissions to the

relevant congressional committees responsible for the RTAA and its triennial renewals also are suggestive of behavioral changes on the part of the
rent-seeker population. As indicated in table 3.3, by 1940, for the first time,
and by a margin of more than two to one, nonlabor and nonagricultural interests testifying before Congress in person or via written brief supported
renewal of the RTAA. The 1940 renewal hearings, which attracted far more
testimony than the original RTAA hearings or the previous and subsequent
renewal hearings, appear to have been perceived as the defining moment for
the future of U.S. trade. By 1940, the full effects of the RTAA program had
become clear. Defeat in 1940 would surely have postponed, and possibly
even ended, America's free-trade experiment. However, it seems apparent
that free traders—including converted flexible rent seekers—rallied to the
free-trade cause. Free trade was not universally supported among U.S. industrialists at the time, but the tide was clearly beginning to turn. In the af-

Table 3.3

Tenor of nonagricultural and nonlabor support for the RTAA and its
renewals, 1934–43

YEAR	COMMITTEE	SUPPORTING[a]	OPPOSING[b]
1934	House Ways and Means	5	9
1934	Senate Finance	3	31
Total		*8*	*40*
1937	House Ways and Means	7	7
1937	Senate Finance	3	6
Total		*10*	*13*
1940	House Ways and Means	90	24
1940	Senate Finance	14	24
Total		*104*	*48*
1943	House Ways and Means	14	12
1943	Senate Finance	2	4
Total		*16*	*16*

Sources: United States (1934a, 1934b, 1943a, 1943b); Brenner (1978, 355–65).

Note: Where a number of companies from the same industry appeared together, their testimony is counted
    collectively as one appearance.

[a]Testimony (oral or written) from industrialists who generally favored the nature and scope of the RTAA.

[b]Testimony (oral or written) from industrialists who generally opposed the RTAA or sought to limit its scope.

termath of the 1940 hearings, there was an inevitability about the direction of U.S. trade.[39]

While the 1943 renewal hearings attracted far fewer depositions, some important issues emerged. One potential reason for the smaller number of pro–free-trade depositions was the fact that larger industrial associations testified in support of free trade for the first time, thereby obviating the need for member industries and firms to testify. For example, the New York State Chamber of Commerce, "the oldest commercial organization in the United States . . . which has a membership that is highly representative of the [n]ation's leading industries, unanimously adopted resolutions [on March 4, 1943] urging Congress to extend the life of the Trade Agreements Act."[40] Similarly, the board of the four-thousand-member New York City Committee on Foreign Trade, Commerce and Industry "unanimously expressed the conviction that the enactment of the Reciprocal Trade Agreements Act is in the best interests of the country."[41] The Business Advisory Council of the Department of Commerce presented a lengthy brief to the House Ways and Means Committee in support of free trade. The brief was signed by, among others, 51 industrialists, many of whom had previously appeared on behalf of their own companies in support of previous RTAA extensions (United States 1943a, 584–605).

Perhaps the most telling testimony of the 1943 hearings came from the NAM. With a membership in 1941 of almost eight thousand, the NAM constituted an important bellwether for the manufacturing sector. Not only did the self-styled spokesman for the nation's industry represent a fairly good cross-section of American business,[42] but it maintained a practice of taking a policy stance only when there was a strong consensus among the voting members (*Fortune* 1948, 165). The NAM had long opposed the RTAA. It had provided depositions in opposition to the act and its renewals to both the House Ways and Means Committee and the Senate Finance Committee in 1934, 1937, and 1940 (United States 1934a, 1934b, 1937a, 1937b, 1940a, 1940b). Its 1940 deposition (adopted at its 1939 annual meeting) before the Senate Finance Committee, for example, leaves no doubt about the organization's protectionist leanings: "Conditions in international trade are so chaotic at present that it is recommended that the National Association of Manufacturers oppose negotiation of further trade agreements, including the revision or expansion of old agreements. . . . The National Association of Manufacturers also recommends that when the Reciprocal Trade Agreements Act expires in June 1940, its further extension in its present form should be vigorously opposed" (United States 1940b, 410).

By 1943, however, in testimony before the House Ways and Means Committee, the NAM had begun to move toward a more liberal position that, while qualified by demands for "fair trade," signified a shift in the NAM's position that would intensify in the postwar era:

> In summary . . . we do favor reciprocal trade agreements in the post-war years. In the light of experience under the act, and particularly in view of the changed conditions which confront the world, we favor renewal of the Reciprocal Trade Agreements Act, with amendments which would, in our opinion, increase the advantages of such agreements by giving a fair starting chance for new industries and new products, and which would give adequate protection of United States industry, agriculture, and labor against dumping, forced labor and property confiscation. This is a position which would provide freer trade, but not free trade, in the post-war years, which would encourage increased post-war international trade carried on in a fair manner (United States 1943a, 717–18).

By the early postwar era, the NAM was in the forefront of the free-trade movement, actively calling on the government to provide greater access to foreign markets (*New York Times* 1952; Humphrey 1955, 158). The organization's trade policy transformation, however, was hardly unique. Watson (1956, 691–92) noted that while the early postwar period witnessed pockets of protectionism within the producer population,

> These business interests came face to face with their economic brethren. Some industry representatives appeared before the Congressional Committees to plunk for the [reciprocity] program. In the early stages this opposition [to protectionism] came in the form of general pronouncements by national organizations such as the Committee for Economic Development and the U.S. Chamber of Commerce. Later, however, the virus of defiance to age-old tariff principles spread throughout the body of the business community. More important, from the standpoint of Congressional pressure politics, it began to localize by settling into strategic nerve tissues of the economy. Specific industries from particular areas came in increasing numbers to testify in favor of the program.

The limited opinion poll data on the subject confirm the point. A 1939 Roper poll showed that while the majority of producers favored higher tariffs, the largest businesses already had shifted their preferences. Thus, while

42 percent of small manufacturers and 47 percent of small retailers favored higher tariffs, only 7 percent of large manufacturers advocated raising the tariff rate.[43] By the mid-1950s, however, businesses of all sizes were overwhelmingly (by a factor of seven to one) in favor of liberalizing trade. Indeed in 1954, asking practically the same questions as in the 1939 poll, and despite the fact that tariffs were far lower at the time, Bauer, de la Sola Pool, and Dexter (1972, 113–16) found that only 5.0 percent of small firms supported raising tariffs. *Fortune* reported in 1955 that over the previous fifteen years, the number of executives favoring a lowering of the tariff rate doubled, while those advocating an increase fell from 31.5 percent to 5.0 percent.[44] The same report showed that given the option of raising, lowering, or maintaining existing tariff levels, 38 percent advocated lowering tariffs and 31 percent preferred the status quo. Thus, 69 percent were satisfied that rent reductions had not gone too far, as opposed to only 5.0 percent who felt that they had. Also worth noting is that roughly one in three of the sample reported that they had changed their position on the tariff since 1941, with more than 75 percent of these shifting from preferring protectionism to freer trade (Bauer, de la Sola Pool, and Dexter 1972, 3). The results were fairly consistent over large (10,000 or more employees), medium (1,000–9,999 employees), and small (100–999 employees) firms. Indeed, as Bauer, de la Sola Pool, and Dexter (1972, 115) found in their study, "The change in attitude from 1939 to 1954 is thus above all a change among smaller businessmen. By 1939, the heads of the biggest firms had already adopted an orientation toward world trade. . . . By 1954, size differences in attitudes had disappeared."

The results of these studies were replicated in other polls. For example, in 1954 the *Saturday Review* (1954) found in a survey of five hundred business and labor leaders that 60.4 percent favored lowering U.S. tariffs, while only 20.9 percent were opposed to lowering tariffs. A few years later, *Dun's Review and Modern Industry* (1962) found that among three hundred executives of large and small industrial corporations, there was widespread (by a margin of more than three to one) support for large, reciprocal tariff cuts between the United States and the European Common Market.

U.S. industry underwent a policy conversion during the interwar and immediate postwar era from an inward-looking, protectionist sector to a lobby that has been at the forefront of internationalism for decades. While internationalism is not universally embraced among the U.S. manufacturing sector—strong pockets of protectionism exist and have done so for decades—a dominant free-trading ethos prevails among industrial producers (see Gilligan 1997, ch. 6).

The shift to internationalism was politically risky. Isolationism was firmly entrenched, effectively ruling out a big bang–type shift in foreign economic policy. Moreover, with agriculture a crucial component of the Second New Deal coalition, the divide-and-conquer strategy also held limited appeal. Thus, Roosevelt and Hull used the iteration strategy as a means of implementing free trade through the gradual conversion of flexible rent seekers. With each reciprocal agreement into which the United States entered (twenty-three between 1934 and 1940), a portion of the rent-seeker population was forced either to restructure or go under. The great advantage for Roosevelt was that while the transformation of the industrial sector was a slow process, his government faced the wrath of only a portion of the rent-seeker population at any given point. Moreover, he was continuously able to read signals from the rent-seeker population, thereby gauging competitiveness. If the costs to industry were too great, the process could have been halted at any time.

Indeed, the administration did not commit itself to a wholesale change in policy absent signals from the rent-seeker population. The RTAA was packaged as an emergency, hence temporary, measure that could have been withdrawn without loss of face at any point that its effects were deemed too harmful to the producer population. Moreover, the somewhat specious no-injury principle ensured that if any one iteration in the rent-reduction process was too extreme, the government would have a remedy at hand that did not signal a lack of resolve or shift in trade policy. As the Australian case (chapter 7) demonstrates, lack of government resolve can fatally undermine the liberalization process by creating an incentive for erstwhile flexible rent seekers to lobby for the restoration of rents. Even so, postwar applications of the no-injury principle, specifically the escape clause and the special-case clause, did serve to extend protection to certain politically sensitive sectors. This qualification to the wholesale shift to trade liberalization helps explain why some sectors have remained protectionist into the 1990s.

This caveat aside, however, it is clear that the iteration strategy worked extremely well for the Roosevelt administration. As early as 1939, most of the big-business sector had committed itself to trade liberalization. By the early 1950s, free trade was institutionalized. It is notable that this trade policy revolution was accomplished in the absence of severe political backlash by U.S. rent seekers.

4

Mexico and the Social Foundations of NAFTA

In 1990, the *Economist* proclaimed of Mexico that "[o]ne of the world's most protected economies has become one of the most open" (quoted in Russell 1994, 217). Despite a half century of economic protectionism, supported by a business lobby so influential that it was able to block Mexico's ascension to the GATT in 1980 (see Story 1982), Mexico has become a role model for trade liberalization in Latin America. After a devastating economic crisis that began in 1982, Mexico slashed its tariff rates, retrenched its generous system of agricultural subsidization, eliminated most of its nontariff barriers to imports, liberalized its laws on foreign direct investment, and sought to maintain greater discipline in its monetary policy. It joined the GATT in 1986 and in 1990 initiated the process that led to the implementation of NAFTA. What is even more surprising is that the popularity of the governing Partido Revolucionario Institucional (Institutional Revolutionary Party, PRI) actually increased during the late 1980s and early 1990s. While the PRI lost the presidency in the election of 2000, that event cannot reasonably be linked to a political backlash from formerly rent-seeking interests. Most of those had either departed from the marketplace or were themselves champions of trade liberalization long before 2000. Instead, the proto-democracy that is emerging in Mexico appears to be a positive externality associated with the expansion of a productive, liberalizing middle class (Drury and Lusztig n.d.), an event anticipated and facilitated by at least some reformers within the PRI during the 1990s (see Rubio 1998).

Two significant events, economic depression and intervention from the world financial community (through the auspices of the IMF and World Bank), laid the groundwork for the transformation of Mexican foreign economic policy. In the aftermath of these events, with the PRI's traditional, corporatist alliance failing, President Carlos Salinas de Gortari sought to reconstruct the party's base of electoral support. Free trade appealed to reformers within the business community—an alliance of businesses that survived the depression of the 1980s and new businesses that emerged in its aftermath. Reminiscent of Roosevelt's Second New Deal coalition, Salinas used free trade to secure the support of the business community to fund an aggressive expansion of the welfare state.

The Mexican case illustrates the opportunities created by structurally imposed rent reductions: both crisis and regime-mandated change. The silver lining of the 1980s debt crisis in Mexico was that it allowed the Salinas administration to gauge the likely response of the producer population to a significant decrease in state-supplied rents under the proposed NAFTA and to benefit politically from trade liberalization. In the aftermath of the debt crisis, it became clear that many former rent seekers favored increased liberalization of trade, whereas the weakest strata of the producer population had been eliminated. As a result, Salinas was able to use the big bang approach, which took the form of NAFTA, to institutionalize free-market reforms in Mexico without suffering serious political backlash. A measure of how well-entrenched those reforms were is that Mexico weathered a serious balance-of-payments crisis, the so-called Peso Crisis of 1994–1995, without meaningful pressure from the business community to revert to protectionism. Indeed, Mexico continues to be in the forefront in negotiations over the proposed FTAA.

The Historical Context

To the extent that it is possible to assign a beginning date to such things, Mexico's twentieth-century economic history was forged during the revolution of 1910–1917. The revolution, in turn, was a reaction to Porfirio Díaz's thirty-one-year reign of oppression and corruption known as the *Porfiriato*[1] —an early attempt by Mexico's president to modernize the economy through export-led growth (largely in primary goods, although there was some industrial development) and increased concentration in the agrarian sector. Ironically, like the new modernizers (or technocrats) of the 1980s and 1990s who led Mexico's "second revolution" (Baer 1993),[2] Díaz surrounded himself with technical advisors (*cientificos*) committed to the construction of a more modern economy based on liberalized trade and foreign investment. Unfortunately for Mexico and for Díaz, this first effort at modernization was not tempered by efforts to redistribute the positive economic benefits to the urban and rural underclasses.[3] Instead, wealth and land were disproportionately skewed in favor of high-ranking *cientificos*, large landholders, and powerful industrialists, many of whom were foreigners. Agrarian centralization was especially pronounced, with the system of land holding conforming to the neofeudal pattern of rural control of landless and impoverished peasants by a small number of immensely wealthy hacienda owners (see Brandenburg 1969). Political control was also highly centralized; the vast majority of Mexican citizens were effectively denied the fundamental political rights that had been entrenched in the liberal constitution of 1857.

The *Porfiriato* ended in violence. Díaz was forced to resign in 1911 after a series of popular uprisings inspired by Díaz's chief political opponent, Francisco Madero. Madero's middle-class revolution, however, succeeded in part on the strength of his alliance with the southern peasantry, mobilized by Emiliano Zapata. When Madero failed to deliver on his promise of land redistribution, Zapata broke with him. In 1913, Madero himself was overthrown in a counterrevolution led by Porfirian loyalist Victoriano Huerta. The effect was to unify the revolutionary forces into a well-organized army consisting largely of peasants, workers, and the petty bourgeoisie. With the defeat of Huerta in 1914, however, the revolutionary alliance unraveled. The next three years witnessed a bloody civil war. The revolution ultimately ended with the victory of the so-called Constitutionalist forces and the construction of a new constitution in 1917.[4] It was the mythology surrounding the revolution that came to inform the future of Mexican politics for the remainder of the twentieth century.

Business retained a fairly powerful voice in the politics of postrevolutionary Mexico until the mid-1930s and the constitutionally limited six-year term (*sexenio*) of Lázaro Cárdenas (1934–1940). Cárdenas's presidency witnessed the construction of the political coalition through which the PRI would dominate Mexican politics for the rest of the century. Founded on a corporatist network that organized the three principal sectors of PRI electoral support (labor, peasantry, and lower middle class, or "popular") into hierarchically structured peak associations, this new coalition was left leaning and steeped in the nationalist mythology of the revolution. That is, the party institutionalized the revolution's putative anti-Porfirian commitment to the protection of the underclasses, as well as the defense of Mexico against foreign economic dominance, particularly by the United States.

Reflecting the party's revolutionary mandate, business nominally was excluded from the PRI coalition. On the other hand, official exclusion did not prevent organized business from enjoying a cozy, clientelist relationship with the PRI. As Lindblom and others have pointed out, even ideologically anti-capitalist governments face the intractable problem that since governments rarely produce things that people wish to buy, there must be at least tacit support for the regime from the private sector to foster and maintain investment and growth; put bluntly, business interests have to be accommodated (see Lindblom 1977; Offe 1984; Goldthorpe 1984). While outwardly the relationship between business and the state was guarded, unofficially ties were quite tight. The government consulted with business leaders before enacting policies that affected business interests; in fact, so institutionalized did this practice become that business enjoyed an implicit policy veto (Tirado 1998, 184). Even more importantly, Mexican business received a wide and generous array of state-supplied rents (import barriers and subsidies) under the auspices of import-substituting industrialization (ISI). These rents provided the means by which the government secured the tacit, if not always explicit, loyalty of the business sector.

By law, as with the "official" components of the Mexican corporatist structure, business was obliged to organize hierarchically. Four traditional business confederations played an important role in the transformation of Mexican foreign economic policy. The oldest are the Confederación de Cámaras Nacionales de Comercio (National Confederation of Chambers of Commerce, CONCANACO) and the Confederación de Cámaras Industriales (National Confederation of Industrial Chambers, CONCAMIN). Created in the immediate aftermath of the revolution, CONCAMIN and CONCANACO have tended to represent Mexico's larger industry associations and firms. The Confederación Patronal de la República Mexicana (Employers' Confederation of the Republic of Mexico, COPARMEX) was founded in 1929 in response to the growing power of the labor movement. A coalition of entrepreneurs from the agricultural, industrial, and retail sectors, COPARMEX traces its roots to the Grupo Monterrey, a dynamic organization of northern business leaders operating since the *Porfiriato*. These three confederations, founded prior to the construction of the PRI corporatist alliance, remained the most suspicious of government intervention in the economy and the least responsive to PRI control. The fourth confederation was a product of state-led industrialization. Beginning in 1941, new businesses that emerged as part of the nascent ISI initiative were required to join the new Cámara Nacional de la Industria de Transformación (National Chamber of Manufacturing Industry, CANACINTRA).[5] Consisting mostly of small and medium-sized businesses, CANACINTRA represents some eighty thousand firms. Born of the ISI process, it tended not to share the suspicion of state intervention harbored by the other three traditional confederations. CANACINTRA was the confederation most durably and intensely committed to protection and other state-supplied rents.[6]

These four business confederations constituted the voice of business through the 1960s and continue to be important players to this day. However, during the early 1970s, in response to worsening relations between state and business, the heads of CONCAMIN, CONCANACO, and COPARMEX joined forces with the leaders of associations representing bankers, insurance institutions, and agriculture to form an elite lobby known as the Consejo Coordinador Empresarial (Business Coordinating Council, CCE).[7] The CCE is massive, retaining more than 1.25 million affiliates.[8] By definition, it is also broadly based. There are two important effects of this. It is vulnerable to internal politics, and when its membership does reach consensus (or at least when internal bargaining generates an equilibrium outcome), it swings enormous clout. The importance of these effects became clear during the 1980s.

Business-state relations were crafted and maintained through the process of ISI—the organizing principle of the Mexican economy for almost forty years.[9] As all Latin American countries that followed this pattern of development found, ISI is an attractive short-term development strategy that contains inherent long-term limitations. ISI is enticing because it provides a means for very late industrializers to modernize their economies in spite of inherent noncompetitiveness in the global marketplace. In this sense, it is reminiscent of the infant industry argument. The principal difference is that advocates of the infant industry strategy envision protectionism as only a short- or medium-term ameliorative.[10] By contrast, under ISI, protection represented a means by which the state could control business by manipulating the supply of import protection. No exit strategy was involved in this development plan; rather than serving as so much scaffolding in the construction of a modern economy, protection itself represented part of the superstructure.

ISI operates according to three fairly clearly defined phases. The first, or easy, phase of ISI is characterized by the emergence of industries dedicated to the production of durable consumer goods (most prominently appliances, electronic goods, and automobiles) for the domestic market. These industries, the "CANACINTRA industries," thrive in the absence of effective foreign competition. In addition, ISI typically involves development subsidies and generous access to capital through state-owned development banks and other credit mechanisms.[11] In Mexico, the early ISI years witnessed the proliferation of numerous small and medium-sized firms. In 1935, for example, there were 7,619 industrial firms in Mexico. By 1940, that figure had nearly doubled to 13,510; five years later, there were again twice as many firms (31,195). Finally, by 1950, near the end of the easy phase, Mexico featured 74,252 industrial enterprises (Story 1986, 19).[12]

Rapid economic growth stimulates investment and creates incentives for further expansion in the industrial sector. This is the second, or exuberant, phase of ISI. In Mexico, economic growth rates during the exuberant phase were impressive, averaging more than 6 percent annual expansion and surpassing all other countries in Latin America for the period 1950–1972 (Ramirez 1993, 174; Basanez 1993, 99). However, the potential for growth beyond the domestic market under ISI is limited. Because ISI involves the importation of established, and therefore often obsolete, technology from abroad, domestic producers typically do not establish world product (or export) mandates. Instead, they seek to exploit market niches, albeit artificially created, in the domestic market.[13] Ultimately, of course, domestic growth potential is exhausted. Profits slow, which in turn depresses investment. Production facilities gradually become outdated, growth rates decline, unemployment rises, and countries that practice ISI are faced with increasingly negative trade balances. Even more problematic, this final, exhaustion phase of ISI sees the economy saddled with a mass of inefficient firms dependent on state-supplied rents for their very survival (Hirschman 1968; Weintraub 1988, 8; Izquierdo 1964, 279–81; Mosk 1950, ch. 5; Vernon 1963, ch. 6).

Throughout the easy and exuberant phases, despite inevitable internal difficulties within the business community—as noted, CANACINTRA tended to be more wedded to state intervention than were the more established confederations—organized business was a largely quiescent, silent partner of the government, content to play but a limited role in the policy-making process. In return, the provision of state-supplied rents was generous. In addition to high tariffs, Mexico increasingly relied on import licenses. In 1956, 28 percent of imports required licenses. Through the 1960s, licenses, on average, covered more than 60 percent of imports; for the 1970s, the average proportion was 70 percent; and by 1985, more than 92 percent of all imported goods required licenses (Lustig 1992, 14–15, 120; Ramirez 1993, 175, 181). The effectiveness of these import barriers is clear from differential growth rates of domestic versus foreign demand for Mexican manufactures. In the 1950s, domestic demand increased by an annual average of 71.8 percent; by contrast, exports grew by an annual average of only 3 percent. For the 1960s, the figures are 86.1 percent and 4 percent, respectively, and for the first half of the 1970s, the trend continued: 81.5 percent to 7.7 percent (Lustig 1992, 14–15).

An important component of the ISI development strategy in this era, and a catalyst for the provision of import licenses, was the construction of industry- or firm-specific industrial development plans. Started in the early 1960s, these plans were designed to create a more integrated domestic manufacturing base, facilitate exports, and construct a Mexican-owned manufacturing structure. To these ends, industrial development plans included generous provision of import protection (typically in the form of the ubiquitous import license), subsidized loans for target groups that realized local content and export objectives, preferred access to government contracts, and limited duty-free importing privileges. In addition, market access to Mexico was restricted further within certain sectors as a means of guaranteeing market shares for existing firms. The program of industrial development plans was expanded throughout the 1960s and 1970s. For example, between 1965 and 1970, about 750 programs were created; roughly 1,200 more were added in the period 1971–1978 (Lustig 1992, 122–24).

The exhaustion phase of ISI, which effectively spanned the terms of Luis Echeverría (1970–1976) and José López Portillo (1976–1982), saw a shift in state-business relations. The era was characterized by a number of important changes. First, as might be expected, government began to play an even more active role in the economy. As growth rates began to slow, government expenditures rose. During the Echeverría administration, for example, the federal deficit increased sixfold (Story 1986, 41).[14] Another indicator of increased government involvement in the economy was the proliferation of publicly owned enterprises. Echeverría's *sexenio* saw the number of such companies rise from 86 to 740 (Story 1986, 41).

Second, as a consequence of the increasingly activist role of government, the business community began to chafe openly against government policy. State expansionism under Echeverría was accompanied by a new antibusiness rhetoric and expressions of solidarity with Chilean Socialist president Salvadore Allende. Even CANACINTRA denounced the new, leftist initiatives of the Echeverría administration. Despite the more conciliatory approach of López Portillo, it was during the 1970s that the first salient political fault lines within the business community began to emerge (Newell and Rubio 1984, 127–28; Heredia 1992, 295; Bensabat 1995, 93–94; Tirado 1998, 186).

The third effect of ISI exhaustion was the reorientation of the Mexican economy. In effect, Mexico was graced with a "soft landing" from the worst economic effects of ISI exhaustion. Economic growth remained positive throughout the 1970s due to the discovery of new oil reserves in Mexico to coincide with the rapid rise in world petroleum prices. The Mexican economy became increasingly reliant on oil to sustain both export-led economic growth and public-sector borrowing. Borrowing was facilitated by the glut of deposits in world banks, largely in the United States, from the oil-rich Organization of Petroleum Exporting Countries (OPEC). These petrodollars were widely available to developing countries and contributed to the severity of foreign debt crises throughout Latin America in the 1980s (see Sampson 1982; Zedillo Ponce de León 1985, esp. 314–15; Roddick 1988). It is estimated that U.S. banks loaned roughly $60 billion to Mexico between 1977 and 1982 (*Economist* 1983). Ultimately, it was overreliance on foreign capital and deficit spending that brought the ISI era to an end and paved the way for trade liberalization.

Trade Liberalization in the 1980s

Crisis and Mandated Change as Catalysts

The proximate cause of trade liberalization in the 1980s was crisis. Crisis forced radical changes on both government and business, and it was crisis that obliged Mexico to follow the liberal orthodoxy of regimes such as the IMF, the World Bank, and later, the GATT. Crisis was a delayed reaction to ISI exhaustion. Although the immediate effects of ISI exhaustion were latent during the 1970s, already there were straws in the winds of impending economic disaster. For example, in addition to the large fiscal deficit, the foreign public debt increased from its average level of $218.7 million in the period 1954–1972, to almost $21 billion by 1976 (Zedillo Ponce de León 1985, 294).

Inflation, which had been low during the period of ISI exuberance, soared to an average of 17 percent in the years 1973–1975 (Lustig 1992, 19). By 1976, dwindling reserves in the Banco de México created severe downward pressure on the peso, resulting in radical devaluation (in 1976 this approached 40 percent), declining industrial output, capital flight, and surging inflation. Mexico was obliged to turn to the IMF, with which it negotiated a loan late in 1976 (Lustig 1992).

The discovery of immense oil reserves after 1976 allowed Mexico to relieve itself of its IMF obligations but did not ameliorate the underlying crisis. Seemingly oblivious, factions within government and private sector alike became infected with unbounded optimism (Wyman 1983; Weintraub and Baer 1992).[15] Despite the notoriously unstable history of most commodity prices, the Mexican government used oil revenues to increase public expenditures rather than attack the structural problems of the Mexican economy. Private investment poured into Mexico. As a result, the high public debt and again-overvalued peso left Mexico vulnerable once more to debilitating crisis. Even with an overvalued peso, inflation in 1980 reached 30 percent (Wyman 1983, 4; Zedillo Ponce de León 1985, 311–13).

Mexican policy makers were not uniformly blind to the precariousness of the economic situation. Even as the late-1970s oil boom was under way, the López Portillo administration made tentative steps toward economic restructuring. Most prominently, in January 1979 the Mexican government responded to a U.S. government proposal by announcing that it would seek membership in the GATT. By October, a protocol of accession agreement was in place.[16] In March 1980, however, López Portillo backed away from the GATT under pressure from "an inbred, uncompetitive, and influential business class whose interests were best protected by opposing economic and financial innovation" (Roett 1993, 1–2; see also Weintraub and Baer 1992, esp. 191).[17]

It is unlikely that GATT accession would have altered significantly the immediate course of Mexican economic history. In 1981, Mexican oil revenues of $14 billion were $6 billion shy of projected income. The shortfall seriously affected the government's balance of payments, and the federal deficit rose to nearly 15 percent of the Gross Domestic Product (GDP) (Wyman 1983, 5). Government expenditures, meanwhile, continued to soar, reaching 42.2 percent of GDP (Newell and Rubio 1984, 250). Moreover, because of the overvaluation of the peso, the country faced a serious trade deficit in nonoil exports. To overcome the shortfall, the government took on increased foreign debt, much of it short term and provided by U.S. banks, even as world interest rates were on the rise.[18]

The following year the bottom fell out of the Mexican economy. On February 17, Mexico devalued the peso by 67 percent. Once again, the usual economic accompaniments, capital flight and inflation, ensued. Equally worrisome, as many of Mexico's short-term notes came due, it became increasingly difficult to find new sources of credit. In August, with the peso still under heavy pressure, the Mexican government announced yet another devaluation and the suspension of dollar trading to protect eroding reserves. More dramatically, the government informed the U.S. Federal Reserve that it would be forced to suspend payments of principal owed and that its foreign debt would have to be restructured. On September 1, the López Portillo administration announced the nationalization of the private banking system and the imposition of exchange controls (Wyman 1983, 8–11; Zedillo Ponce de León 1985, 315–17; Kuczynski 1988, 82–85). The results were as might have been expected. Inflation for the months September through November 1982 jumped to 103.6% over that of June through August, and an estimated $6.58 billion in private-sector funds left the country in 1982 (Newell and Rubio 1984, 258).

The crisis of 1982 severely limited Mexico's economic policy options. Control of foreign economic policy passed largely out of the hands of the Mexican government and its rent-seeking constituents and into those of foreign banks and international regimes. Thus, even as the business sector (including CANACINTRA) pilloried the government for economic mismanagement and overreaction to the crisis, the seeds of economic renewal were sown (see Baer 1991; O'Brien 1995, 707–8).

Crisis had numerous important effects. First, it obliged the government to wean inefficient business off the public purse. Subsidies to industry were slashed—not because government had finally mustered the resolve to do so, but because the state could no longer afford to foot the bill. Thus, not only did businesses have to learn to adjust to a less-comfortable economic environment, but it was clear that no amount of lobbying could restore precrisis levels of state-supplied rents. Second, as a consequence, rent-seeking interests became less committed to the status quo and began to engage in compensatory activity. In the case of flexible rent seekers, this entailed restructuring for global competition. Third, the international orientation of business and state alike was reinforced by the fact that crises typically are partially a function of unsustainable trade deficits. Certainly this was the case in Mexico when oil prices declined. To compensate, export-led growth became increasingly attractive. Finally, because crises are also typically a function of insufficient access to credit, lenders of last resort such as the IMF and World Bank, as well as private-sector bankers, tend to stiffen the resolve of reforming governments by insisting on economic orthodoxy as a prerequisite for emergency loans.

All of these effects came together rapidly in early-1980s Mexico. The IMF, the World Bank, and to some extent the U.S. government ensured that the administration of Miguel de la Madrid Hurtado (1982–1988) became less attentive to the political business cycle and more so to the prerequisites of economic recovery. In November 1982, Mexico and the IMF reached a bailout agreement in which Mexico agreed to eliminate exchange controls and slash its public debt (Alvarez Bejar and Mendoza Pichardo 1993; O'Brien 1995). The World Bank maintained strict vigilance over the reform process, insisting not only on fiscal reform, but also on deregulation, privatization, elimination of price controls, and liberalization of foreign investment and trade. Moreover, the IMF and World Bank employed a policy of cross-conditionality, whereby neither institution would lend money unless the conditions specified by both were satisfied (Bensabat 1995, 142–43; see also Cypher 1990; Russell 1994, ch. 4).

The de la Madrid *sexenio* saw strict IMF-sanctioned reforms take hold. The federal budget went from an operating deficit of 7.3 percent in 1982 to a surplus of 4.2 percent the next year (these figures are net of debt-servicing costs, which were enormous and which by 1988 consumed around 60 percent of the federal budget) (Lustig 1992, 30; Cleaves and Stephens 1991, 188–89). Public capital expenditures fell from 12.9 percent of GDP in 1981 to 5.5 percent in 1987 (Weintraub 1993, 68). In 1983, Mexico doubled the proportion of tariff-exempt imports from 21 to 42 percent. More significantly, in 1985 import licensing was removed from almost 60 percent of import classifications, and the percentage of import value subject to licensing fell from 85 percent in 1981 to 37 percent in 1985 and 31 percent the following year (Ramirez 1993, 181; Vega-Canovas 1994, 204). In large part, reductions in import licensing were a function of the dismantling of the industrial development plans. Although industry-specific import protection was not eliminated, government procurement advantages, energy subsidies, and tax credits were reduced (Lustig 1992, 124).

The early de la Madrid years also saw a slight liberalization of the in-bond (*maquiladora*) program. Begun in 1965 as a means of allowing Mexican labor to be incorporated into U.S. production on a strict for-export-only basis, the system was reformed in 1983 to allow for modest domestic sales. Moreover, whereas in the past, the *maquiladoras* were obliged to locate in the border region, after 1983 construction was allowed further into Mexican territory (Russell 1994, 204).

The government also took steps to institutionalize Mexico's reorientation toward trade liberalization. In 1983, the rent-seeker-friendly Trade and Industry Ministry was reorganized into the Secretaria de Comercio y Fomento Industrial (Secretariat of Trade and Industrial Development, SECOFI). The reorganization included recruitment of committed free traders and the insulation of trade policy makers from rent-seeking special interests (Pastor and Wise 1994, 478; see also Centeno and Maxfield 1992).[19]

However, the short-term effects of the reforms of the early de la Madrid years were not terribly positive. Inflation continued to run higher than projected, and the liberalizing trend, combined with steadily declining oil prices,[20] exacerbated the balance-of-payments problem (see Cornelius 1986). The deepening crisis reinforced de la Madrid's commitment, manifested in the 1984 Programa Nacional de Fomento Industrial y Comercio Exterior (Program to Promote Industrialization and Foreign Commerce, PRONAFICE), to expose the Mexican economy to the forces of the international market (see de Maria y Campos 1987). In late 1985, Mexico took this commitment one step further by petitioning once again for membership in the GATT and joining the following year. A number of reforms resulted. By 1987, Mexico had ceased to subsidize exports, subscribed to the Tokyo Round codes on nontariff barriers, and surpassed the standards of trade liberalization set by both the GATT and World Bank as a condition of its loans to Mexico. Indeed, the average nominal tariff rate fell to 16 percent; 90 percent of imports were no longer subjected to import licenses (Bensabat 1995, 147–48; de Maria y Campos 1987, 72–73; O'Brien 1995, 708; see also Weintraub 1988; Ramirez 1993).

Despite the deepening of the government's commitment to free-market reforms, economic conditions in Mexico continued to deteriorate in 1986 and 1987. Oil prices bottomed out, and the global stock market crash of October 1987 intensified the misery index. GDP fell by 3.8 percent in 1986, and inflation for 1987 averaged almost 132 percent (Lustig 1992, 40–41; see also Reynolds 1993; Gould 1996, 23–26). The economic crisis of 1987 stimulated the final major initiative of the de la Madrid administration: the Pacto de Solidaridad Económica (Economic Solidarity Pact, PSE). Announced in December 1987, the PSE constituted a neocorporatist agreement between state, agricultural, industrial, and labor leaders to stabilize the economy through

wage and price controls (ultimately freezes) and fiscal and monetary re-
straints. The latter manifested itself in the pegging of the peso to the U.S.
dollar (Reynolds 1993, 80; Ten Kate 1992, 666).

The PSE and its successor, the Pacto para la Estabilidad y el Crecimiento
Economico (Pact for Economic Growth and Stability, PECE) established
under de la Madrid's successor, Carlos Salinas, yielded rapid results. Inflation
fell markedly by 1989, averaging a manageable 20 percent for that year. Private-sector investment increased by almost 11 percent (Lustig 1992, 40–41).
Equally encouraging was the shift in Mexico's export profile. In 1982, manufactured goods accounted for 14 percent of all Mexican exports. By 1989 that
figure had reached 55 percent (Baer 1991, 133). Clearly the de la Madrid reforms of the mid-1980s had finally begun to pay off by decade's end.

The Big Bang Strategy

Reforms intensified under Salinas (1988–1994). By the early 1990s, import licenses had been eliminated in all but the agricultural and automotive
sectors and covered less than 2 percent of imports. Tariffs ranged from 0 to
20 percent, with the average weighted rate at about 10 percent. To put the
speed with which Mexico liberalized trade into context, Mexico liberalized as
rapidly in the six years 1985–1991 as did the United States in the forty years
following the Smoot-Hawley Tariff of 1930 (Weintraub and Baer 1992;
Gould 1996, 29). However, by the early 1990s it had become clear to Salinas
that Mexico's economic recovery, to say nothing of his own party's political
recovery, necessitated one more large reduction in rents—a free-trade agreement with the United States. Thus, aided by the structurally imposed rent reductions of the 1980s, which had eliminated many inflexible rent seekers and
demonstrated the competitiveness of the remainder of the producer population, Salinas relied on the big bang approach to institutionalize free trade in
Mexico.

Salinas came to power in 1988 with the twin objectives of completing
the task of economic recovery and of reconstructing his party's electoral
dominance (see Morris 1992; Smith 1992). His presidential victory was almost certainly an artifact of the PRI's control of the electoral process. In reality, his electoral coalition had fallen away, with much of the business sector
having defected to the free-market Partido Acción Nacional (National Action Party, PAN), while a great deal of labor and peasant support had been si-
phoned off by the leftist Partido de la Revolución Democrática (Party of the
Democratic Revolution, PRD; see Klesner 1993). With the public finances in

disarray, the PRI had few resources with which to bind its electoral coalition.

The crisis years had put enormous pressure on the PRI. The party retained its political support through a corporatist network of client relations between the party and key societal peak associations. The organization was able to stay afloat as long as the state could generate sufficient revenues to satisfy all of its societal clients (see Purcell and Purcell 1980, 201). However, with the economic decline of the 1980s, the state lost its capacity to finance control of its erstwhile societal supporters.

In the same manner as Roosevelt in the construction of his Second New Deal coalition, Salinas undertook an ingenious strategy to rebuild his coalition. The greatest threat to the integrity of the PRI coalition was the disintegration of the left—it was the PRD that had secured the most electoral gains in the 1988 elections. While the loss of business support during the 1980s had been costly, it was the potential loss of the lower classes, and their millions of voters, that could have spelled the end of PRI dominance, or even of the party itself. To combat the threat on the left, Salinas undertook what amounted to construction of the welfare state in Mexico. Under the auspices of the Programa Nacional de Solidaridad (Program of National Solidarity, PRONASOL), Salinas instituted massive reform of the ways in which the most needy Mexicans interacted with the state. Rather than relying on the bloated and corrupt PRI corporatist network, PRONASOL was designed to direct state funds to projects and neighborhoods that were most in need (and most vulnerable to PRD infiltration).[21] PRONASOL completed a great deal in fairly short order. By the 1991 midterm elections, in which the PRI rebounded electorally, PRONASOL had provided funding for projects in more than fifteen hundred municipalities and had introduced electricity into the homes of five million Mexicans and running water into the homes of three million. However, the program was costly. By 1991, PRONASOL consumed 44 percent of the programmable federal budget (Reynolds 1993, 85; Camp 1993, n. 57; Salinas de Gortari 1991; Fox 1994).

It was the imperative to fund PRONASOL that motivated Salinas to undertake one final, big bang rent reduction: NAFTA.[22] NAFTA was critical to the reconstruction of the PRI electoral alliance for two reasons. First, it would solidify Mexico's financial situation by stimulating investment, foreign and domestic, in the Mexican economy. (The flow of private capital into Mexico went from $1 billion in 1987 to $14 billion in 1991, the year after Mexico's NAFTA decision was announced [Weintraub 1993, 72].) In turn, this would increase Mexico's tax base while generating employment and taking some financial pressure off the state.[23] Again, this would complement funding of welfare-state initiatives such as PRONASOL, which saw its budget increased from $500 million in 1989 to $2.4 billion by 1993 (Mexico 1993, 18). Second, it would appeal to disaffected, free-market portions of the business sector that had defected to the PAN (Baer 1993, 57).

Free trade with the United States, however, had not been Salinas's optimal preference. Mexico has a long tradition of economic and cultural nationalism. In large part, this tradition has been manifested as a reaction to the perceived threat of U.S. imperialism—a threat that given events of the nineteenth century was not without basis. Both ISI and Mexico's corporatist structure (which institutionalized the ideals of the revolution) can be seen as reactions to the threat of economic dominance by the United States.[24] However, circumstances left him with few options. Unable to generate much interest in Europe or Japan, Salinas ultimately turned to the United States.

In October 1989, Salinas traveled to the United States for talks with President George H. W. Bush. The two leaders agreed to "consider" a North American free-trade deal. Publicly, Salinas downplayed the significance of the trip, suggesting that the unevenness of the two economies made the prospects of a comprehensive trade deal unrealistic. In the interim, however, the two countries signed several bilateral sectoral agreements to liberalize cross-border trade, especially in the steel, textiles, automotive, and electronics sectors. In addition, Mexico liberalized its rules on U.S. foreign direct investment (see Pastor 1990, 15–16; Bensabat 1995, esp. 204–7).

According to the *Wall Street Journal*, representatives of the two countries met again in February 1990 and agreed to negotiate a free-trade deal (Truell 1990). There was a good deal of secrecy surrounding these talks. Given past relations between the two countries, Salinas was not keen to show his hand early, lest the political backlash at home be overwhelming. Indeed, as a presidential candidate, Salinas had gone on record as saying that "For Mexico, the integration of a common market in the Northern Hemisphere is not a viable option" (quoted in Russell 1994, 335). After the *Wall Street Journal* story broke in late March, Salinas reiterated, "Mexico will not cooperate with the formation of economic blocks" (quoted in Russell 1994, 336). In June, Salinas once again went to Washington. This time he announced publicly that Mexico and the United States had agreed to negotiate a free-trade deal.

Salinas, whose cautious approach indicated his understanding of the political risks involved, did not play into a blind game with NAFTA. Unlike Peel in 1846 or Gough Whitlam in Australia in 1973 (see chapter 7), Salinas's big

bang approach came on the heels of significant structurally imposed rent reductions. Thus, his government was in a position to gauge the profile of the
producer population. Indeed, many former rent seekers, represented most
prominently by CONCAMIN, CONCANACO, COPARMEX, and increasingly the CCE, had already become proponents of more liberal trade. On the
other hand, NAFTA was not expected to be popular with organized labor,
nationalists, and the large remaining bloc of rent seekers largely concentrated within CANACINTRA.

The advantage of the big bang approach was that it would institutionalize reform while signaling the government's commitment to free-market
economics. The disadvantage was the strong potential for political backlash.
Salinas and his advisers were cognizant of the risks involved. As Salinas's
chief of staff, José Cordoba (1994, 233), summarizes the problem of estimat-
ing the optimal size of the rent reduction, "[E]ven if the overall policy objectives are clear, how are the steps toward change going to be defined? Where
are the guarantees that these steps will not go beyond what is acceptable to
the most significant social groups and tolerable to the population as a whole?
How, on the other hand, can one be sure that these steps are not short and
shy ones that will erode people's patience and trust in change itself?"

The Salinas team also knew that once the reform was in place, it was critical to hold steadfast to the decision. The institutionalized nature of NAFTA
made it especially desirable. "Credibility is the key: when businessmen become convinced that there is no chance of reversing trade liberalization, they
quickly try to adjust to the new production patterns" (Cordoba 1994,
244–45). The big bang approach did not fail Salinas. While controversial,
NAFTA came to be widely recognized as a boon to the Mexican economy.[25]
As he had certainly recognized, the weakest strata of the rent-seeking population had been early victims of the 1980s crisis. Most of those who remained, or who had emerged in its wake, were not committed to the old
ways that ultimately had led to such unmitigated economic disaster.

In the end, of course, NAFTA's passage did not spell the end of Mexico's
economic troubles. As has so often happened at the end of a presidential *sexenio*, the Ernesto Zedillo administration (1994–2000) came to power and
was immediately faced with yet another currency crisis. As a result, the first
two years of the Zedillo government were catastrophic. On the other hand,
the combined result of a United States–led bailout of Mexico in 1995 (now
completely repaid) and a diversified export sector has generated an economic recovery in Mexico that, while still vulnerable to decreasing oil prices

and investor uncertainty, has rebounded strongly. Significantly, the Mexican industrial sector has not backtracked in its commitment to free trade, and Mexico remains a leader in the push for an FTAA.

Fate of the Rent Seekers

Inflexible Rent Seekers

Under the best of conditions it is difficult to assess the impact of rent reductions on inflexible rent seekers. Businesses fail for myriad reasons. Moreover, because rent reductions often occur during economic crises, which in and of themselves axiomatically lead to business failures, it is often difficult to separate the effects of crisis from those of rent reduction. The problem is compounded in underdeveloped countries such as Mexico, in which economic statistics are not terribly comprehensive, nor, in the case of bankruptcies, very accurate (Ramirez 1993, 183). As a consequence, analysts have been divided in assessing the impact of liberalization on rent seekers. Lustig (1992, 122), for example, looking at aggregate numbers, implies that the rent-seeking population in Mexico was largely flexible. "Trade liberalization did not produce massive bankruptcies and layoffs as some had feared. The number of plants actually grew between 1985 and 1988, and the contraction of manufacturing employment was small. This may be indirect evidence for something that authors and policymakers in favor of free trade had stated all along, namely, that protectionism resulted in attractive rents for producers, many of whom had cost structures that allowed them to compete against foreign producers."

Others, however, insist that trade liberalization had a strongly negative effect on inflexible rent seekers. Russell (1994, 222) argues that the "flood of imports has devastated Mexican producers" and that the combined effects of the 1982 crisis and 1985 GATT decision were important contributors. Even in the dynamic Monterrey region, the negative effects of trade liberalization were felt strongly. By 1992, imports had taken over about a third of the domestic market share in plastics, paper, steel, and textiles. The Monterrey Manufacturers' Association claimed to lose more than thirty-seven hundred members between 1987 and 1992 (*Economist* 1992b). This phenomenon does not appear to be restricted to the Monterrey region. Table 4.1 suggests that, using 1985 as a base year, the number of establishments in production fell across a wide range of industrial sectors. While some of this decline reflects a global (at least as reflected in Organisation for Economic Co-operation and Development [OECD] countries) phenomenon, certain sectors appear to have been hit comparatively hard. This is especially true of the textiles, chemical, basic metals, and fabricated metals sectors. Roughly 10 percent of Mexico's ninety thousand small and medium-sized businesses were wiped out between 1990 and 1992 alone, taking with them an estimated one hundred thousand jobs. This is on top of an estimated twenty-eight thousand small-business failures in the second half of the 1980s (Rubio 1993, 37; Morici 1993, 52; Pastor and Wise 1994, 466; Poitras and Robinson 1994; Bensabat 1995, 198). In sum, as Javier Ortíz, senior economic adviser for the Canadian embassy in Mexico City, put it in 1992, "There are two kinds of industry in Mexico, those that are booming because they capitalized their enterprises and are not debt burdened, and those that go bankrupt" (quoted in Bensabat 1995, 197).

It appears that independent of the effects of the economic crisis, many Mexican businesses failed due to the elimination of state-supplied rents. While bankruptcy records in Mexico are notoriously inaccurate (hence the widely differing analysis on the effects of rent reductions by experts on the Mexican economy) it is reasonable to expect that most of the victims came from the small and medium-sized business sector. Certainly CANACINTRA had predicted such carnage in the context of the 1980 GATT decision. Small and medium-sized businesses typically shoulder most of the initial free-trade costs. Berry (1996, 58–60) identifies a number of reasons for this. Small and medium-sized enterprises tend to be comparatively weak in their ability to influence state actors, they have a propensity to be located outside of export-niche sectors, their relative undercapitalization limits their ability to ride out crisis and regime transition, and they suffer from competitive disadvantage vis-à-vis larger enterprises in accumulating information necessary to engage in newly competitive markets. The flip side, of course, is that larger firms tend to be more adept at engaging in the sorts of adjustments that characterize flexible rent seekers. For example, in the case of Mexico, by 1988, large firms' share of total fixed investment was 87.3 percent; small firms accounted for just 3.2 percent (Thacker 1998). It is this asymmetry in the ability to adjust that explains the disproportionate costs borne by small and medium-sized businesses during the 1980s. It also explains why the conversion to free trade was much more rapid on the part of the confederations that represent larger businesses than was the case with CANACINTRA.

Flexible Rent Seekers

The fault line between flexible and inflexible rent seekers in Mexico emerged as early as the first GATT decision of 1980. While it was an impor-

Table 4.1

Establishments in production by industry, Mexico and OECD average

	Food, Beverages, and Tobacco		Textiles, Apparel, and Leather		Paper, Paper Products, and Printing		Wood, Wood Products, and Furniture		Chemical Products		Basic Metal Industries		Nonmetallic Mineral Products		Fabricated Metal Products	
	Mexico	OECD Average	Mexico	OECD Average	Mexico	OECD Average	Mexico	OECD Average	Mexico	OECD Average	Mexico	OECD Average	Mexico	OECD Average	Mexico	OECD Average
1985	100.00	100.00	100.00	100.00	100.00	100.00	100.00	100.00	100.00	100.00	100.00	100.00	100.00	100.00	100.00	100.00
1986	99.66	99.32	100.00	100.04	100.00	101.33	98.91	98.19	99.57	102.05	100.00	96.17	100.00	99.38	100.00	100.02
1987	99.49	98.18	98.81	97.28	99.52	99.77	97.83	97.06	98.85	98.93	96.03	93.30	99.50	96.77	99.34	98.32
1988	98.30	98.10	97.02	98.15	99.52	102.59	94.57	95.85	97.98	103.67	94.44	94.62	98.49	97.18	98.15	102.34
1989	98.13	96.67	95.83	95.96	99.03	101.13	92.39	95.27	97.84	103.11	94.44	93.83	97.99	96.60	96.43	101.95
1990	98.13	98.69	95.24	96.49	99.03	105.14	91.30	97.40	97.12	106.46	94.44	95.68	94.47	99.88	96.17	107.19
1991	94.05	96.11	93.85	93.36	98.55	102.47	89.13	93.88	95.82	106.26	92.86	93.83	91.96	99.16	93.00	106.40
1992	91.50	93.37	91.47	88.69	96.14	102.32	89.13	90.58	92.51	105.18	92.86	90.90	89.45	97.38	90.09	103.82
1993	89.80	84.30	86.71	97.99	95.65	102.24	89.13	76.95	89.91	124.31	88.89	102.67	84.40	105.02	86.13	113.60

Source: Organisation for Economic Co-operation and Development (1997).

Note: Base year 1985 = 100.

tant illustration of the residual power of Mexican rent seekers, the GATT controversy also revealed clear divisions within the business community. Tirado (1998, 185) identifies three distinct factions: nationalists (who correspond to inflexible rent seekers), moderates, and radicals (flexible rent seekers). This typology is useful in that it helps to elucidate the state-business politics associated with the first GATT decision; it also illustrates how rapidly these politics changed in the aftermath of the 1982 crisis.

The nationalists were the staunchest advocates of the status quo and hence the most committed opponents of GATT entry. Represented most effectively through CANACINTRA, and therefore also having a strong voice in the CCE, the nationalists represented the hardest core of the rent seekers. As the outcome of the 1980 GATT decision suggests, the nationalists were also the faction most intensely preferential with respect to trade policy. CANACINTRA made the argument, probably accurate as it turned out, that significant liberalization of trade would prove fatal to large portions of the uncompetitive small-business sector. While the crisis of the 1980s would doom these firms in later years, it was these dislocation costs that appear to have persuaded López Portillo that the timing of liberalization was not propitious (Story 1982, 785–86; Escobar Toledo 1987, 68–75; Thacker 1998).

The other two identifiable factions, moderates and radicals, were dispersed throughout the remaining dominant confederations. The moderates represented the historical policy stances taken by CONCAMIN, CONCANACO, and COPARMEX during the years of ISI exuberance. Moderates were generally supportive of import protection and subsidies but wary of excessive statism. Moderates opposed entry into the GATT, and they carried the day within CONCANACO and the CCE.[26] While the leaders of these confederations equivocated, they publicly voiced support for López Portillo's ultimate decision to reject the GATT.

Finally, as would be predicted for flexible rent seekers, radicals supported GATT entry as a means of escaping from the clutches of ISI exhaustion. While radicals were represented in CONCANACO and the CCE, they were more successful in influencing COPARMEX and CONCAMIN. COPARMEX, led by the more dynamic industrialists from the north, vacillated on the GATT question. As late as February 1980 it refused to take a firm stance. But just one month before López Portillo declared that Mexico would not join the GATT, COPARMEX president Manuel Clothier claimed that without GATT membership, Mexico could not hope to become an economic power (Escobar Toledo 1987, 70; see also Story 1982, 788). CONCAMIN was even more forceful, stressing the opportunity costs of failing to abandon a protectionist system that clearly promised diminishing marginal returns (Escobar Toledo 1987, 68, 72).

By 1982, the economic crisis rendered the moderate middle ground untenable. Moderates were forced to choose between the radicals and the nationalists, as the business community polarized. Inflexible rent seekers, still fighting for their survival, remained as intensely preferential as they had in the past. What changed was the increased commitment and growing influence of the flexible rent seekers (Bensabat 1995, 116–27; see also Luna, Tirado, and Valdes 1987, esp. 23). The transformation was rapid and was manifested by three important bellwethers. By the mid-1980s, flexible rent seekers had taken control of the influential CCE. Whereas the old radical faction had enjoyed only marginal influence in the CCE during the 1980 GATT controversy, by 1985 it was the inflexible rent seekers who were marginalized. Also, most of the major business confederations, including the CCE, strongly supported Mexico's accession to the GATT in 1985. Only CANACINTRA remained firmly opposed (Luna, Tirado, and Valdes, 1987, 22–23; see also Camp 1989, ch. 2; Bailey 1986). Finally, the shift in economic policy preference was sufficiently sharp on the part of flexible rent seekers that in spite of the free-market reforms undertaken by the de la Madrid administration, many flexible rent seekers abandoned the PRI in favor of the more radical PAN (Bensabat 1995, 127; Thacker 1998).

Finding itself isolated in the second half of the 1980s, CANACINTRA portrayed the schism in the business community as one between large firms on the one hand and small and medium-sized firms on the other. While not wholly specious, such a complaint obscures an important dynamic. The crisis of the 1980s was like a forest fire, the effects of which were more devastating to the weak and vulnerable. But after every forest fire there is regrowth. Doomed was the deadwood of the ISI era; from the ashes rose a new, more robust cadre of small and medium-sized businesses. Indeed, even as the Monterrey Chamber of Commerce decried the aforementioned loss of thirty-seven hundred members during the period 1987–1992, five thousand new ones joined (Tirado 1998, 185). While smaller firms may have had a more difficult time adjusting than did their larger brethren, the economic revolution of the 1980s affected small and medium-sized businesses as well (Russell 1994, 179; Pastor and Wise 1994, 466–67; Bensabat 1995, 201–2). Ultimately, this replacement effect within the small and medium-sized business sector seems to have had the effect of shifting, albeit belatedly, CANACINTRA's trade preferences as well (see Russell 1994, 179; Pastor and Wise 1994, 466–67; Bensabat 1995, 201–2; Thacker 1998).

Figure 4.1: Export of manufactured goods as a percentage of merchandise exports

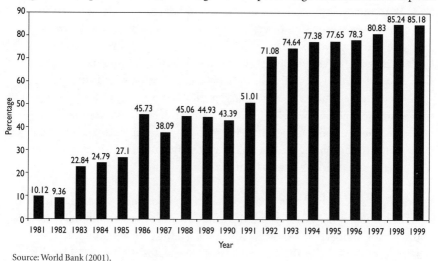

Source: World Bank (2001).

The shift in policy preference articulated by most of the business confederations in Mexico was reinforced by their members' changing production profiles. As figure 4.1 indicates, the immediate post-GATT years saw a large increase in manufactured goods as a percentage of total exports. The implications are inescapable. Denied oligopoly market shares at home, Mexican businesses altered their production profiles to become more globally competitive. As the limits of rent seeking model predicts, and figure 4.1 bears out, this export orientation appears to have been stimulated by the GATT accession in 1985. The second large jump in manufactures as a share of exports, in 1992, is interesting in that it occurred after the announcement that NAFTA would be negotiated but prior to the implementation of that agreement. Clearly then, much of the Mexican producer population was willing and able to adjust to new market conditions during the early 1990s. It is difficult to imagine that a population of inflexible rent seekers would react in the same way. Instead, the reasonable assumption is that inflexible rent seekers would take advantage of the time lag between announcement and implementation of NAFTA to mobilize in opposition. A population dominated by inflexible rent seekers might be expected to act as Mexican producers did during the first GATT decision. Manifestly, that option was not chosen by a majority of the business community. Instead, major business confederations led the charge for NAFTA. As Poitras and Robinson (1994, 14) point out,

> With only minor reservations, most state-recognized business associa-
> tions were strong supporters of free trade. . . . COPARMEX, known as
> the conservative conscience of the business community, endorsed free
> trade with the United States along with other pro-business measures. So
> too did . . . CONCAMIN, the national confederation of industry, which
> stressed the benefits of economic growth while warning of the potential
> harm to small business. . . . CONCANACO, the national association of
> chambers of commerce, took its support one step further, not only
> staunchly defending the free-trade agreement, but also advocating that it
> might be extended to petroleum as well.[27]

Indeed, Mexican business spoke with more than just words. During the
NAFTA debates in Washington, Mexican businesses spent millions of dollars
lobbying members of Congress and their staffers in the attempt to secure
passage of NAFTA in the United States (Lewis and Ebrahim 1993; Russell
1994, 345).

As had been the case with the 1985 GATT ascension, among the major
business confederations, only CANACINTRA stood opposed to NAFTA.[28]
However, even in that organization, opposition eventually fell away by the
early 1990s. In part, CANACINTRA's opposition to free trade crumbled in
the face of its shifting internal makeup. In part, CANACINTRA was forced to
accept the new reality in the face of the strong coalition of business and state
actors committed to freer trade. As one analyst summarized the liberalization initiatives of the mid- to late 1980s, "A lesson learned from these
changes is that once implemented, they release new economic forces which
then call for further changes" (Ramirez de la O 1991, 13). Consistent with the
logic of the limits of rent seeking model, CANACINTRA found that its
major adversary was no longer merely the government, but its erstwhile
business allies as well. In 1990 business and government forged even tighter
links. Business groups and government created the Coordinadora de Organ-
ismos Empresariales de Comercio Exterior (Coordinating Body of Foreign
Trade Business Associations, COECE) to serve as the official link between the
business community and the government in coordinating trade policy.
COECE was closely integrated, in ideology, policy positions, and even personnel, with SECOFI and other organs of the state directing trade policy.[29]
CANACINTRA found itself under strong pressure from the CCE and
COECE to drop its opposition to NAFTA and to get in line with the other
major business organizations (Bensabat 1995, 212; Luna 1995, 86–87). In

1992, CANACINTRA finally not only capitulated on the NAFTA issue, but actually moved to support it. In a letter of February 11, 1992, to commerce secretary Jaime Serra Puche, CANACINTRA president Roberto Sánchez offered his organization's full support for NAFTA (Cámara Nacional de la Industria de Transformación 1992). Since that time, CANACINTRA has retained its commitment to trade liberalization, admitting more recently that its members' technological shortcomings and inefficiencies will not be ameliorated by protectionist measures (*Reforma* 1997).[30]

The Mexican case provides excellent validation of the limits of rent seeking model. Because the case played out over a number of years, it is possible to identify discrete stages in the behavioral modification of flexible rent seekers. After World War II, Mexico's producer population was almost uniformly in favor of the network of subsidies and import protection that characterized the ISI era. It was not until the period of ISI exhaustion in the 1970s that a small, radical rump within the business community began to consider alternatives to protectionism and to support the López Portillo administration's GATT initiative. However, this nascent free-trade coalition was too small, and the initiative died.

Deepening crisis after 1982 and the support of more flexible rent seekers forced from the middle ground led to de la Madrid's successful 1985 GATT initiative and deep cuts to state-supplied rents. By the early 1990s, even the relcalcitrant CANACINTRA, along with the rest of the business community, was supporting free trade. The successful transition from a protectionist to a free-trading society was born of crisis, but managed according to strategic considerations, particularly by Salinas. His predecessor, de la Madrid, had had very little policy maneuverability and had been more reactive than proactive in the liberalization of trade.

From the perspective of the limits of rent seeking model, it is difficult to find fault with de la Madrid's actions. He signaled his administration's commitment to the permanence of trade reform in a number of ways. First, he populated his cabinet and key advisory posts with *technicos* who were widely known to be firm advocates of free-market reform, including trade liberalization. Indeed, his selection of Salinas as (in effect) the next president of Mexico underscored that commitment. Second, upon his realization that trade liberalization was necessary to right the economic fortunes of Mexico, he chose a mechanism, entry into the GATT, that would institutionalize reform by making it extremely difficult for rent seekers to lobby for a policy reversal.

In one sense, then, de la Madrid accomplished much of the hard work to transform Mexico into a free-trading economy. But Salinas took office with the large portion of the business community represented by CANACINTRA still opposed to further liberalization of trade. Moreover, the Mexican economy had not fully recovered, and what was perhaps more problematic, the PRI electoral coalition had splintered on the left and the right. Indeed, if not for wide-scale electoral fraud in 1988, Salinas would never have had the opportunity to complete the transformation of the Mexican economy.

Salinas also demonstrated acute political skills. With a proto–free-trade coalition already in place in the aftermath of the structurally imposed rent reductions of the 1980s, Salinas recognized the political and economic opportunities that would be provided by one last, big bang reduction in rents. Salinas pursued NAFTA, therefore, because it would satisfy a large component of the industrial producer population, because it would stimulate investment (both foreign and domestic) in Mexico, and because this investment, in turn, would create sufficient revenue streams for government to continue to fund PRONASOL. PRONASOL, moreover, was a critical component of Salinas's electoral strategy of rebuilding the decimated PRI coalition that had largely disintegrated with the demise of Mexico's corporatist system in the mid-1980s.

The big bang approach was a risk, but a calculated one. Unlike in the British or Australian (chapter 7) cases, Salinas was fairly certain about the makeup of the industrial producer population. He calculated correctly that one final rent reduction would force the remaining protectionist core, CANACINTRA, to modify (and indeed reverse) its position on trade liberalization. In this calculation he was proven correct. Mexican producers have continued to support free-trade initiatives, with other Latin American countries, and under the broader rubric of the proposed FTAA (see Ortiz 2000).

5

From Protection to Free Trade in Canada

Canada represents an unusual case among industrialized nations. Its proximity to the United States makes it akin to a candle in the sun. An economic power in its own right, Canada is dwarfed economically and culturally by its giant neighbor to the south; its geographic isolation from other centers of commerce further magnifies America's importance. The result is that while the two countries are economically interdependent, Canada has long felt a need to assert its national identity in matters of intercontinental affairs. One manifestation of this has been a long tradition of left-nationalism, which has stressed the importance of maintaining an arm's-length economic relationship with the United States.

While persistent, left-nationalism in Canada has not been a great success in limiting commerce and investment between the United States and Canada. Each is the other's largest trading partner, with more than three-fourths of Canada's trade volume crossing the U.S. border. However, left-nationalists, in combination with a historically coddled population of industrial rent seekers, represented a powerful protectionist alliance in Canada. Thus it was surprising that in 1985, Canadian prime minister Brian Mulroney approached U.S. president Ronald Reagan about the possibility of an intercontinental free-trade agreement. Mulroney's decision, while predicated largely on regime-mandated change, was facilitated by the almost uniformly protectionist industrial sector rapidly altering its trade policy demands between 1979 and 1985.

The Canadian experience is also a clear illustration of the limits of rent seeking model. When the Tokyo Round of the GATT ended in 1979, its signal triumph was the creation of a set of codes designed to limit the use of nontariff barriers (NTBs) in global industrial trade. For Canada, the liberalizing effects of the Tokyo Round were magnified by the fact that Canada was obliged to accept the significant industrial tariff cuts that most of the world already had faced in the preceding Kennedy Round in the 1960s. Throughout the Tokyo Round negotiations, Canadian business leaders made it clear to their government that the proposed reductions to tariff and nontariff barriers under the GATT would spell doom for the industrial sector in Canada. However, upon the signing of the Tokyo Round agreement, Canadian business organizations radically altered their trade policy demands. As early as 1981, business leaders began to lobby the government for the expansion of continental trade in the form of a free-trade agreement with the United States.

The coincidence of a severe global recession with the effects (and anticipated effects) of the Tokyo Round cuts to industrial import protection in Canada transformed the production profile of Canadian industrial producers. Large numbers of the least efficient enterprises failed. Those that survived, faced with increased import penetration, sought to expand export markets in the United States. This rapid transformation, moreover, sent a clear signal to the Canadian government. Despite the fact that Canadian history had proven free trade to be a politically suicidal policy choice, and despite Mulroney's 1983 statement that continental free trade was antithetical to Canada's interests (Cameron 1986, xiv), the transformation of flexible rent seekers after the Tokyo Round made it clear to Mulroney that the political risks of free trade were greatly mitigated in the mid-1980s (Langille 1987). In many ways, the Canadian case is similar to that of its NAFTA partner, Mexico. Like President Carlos Salinas, Mulroney used the big bang approach in the aftermath of structurally imposed rent reductions that had triggered the demise of many inflexible rent seekers and stimulated behavioral change on the part of flexible ones.

The Historical Context

Canada's economic history is a product of its demography and its colonial past. Both conspired to elevate the fur trade to the status of what Innis

(1962) characterized as the foundational event in the creation of Canada. Fur represented the staple commodity of New France; it led to the founding of the Northwest and Hudson's Bay companies, to the creation of a banking structure to fund the enterprise, and ultimately to settlement patterns in British North America. Upon the British conquest of New France, the colonial market, with its system of imperial preferences, became critical for the sale of Canadian goods. New staples, including agriculture and timber, tied the British North American economy ever more closely to that of Great Britain. Agricultural production, a function of the territorial expansion generated by the fur trade, gradually overwhelmed the latter, as homesteading and land-use patterns destroyed the habitats of fur-bearing animals. Agricultural expansion was further aided by preferential access of Canadian wheat to the British market following the Napoleonic Wars.[1] Finally, timber also was vital to the early nineteenth-century economy. By the mid-1820s, roughly 60 percent of Canada's exports were in lumber (Lower 1933). At the height of its importance, Canadian timber represented one-seventh of all British shipping (Cross 1971, 1).

As with wheat, Canadian producers enjoyed duty-free access to the British market. Within each of these industries, powerful vested interests emerged and aligned with a growing merchant class based largely in Halifax and Montreal. These groups lobbied hard for continued (and expanded) preferential access to the imperial market, as well as tariff protection from the United States (see Brooks and Stritch 1991; White 1989; Forster 1986). The early nineteenth century witnessed the evolution of Canada's earliest rent seekers.

It was therefore a source of grave concern when Britain embraced free trade, with the repeal of the Corn Laws and concomitant reduction of timber preferences in 1846.[2] Powerful Canadian merchants subsequently mobilized in support of the 1849 Annexation Manifesto, whereby the Province of Canada would have been absorbed into the United States. Politics (and economics) in both countries interceded, however. British nationalism precluded annexation in the minds of many Canadians. At the same time, fear of adding more northern states made incorporation of Canada an unpopular idea in the U.S. South. Finally, the California Gold Rush had elevated commodity prices in the United States, making Canadian imports more attractive. Canada's competitive advantage in the U.S. market made increasing existing trade ties, rather than political incorporation, a more attractive option for many Canadian merchants (Easterbrook and Aitken 1967, 354–55).

By 1854, panic having subsided, Canada sought preferential access to the

U.S. market with the Elgin-Marcy (Reciprocity) Treaty.[3] This solution was short lived, as the United States exercised its option to abrogate the treaty in 1866. A function of rising protectionism in the United States as well as resentment over latent British support of the South in the Civil War, the U.S. decision to terminate the Reciprocity Treaty ultimately led to Canada's Confederation in 1867.[4] This economic dynamic in Canada's national founding was reinforced by the fear that Canada would lose its western territories in the face of postwar American expansionism. With the victorious Northern army at its disposal, the United States constituted a serious threat to the largely unsettled land between Manitoba and the vulnerable Pacific colony of British Columbia.[5]

After Confederation, Canada's first prime minister, Sir John A. Macdonald, sought to reestablish reciprocity by forcing concessions from the United States through Canada's imposition of higher tariffs against American manufactures. American indifference was resounding. Indeed, the most pertinent effect was to increase tariff dependence on the part of Canadian businesses. A secondary implication was that, having been denied reciprocity, Macdonald's Conservative Party, which dominated Canadian politics during the last quarter of the nineteenth century, evolved into the party of industrial protectionism. This protectionism came to dictate the structure of Canadian economic development in the coming century as thoroughly as the fur trade had in the previous one.[6]

While American recalcitrance may have stimulated Canadian protectionism during the nineteenth century, it cannot be cited as the sole cause. Trade liberalization also was greatly undermined by British Columbia's 1873 terms of entry into the union, which included the guarantee of a Canadian transcontinental railway. To make the railway cost effective, it was imperative to settle the Canadian West. It was the railway, then, that created an east-west economic dynamic that replaced the prevailing north-south flow of Canadian commerce. The resulting internal development strategy, reminiscent of Henry Clay's American System,[7] was known as the National Policy (1879).

The National Policy was an omnibus platform that served as an electoral vehicle for Macdonald. In the main, it entailed three principal objectives: to finance completion of the railway, to seek immigrants to the West, and to create a dynamic manufacturing base in Ontario and Quebec by virtue of high tariff barriers. The rationale was that the railway would attract settlement to the prairies. The newly settled West would serve as an internal market for Canadian manufactured goods. And high tariff walls would stimulate a vibrant manufacturing sector. Of course, these import barriers would also create a powerful constituency for their own retention. As Ellis suggests, the National Policy "produced in the Dominion a situation comparable to that in the United States after the Civil War: the emergence of a tariff-fed group of industrialists with connections interweaving the fabric of Canadian economic life" (1939, 4).[8]

The extent to which protectionism was institutionalized in Canada would not become wholly apparent until after the administration of Sir Wilfrid Laurier (1896–1911). By the early twentieth century, Canada's comparative advantage in agricultural production in the fertile western prairies had made the National Policy tariff structure unpopular in the West. Not only did the tariff structure preclude greater reciprocal access to natural markets in the United States, but it raised the price of manufactured farm equipment. The National Policy, then, was the first of many policy initiatives that stoked the fire of what has come to be called western alienation. This western alienation would come to play a critical role in the decision to embrace free trade during the 1980s. With the rapid settlement of the Canadian West following the wheat boom of the late nineteenth century, roughly a quarter of Canada's population resided on the prairies. The importance of western voters to the Laurier administration was magnified by the fact that the government's support of a freestanding Canadian navy had generated significant opposition in the traditionally Liberal province of Quebec (Morton 1963, 413).[9] Laurier resuscitated traditional Liberal support for free trade as a means of expanding his party's electoral fortunes westward.

South of the border, meanwhile, partisan politics had begun to force a revision of the tariff question as well. While the Republican Party in general was still closely aligned with industrial rent seekers, the Progressive wing of the party had begun a strong campaign for moderation of the tariff. The 1909 Payne-Aldrich Tariff was the catalyst for a new era of more moderate protectionism. The act itself was no liberalizing tour de force. Indeed, Payne-Aldrich gave the U.S. government the power to impose trade sanctions against countries that discriminated against the United States even by indirect means. However, an externality of the act was to move the Taft administration away from traditional U.S. indifference to free trade with Canada. Free-trade discussions between Canada and the United States technically came about as a result of a bilateral trade deal between Canada and France. Under the terms of that deal, French imports were granted preferential treatment in the Canadian market; the question was whether this constituted indirect discrimination against U.S. goods and should thus trigger sanctions under the terms of the Payne-Aldrich Act (Skelton 1916, 260–63; Ellis 1939, 36).

With negotiations under way, political dynamics in both countries took over. President Taft, under increasing pressure from low-tariff Republicans in the Northeast and Midwest, sought to expand trading relations with Canada as a means of signaling moderation on the tariff question. Reciprocity served this purpose. Laurier, with his own domestic problems, saw reciprocity as a means of satisfying western farmers. The resulting agreement, reached in January 1911, was almost as broad as the Elgin-Marcy Treaty had been, albeit with most of the liberalization restricted to the primary sector.[10]

There was no reason to suspect that reciprocity would be terribly controversial in Canada. Although Canada maintained high industrial tariffs, free trade in primary goods had been the nominal objective of Canadian governments of both stripes since Confederation. Moreover, the treaty would not affect the system of imperial preferential tariffs between Canada and Britain that many nationalists saw as a critical link to Canada's British heritage. However, as democratic governments the world over would come to realize, there exists a world of difference between enthusiasm for free trade in theory and support for specific agreements. Even though the reciprocity agreement made only marginal inroads into industrial protectionism, nationalists and manufacturers maintained that the agreement put Canada on the slippery slope to greater economic integration with the United States. The rent-seeking interests that had benefited from the National Policy tariff structure found increasing support within the Conservative Party, which used the trade issue as yet one more piece of evidence that the Liberals were intent on abandoning Canada's British heritage in favor of continentalism.

In the end, for the reasons that public choice theorists have long articulated, protectionist forces won out. Led by the Canadian Manufacturers' Association (CMA), as well as financial, insurance, and transportation interests, the protectionist movement captured popular support through the Ontario manufacturing belt (Skelton 1916, 263–66; Ellis 1939, 141–42; McInnis 1947, 402–3; Brown and Cook 1974, 181–85; Canada 1985a, 1:222–23). While support for the Liberals remained fairly strong in the West and in Quebec, the Conservatives secured a commanding victory in the election of 1911. The lesson that emerged was clear and lasting: free trade was a political nonstarter in Canada.[11] It would remain that way until the mid-1980s.

After 1911, the Canadian manufacturing sector continued to produce largely for the protected domestic market, which provided small economies of scale and hence encouraged the emergence of small indigenous firms.

While this led to a proliferation of industrial enterprises in the central Canadian provinces of Quebec and Ontario, it reinforced the dependence of industrial producers on state-supplied rents. Firms eschewed technological innovation and instead found it more profitable to import technology, largely in the form of licensing agreements, from the United States. This strategy of ISI characterized industrial development in Canada for much of the twentieth century (Williams 1994, ch. 2).

The interwar era saw the emergence of an important trend that reinforced industrial rent seeking. High tariff walls created the incentive for American firms to establish a presence in Canada by erecting branch plants.[12] The proliferation of U.S. subsidiaries operating in Canada contributed to a bias against the construction of an internationally competitive manufacturing class. Branch plants were established in Canada solely for the purpose of servicing a regional market. Product innovation, a vital spur to the construction of a viable export sector, was not part of the mandate of a regional subsidiary. Indeed, exports merely served to encroach onto the regional domain of another regional subsidiary within the same firm (Williams 1994, ch. 6). U.S.-owned branch plants, then, were enthusiastic partners of domestic firms in the lobby for retention of state-supplied rents.

Even the era of global trade liberalization following the implementation of the RTAA in the United States did little to alter the structure of Canadian industrial protection. In 1935 Canada and the United States extended most-favored-nation treatment to one another, and in 1938 Canada, the United States, and Great Britain agreed to lower trade barriers even further (Stone 1984, 11–12). During World War II, moreover, a source of western frustration was finally eliminated when the United States and Canada agreed to duty-free trade in agricultural implements (Reisman 1984, 38). However, while they were symbolically important, the economic impact of these deals was limited.

The end of the Second World War ushered in a new era of international cooperation. The political and economic instability of the preceding decades had persuaded Western nations of the need for closer military and economic interaction. Canada embraced multilateralism and was a founding member of the GATT. However, GATT membership did not represent the shift in Canadian trade policy that it might have. Although trade was liberalized across most sectors, tariff reductions in secondary manufacturing were marginal.[13] Indeed, Canada's entry into the GATT permitted a continuation of its historical pattern of parallel development—export-led growth in the resource sector and domestic protection for manufacturing—while allowing Canada to enjoy the increased prosperity born of the postwar global expansion of trade (Hart 1985; Salembier, Moroz, and Stone 1987).

The only real threat to comprehensive industrial protection in Canada during this time came in the immediate aftermath of World War II. In 1947, the administration of Mackenzie King went so far as to negotiate a free-trade agreement with the United States. The agreement was never made public, however, as King lost his resolve to carry through with the deal (Reisman 1984, 39–40). Six years later, the administration of Louis St. Laurent rebuffed American overtures to resurrect free-trade negotiations (Barry 1987).

Sectoral free trade was slightly more successful. The 1965 Auto Pact institutionalized free trade in automobiles and automotive parts. By the mid-1980s, the auto trade constituted one-third of all trade in manufactured goods between the two countries (Winham 1988, 51).[14] However, the Auto Pact was the exception to the general rule of industrial protectionism, and it was not until the Kennedy Round of the GATT (1963–1967) that Canada's protectionist trade policy once again became an issue.

The Kennedy Round featured conflicting objectives among the world's industrialized nations. Most sought to implement the so-called Swiss formula of comprehensive, across-the-board tariff reductions, a radical departure from the procedure used in earlier GATT rounds. These rounds had tended to constitute a series of commodity-specific bilateral accords that, by virtue of the unconditional most-favored-nation principle, extended benefits to all other member countries. Canada, along with Australia and New Zealand, lobbied against comprehensive reductions, insisting that because most of its exports were in low-tariff resources, while the majority of its imports were in price-sensitive manufactured goods, the Kennedy Round tariff cuts would be unduly punitive and would provide few benefits (Canada 1983b, ch. 7; Hamilton and Whalley 1985, 9).

In the end, the Kennedy Round saw most industrial countries reduce industrial tariffs by an average of approximately 40 percent (representing 70 percent of the value of dutiable goods). About two-thirds of these products featured tariff reductions of 50 percent or more. Canada, Australia, and New Zealand, however, were permitted to opt out of the Swiss formula tariff reductions and were permitted to maintain higher industrial tariffs. Moreover, by virtue of the GATT's unconditional most-favored-nation rule, these countries enjoyed the benefits of tariff reductions abroad (Hamilton and Whalley 1985, 9–10). This anomaly would not continue indefinitely. By the Tokyo Round, Canada's trading partners would deem its industrial tariff structure anachronistic and incompatible with the global trading regime.

Trade Liberalization in the 1980s

Mandated Change as Catalyst

The Tokyo Round, also known as the Multilateral Trade Negotiation (MTN), began in 1973, although substantive negotiations took place after the 1976 U.S. presidential elections. In some ways the Tokyo Round was a remarkable achievement, and in some it was merely a natural follow-up to the Kennedy Round. The economic dislocation of the early 1970s brought strong protectionist pressures to bear on most GATT nations. More ominously for Canada, given the importance of the U.S. market, the United States appeared, at best, ambivalent about sustaining and underwriting the global trading order. In 1971, President Richard Nixon had imposed a unilateral surcharge on all imports into the United States. The United States also abandoned the gold-dollar standard that had served to stabilize the international economy. Finally, the 1974 Trade Act lowered the bar considerably for the industries harmed by international trade seeking escape-clause relief.[15]

On the other hand, the 1974 Trade Act did not signal, as many feared, a retreat into protectionism by the United States. The act introduced the fast-track procedure, which expanded the authority of the president to negotiate reduction of nontariff barriers (NTBs).[16] It also granted the administration fast-track authority for the ongoing GATT negotiations.

The apparently ambivalent approach to trade policy in the United States during the period 1971–1974 was a consequence of America's dissatisfaction with the status quo following the Kennedy Round. This dissatisfaction was born of irritation that its trading partners were compensating for mandated tariff reductions with increasingly complex NTBs. (In addition, of course, countries such as Canada continued to rely on high tariffs, having escaped the Kennedy Round reductions.) Seen in this light, the MTN was an essential complement to the previous round of multilateral negotiations, consolidating the gains from tariff reductions. It also served to relieve the United States of the burdens of subsidizing the global trading order (see Stein 1984).

The new world trading order rapidly had an impact on the Canadian tariff structure. Unlike previous rounds of the GATT, the Tokyo Round was dominated by negotiations between the United States and the European Community, as it was then known (Winham 1986, 26–27). The result was that smaller countries such as Canada found themselves with decreasing leverage during the negotiations, playing the role of price takers on issues such as industrial tariffs, for example, over which they had previously exercised more influence.

Canada's more marginal role did not prevent rent seekers from attempting to stiffen the protectionist resolve of their government, however (Winham 1986, 334). Insight into this lobbying process can be gleaned from submissions to the interdepartmental Canadian Trade and Tariffs Committee (1974–1978) and to the Senate Standing Committee on Foreign Affairs (1976–1977). While some industries, most notably mining, favored trade liberalization, Canadian industry as a whole maintained its strong, united defense of protectionism during the Tokyo Round negotiations.[17] The general tenor of submissions was that the existing tariff was a bare minimum necessary for the viability of the relevant sector in Canada.[18]

Despite their pleas, however, Canadian rent seekers were not to be gratified during the Tokyo Round. In the aftermath of the MTN, Canada's industrial tariffs were reduced significantly, seriously undermining for the first time the historic protection afforded by the National Policy tariffs. These reductions were large, averaging 34–40 percent across industrial sectors and lowering the average import duty on manufactured goods from approximately 15 percent to roughly 9–10 percent over an eight-year period (Finlayson and Bertasi 1992, 30). In addition, Canada accepted the six Tokyo Round codes regulating the use of nontariff barriers. These codes, particularly as they pertained to customs valuation and government procurement, further undermined the level of effective import protection in Canada through the 1970s (Canada 1983b, ch. 7).

The Canadian government failed to gratify the demands of industrial rent seekers in the 1970s because during the Tokyo Round it found itself caught between foreign and domestic policy objectives. While it continued to seek the most favorable terms possible for domestic rent seekers, at the end of the day, Canada was obliged to accept the GATT's mandate for liberalization of its industrial sector. Canada's proximity to, and hence dependence on, the United States has tended to make multilateralism, embodied significantly by the GATT, the centerpiece of Canadian postwar foreign policy. As early as 1957, prime minister John Diefenbaker, concerned that the United States was the basis of too much of Canada's foreign trade, announced Canada's intention to divert 15 percent of its cross-border trade to overseas markets. Similarly, in the early 1970s the government of Pierre Trudeau attempted a similar strategy with its so-called Third Option, whereby Canada again made a conscious effort to reduce its export dependence on the United States. Finally, even in the post-NAFTA environment of the twenty-first century, Canada is an enthusiastic supporter of the proposed FTAA as a means to balance U.S. economic influence. This perpetual quest for a multilateral counterweight to U.S. dominance accounts in large measure for Canada's support of international regimes such as the United Nations. It also accounts for Canada's historic support for the GATT even while maintaining formidable import barriers. Most importantly, it explains the Canadian government's willingness to accept the GATT's mandate under the terms of the Tokyo Round (see Winham 1986, 334–41).

Significant as the Tokyo Round rent reductions were, few could have foreseen that the ultimate effect would be a fundamental reorientation of Canadian trade policy. It was the Tokyo Round rent reductions that triggered the transformation of industrial producers from staunch supporters of protectionism into proponents of continental, and possibly hemispheric, free trade. Of course, while the Tokyo Round rent reductions can be characterized as the proximate cause of the behavioral shift of Canadian rent seekers, four other factors also contributed to the government's receptivity to free trade in the 1980s.

First, there was growing alarm over Canada's trade dependence on the United States. This had long been a source of concern, but by the early 1980s there was a sense of urgency. In the early 1970s, the left-nationalist, Liberal government of Pierre Trudeau had introduced its Third Option. The policy was an unqualified failure. In 1972, less than 70 percent of Canada's exports went to the United States. By the mid-1980s, and in spite of the Third Option, the U.S. market absorbed 76.6 percent of Canada's exports (Canada 1985a, 1:263). The palpable danger in the early 1980s was that rumblings of protectionism in the U.S. Congress could leave Canada shut out of its dominant export market.

Another factor that helped pave the way for government's acceptance of free trade was the poor performance of the Canadian economy during the 1970s. In part, Canada's woes during that turbulent decade were a function of larger global phenomena. Thus, like most of the developed world, Canada experienced a marked decline in GNP, as well as a spike in the inflation rate. What made these indicators especially worrisome, however, was Canada's weak performance during the 1970s as compared to the United States and other major industrialized economies, especially in productivity decline and unemployment. This comparative weakness was emphasized by the severity of the 1981–1982 recession, which hit Canada far harder than most other industrialized countries (Canada 1985a, 2:44–51; Cameron 1986). Indeed, the perception began to grow that there were fundamental structural pathologies within the Canadian economy. These could be traced to the National Policy tariff structure, ISI, and the branch-plant economy. By 1980, Canada stood alone among the world's industrial leaders in that less than half (in fact, only 32 percent) of its exports were in finished manufactured goods. About one-third of these were in the automotive sector (Finlayson 1985, 30).

Together, increasing dependence on the U.S. export market and economic vulnerability led to a third important additional factor—the establishment of a royal commission of inquiry into the economy in the fall of 1982. Titled the Royal Commission on the Economic Union and Development Prospects for Canada, but more commonly known as the Macdonald Commission, it was notable for the thoroughness of its research (its report was almost two thousand pages in length, and the commission generated 280 background studies in seventy-two book-length volumes). More importantly, the Macdonald Commission is widely credited with helping to place the continental free-trade issue on the policy agenda. The Macdonald Commission Report was the culmination of an emerging sense within various agencies of the national government and Parliament that the trade policy status quo was untenable. As early as 1975 the Economic Council of Canada had presented continental free trade as a meaningful option for Canada (Canada 1975). Similarly, despite the remonstrance of rent seekers, the (unelected) Senate's Standing Committee on Foreign Affairs had come out strongly in favor of continental free trade.[19] Finally, within the Department of External Affairs, a cadre of internationalist trade specialists had begun to push for a fundamental reorientation of Canadian trade policy (Canada 1983a; see also Wright 1985). However, it was the enormous visibility of the Macdonald Commission that made its report authoritative. It is significant that the prime minister, Mulroney, committed to negotiate a free-trade deal exactly three weeks after the release of the Macdonald Commission Report.

The final factor that reinforced the decision to reorient trade policy in Canada was the unlikely intrusion of constitutional politics into the trade policy sphere. In 1984, the Conservative Party won a landslide election, bringing Mulroney to power. The next four years saw the intricate weaving of complex economic and constitutional issues, which led to free trade, constitutional crisis, and, very nearly, the breakup of Canada.

The central players in the juxtaposition of trade and constitutional politics in Canada during the 1980s were the increasingly alienated West, the predominantly francophone province of Quebec, and the Liberal Party of Pierre Trudeau. While the Liberals had been the champions of free trade in the nineteenth century, their ardor for continental free trade had gradually cooled through the twentieth. Indeed, by the time that Trudeau became prime minister in 1968, the Liberals had become established as the party of left-nationalism, dedicated to ensuring Canada's cultural identity within

North America. To achieve this, Canada sought to distinguish itself from the United States in its politics, economics, and culture. The Third Option was a prime example. Even more important was the National Energy Programme (NEP), which was destined to fan the flames of western alienation and mobilize the free-trading West in the constitutional battles to come.[20]

The NEP institutionalized a two-tiered pricing scheme for domestic and international consumers of Canadian oil and natural gas. The pricing schedule was set unilaterally by the federal government and ensured that domestic energy demands were satisfied.[21] The result was that producers, located largely in the western province of Alberta, were legally mandated to subsidize consumers, the majority of whom lived in the population (and vote concentration) centers of Ontario and Quebec. In addition, the NEP sought to "Canadianize" the oil patch by significantly increasing federal taxation and using the additional revenue to purchase greater ownership of the oil patch from U.S. multinational corporations.[22]

The NEP left bad feelings in both the United States and western Canada. For the United States, the fact that Canada would seek to limit oil exports during a period of crisis was a sign of bad faith toward a long-time consumer of Canadian petroleum. Indeed, one of the key objectives of the United States during the Canada-U.S. free-trade negotiations was to ensure that Canada could not restrict supply during times of shortage. In western Canada, feelings were even more intense. Western alienation reached fever pitch with the NEP, which many saw as economic theft by a government all too sensitive to the demands of central Canada.[23] The former premier of Alberta, Peter Lougheed, estimated that the NEP had cost his province roughly $60 billion in consumption subsidies and federal taxes (Lougheed 1988).

The cavalier treatment of western interests was not surprising. The political base of the Liberal Party has long been in central Canada, and particularly Quebec. Quebec was Canada's version of the "solid South," delivering a steady string of national electoral victories to the Liberal Party, which dominated politically during the first eight decades of the twentieth century.[24] Between 1900 and 1980, in the seventeen elections won by the Liberal Party, an average of 79.2 percent of the ridings in Quebec went Liberal. In the five elections contested by Pierre Trudeau (four of which he won), 83.9 percent of the Quebec seats went to the Liberals.[25] By contrast, the postwar trend that saw the Conservatives dominate the West intensified during the Trudeau years. In British Columbia, the Trudeau Liberals averaged 23.2 percent of the seats (although only 12.7 percent after 1968); the other western provinces were even less supportive: Manitoba averaged 19.4 percent, Saskatchewan

9.0 percent, and Alberta 4.0 percent. Western antipathy suggests that Trudeau was fairly safe in alienating westerners with the NEP and economic nationalism in general.

However, Trudeau miscalculated badly in Quebec. Trudeau's vision of Canada, whereby the country would become universally bilingual and bicultural, was not wholly embraced in Quebec. The "quiet revolution"[26] had unleashed a powerful separatist movement that found voice in the provincial Parti Québécois (PQ). The 1976 election of a PQ government in Quebec brought the forces of Quebec and Canadian nationalism to a head. The new PQ government announced that a referendum would be held in May 1980 to seek a mandate from the people of Quebec to negotiate the terms of independence from Canada. In the days leading up to the referendum, opinion polls indicated that the separatist forces were headed for victory. Trudeau responded with a rousing speech in Montreal promising constitutional reforms that would satisfy Quebeckers' demands for meaningful change. The speech turned the tide of the referendum, but delivering on the promise proved difficult. In 1981, Trudeau was able to entrench significant constitutional reform with the support of nine of the ten provinces.[27] Significantly, though, Quebec was the lone holdout. The promise that had won the referendum ultimately came to be seen as a stab in the back.[28] Quebeckers took their revenge in the next federal election, helping to sweep Mulroney and the Conservatives into power.

The Trudeau years witnessed two phenomena of interest to the juxtaposition of constitutional and trade politics: tension between the federal government and the West and tension between the federal Liberal Party and Quebec. Both played a critical role in convincing the Mulroney government to take the gamble of initiating a comprehensive free-trade agreement with the United States.

The Big Bang Strategy

There is not general agreement as to what motivated Mulroney, a quintessential brokerage politician, to engage in Canada's boldest free-trade experiment since the disastrous and ill-fated 1911 deal with the United States. Much of the left-nationalist literature reduces to standard class-based analysis: the Conservatives brought with them a neoconservative agenda that included seeking to gratify their big-business constituents (see, for example, Cameron 1986; Rocher 1991; Richardson 1992). There is some truth to this position—the business community was a driving force behind the decision to pursue free trade. However, the left-nationalist literature is silent as to why the business community shifted its position from the strident protectionism of the 1970s to commitment to free trade just a few years later. Moreover, it is unclear why the centrist, tax-and-spend Mulroney administration, which could scarcely have been confused with a true neoconservative government, would choose such a controversial issue with which to curry favor with the business sector.

The 1984 election produced the first Conservative Party majority since 1958. Mulroney was under few illusions about the reasons for his party's success. Like the 1958 landslide, the Conservative victory was less an affirmative vote for the party than a reaction against a long period of Liberal rule. Recognizing the interim nature of Conservative governments in Canada, one of Mulroney's primary objectives upon coming to power was to alter the political landscape that had seen the Liberals reign as the country's "natural governing party." The obvious target was the Liberal stronghold of Quebec. As Mulroney (1980) himself had noted as early as the 1980 election, "With few if any exceptions, the Conservative Party has been consigned to the Opposition benches for one reason alone—its failure to win seats in the French-speaking areas of the nation. . . . Though the prospect is daunting, the challenge is clear. The duty of the Conservative Party is to deal on a priority basis with this, its major problem."

The conventional wisdom in Canada had long been that there were three important electoral regions—Quebec, Ontario, and the West. The party that could win two of the three would form the government. The Conservative Party's base of support had long been in the agrarian western provinces of Manitoba, Saskatchewan, and Alberta and in British Columbia. The trick, therefore, was to effect an electoral realignment that would couple existing western support with a far greater electoral presence in Quebec. Trudeau's constitutional fumble in 1981 appeared to open the door for just such a realignment. If Mulroney could deliver meaningful constitutional reform to Quebeckers, he was confident that the French Canadian vote would shift from the Liberals to the Conservatives.[29] This logic likely was quite sound. In fact, Mulroney did manage to effect an electoral realignment in Canada; however, shoddy execution of his plan meant that the spoils went to two new parties, the Bloc Québécois in Quebec and the Reform Party (now called the Alliance) in the West.

Mulroney sought to put his plan into effect during the 1984 election campaign. Although Trudeau's constitutional amendments of 1982 (which had featured a Charter of Rights and Freedoms and a new formula for amending the constitution) were binding on all provinces, Quebec had signaled its dissatisfaction symbolically, by refusing to sign (essentially ratify) the new package. Mulroney sought to rectify this anomaly, announcing a plan for constitutional change that would allow Quebeckers to embrace the constitution with "honour and enthusiasm" (Mulroney 1984). Immediately upon his election, Mulroney elicited from the government of Quebec its minimal demands for symbolic acceptance of the prevailing constitutional structure. He then set about to broker an agreement with the other nine provincial premiers.

The result was the Meech Lake Accord. Signed in 1987, the Meech Lake Accord was a remarkable achievement in that it had the nominal, and constitutionally necessary, support of all ten premiers.[30] This support, however, while unanimous, was hardly universally enthusiastic. Most pertinently for the issue at hand, the premiers of the western provinces were, at best, ambivalent about the Meech Lake Accord. For the western premiers and their constituents, Meech Lake smacked of pandering to Quebec—something that in the minds of many in the West had been a recurring problem since Confederation (Gibbins et. al. 1988). Western alienation was a tricky issue for Mulroney. Whereas Trudeau's Liberals, a marginal presence in western Canada, had been pleased to give the back of their hand to the region, the West was strategically vital for Mulroney. Desperate to build an electoral coalition between two mutually antipathetic regions of the country, Mulroney had to offer westerners something in exchange for their support on the constitutional issue. Quebec would get its constitutional reforms; western Canada would finally receive its long-standing policy demand, dating to the National Policy, of free trade with the United States.[31]

Mulroney had not been an avid supporter of free trade. During the 1983 campaign for the Conservative Party leadership, Mulroney had taken a strong stand against continentalization: "Free trade with the United States is like sleeping with an elephant. It's terrific until the elephant twitches, and if the elephant rolls over, you're dead.... Canadians rejected free trade with the United States in 1911. They would do so again in 1983" (quoted in Ritchie 1997, 43). However, its usefulness as a side payment for western premiers' support for Meech Lake, coupled with the fact that flexible rent seekers within the business community had begun to lobby hard for free trade in the aftermath of the Tokyo Round, convinced the otherwise-timid Mulroney that free trade was an acceptable risk.

In the fall of 1985, Mulroney approached Reagan with a request to negotiate a comprehensive continental free-trade agreement. The resulting Canada-U.S. Free Trade Agreement (CUFTA), the precursor to NAFTA, was successfully negotiated in 1987 and was to come into effect on January 1, 1989, subject to legislative ratification in both countries. While Mulroney's Conservatives held a massive majority in the House of Commons, the opposition, anti–free-trade Liberals controlled the Senate. Although the Senate is unelected and conventionally does not veto legislation, Liberal senators claimed that Mulroney had not campaigned on the free-trade issue in 1984 and that therefore he had no democratic mandate to negotiate a free-trade accord. The only way the Senate would relent was if the Mulroney government went to the polls and won an electoral mandate for free trade.

The 1988 general election, like that of 1911, was fought almost exclusively over the issue. But this time, although labor unions, left-nationalists, feminists, and other groups lobbied hard against free trade,[32] the result was different: the sponsoring Mulroney Conservatives won a majority government. This was more than just blind luck. It is clear that the Mulroney government had anticipated the political risks of free trade well before the Senate blindsiding of 1988 and had taken steps to ameliorate them. A 1985 memo from the prime minister's office, leaked to the *Toronto Star*, provides rare insights into the politics behind the free-trade decision. The memo cautions that public-opinion polling on free trade is notoriously inaccurate, largely because the complexities of the issue are not well understood by most of the population. To mitigate the risk, the memo suggests that the government allow prominent interest groups to take the lead in promoting the free-trade issue. "Where support exists, efforts should be pursued to enlist in promoting the initiative. Groups willing to be counted should be clearly identified and amplified to a level that would serve to support the notion of a national consensus and act as a counterbalance to the opposition" (Canada 1986b, 8).

The most important of these groups clearly was the business community. In fact, it is no exaggeration to claim that without the support of the business community, the Mulroney government could not have been persuaded to take its free-trade gamble. The administration was satisfied as early as the spring of 1985 that the formerly protectionist business sector would be strongly supportive of a big bang free-trade initiative.

The Fate of the Rent Seekers

Inflexible Rent Seekers

One of the fortuitous circumstances (at least from a macroeconomic perspective) associated with the Tokyo Round rent reductions is that they were followed by a severe recession in 1981–1982. Although the crisis paled in comparison to the contemporaneous one in Mexico, it had a similar effect. Destructive and unfortunate, it also paved the way for regeneration. The great recession of the early 1980s hit Canadian manufacturing especially hard. By 1983, for example, employment in manufacturing had declined 11.5 percent from its 1980 level, representing a net loss of 583,000 jobs. Total unemployment as a percentage of the civilian labor force rose from 7.5 percent to 11.9 percent (Organisation for Economic Co-operation and Development 1984, 28).

Bankruptcies during this period also increased markedly. Whereas the total number of industrial bankruptcies and insolvencies was 6,595 in 1980, the figure soared to 10,765 by 1982 (Canada 1985b, 584–86). On the other hand, amid all this dislocation, the number of manufacturing firms in production stayed remarkably flat, from 34,578 in 1979 to 35,287 in 1983 (Canada 1987, 16). Thus, while the recession hastened the demise of the most vulnerable producers, the post–Tokyo Round era paved the way for new, apparently competitive, industries to emerge. More importantly, the elimination of the weakest strata of the economy facilitated an extremely rapid, and widely supported, shift in policy preference within the flexible rent-seeker population. While not nearly as pronounced or dramatic, the same dynamic that culled the hardest core of Mexican protectionists also operated in Canada during the early 1980s. As in Mexico, the effect was to strengthen the hand of the flexible rent seekers.

Flexible Rent Seekers

Rent seeking in Canada enjoyed a long and successful tradition. From the National Policy through the completion of the Tokyo Round in 1979, it was the rare industrial trade organization that came out in favor of lower import barriers. By the early 1980s, however, the Tokyo Round rent reductions had forced Canadian business into the unenviable position of insufficient import protection to ensure profitability but too much to allow for international competitiveness. The prevailing system of import protection, neither fish nor fowl, raised the price of imported factor inputs and, by virtue of the logic of reciprocity, restricted market access to Canada's principal export market. In the words of Ted Newall, chairman of Dupont Canada, "We, manufacturers, are caught in a catch 22 situation. On one hand, the tariffs in Canada are no longer high enough to offset the costs of producing solely for the Canadian market. On the other hand, even modest tariffs into the United States can make it difficult, if not impossible, to set up production in Canada to export into that market. . . . Unless we can negotiate increased and assured access to the U.S. market, Canadian industry will be unable to take the risks involved in making the substantial investments required to operate on a North American basis."[33]

As was the case in the United States and Mexico, it was organizations representing larger firms that were the first to shift from protectionism to advocacy of free trade. Led by the Business Council on National Issues (BCNI), now called the Canadian Council of Chief Executives, big business started to lobby the federal government for a free-trade agreement with the United States almost immediately upon the completion of the Tokyo Round negotiations. By the second half of the 1980s, small and medium-sized enterprises also had taken up the cause of free trade as a means of ensuring institutionalized access to the U.S. export market.

Founded in 1976, the BCNI, the Canadian equivalent of the U.S. Business Roundtable, is composed of the chief executive officers of the 150 largest corporations in the country. Its mandate is to allow big business to speak with one voice in articulating its public policy demands, to make those demands clear to government and public alike, and make sure that the business community is as informed as possible about the policy choices that affect it.[34] The BCNI quickly allied with the much broader-based CMA in lobbying for free trade during the early 1980s. The CMA has a much longer history. As early as the National Policy debates in the 1870s, the forerunner of the CMA served as an advocacy group for Canadian business. Open to any firm with at least five employees, the CMA seeks to use its vast membership as political clout. By 1986, the CMA had thirty-eight hundred member firms, 80 percent of which came from Ontario and Quebec.[35] Like the NAM in the United States, the CMA, now called Canadian Manufacturers and Exporters, constitutes an effective bellwether for the policy preferences of the nation's manufacturing sector.

Both the BCNI and the CMA were recent converts to free trade during the 1980s. The embryonic BCNI had not taken a strong protectionist stance during the Tokyo Round negotiations and did not strike a committee on trade until 1981. However, its leadership appears to have been well satisfied with protectionism through the 1970s (Doern and Tomlin 1991, 47). The CMA played a much greater role during the trade politics of the 1970s and was in the forefront of the fight for continued protectionism. In its brief to the Trade and Tariff Committee, for example, the CMA wrote in 1974, "We present here an overall view that is representative of a broad cross-section of manufacturing industries. In order to achieve this, we have contacted a wide range of industry associations, have reviewed a large number of briefs, have worked closely with many industry specialists and have reviewed some of the basic manufacturing trends. . . . We do not favour the adoption of general tariff-cutting formulae in the [Tokyo Round] negotiations. Any attempt to reduce an entire tariff structure to a few simple numbers would not be helpful and might be damaging."[36]

By 1981, however, representatives of the BCNI and CMA approached cabinet secretary Michael Pitfield about the prospect of a free-trade agreement with the United States. Pitfield, closely associated with the nationalist Liberals, rebuffed the proposal. The BCNI and CMA found a more receptive ear within the soon-to-be-constituted Macdonald Commission (Cameron 1986, xv). While there is no direct evidence that Commissioner Donald Macdonald's own conversion from protectionism to free trade was a result of influence from the business community, the commission was certainly bombarded by business pressure. As Cameron (1986, xv) puts it, "The concerted effort of dozens of corporations heralding the free trade option in public appearances before the commission in 1983 and 1984 had had a great effect, not only in swaying the commission and influencing its work, but also in putting free trade on the political agenda by 1985."

Behind the scenes, business leaders were also extremely busy. Throughout 1982 and 1983, the BCNI, along with the Canadian Chamber of Commerce and the CMA, engaged in numerous discussions with representatives of American business organizations about the merits of a comprehensive free-trade agreement. They also sought to solidify support among other business confederations that had, until very recently, been staunch defenders of protection (Langille 1987, 67). An excellent example is the Canadian Federation of Independent Business (CFIB).

The CFIB was founded in 1970 as a means of giving small-business owners in Canada some political influence. By the mid-1980s, the organization had more than seventy-one thousand members, making it the largest (direct-member) business organization in the country. With membership dues capped at a modest level, the CFIB seeks to limit the influence of large corporations on its policy positions. Instead, through its mandate program, the CFIB engages in monthly surveys of its members on relevant policy issues (Coleman 1988, 87–88). Like the CMA, the CFIB had been an ardent defender of the trade policy status quo during the Tokyo Round negotiations on Canadian industry. CFIB president John Bulloch testified before the Senate Standing Committee on Foreign Affairs on May 26, 1977, that his organization could support free trade only after a ten-year program of strengthening Canada's productive sector.[37] Ten years later, however (and in the absence of a ten-year program for strengthening the productive sector), Bulloch testified before the House Committee on External Affairs and International Trade that his members supported free trade by a rate of over 2.5 to 1.[38]

The CFIB, moreover, was hardly an isolated example of a business organization that changed its policy preference since the 1970s. Other notable organizations to do so include the Canadian Chamber of Commerce,[39] the Canadian Association of Toy Manufacturers,[40] the Canadian Chemical Producers' Association,[41] the Machinery and Equipment Manufacturers' Association of Canada,[42] the Rubber Association of Canada,[43] and the steel industry.[44]

With the electoral victory of the Conservatives under Mulroney in 1984, free-trade activists within the business community accelerated their campaign. To this end, in the autumn of 1984, the business community formed the Task Force on Canada–United States Trade Policy, consisting of forty-five business and trade association leaders. Ostensibly created to advise the government on potential free-trade negotiations, the task force was designed to demonstrate the unified support of the business community for free trade to the incoming Mulroney government. The influential position of the BCNI allowed its leadership direct access to the prime minister. According to BCNI president Thomas D'Aquino, Mulroney's conversion to support of free trade was partially due to the influence of the business community. "Brian had sufficiently high regard for the BCNI that if we thought it was a really important issue, he felt he should at least take a good hard look at it. And he did. By the end of that autumn [1984], he had bought the argument" (quoted in Newman 1998, 157).

A secondary target was international trade minister James Kelleher, who was strongly pressured by the business community to support free trade during the crucial early months of 1985. After touring the country to get a fix on business and labor attitudes toward free trade, Kelleher announced in May that "we have found conviction—not unanimous, but fairly general— among Canadian business people that they can compete, and will be happy to compete, with American business on any reasonable terms.... The feeling has been close to unanimous that we have to do something of substance to secure and enhance our access to the United States, and that we should act fairly quickly to do it" (Gherson 1985).

The free-trade activism of former rent seekers did not stop with the Mulroney government's decision, in September 1985, to pursue continental free trade. Between 1985 and the general election of 1988, in which free trade was the central issue, the BCNI alone spent some $20 million lobbying for free trade (Newman 1998, 156). More recently, the business community once again stood almost united in its support for NAFTA. Indeed, industrial producers today are as resolute in their support of free markets as they were in support of protection through the century from the National Policy until the end of the Tokyo Round.

The Canadian experience is important because the business community's conversion to free trade preceded even that of the government. From a century-long tradition of protectionism that extended well into the MTN negotiations of the late 1970s, the Canadian business sector emerged from the recession of 1980–1981 as one of the most important catalysts for a continental free-trade accord. Moreover, the conversion was all but universal, with the country's major trade confederations publicly shifting their policy preferences within a four- to five-year span.

The rent reductions associated with the Tokyo Round of the GATT conspired with the great recession of the early 1980s to produce several conditions that facilitated free trade. The MTN rent reductions forced flexible rent seekers to adopt production profiles that allowed them to be competitive outside of the (subsequently much less protected) domestic market. Institutionalized access to the U.S. market was a critical component of this new production strategy. Inflexible rent seekers were victims of the great recession and thus were not around to obstruct a radical trade policy shift. The structurally imposed rent reductions sent a clear signal to the federal government that an enormous obstacle to trade liberalization had been removed. The coalition of rent-seeking producers was now at the forefront of a new proto-coalition in support of free trade.

The early 1980s were even more favorable: a Royal Commission came out in favor of free trade, legitimizing the shift away from protectionism. The incoming Conservative government of Brian Mulroney was desperate for a popular issue in Quebec. Constitutional reform was such an issue; the price for its realization was a strategic side payment to the pro–free-trade premiers of western Canada. This side payment was CUFTA.

Free trade was a risky policy choice for Mulroney, a prime minister with few political convictions. Even with the potential prize of electoral realignment in Quebec, it is inconceivable that Mulroney would have chosen the big bang strategy had he not been comfortable with the fact that the business community was on board for free trade. However, the signals from the business community in the aftermath of the structurally imposed rent reductions of the late 1970s—which took the form of regime-mandated change—suggested that the risks were manageable.

The consummation of the free-trade agreement in 1989 seems to have put to rest any further controversy over trade liberalization in Canada. The subsequent Liberal government of Jean Chrétien, for example, ratified NAFTA, even though the Liberals had been staunch opponents of the 1989 trade deal. Since that time, moreover, the Chrétien government has been at the forefront of efforts to liberalize trade throughout the hemisphere, as well as in Asia.

Ironically, although Mulroney was able to secure passage of the free-trade agreement without significant backlash—the Conservatives were elected to a second majority government in the "free-trade" election of 1988—he was to reap no lasting electoral rewards. The Meech Lake Accord unraveled in the aftermath of free-trade ratification. Disillusioned Quebeckers turned to the more nationalist Bloc Québécois as a vehicle for the realization of their constitutional objectives. And in the cruelest cut of all, the majority of western Canadians also abandoned the party that had finally delivered on the promise of free trade, shifting first to the Reform Party and then to its successor, the Alliance Party. The Conservatives, as of this writing, have been reduced to a rump on the verge of disappearance.

It is important not to read too much into the demise of the Conservative Party in the aftermath of the Mulroney era. Ironically, Mulroney's downfall appears to have been more a function of poor handling of the constitutional issue than of the (apparently) more dangerous free-trade one. As was the case in Mexico, the successful free-trade initiative, relying on the big bang strategy, worked well. It was the constitutional issue that was a strategic disaster.[45] Indeed, the lesson of the Canadian experience—that the big bang approach is a relatively costless strategy in the context of appropriate signals from the business community in the aftermath of a significant structurally imposed rent reduction—should not be obscured by political blundering on the constitutional initiative.

6

New Zealand
Social Democrats, Free Markets

Economically speaking, New Zealand was slow to emerge from the shadow of colonialism. As late as 1960, 53 percent of its exports went to the United Kingdom—largely in the form of primary products (Hazeldine 1993; Bollard 1994). The 1965 signing of the New Zealand–Australia Free Trade Agreement (NAFTA) did little to alter the pattern of New Zealand's trade, and as the 1970s dawned, New Zealand shared with Australia the dubious distinction of being the OECD's most protected economy (Nieuwenhuysen 1989; Garnaut 1994a). The early 1980s witnessed two seminal events. In 1983, following an economic crisis born of decades of high protectionism, and against the wishes of the business community, New Zealand entered into the Australia–New Zealand Closer Economic Relations Trade Agreement (ANZCERTA, or, more commonly, CER). Then, a Labour Party government led by David Lange was elected the following year. The Lange government undertook significant microeconomic reform, including the elimination of export subsidies and import licensing and the reduction of tariff protection.

The irony of the New Zealand case is that the Labour government that instituted free-market economic reform was not led by a fiscally conservative right-wing party but by a social democratic one. At second glance, however, the political logic is clear. The economic crisis born of generations of industrial and (to a lesser extent) agricultural featherbedding had profound redistributive implications. At some point excessive statism becomes costly to the traditional clientele of the state (labor unions and the urban and rural underclasses). Indeed, as crisis forces the state to become increasingly sclerotic in its fiscal maneuverability, statism ceases to be progressive and becomes regressive—the poor pay a disproportionately high share of the cost of economic inefficiency. Given the severity of the economic climate in New Zealand, elimination of the corporate welfare state became a prerequisite to the retention of the traditional welfare state.[1]

The New Zealand case provides important validation of the limits of rent seeking model. As in other countries, flexible rent seekers were quick to shift their trade policy preferences upon the demonstrated imperative to reform in the face of the reduction of state-supplied rents. Moreover, the strategy employed by the Labour and later National Party governments generated fairly little political backlash. Employing the divide-and-conquer and iteration strategies under the direction of finance minister Roger Douglas, the Lange government concluded that the agricultural sector would offer the least initial resistance to a reduction in import protection and subsidies. Rents were quickly and deeply slashed, and as the limits of rent seeking model predicts, farmers either restructured or exited the market. Within three years, moreover, the government had an effective and vocal ally in the quest to reduce industrial rents. Meanwhile, industrial rents had been incrementally reduced in the early years of the Lange government. By the time that the agricultural rent reductions were completed, the government was comfortable that industrialists could withstand large-scale rent reductions. Thus, industrial rents were attacked with the same vigor that agricultural rents had been and with similar results. By the early 1990s, not only was free trade apparently entrenched, but it was producers themselves who signaled their intention to resist any backsliding on the part of potentially protectionist future governments.

The Historical Context

Until the 1980s, New Zealand had had little experience with significant liberalization of trade. In 1841, tariffs were introduced for revenue purposes only, although the depression of the last quarter of the nineteenth century created strong pressure for a protectionist tariff. In 1888, the tariff rate on most items was doubled, creating an average tariff rate of 20 percent. Although the tariff would be extended to an increasing range of products over the succeeding several decades, the average rate of tariff protection remained roughly the same, in large part due to the British system of imperial preference. Britain was far and away New Zealand's most important trading partner during the nineteenth and twentieth centuries. Exports to Britain, largely in agricultural products and gold, constituted 75–80 percent of New Zealand's total exports from the 1880s through the end of the Second World War (Hawke 1985, 57).

Population increases in the first decades of the twentieth century generated incentives for diversification of economic production. Like many countries with small economies, New Zealand introduced ISI as a means of growing a domestic manufacturing base. Domestic manufacturing tended to be inefficient, featuring small economies of scale and too much reliance on state support. The primary objective, however, as articulated by the sponsoring Labour government, was to maintain long-term full employment that was not vulnerable to global economic cycles. Secondary benefits were increased economic independence and fairly robust rates of economic growth (Maitra 1997, 25–29).

A severe foreign exchange crisis led to the introduction of import licensing in 1938 under the traditionally protectionist Labour government. Licensing survived the crisis and was maintained as a core instrument of public policy in New Zealand despite pressure from the United States and Britain at the Bretton Woods and later the GATT talks. The return of a National Party government in the late 1940s witnessed some relaxation of import licensing. In 1948, 100 percent of all imports required licenses; by 1957 just 20 percent did so. But when Labour resumed office in 1957 a new round of protectionism, aimed at providing long-term security for manufacturing industry, prevailed (Wooding 1987; Lattimore 1987; Rayner and Lattimore 1991).[2]

One reason for the reimposition of import controls was the fragility of the manufacturing sector. Although ISI and the wartime boom had stimulated manufacturing industry—especially in light engineering, metal work, electronics, and clothing—the first post–World War II decade had witnessed the inevitable stagnation associated with import substitution, as industrial employment growth barely kept up with overall expansion of the labor market. As a result, between 1949 and 1961, New Zealand featured one of the slowest annual rates of growth in the developed world (see Gould 1982, 73; Douglas 1993, 24).

The problem, of course, was ISI. While superficially justifiable as an entrée into world industrial markets, ISI tends to become an end in itself. Rather than develop world product mandates, invest in new technologies, and engage in product specialization, industries concentrate on production for the domestic market, substituting monopoly profits for riskier, if potentially greater, rewards in the free market. As Rayner and Lattimore (1991, 76–77) note in the context of New Zealand, "The very substantial import protection had permitted the import substitute industries to shirk the reorganization and restructuring that would have been forced on them by overseas competition. . . . It had become increasingly clear that some of the 'infant industries' simply developed into chronic invalids tied to ever more costly life support systems." Given industrial inefficiency, New Zealand relied heavily on traditional agricultural exports such as wool, tallow, cheese, meat, and butter. In the postwar era, some effort was made to diversify export markets. Beef exports to the United States increased markedly in the 1950s. Similarly, New Zealand signed a trade pact with Japan in 1958 to facilitate the exportation of farm products. These initiatives had limited effect in New Zealand's natural Pacific Rim export sphere, however. As late as 1955, more than 50 percent of New Zealand's exports (largely in agricultural goods) still went halfway around the world to Great Britain (Gould 1982, 102). By contrast, only 4 percent of exports went to New Zealand's most natural trading partner, Australia (Hoadley 1995, 23).

It was not until 1960 and the prospect that Britain might join the European Economic Community (EEC) that New Zealand and Australia set up the Australia/New Zealand Joint Consultative Committee on Trade as a forum to discuss bilateral trade liberalization (see Burnett and Burnett 1978, esp. ch. 4). Both countries were alarmed at the prospect that EEC membership would terminate Britain's Commonwealth Preference tariff system, but the effects on New Zealand were potentially more dramatic.

The need for new export markets created for producers a mandate for more efficient production and specialized market niches. On the other hand, this reorientation extended only to traditional export sectors—that is, those that already were fairly competitive internationally. Industrialists, who produced largely for the domestic market, were not obliged to respond to the potential crisis and focused their efforts at seeking to retain their ample network of state-supplied rents in the face of the potential threat of free trade with Australia. They need not have worried.

Australian producers were no more enthusiastic than their New Zealand counterparts about seeing their rents dissipated. Although the resulting free-trade deal—NAFTA—permitted roughly one-half of the goods traded be-tween the two countries to be imported duty free, it did little to affect the production profiles of import-competing industries in either country.

The heart of the accord was a master list of items that could be traded tariff free, known as Schedule A. Superficially impressive, Schedule A was constructed to ensure that freer trade did not actually expose industry in ei-ther country to a great deal of foreign competition. Where Schedule A com-modities did threaten domestic producers, both countries were permitted to impose quantitative import restrictions or provide compensatory domestic subsidies. Although both countries committed to expand the range of goods covered under this schedule, and it eventually grew to cover about two-thirds of bilateral trade, the impact was more symbolic than economic. As a result, NAFTA was more an exercise in trade diversion than trade creation. It con-stituted a redirection of exports from sectors that were already globally com-petitive rather than providing a stimulus for restructuring inefficient sectors.[3]

By 1970, despite NAFTA, New Zealand's was the most regulated econ-omy outside of the communist bloc. More half-hearted reforms were at-tempted when Britain ultimately did join the European Community in 1973. In 1972 Australia proposed that the effectiveness of Schedule A could be ex-tended if the two countries considered goods for inclusion on an industry-by-industry basis rather than the prevailing commodity-by-commodity formula. In this way, incremental reform of inefficient industries could work to maximize comparative advantage on both sides of the Tasman. Manufac-turers in both countries, however, resisted this initiative and it was aban-doned. The following year, both governments decided that a larger number of products would be considered as target commodities for eventual inclu-sion under Schedule A. This was a less-ambitious plan to give potentially tar-geted producers fair warning of the need to restructure for limited competition from abroad. Once again, rent seekers successfully protested the scheme. Finally, in 1975–1976, the New Zealand government floated the bolder step of creating a comprehensive free-trade list with its "all the way with Schedule A" initiative. Under this scheme, all commodities not explicitly excluded would be on the duty-free list. For the third time, rent seekers blocked plans to reform NAFTA (Gold and Thakur 1981; Hoadley 1995, 27).

Efforts toward substantive reform of NAFTA were disappointing for two principal reasons. While both governments nominated numerous com-modities for inclusion on Schedule A, neither successfully resisted demands of industry leaders to desist from significant rent reductions. Furthermore, many of the NAFTA negotiations, incredible as it might seem, were undertaken by representatives of potentially affected firms and industries. To relieve themselves of the administrative (and political) burden of meaningful trade liberalization, the two governments devolved significant negotiating power to industry panels (Burnett and Burnett 1978, 132–33; Hoadley 1995, 27–28).

The failure to reform the least efficient portions of New Zealand's economy began to tell on economic performance during the mid-1970s. Economic growth slowed precipitously between 1974 and 1976, and unemployment rose from a monthly average of 1,250 in 1974 to 11,500 two years later (Gould 1982, 141). The next eight years witnessed scant improvement. Under the premiership of National Party leader Robert Muldoon (1975–1984), New Zealand maintained rigid policies of economic intervention. Relying on wage and price controls, subsidies, and artificially low interest rates, the Muldoon administration was unable to defend the New Zealand economy against steadily deteriorating economic performance (Bassett 1993; Bertram 1993; Bollard 1994).

Meanwhile, things were not going well on the trade front. Australian producers were increasingly vocal about what they saw as unfair trading practices by New Zealand. Most irritating were import licenses, which Australia had long since abandoned and which made access to the New Zealand market difficult for a number of producers. To cite just one example, Hoadley notes (1995, 30–31) that Australian officials were obliged to negotiate approximately three hundred licenses to export furniture worth a total of $A6.5 million into New Zealand. Such bureaucratic obstacles created predictable discrepancies in reciprocal market access. Between 1965 and 1982, using constant dollar measures, New Zealand's exports to Australia increased sixfold, while imports from Australia only doubled.

By 1978, Australia had grown sufficiently weary of New Zealand's tenacious commitment to import licensing that it threatened to pull out of NAFTA and reorient its trade efforts to other countries in Southeast Asia (Alchin 1990). Given the growing importance of the Australian market, the threat was taken seriously in New Zealand. The Muldoon government responded in two ways. It articulated small reforms in its 1979 budget; while these were largely marginal, they constituted the basis for more significant restructuring under the Lange administration. More importantly, it sought to expand the impact of NAFTA by negotiating a new arrangement with Australia.

The government announced three initiatives in the 1979 budget. In an attempt to inject market mechanisms into the import-protection structure, import licenses for some consumer goods were put up for tender. Of course, while this was merely a means by which superfluous licensing arrangements could be identified, it constituted the first step in what was to become the elimination of import licensing in New Zealand.[4]

Second, as a means of weaning less-competitive sectors from their dependence on state-supplied rents, the government identified strategic but underperforming industries that ultimately might be capable of responding to market pressures. These industries were subject to a program of neocorporatist industry plans developed by the Industries Development Commission or by other relevant departments of government in conjunction with industry leaders. The goal was to phase out licensing protection slowly and to review the extent to which alternative forms of industry protection would be needed in the future. Industry-plan industries were identified as carpets, ceramics, eggs, electric motors, electronics, footwear, fruit growing, general rubber, glassware, milk, motor vehicles, packing, plastics, shipbuilding, starch, textiles, tires, tobacco, wine, and writing instruments (Wooding 1987; Rayner and Lattimore 1991; Birks 1992).

Finally, under the auspices of the "think big" plan, export subsidies were increased as a means of helping larger New Zealand industries crack export markets. Typically the think big industries were so weak internationally that they were not included in the industry plans. Instead, protection was maintained at current levels, while the state stepped in to assist in the creation of large, competitive enterprises. The principal vehicle for this was the Export Performance Taxation Incentive (EPTI), in which firms received a tax credit of 14 percent of the domestic value added for foreign exchange earned and remitted to New Zealand (Lattimore and Wooding 1996, 329).

In all, the reforms outlined in the 1979 budget were fairly tepid. Still, they marked the first apparent realization by the Muldoon administration that the status quo was untenable. In 1965 New Zealand had enjoyed the eighth highest standard of living in the world. By 1978 it had slipped to twenty-second, and by the early 1980s it ranked twenty-fifth. In terms of real income, New Zealanders' per capita share was 40 percent of that of the average Swiss. Between 1960 and 1984, New Zealand had an average growth rate of 1.2 percent—lowest in the OECD. New Zealand workers received the same incomes in real terms in 1987 as they had in 1960 (Rayner and Lattimore 1991, 8, 69; Douglas 1993, 14, 24–25; Sloan 1994). The impending crisis also obliged the government to seek changes in bilateral trade relations with Australia. Later, the crisis would compel the Labour government of David Lange to adopt radical supply-side changes, known as Rogernomics (in honor of finance minister Roger Douglas, architect of the post-1984 reforms) (Atkinson 1997).

Trade Liberalization in the 1980s

Crisis as Catalyst

The stimulus for economic reform in New Zealand was structural. Starting with the threat of Britain's membership in the EEC, circumstances had buffeted a series of reluctant New Zealand governments along the path of limited trade liberalization. Australia's threat to abandon NAFTA in 1978 continued the trend. However, that danger paled in comparison to the looming presence of a severe economic crisis that was brought to a head with the recession of 1980–1981.

The decade 1974–1984 saw New Zealand's debt balloon drastically. The oil shocks, the recession of the early 1980s, and Muldoon's interventionist economic policies conspired to run up a debt of $NZ35 billion for a population of just over three million. Moreover, there was little hope that staying the course would see the economy through. Unemployment was on the rise, inflation was high, and the deficit continued to grow as the service charges on the debt crept to 20 percent of revenues. Between 1977 and 1982, New Zealand suffered consecutive years of net emigration.

In large part, deficit financing fueled New Zealand's economic woes. As in Canada and Mexico, New Zealand's public finances fell out of equilibrium in the 1970s. Throughout the 1960s, the New Zealand government spent at a rate of between 26 and 29 percent of GDP. By fiscal 1975–1976, that figure had ballooned to 38 percent of GDP, and by 1983–1984 had reached 40 percent. The annual budget deficit for 1984–1985 was an unhealthy 9.1 percent of GDP. Indeed, the government's real net debt tripled between fiscal 1974–1975 and 1978–1979 and tripled again by fiscal 1984–1985. To put the enormity of these figures into perspective in a small economy like New Zealand's, every household in New Zealand owed at least sixty thousand dollars in per capita public debt. The interest alone on such a debt was one hundred dollars per week per household (Douglas 1993, 19–23).

Thus, by the early 1980s, it was becoming increasingly clear, even to the Muldoon administration, that reforms at the margins would not suffice to right the economy. As the crisis deepened, reform elements within the bureaucracy, aided by certain influential members of the cabinet, including trade and industry minister Hugh Templeton, as well as export-oriented producers (most notably the Farmers' Federation), began to argue the need to overhaul, not merely tinker with, the ISI system (Thakur and Gold 1983; Alchin 1990; Bollard 1994). This reform coalition pushed hard to replace NAFTA with a genuine free-trade agreement, which ultimately took the form of the CER. As Templeton noted in the context of the burgeoning CER negotiations, "I believe it would be nonsense to disregard [CER] on the basis that we can continue as we are. It's obvious that we can't" (*Manufacturer* 1982a).

As had occurred in the 1970s, rent seekers attempted to block expansion of the trade agreement. In this they were aided by patrons more committed to state intervention, both within the Muldoon administration and in the bureaucracy. As Bertram notes (1993, 47–48), reform was once again opposed by "powerful, self-interested bureaucratic elites which were selectively responsive to the lobbying demands of particular constituencies, and shaped policy accordingly, often with little regard to the ostensible checks and balances of democratic politics."[5] Among rent seekers, the most vocal opponent of the proposed CER was the Manufacturers' Federation (Manfed; Roper 1993). In 1981, the Manfed issued its *Manufacturers' Manifesto*, which declared, "In a world where government interventionism is the name of the game, a free trade policy for New Zealand would be totally insane—it would quickly wreck the economy creating commercial and social havoc right across the country" (Roper 1992, 7).[6]

The pervasive nature of the crisis, however, blunted the traditionally decisive impact of the rent-seeking coalition. Indeed, as the CER became increasingly likely, the Manfed, for once, found itself on the defensive. While maintaining its official opposition to the CER, the Manfed articulated its minimally acceptable conditions: that reductions in import controls be bilateral and gradual, proceed only with the consent of a majority of manufacturers in the regions affected, and be accompanied by compensation for adversely affected industries (Roper 1992, 6; see also *Manufacturer* 1982b, 1982d). The Manfed resisted the elimination of quantitative import controls. In the words of then-president Laurie Stevens, "The statement in the Budget that Government is prepared to replace import licensing gradually with tariff-based protection is completely unsatisfactory from the manufacturers' point of view and we believe it is not in the best interests of the country as a whole" (*Manufacturer* 1981).[7]

The CER came into effect at the start of 1983. A comprehensive accord, it explicitly bound both parties to a liberalization timetable, thereby providing a minimum of policy maneuverability. As a result, both sides committed to "binding their hands" as a means of limiting the impact of rent-seeking interests who might try and overturn some of the accord's provisions (Bollard 1986).[8] The agreement called for all tariffs to be phased out between the two countries by 1988, except for those on commodities granted specific exemptions at the time of the original negotiations. Unlike NAFTA, which applied only to the commodities explicitly specified, the CER was designed according to the principle of automaticity—the default position is that all commodities are included except those agreed on in advance.

Even more important was the issue of import licensing. The CER called for the elimination of licensing between the countries by 1995. The phasing out of licenses was to be gradual, with access to be increased annually. The impact on New Zealand manufacturers, however, was mitigated by the fact that the CER did not obligate New Zealand to eliminate licensing against third-party producers. Rather, the licensing system was retained, and Australian producers were allowed increased access through the use of Exclusive Australian Licenses.

The CER also contained provisions on other potential trade irritants. Certain export incentives were identified in both countries as violating the CER, and a timetable was included for their removal by 1987. Continued agricultural stabilization and support was permitted, subject to conditions listed in the agreement. The two countries agreed to work toward ending discrimination in government procurement, although this provision was not to extend to the state governments in Australia. In addition, the agreement contained standard antidumping and countervailing actions. Finally, special provisions were made for New Zealand's industry-plan industries to be incorporated into the CER at a more gradual rate than other industries.[9]

The introduction of the CER did not forestall the economic crisis of the early 1980s. The day after the election was called in 1984, $NZ110 million in investments was moved offshore. The country faced a massive foreign-exchange crisis, and the public debt reached 64.7 percent of GDP (Coddington 1993; see also Albinski 1986). The foreign-exchange crisis was so severe that the new Lange government's first task was to devalue the dollar by 20 percent. The chairman of Gibbs Securities later described the state of the New Zealand economy at the end of the Muldoon era as "a combination of a Polish shipyard in economic terms and a banana republic in our politics" (quoted in Coddington 1993, 51). The next few years were dedicated to the systematic rebuilding of the economy and dismantling of the state as the austerity program of finance minister Roger Douglas took hold.

The Divide-and-Conquer and Iteration Strategies

With the CER, New Zealand took an important first step in reversing its traditional protectionist trade policy. However, the Lange government also recognized the importance of building on the late-day reforms of the Muldoon administration. The new Labour government enjoyed a degree of policy autonomy that its successor had not. Although Labour had long advocated statism, it was not wedded to a rent-seeking constituency of producers to the same extent that the National Party had been. In this sense, while the prevailing crisis compelled the new government to extend the tepid reforms of the late Muldoon era, Labour was helped by the fact that its core constituency actually was beginning to suffer under the weight of the excessively generous provision of state-supplied rents. A secondary advantage was that the producer population clearly was not equally committed to the prevailing structure of import protection. While farmers had certainly benefited from state-supplied rents, New Zealand enjoyed comparative advantage in agriculture. This made the agricultural sector an attractive potential ally in the quest for free trade.

Upon committing itself to fundamental reform of the economy, the Lange government relied on a two-pronged approach: simultaneous use of the divide-and-conquer and iteration strategies. Iteration was practiced in the industrial sector, where rents were reduced serially and increasingly deeply. Divide and conquer was more complicated. Its clearest manifestation was with the use of large rent reductions in the agricultural sector even as industrial rents were reduced only incrementally. At the beginning of the reform process, the most pressing need was to construct a pro–free-trade alliance. The natural ally was agriculture. The Farmers' Federation had supported the CER as a means of reducing industrial rents and indeed was frustrated with the deadweight costs associated with an inefficient manufacturing sector. At the same time, however, the agricultural sector was not ideally situated to cast stones. In the early 1980s, New Zealand agriculture benefited from a wide range of subsidies that had been provided incrementally throughout the 1970s as a means of compensating farmers for the loss of their principal export market in Great Britain after its admission to the European Community in 1973 (Johnston and Frengley 1994, 1034–35; see also Atkinson 1997). As late as 1984, levels of agricultural support were 34 percent of pastoral output (Sandrey and Scobie 1994, 1041).

The Lange government resisted the temptation to curry favor with the agricultural sector by leaving their subsidies intact and focusing instead exclusively on the reduction of industrial import protection. Instead, employing the divide-and-conquer strategy, farmers became the first target of fundamental reforms, as the government began an assault on agricultural subsidies. The logic was that since the agricultural sector had demonstrated its ability to compete in world markets, large and rapid reductions in state-supplied rents would not be catastrophic. It was likely that the agricultural sector was largely populated with flexible rent seekers, and the political backlash would be expected to be relatively small.

The transition to freer agricultural markets in New Zealand was extremely quick. By 1987, the rate of government assistance to agriculture had fallen to 23 percent (not counting the forgiveness of nearly $NZ1 billion in loans), and by the end of the decade the effective rate of assistance was actually negative, if artificially inflated factor input costs (due to the persistence of industrial protection) are considered (Johnston and Frengley 1994, 1036).[10] While supply-marketing boards still persist in New Zealand, they remain the only anomaly in the freeing of agricultural trade.

Douglas confirms (1993, 226) that the decision to target agriculture was part of a carefully orchestrated plan consistent with the logic of the limits of rent seeking model and the divide-and-conquer strategy:

> Before you remove the privileges of a protected sector, it will tend to see change as a threat which has to be opposed at all costs. After you remove its privileges and make it plain that the clock cannot be turned back, the group starts to focus on removing the privileges of other groups that will hold up its own costs. . . . Farmers in New Zealand have traditionally loathed the Labour Party. But moves on that scale convinced them that we meant business in getting their costs down as well as removing their subsidies. Federated Farmers became one of the first major interest groups to endorse the principles behind our reforms.

Despite Douglas's conviction that speed is the ally of reformers, however, movement on rent reductions in the industrial sector was not as rapid. Manufacturers had not been exposed to the chill winds of market forces, and it was not as easy to gauge how they would respond to large-scale reductions in rent. If industrial producers were largely inflexible rent seekers, in other words, the political cost could have been considerable. As a result, and against the advice of Douglas, the Lange government used the iteration strategy be-

fore a significant reduction in industrial rents. Moreover, even when industrial rents were cut deeply in the early 1990s, industry-plan industries continued to receive higher levels of tariff protection than less politically important
sectors. In this sense, reminiscent of "special cases" in the United States and
industry-plan industries in Australia (chapter 7), New Zealand's reform
process remained, in the title of Douglas's memoirs, *Unfinished Business*. On
the other hand, unlike the Australian case, industrial rent reductions ultimately were sufficient to force change on the part of industrial rent seekers.

The reforms to the industrial sector by the Lange government affected a
wide range of economic policies. The new Labour government made strides
in the imposition of fiscal discipline, tax reform, deregulation, and privatization.[11] In the field of trade and investment, the government moved quickly to
eliminate the dense web of state-supplied rents that sheltered protectionists
in spite of the CER. Just weeks after the 1984 election, the government announced that the 20 percent currency devaluation obviated the need for the
EPTI. As a consequence, export incentives were halved in fiscal 1985–1986
and again in 1986–1987. By April 1, 1987, they were completely eliminated.

Import licenses were the next target for the Lange government. In the
1984 budget it was announced that the import-licensing tendering system
introduced in 1979 would be greatly expanded. In the November 1984
round, for example, licenses were tendered for 10 percent of domestic products (outside of industry plans). This was twice the rate of the previous
round. For products that generated little demand for licenses, licensing
would be removed. In September 1985, the government announced that tendering would occur annually, with increases each year of 5 percent of non–
industry-plan domestic production. Finally, in November 1986, the government announced that import licensing would end on July 1, 1988 (Wooding
1987, 98–99; *Business Line* 1997).

The government also moved to increase the flow of foreign capital into
and out of New Zealand. Beginning in 1985, New Zealand radically liberalized its rules on foreign investment—portfolio, direct, or equity—which
now is almost free from state regulation. Similarly, currency-exchange controls were lifted, which significantly boosted trans-Tasman trade. Finally, discriminatory restrictions on foreign-owned companies, especially with
respect to repatriation of profits, have been eliminated.

The final pillar of protectionism at which the government took aim was
the tariff structure. Tariffs were a touchy issue, as the Muldoon government
had linked the provision of a means-based tariff with the implementation of
the CER. After perfunctory talks with manufacturers, the government "ac-

knowledged the agreement made between the previous government and the Manufacturers' Federation but set about increasing the pace of reform without being hampered by consultations with the federation" (Wooding 1987, 97). In September 1985, the government announced its tariff-reduction schedule. For the first time in its history, New Zealand lowered its tariff rates comprehensively, albeit tentatively. Tariff rates below 25 percent were to remain untouched. Rates above 25 percent were to be lowered by 5 percent in 1986 and a further 10 percent in 1987.

Significant liberalization of trade continued after Labour was reelected in 1987. By this time, the worst cuts to the agricultural sector were over, and farmers were showing strong signs of recovery. Moreover, incremental industrial rent reductions beginning with the CER had demonstrated that industry was capable of meeting the challenge of increased market competition. As a result, in 1988, Australia and New Zealand completed a review of the CER and agreed to a number of new initiatives, including a Protocol on Trade in Services, which pledged the two countries to strive for free trade in services by 1994, and the realization of full free trade in goods in 1990—a full five years ahead of the schedule agreed to in 1983. Australia and New Zealand also sought to eliminate means of "back door" protection, by abolishing antidumping measures against one another and reaching agreements on standards and quality.

In the election of 1990, Labour was ousted from power, although not as a result of political backlash from the reform process. Indeed, the National Party government led by Jim Bolger continued liberalization. In its first year in office, the Bolger government announced that it would reduce New Zealand's world nominal tariff rate to 10 percent by July 1996 for non–industry-plan industries. By the early 1990s, liberalization was supported by a portion of the business community. A large and significant exception, however, was the Manfed, which vowed to fight "tooth and nail" to prevent further reductions in industrial import protection (*National Business Review* 1990). Manfed director Wally Gardner complained that "it would be impossible for many New Zealand manufacturers to compete with even cheaper imports when tariffs were cut to 10 percent in 1996" (Reuters News Service 1990b).

Even before that date was reached, however, the government announced, in December 1994, its intention to eliminate virtually all import protection in New Zealand. Tariffs on most items would be reduced to 5 percent or less by 2000. Significantly, even industry-plan industries would have a top tariff rate of 15 percent by the turn of the century. In 1997 the government announced its intention to reduce all tariffs, even in industry-plan industries, early in the new century. Thus, New Zealand avoided the fatal error of following the path of least resistance, by signaling to industry-plan industries that they too would be obliged to restructure for global competition. Finally, further reduction of trans-Tasman trade continued apace. In 1995 Australia and New Zealand agreed to discuss a Trans-Tasman Mutual Recognition Agreement, which would eliminate all remaining NTBs between the two countries.[12]

The transformation of the New Zealand economy since 1983 has been revolutionary. While adjustment costs were heavy (unemployment reached a peak of almost 11 percent in 1991), the results have been impressive. As of 1996, unemployment had fallen to 6.2 percent. Inflation, which was over 15 percent in the mid-1980s, ran between 0 and 2 percent for most of the period 1991–1996. Private-sector investment reached record highs in the mid-1990s (Brash 1996; *Business Line* 1997).

The free-market economy that prevails today is a far cry from the overly regulated one of just a few years ago. Prior to the reforms, New Zealanders required exchange-control approval to subscribe to foreign periodicals and a doctor's prescription to purchase margarine. Consumer choices were extremely limited. For example, there were only two types of refrigerator on the market—both made by the same company and both according to the same specifications (Brash 1996). Reform has created a sea change in consumption patterns in New Zealand.

Trans-Tasman trade increased markedly, with Australia emerging as New Zealand's most important trading partner. Between 1984 and 1997, bilateral trade expanded by 370 percent in value terms (Organisation for Economic Co-operation and Development 1998, 75). Moreover, increased trade with Australia was not a function of trade diversion from the rest of the world, as non-Australian trade increased as well. In recent years, New Zealand has sought to institutionalize trading links with other nations. Both Australia and New Zealand are eager to establish stronger trade with Chile, there is talk of a free-trade deal with the United States, and the Tasman governments have looked into the possibility of establishing formal links between the CER and the South American Common Market (MERCOSUR). Finally, New Zealand also is eager to establish links with the Association of South-East Asian Nations Free Trade Association.

Fate of the Rent Seekers

As usual, the distribution of rent seekers can only be determined with the benefit of hindsight. In New Zealand, while a large number of inflexible rent seekers were part of the producer population, it seems quite clear that the majority of producers, both agricultural and industrial, were flexible. As for the optimal size of rent reductions, the government felt comfortable that traditional exporters in the agricultural sector could survive without state-supplied rents. In the industrial sector, the pace of reform was more delicate. Iterative rent reductions, both in industry-plan industries and among industrial producers in general, allowed the government to gauge the producer profile and make subsequent cuts accordingly.

Inflexible Rent Seekers

Rent reductions in the manufacturing sector began to take their toll in the mid-1980s. Between 1986 and 1991, employment in manufacturing fell from 330,000 to 240,000 (Bollard 1994, 83). While some of this job loss may be attributable to restructuring within viable industries, some sectors of the economy were decimated. The ceramics and consumer electronics industries, for example, were wiped out entirely in New Zealand (Coddington 1993, 56–57; Bollard 1994, 83). Indeed, as Roger Douglas (1993, 27) put it, "One of the enduring myths about the reforms begun in 1984 has been that they were done to benefit big business. In fact it was the previous policies that protected and benefited big business. The removal of protection cost major companies tens of millions of dollars as they were forced to restructure their operations. In some cases businesses were forced to close once the protection of import barriers was taken away." Similarly, Alan Gibbs, an executive with the defunct Crown Lynn Pottery, reflected with remarkable introspection,

> Based on the infant industry theory and very talented lobbying, Crown Lynn was able to obtain protection for 70 per cent of the New Zealand crockery market. You would think that with this base of business we could build an industry that would be internationally competitive. Unfortunately, the more protection we obtained, the more we needed. The problem was that rather than concentrate on a few products and develop real skill and talent in depth, we tried to make the whole spectrum of crockery to supply that 70 per cent of the New Zealand market. We concentrated on the home market because it was easier and guaranteed. . . . In addition, under this protection regime, our management let their guard down and our unions were able to entrench totally uneconomic work practices. . . . Protection destroyed Crown Lynn (quoted in Douglas 1993, 28).

With more significant tariff reductions in the early 1990s, there were even more casualties. Between 1988 and 1990, for example, the plastics industry lost two thousand jobs (roughly 25 percent of its workforce) and sixty manufacturers (*New Zealand Herald* 1990b). Indeed, with unemployment running at almost 11 percent in 1991, the director of the New Zealand Trade Section in Canberra was forced to admit that "a lot of New Zealand manufacturing has gone to the wall" (Nutt 1992).

On the other hand, it seems quite clear that the majority of New Zealand's industrial rent seekers were fairly capable of weathering the effects of rent reductions. One way to measure the effects of rent reductions is to examine the number of manufacturing establishments in production during the period of rent reductions. As table 6.1 indicates, each of the major industrial sectors suffered an absolute decline in the number of establishments in production between 1988 and 1993.

The early 1990s, however, constituted a period of global recession, and it is imperative to control for the effects of economic downturn. A means to accomplish this, especially given the increased interdependence of the world economies, is to compare the decline of New Zealand's manufacturing establishments, in particular sectors with those in other OECD countries for which there are complete data. While some sectors, such as chemicals, metals, and nonmetallic minerals, were hit hard, even controlling for the effects of recession, most industrial sectors experienced establishment losses in line with those suffered in countries that did not reduce industrial rents as significantly during this time.

In sum, while rent reductions had negative short-term effects on the New Zealand economy, it appears that the most negative effects were a function of the recession. By global standards, New Zealand does not appear to have been saddled with a disproportionately large population of inflexible rent seekers. Of course, many enterprises did fail during this period. Whether due to recession or rent reduction, the weakest strata of the producer population were forced to exit the market, removing those most committed to protection from the political debate.

Flexible Rent Seekers

For flexible rent seekers, the New Zealand case supports the limits of rent seeking model. Indeed, within the business community there was a slow realization that the reduction of state-supplied rents necessitated fundamental change in the strategies by which producers secured profits. The iterated rent-reduction strategy employed by the New Zealand governments beginning in 1983 led to the transformation of the producer population from one

Table 6.1

Establishments in production by industry, New Zealand and OECD average

	Food, beverages, and tobacco		Textiles, apparel, and leather		Paper, paper products, and printing		Wood, wood products, and furniture		Chemical products		Nonmetallic basic metal industries		Fabricated mineral products		Metal products	
	New Zeland	OECD Average	New Zeland	OECD Average	New Zeland	OECD Average	New Zeland	OECD Average	New Zeland	OECD Average	New Zeland	OECD Average	New Zeland	OECD Average	New Zeland	OECD Average
1984	100.00	100.00	100.00	100.00	100.00	100.00	100.00	100.00	100.00	100.00	100.00	100.00	100.00	100.00	100.00	100.00
1985	72.85	74.30	77.49	74.60	79.25	73.80	76.56	77.33	99.39	80.88	95.15	70.97	98.13	76.08	102.70	77.34
1986	94.38	72.36	92.38	74.33	102.53	78.52	101.66	73.25	112.58	78.41	112.73	68.85	114.74	74.08	135.50	76.03
1987	104.90	71.53	114.11	72.28	119.17	77.31	134.78	72.41	107.29	82.16	121.82	69.83	109.71	74.40	140.47	79.13
1988	104.01	71.47	115.19	72.92	123.23	79.50	137.71	71.51	102.60	81.72	120.00	69.24	105.85	73.96	138.43	78.83
1989	106.61	70.43	111.29	71.30	127.87	78.37	135.23	71.07	101.47	84.37	115.15	70.61	101.05	76.46	135.05	82.89
1990	106.67	71.90	108.00	71.69	127.20	81.48	133.39	72.66	77.19	84.21	95.15	69.24	77.43	75.91	123.08	82.27
1991	88.39	70.02	98.73	69.36	149.58	79.40	128.38	70.04	81.01	83.36	98.18	67.08	76.26	74.56	125.48	80.28
1992	93.23	68.02	101.03	65.90	156.25	79.28	98.39	67.58	77.45	98.52	100.61	75.77	80.47	80.40	124.55	87.85
1993	94.58	61.42	102.35	72.81	122.55	79.23	134.47	67.38								

Source: Organisation for Economic Co-operation and Development (1997).

Note: Base year 1985 = 100.

dominated by protectionist rent seekers to one in which, by 1994, free traders were virtually hegemonic.

For agriculture, the evidence suggests that although the principal farm lobby—the Federated Farmers—supported the CER, the severity of the reductions in state-supplied rents threatened the cohesiveness of the agricultural sector. In some ways this is not surprising. Agricultural supporters of the CER saw the accord as a means of reducing industrial factor input costs and eliminating industrial rents. To suggest that farmers were in favor of freer trade, then, is not to argue that all desired elimination of agricultural subsidies and implementation of free-market reforms.

The years 1985–1988 were especially hard on New Zealand farmers. Land area farmed and agricultural employment rates both fell steeply in this period, generating significant pain in the agricultural sector. As Johnston and Frengley (1994, 1039) note, "Farmers, who first had expectations of manageable adjustment and improved profitability reinforced early on by the 1985–86 "profit bubble," experienced considerable adjustment difficulties. This was especially true for newer, younger entrants and leveraged entrepreneurs. . . . Federated Farmers leadership was under particular strain to alter the course of reform."

However, the farm lobby held firm. Although the real net incomes of beef and sheep farmers, for example, fell by more than one-half between 1984 and 1991, the Federated Farmers focused attention on a call for reduced rates of protection in the industrial sector (*Economist* 1991). The strategy paid off. Farm incomes rebounded to the extent that by as early as 1992, agriculture minister John Falloon noted that "farmers in New Zealand would move a vote of no confidence in a minister who advocated subsidies for them or anyone else in the economy" (*Economist* 1992a).

The case of industry is more dramatic. Rent seeking in the industrial sector persisted after the introduction of the CER in 1983 and the deepening of that agreement in 1988. The change in trade policy preferences within the business community occurred incrementally. Some businesses, especially the larger ones (represented by the Business Roundtable), converted to freer trade during the mid-1980s, creating a schism in the formerly cohesive front presented by the industrial sector (Roper 1990, 158).[13]

This schism was played out within the Manfed, which remained staunchly protectionist into the 1990s. However, the Manfed's consistent stance masked growing cleavages. As more and more companies were able to read the handwriting on the wall of New Zealand's trade future, the profile of industrial production changed in that country. Increasingly, companies

began to rely on exports. Table 6.2 and figure 6.1 indicate the inverse relationship between rates of protection and exports in New Zealand. Export
rates are indicated by grouped standard industrial trade classification (SITC)
industries.

The effects of free-market reforms, including the deepening of the CER
in the late 1980s, and the promise of more reforms in the 1990s, had a remarkable effect on most industrial sectors. For most, exports (measured in
1990 U.S. dollars) rose sharply and consistently after the introduction of the
CER and the election of the Lange government. The effect of these underlying changes in production profiles ultimately undermined the protectionist
stance of the last great pillar of industrial protectionism—the Manfed.[14]

By 1994, when the government announced a further round of tariff reductions after 1996, most industry groups, including the Manfed, supported
the program (New Zealand 1994; Graham 1994). Moreover, this support was
not merely passive, but instead entailed active lobbying. When the new Alliance Party, for example, suggested that import tariffs be raised by 10 percent in New Zealand, one of the harshest critics of the proposal was none
other than the erstwhile protectionist Manfed. The Manfed estimated that
the tariff hike would cost the manufacturing sector $NZ1 billion per year
(Reuters News Service 1996b). Manfed chief executive Simon Arnold suggested that among the key policies necessary for the continued success of the
New Zealand economy was "no further tariffs or barriers to trade and investment" (Reuters News Service 1996a). The Manfed also has lobbied hard
in recent years to liberalize trade faster under the CER. Specifically, it wants
local content rules liberalized to allow for even freer trade across the Tasman
(Barber 1997).

Table 6.2
Rates of protection in New Zealand, 1989–2000

Indicator	1989	1996	2000[a]
		%	
Bound tariff lines	55.0	100	100
Duty-free tariff lines	36.1	50.1	n.a.
Simple average applied tariff rate	14.5	8.7	3.1
Import coverage ratios (all NTBs)	11.5	0.2	n.a.

Source: Organisation for Economic Co-operation and Development (1998, 73, 75).

Note: n.a. = not applicable.

[a]Projected.

Perhaps even more remarkable than the about-face by the Manfed was that of the Apparel and Textile Federation of New Zealand (ATFNZ). As late as 1994 the industry was opposed to further tariff reductions. However, in 1997, in a meeting with federal cabinet ministers to discuss the overvalued New Zealand dollar, the ATFNZ stated, "Despite the high value of our dollar favouring imports, our exports have gone up nearly 400 per cent since 1988. . . . We face competition internationally on a pretty roughed up and unlevel playing field with high tariffs and non-tariff barriers in other markets. An example (is) Australia whose industry is generously assisted through their export credit scheme. . . . *But we are not asking for any special consideration*" (Matthew 1997; emphasis mine). Even the most protectionist elements of the New Zealand manufacturing community appear to have accepted, and now even support, further liberalization of trade.

Figure 6.1: New Zealand exports by commodities, in constant U.S. dollars

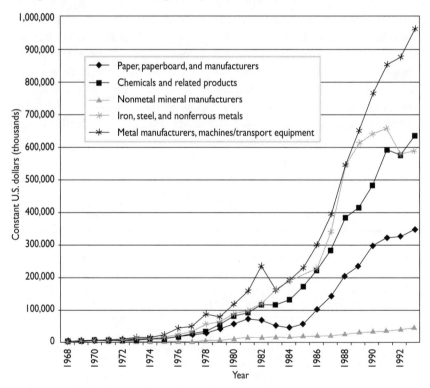

Source: Orgaanisations for Economic Co-operation and Development (1966).

In many ways, New Zealand serves as a textbook illustration of the limits of rent seeking model. An overwhelmingly protectionist country through the 1970s, New Zealand's protectionist rent seekers dominated the trade policy process for much of its history. However, within a ten-year period, producer groups in New Zealand radically reoriented their trade policy preferences. The same groups that had been die-hard protectionists as recently as the late 1980s—the Manfed is an excellent example—are currently in the forefront for retention and expansion of the trade liberalization process. The logic of the model dictates that they will continue to support trade liberalization far into the future.

In contrast to the experience of Australia (chapter 7), the New Zealand governments of David Lange, (briefly) Geoffrey Palmer, and Jim Bolger employed both the divide-and-conquer and iteration strategies. Following the lead of the Muldoon government, they used the prospect of severe economic crisis as the catalyst for trade liberalization, thereby generating as much political camouflage as possible.

Crisis allowed for two major rent reductions. The CER was deemed necessary after reforms failed to stimulate the economy. That agreement, unlike NAFTA, had a major impact on the production profile of a number of New Zealand producers. Indeed, although the CER was not significant enough in Australia to trigger much change in the behavior of flexible or inflexible rent seekers, its impact was magnified in the much smaller New Zealand economy. It was with the CER that a nascent free-trading coalition emerged within the still largely protectionist manufacturing sector.

The second crisis-inspired rent reduction was the elimination of export subsidies (the EPTI) beginning in 1984 under the new Lange government. The impact of this rent reduction was coupled with a compensatory 20 percent devaluation of the New Zealand dollar. However, while the dollar would ultimately be able to float to its equilibrium price, the EPTI was gone forever.

After these initial rent reductions and the end of the recession, the Lange government was obliged to continue the job of restructuring the New Zealand economy without the political cover of a crisis. The government had three main rent-seeking constituencies: the agricultural sector, which benefited from large subsidies; the majority of the manufacturing sector; and the least competitive manufacturing industries—the industry-plan industries. Each of these constituencies was treated differently, but none was spared the imperative to reform. The Lange government was confident that most farmers were competitive, the farm sector was the least committed to import protection, and the farmers were thus the first targets of reform. Subsidies were removed very rapidly with the effect that, although the years 1985–1988 were difficult ones, the agricultural sector was more firmly committed to free trade than it ever had been. Henceforth, the government could place itself in the politically comfortable position of reacting to pressures from a committed free-trade lobby rather than appearing to be in the forefront of the campaign to reduce state-supplied rents. In short, the New Zealand government played the divide-and-conquer strategy to perfection.

The success realized by the New Zealand government was also a function of its ability to stand firm in the face of rent-seeking pressures. Rather than cave in to political pressures, the government signaled its resolve to stay the course of rent reduction.[15] Finance minister David Caygill noted in early 1990, "New Zealand's manufacturing is still one of the most protected in the OECD, [but] you'd hardly think so listening to the pathetic bleating of their national spokesmen. . . . I expect that there'll be some pretty tough lobbying from their [manufacturers'] association and from individual companies as they confront the prospect of lower tariffs, [but] I think it's important to remind ourselves that of all our producers, manufacturers are the only group that are still substantially protected from international competition" (Reuters News Service 1990a). The sentiment was reinforced by Lange's successor as prime minister, Geoffrey Palmer: "The manufacturing sector has to face the reality that the days of protection and subsidies have gone. . . . How can we block off imports from one source while taking every advantage of free trade in another direction? [i.e., agriculture] . . . The changes . . . were essential to the future well being of all New Zealanders. We couldn't go on living in Alice's Wonderland" (*New Zealand Herald* 1990a).

The remarkable success of the New Zealand reforms has led many analysts to seek to explain the means by which radical economic reform can be effected without a great political backlash.[16] The governor of the Reserve Bank of New Zealand, for example, has suggested that the New Zealand case "was probably the world's first example of a 'big bang' approach to reform" (Brash 1996). Indeed, he cites Roger Douglas's prescription (1993, 220–21) that successful reform does not advance a step at a time, but rather in quantum leaps.

However, the evidence suggests that the genius of the New Zealand reform package was that it avoided the pitfalls of the big bang approach. Instead, the New Zealand government sought to gather as much information as it reasonably could on the profile of the rent-seeker population before it implemented reforms (Douglas 1993, 222–24).[17] In this respect, the government did not follow Douglas's prescription: "Speed is essential. It is almost impossible to go too fast."

Ironically, analysis of several cases suggests that speed can create political backlash that is avoided with a more prudent approach.[18] Instead of effecting reform as rapidly as possible, the government acted to provide sufficient lead time for rent seekers to be able to determine their objective status as flexible or inflexible, while signaling that reform was inevitable down the road. Industrial rent reductions occurred over a period of roughly thirteen years, with significant cuts coming at two- to four-year increments. The result might have been too slow for Douglas's taste, but the advantage of hindsight makes it difficult to quibble with the result.

Australia and the Triumph of the Rent Seekers

Australia represents an interesting case for students of trade liberalization because its circumstances closely mirror those of its cross-Tasman neighbor, New Zealand. In fact, by the middle of the 1970s, Australia appeared the far more able of the two countries to deal with the effects of economic decline born of pathologically inefficient industrial sectors. Certainly Australia was the first to attempt to deal with the problem in a meaningful way when, in 1973, the government of Gough Whitlam introduced an across-the-board tariff reduction of 25 percent. Moreover, because Australian producers enjoyed a larger domestic market, reason would indicate that they would have an easier time adjusting than their counterparts in New Zealand. However, hindsight shows New Zealand to be far and away the more successful case of trade liberalization.

Within two years of Whitlam's big bang tariff reduction, a protectionist backlash from business, the civil service, and even members of his own party forced retrenchment. Subsequent administrations have been at least on their face committed to trade liberalization. The governments of Malcolm Fraser, Robert Hawke, and Paul Keating each lowered the overall level of import protection in Australia. Indeed, the Hawke administration lowered tariffs on manufacturing industry significantly in 1988 and again in 1991. The results,

150

however, have been disappointing. There is only limited evidence of behavioral modification on the part of flexible rent seekers, and a powerful protectionist lobby persists.

Australian rent seekers failed to act as the limits of rent seeking model predicts. Suboptimal strategic choices on the part of successive Australian governments served to preserve a hard core of inflexible rent seekers while providing flexible rent seekers with alternatives to restructuring for competition in world markets. Whitlam's disastrous use of the big bang strategy was but the first in a series of missteps. The second was Whitlam's reaction to the furor created by his trade reform. He failed to remain resolute, softening and even reversing the effects of rent reductions in response to political mobilization on the part of rent seekers.

If Whitlam (at least initially) was recklessly bold, his successors were far too cautious in their attempts to liberalize Australian trade. Faced with a burgeoning economic crisis that mandated reform, these successor governments committed the third, and most grievous, misstep by seeking a compromise solution along the notorious path of least resistance strategy. Specifically, these governments maintained a Janus-faced commitment to trade liberalization by compensating those injured by trade liberalization with a generous network of selective side payments. There were at least three negative effects. The existence of compensatory rents created a disincentive for erstwhile flexible rent seekers to adjust for global competition. Rather than seeking to become more competitive, these producers tended to dissipate resources by lobbying for subsidies. Second, compensatory rents helped sustain erstwhile inflexible rent seekers, ensuring that the least efficient producers survived to retard further progress toward more market-based foreign economic policy. Finally, compensatory rents precluded the emergence of a free-trade coalition that could assist the government, or possibly even take the lead, on future free-trade initiatives.

It is important not to overstate the problem. The administrations of Hawke and Keating (1983–1996) enjoyed some success in slashing state-supplied rents while absorbing limited political damage. However, the long-term prospects for meaningful trade liberalization remain bleak. Rent seekers remain sufficiently powerful to have dissuaded the current administration of John Howard from following through on even the modest reforms of his predecessors. Thus, even as Australia begins to assert a larger role for itself in multilateral trade organizations such as the WTO and the Asia-Pacific Economic Cooperation (APEC) initiative, the Australian government appears to have lost any remaining zest for reform.

The Historical Context

Much of Australia's early economic history was shaped by the tariff. As Garnaut (1994b) has argued, Australia was born a free-trading country in 1901, but within a decade of its founding adopted a policy of industrial import protection. By 1927, the League of Nations deemed that Australia ranked behind only the United States as the most protectionist in the developed world. Its average tariff rate almost doubled during the 1920s; the onset of the Great Depression saw it double yet again (Capling and Galligan 1992, 70). While British Commonwealth preferential tariffs declined slightly during the Depression, Australia's general rates remained extremely high. The economic stimulus provided by the Second World War affected Australian manufacturing in a positive way. However, unlike much of the developed world, Australia eschewed postwar liberalization of trade, refusing to participate in the Dillon and Kennedy Rounds of the GATT on the rather dubious grounds that exclusion of agriculture from the talks would create no incentive for Australia to reduce industrial tariffs (Anderson and Garnaut 1986, 174; see also Snape 1994).

Australia's manufacturing profile in the first half of the century is unusual by comparative standards. By the 1950s, roughly one-third of Australia's GDP and employment were generated by the manufacturing sector. This figure is roughly compatible with those of other industrialized countries at the time. However, manufacturing constituted only about 10 percent of exports—about the same proportion as in 1910 and well below the 70–80 percent of exports experienced by the more dynamic industrialized economies (Anderson and Garnaut 1986, 164–65).

Instead of focusing on export-led growth, reminiscent of Clay's American System and Canada's National Policy, Australia sought to parlay its postwar prosperity into a development strategy that would attract significant immigration and industrial development. To ensure that the economy could absorb the anticipated influx, the industrial sector was granted even higher levels of protection against import penetration. As a consequence of this policy of McEwenism (after the minister of trade and industry, Sir John McEwen), Australia supplemented its high tariff walls with a system of import licensing.[1] By 1970 only New Zealand had comparable levels of import protection within the industrialized world.[2]

In part, Australia continued to maintain high levels of import protection because the Tariff Board—the functional equivalent of the U.S. Tariff Commission—served as an inadequate counterweight to the power of rent-seeking manufacturers. The board's mandate was to serve as a guardian of the public good. However, for much of its early existence, the Tariff Board was ineffective, constituting an excellent case study in bureaucratic capture. In part, this ineffectiveness was a function of the board's operating procedures. Prior to the mid-1960s, the Tariff Board considered tariff rates on a com-modity-by-commodity basis, usually after being requested to inquire, often by a rent-seeking manufacturer who wanted commodity-specific import protection. Such a practice not only limited the scope of the board but also influenced its mandate. Equally problematic, the Board used the antiquated cost-equalization principle, whereby effective rates of assistance for a partic-ular good were established by subtracting the production costs of the lowest-priced Australian producer from the landed-in-Australia price of the cheapest foreign producer (Rattigan 1986, 12, 22). As in America, the effect was to obviate comparative advantage by compensating for inherent ineffi-ciencies. Adding to the impotence of a defanged Tariff Board, McEwen, as minister for trade, was able to create institutional innovations to facilitate the growth of protection. The Special Advisory Authority (SAA) was set up as a means of providing short-term tariff protection to companies that ap-plied for it in lieu of longer-term Tariff Board recommendations. Sir Frank Meere, who headed the SAA from its inception in the early 1960s, was fa-mous for his philosophy of "you make it, and I'll protect it" (quoted in Dys-ter and Meredith 1990, 253).

Industrial protection in Australia, of course, brought with it a powerful constituency committed to its retention. Even sectors that were harmed by protection—largely in the resource extraction and agricultural sectors—found it fruitless to lobby for policy change (Garnaut 1994a). Advocates of protectionism used a variety of standard arguments to ensure that the state continued to supply generous levels of protection: specifically, Australia re-quired import protection to nurture a diversified industrial base; protection-ism raised real wages and allowed for the employment of a larger workforce; and protectionism served to redistribute wealth from landowners to the urban class (Anderson and Garnaut 1986, 165–68; Garnaut 1994b, 229–31). The hegemony of protectionism was so complete, according to Higgins (1991, 104), that the manufacturing sector "in its heyday, by the mid-1960s . . . employed a quarter of the workforce—a vast sheltered workshop for bel-ligerent, inward-looking managers, occupationally fragmented work prac-tices and labour organizations, and under scaled and antiquated plants producing variegated, poor quality merchandise in unviably short produc-tion runs."

Australia did enter into a bilateral trade deal with New Zealand beginning in 1965. This NAFTA, however, did very little to liberalize trade between the two countries, focusing instead almost exclusively on goods that had already traded freely across the Tasman Sea. Where imports competed with domestic industries, NAFTA had virtually no impact. It was not until the late 1960s that the dominance of the rent seekers was challenged. This challenge came from an unlikely source. In 1963, the McEwenite Tariff Board underwent an internal transformation with the appointment of Alf Rattigan as its chairman. Rattigan, who turned out to be a committed free trader, sought to reassert the Tariff Board's role as the conscience of Australian trade policy. In its 1967–1968 annual report, the Tariff Board (1968) came out against high uniform levels of protectionism, suggesting that industries should receive variable rates of protection according to their needs. With this rather innocuous proposal, the Tariff Board (later renamed the Industries Assistance Commission [IAC] and still later the Industries Commission [IC]) fired the first volley in what would become a long feud with much of the manufacturing community.

Not surprisingly, the response of the business community to the Tariff Board report was entirely hostile, with not a single manufacturers' organization publicly endorsing the board's proposal (Glezer 1982, 100). The Associated Chambers of Manufacturers of Australia (ACMA) condemned the report and sought to have it quashed on the grounds that its publication would have "real and psychological side effects . . . in the so-called high protection industries . . . affecting future employment investment and share values" (Glezer 1982, 100).[3] The Manufacturing Industries Advisory Council, the government's advisory committee from within the industrial sector, also uncomfortable with any challenge to the provision of high rents to Australian industry, suggested that publication of the report would be "quite perverse" (Glezer 1982, 100). One year later, in 1969, the ACMA was even more remarkably candid, claiming that "there is the strongest possible objection within the manufacturing industry as a whole to the proposition that the tariff instrument should be used to direct national resources into the areas where they will do the most good" (Bell 1993, 56).

The Tariff Board, however, continued to press for further rent reductions. In its 1969–1970 annual report (Tariff Board 1970), it declared that "the average effective rate of protection needed by manufacturing industry to compete with imports is below—and probably significantly below—the average effective rate of protection afforded by the Tariff." As a result, the board proposed a Tariff Review Program with an eye toward a threefold classification of industries. "High-cost" industries would require tariff rates of greater than 50 percent, while "medium-cost" industries would require 25–50 percent tariffs, and "low-cost" sectors would have to make do with tariffs lower than 25 percent (Bell 1993, 48–49). To this end, the Tariff Board began an industry-by-industry review of tariff levels that continued throughout the 1970s (Nieuwenhuysen 1989). By 1971, rent-seeking industrialists, feeling increasingly harassed by Tariff Board investigations, reacted even more strongly than they had in the past. A joint statement of the ACMA and Metal Trades Industry Association (MTIA) declared that "manufacturers are getting sick and tired of being pushed around. . . . It is not a threat but merely a statement of fact to suggest that the present Government would be out of power in quick time if it monkeyed about too much with tariff levels" (Bell 1993, 57).[4]

With the election of the Whitlam government in 1972, industrialists were confronted with a more powerful adversary than the Tariff Board. Although he led a Labour government, Whitlam made it clear from the start that his was Australia's "first free enterprise government in 23 years" (Whitlam 1973) and that he was a "strong Rattigan man" (Bell 1993, 56). To this end, in July 1973, his government implemented an across-the-board 25 percent tariff reduction. This reduction, the largest in Australian history, had its origins partly in ideology and partly in economics. Whitlam's strong opposition to industrial featherbedding was consistent with his party's political orientation (Whitlam 1973). Indeed, a decade later the New Zealand Labour Party would attack that country's import barriers for ideologically similar reasons. At the same time, a large balance-of-payments surplus seemed to provide some flexibility on the tariff question, while a reduction in tariffs could dampen Australia's increasingly serious battle with inflation (Glezer 1982, 117). The timing seemed propitious for a political battle with the country's coddled industrialists. In retrospect, as Canada's Wilfrid Laurier had discovered decades previously, the big bang approach to rent reductions is a foolhardy strategy in the absence of mitigating conditions such as crisis or regime-mandated change.

The reaction to the tariff cut among manufacturers was predictable (see Gruen 1975; Bell 1993, ch. 3). The ACMA and the Confederation of Manufacturing Industry Associations (CONMIA), among other manufacturers' organizations, pursued the option of mounting a legal challenge to the tariff reduction. They were supported by the opposition parties and, at least implicitly, by portions of the bureaucracy as well (see Glezer 1982, 118–20; Bell 1993, 57–58). Whitlam's fortunes were further harmed by the economic downturn following the 1973 oil shock. As the economy worsened, key members of the government began to question the political wisdom of the tariff reductions. Whitlam, despite blasting the "nervous nellies" in his own party (Glezer 1982, 128), ultimately was forced to retrench. In September 1974, the government devalued the dollar by 13.5 percent as a means of raising the price of imported goods. Devaluation, according to one study, raised the effective rate of protection by 50 percent (Glezer 1982, 128). In November, the government lowered corporate and personal tax rates, instituted a mild form of wage controls, and increased the use of temporary assistance measures. The latter was possible under the auspices of a new Temporary Assistance Authority (TAA). The TAA could hear appeals from adversely affected industries and, where it felt appropriate, make recommendations to the government for short-term increases in protection levels. By the mid-1970s, twenty-two industries had received temporary assistance through government acceptance of TAA recommendations (Glezer 1982, 156). Finally, despite the fact that highly protected industries such as the passenger motor vehicle (PMV) and textile, clothing, and footwear (TCF) sectors had been specifically targeted for significant tariff reductions, the government made numerous concessions beginning in 1974. Indeed, during the period 1973–1974 to 1981–1982, effective rates of import protection jumped from 35 to 54 percent for textiles, 64 to 204 percent for clothing and footwear, and 38 to 124 percent for motor vehicles and parts (Anderson 1987, 178; Nieuwenhuysen 1989; Garnaut 1994b).[5]

The PMV and TCF sectors were privileged for a number of reasons. They had had the most established lobbying capacities in the pre-1973 period due to their historic dependence on import protection. In addition, between them these sectors accounted for roughly one-fifth of the manufacturing workforce in Australia; these industries had been especially badly affected by the 1973 tariff reduction (see Capling and Galligan 1992). In short, these industries had the greatest incentive to lobby the government for the restoration of state-supplied rents, and given the importance of these sectors, the government had great incentive to heed their demands (Anderson and Garnaut 1986, 175–76). On the other hand, the government's unwillingness to hold the line on economic reform in these sectors had negative longer-term consequences. As Jim McClelland, minister for manufacturing industry, remonstrated to his cabinet colleagues at the time, if the government continued its stop-go policy of restructuring, "No one has any reason to believe we are serious" (quoted in Bell 1992a, 43). This statement would prove prophetic.

In 1975, the governor general dismissed the Whitlam government, which was unable to get its budget through the Senate, and a national election was held. Running on a platform of economic protectionism, the conservative coalition parties (Liberal and National County) formed the government under Malcolm Fraser. Whitlam's defeat was a further, clear signal that rent-seeking interests in Australia were not at bay. In retrospect, the Fraser government was critical to the future direction of Australian trade. Faced with a range of options, from reinstituting reform to retreating back into McEwenite protectionism, the Fraser government opted for a middle road.

Intuitively, the drift back to protectionism seemed to be the safest option. Tried and true, it would have ensured the support of an industrial sector sufficiently powerful to have beaten back the Whitlam government's reform initiative. However, while unsuccessful on its face, the Whitlam reforms had unleashed new forces in Australian politics. For example, the liberalization crusade begun by the Tariff Board had found fertile ground in the economics profession, and public-opinion leaders became increasingly outspoken about the costs of protection. While there was still little public sentiment in favor of wide-scale liberalization, there was a growing assertiveness on the part of those hurt by protection of the costs of state-supplied rents (Anderson and Garnaut 1986, 174–75; Bell 1995).

The heaviest burden fell on farmers. Not only did industrial protection increase the costs of factor inputs, but other countries responded to protectionism in Australian industry by placing import barriers on Australian farm exports (Nieuwenhuysen 1989). By the late 1970s farmers and graziers had grown impatient with Fraser's ambivalence about trade liberalization. Agricultural lobbyists brought tremendous pressure to bear on the coalition government—especially the smaller National County Party, which was traditionally the party of the countryside—to lower the levels of industrial protection (Bell 1992a; see also Connors 1981). Similarly, interests such as export-oriented manufacturing and mining also lobbied the government to reduce import barriers. Finally, Australia's trade partners, especially in Southeast Asia and the former European Community, strongly pressured the Fraser government to open up the Australian market (Anderson and Garnaut 1987; Bell 1993, 104–5; Fagan and Webber 1994, esp. 128).

On the other hand, while the spur to reform was apparent, the Fraser government feared suffering the same political fate as Whitlam. As a result, it maintained a Janus-faced trade policy that publicly decried the need for lowering of effective rates of protection but at the same time accepted a large number of IAC recommendations for tariff reductions. Even as Fraser complained that "[i]t must be a matter of concern ... when industry believes that the IAC is a body to be feared" (Glezer 1982, 150), aggregate effective rates of import protection fell quite sharply for non-TCF and non-PMV sectors between 1973–1974 and 1981–1982.[6] These figures are deceptive, however. While import protection fell in some sectors, the most heavily protected industries saw their protection rates rise significantly (Garnaut 1994a, 63).

Fraser was never able to reconcile his conflicting objectives over the tariff issue. The principal problem was that while his strategy of maintaining an outwardly hostile position toward the IAC provided a modicum of protective camouflage for the rent reductions of the later 1970s, it precluded a proactive policy of import protection. The government painted itself into the position of acting as the friend of industry, while forcing the IAC to make the unpopular recommendations that government would "reluctantly" follow.

Fraser's middle road also extended to the provision of direct subsidies to industry. In 1977, the government's "White Paper on Manufacturing Industry" proclaimed that as part of the reform process, special assistance to vulnerable sectors would be made available, but only on a temporary basis. During that time, it was expected that real efforts would be made by industry itself to improve its structure and efficiency (Australia 1977, 24–25). Obviously this was pie in the sky. As Bell points out, the White Paper provided no enforcement provisions to entice inefficient industries to restructure. Instead, the propensity of the Fraser government to leave industrial reform to the industrial sector helped to erode the government's credibility on the issue of industry restructuring. It also reduced industry's commitment to restructuring goals and tended to set it on the defensive (Bell 1992a, 44; see also Industries Assistance Commission 1980, ch. 2).

The most damaging aspect of the Fraser government's approach to reform was that it created a perverse incentive structure. Those willing to undertake reform were functionally penalized for doing so. Not only would they reap no benefit through subsidy, they would, in fact, have to subsidize weaker firms and industries. Even worse is that the policy created obvious rewards for those most committed to the retention of state-supplied rents. The most committed rent seekers quickly recognized that they could win government sympathy on the grounds that rent reductions would lead to job losses. Moreover, they learned to play the "declining confidence game"—poor industry performance was a function of declining industry confidence in the face of threatening recommendations from the IAC. State-supplied rents, apparently, were necessary to recapture some sort of industrial self-esteem. As Glezer suggests (1982, 139–40; see also 151, 159), the government's unwillingness to make difficult decisions was "an indication for some business analysts and lobbyists . . . that there was money to be made if pressure was applied."

There were two legacies of Fraser's middle-of-the-road rent-reduction policy. Protectionism was still prevalent in Australia a decade after the 1973 tariff cuts. This is manifest in the persistent opposition to the ANZCERTA on the part of Australian industrialists (Thakur and Gold 1983). Also, having witnessed a lack of resolve on the part of successive Australian governments, a powerful core of industrial rent seekers was conditioned to believe that victory in the rent-reduction game was possible in the face of strong political pressure.

Trade Liberalization in the 1980s

Crisis as Catalyst

When Labour returned to power following the 1983 election, there was not much reason for optimism among advocates of trade liberalization. The previous year the Australian Labour Party (ALP) had released its misleadingly titled position paper "New Directions for Australian Industry" (1982), which recommended a healthy dose of industrial protectionism. However, the new government led by Robert Hawke soon came under the same sorts of cross-pressures that had bedeviled Fraser. Australia's poor economic performance through the 1970s and early 1980s strengthened the commitment of those opposed to economic protectionism. By the mid-1980s, Australia was faced with a serious balance-of-payments crisis that put enormous pressure on the dollar and eliminated the option of clinging tenaciously to the middle ground.

The crisis had its roots in the 1970s. Australia's failure to restructure its economy in the boom years of the 1960s limited its maneuverability in the crisis years to follow. In keeping with the global stagflation crisis, inflation ran at roughly 14 percent, while economic growth was marginal; Australia's balance-of-payments deficit triggered a 17.5 percent devaluation in late 1976 (Dyster and Meredith 1990, 272). The move, while inflationary, had only a short-term impact. The Australian economy continued to stagnate, with sustained deficits in both the current accounts and trade balances. In 1979–1980, for example, Australia's manufactured output in constant dollar terms was 5 percent lower than that of 1973–1974 (Anderson 1987, 174). Perhaps more significantly, Australia became extremely debt dependent by the early 1980s. In June 1980, Australia's net external debt was $A7.3 billion, or 6 percent of GDP. By 1985, those figures had ballooned to $A52 billion and 25 percent of GDP. To put this in perspective, by fiscal 1984–1985, 33 percent of export earnings were required merely to cover foreign debt repayments (Drake and Nieuwenhuysen 1988, 9).

By the time the Hawke government came to power in 1983, Australia, far from mirroring global trends of recovery from the recession of the early 1980s, continued to wallow in economic misery. In 1982 Australia had faced its worst economic year since the Great Depression. The first five months of 1983 were even worse (Pagan 1987, 125–27). Unemployment in 1983 averaged 9 percent in an economy with an annual inflation rate of 11.5 percent. The real GDP growth rate was negative 2 percent (Capling and Galligan 1992, 119). As treasurer Paul Keating noted in 1986, "We must let Australians know truthfully, honestly, earnestly just what sort of an international hole Australia is in. It's the price of our commodities—they are as bad in real terms as since the Depression. That's a fact of Australian life now. . . . If this government cannot get the adjustment, get manufacturing going again . . . then Australia is basically done for. We will end up being a third rate economy . . . a banana republic" (quoted in Bell 1992b, 192).

The first five years of the Hawke administration were largely a continuation of Fraser's middling approach. It was not until 1988 that the government became (if only briefly) committed to more significant trade liberalization (see Leigh 2002).

The Path of Least Resistance Strategy

The Hawke and, to some extent, Keating years clearly constituted a period of reform for Australian foreign economic policy. Industrial tariff rates fell, and Australia emerged from isolationism to take a stance on global and Asian trade reform. The effects of these reforms, however, have been disappointing. Protectionism remains widespread. Indeed, Australia was widely condemned by its major trading partners in a 1998 WTO report that accused Australia, in part, of using antidumping, quarantine restrictions, particularistic country-of-origin labeling, and industrial policy (especially in the automotive and TCF sectors) as significant distortions to liberal trade (Marshallsea 1998). In large part, this is a function of the Hawke and successor governments' decisions to continue the path of least resistance strategy pioneered by Fraser.

Under Hawke's premiership, early attempts at reform were carried out under the direction of the minister of industry, technology, and commerce, Senator John Button. Button had been influenced by Sweden's attempts to come to terms with its own financial difficulties in the late 1970s and early 1980s. As a result, in addition to continuing the Fraser government's program of seeking to educate business about the need to reform voluntarily, he sought to underwrite some of the risk of reform through an interventionist industrial policy. Specifically, Button relied on industry-specific adjustment plans and direct, compensatory subsidies to industry. Button (1985, 69) summed up the rather tenuous logic of his position by suggesting that "because Australian industry has been protected for too long, we need to move to a regime of positive assistance which reinforces movements in the right direction."

Neocorporatist industry plans were drawn up for a number of key industries, with the most generous and persistent in the PMV and TCF sectors (Stewart 1994). Each was constructed with input from government, labor, and business leaders in the relevant sector of the economy. Industry plans were to provide a blueprint for the means by which industries would restructure for competition in global markets. They also were designed to determine the degree of import protection that would be necessary at each stage of the reform process. Logically, it was expected that protectionism would decrease in proportion to the extent of industrial adjustment.[7]

The subsidy program was comprehensive, being available to a wider range of industries than were the industry plans. The program entailed two distinct phases. In the first phase, which coincided with the comparatively protectionist era 1983–1986, government subsidies were provided to assist industries in the production of goods for which Australia suffered comparative and competitive disadvantage. In the second, post-1986 phase, subsidies continued, but no longer as a means of providing an alternative to innovation and industrial restructuring. Instead, subsidies were designed to assist with product development, marketing, and export. These subsidies included 150 percent tax concessions for research and development, Export Market Development Grants, and diesel fuel rebates. Moreover, the government facilitated the process of seeking relief from unfair trade practices abroad by justifying subsidies on the grounds of predatory trade practices abroad (Stewart 1990). Even as industries were forced to withdraw from the production of uncompetitive goods, the risk of product innovation was subsidized by the government. This practice continued into the late 1990s; Australia is one of the world's most prodigious employers of antidumping procedures (Spencer 1998).

Not surprisingly, Button's objective of creating a business-friendly environment in which to reduce rents was unsuccessful in the early and mid-

1980s. His program entailed too much carrot and not enough stick. Not only were rent seekers accorded too much input into the policy process, government subsidization of industry removed the incentive to undertake serious structural adjustment required for global competitiveness. As the chief of staff to Carlos Salinas in Mexico's much more successful attempt to liberalize trade noted, "[I]t is almost impossible to negotiate trade liberalization measures with the business community: they have to be imposed and sustained over businesses' protests" (Cordoba 1994, 244).

Another problem with the Button approach is that exposure to risk is a critical component of the reform process. Businesses unsure of their global competitiveness will be unlikely to risk the safety of state-supplied rents for the uncertainty of the marketplace. Indeed, this explains why many flexible rent seekers prefer state-supplied rents to the potentially greater rewards offered by free-market competition. As another architect of successful reform argues, "Vested interests continuously underestimate their own ability to adjust successfully in an environment where the government is rapidly removing privilege across a wide front" (Douglas 1993, 223). It is imperative that reforming governments force industries to take risks that they otherwise would not. Instead, like an overanxious parent teaching a child to ride a bicycle, with the Button plan the Australian government refused to remove the metaphorical training wheels long after they had become counterproductive.

Finally, the Button plan failed because it was insufficiently grounded in market forces. Industrial policy axiomatically constitutes compensation for the harshest effects of the marketplace. However, these effects are part and parcel of effective reform. Artificial protection of inefficient industries skews resources away from efficient sectors, thereby undermining the productiveness of such sectors. Moreover, as the limits of rent seeking model suggests, it keeps alive producers who will fight against future reforms.

Frustrated with the lack of success of his early reform initiatives, Button targeted certain sectors, specifically telecommunications, plastics, and chemicals, with specific tariff reductions in 1985 and 1986, on the grounds that these sectors were performing well abroad. This constituted the first step in a serious attempt to reduce industrial rents in Australia. In the targeting of sectors that demonstrably could withstand market competition, the nascent emergence of what could have been a divide-and-conquer strategy can be seen. The plan worked quite well, with leaders of the plastics and chemicals industries shifting their trade policy preferences in favor of liberalization (Stewart 1990, 112–13). On the other hand, promising developments in the mid-1980s did not constitute a shift away from the path of least resistance approach. For example, the notoriously inefficient PMV and TCF sectors were spared tariff reductions in 1985–1986 (Stewart 1990, 110–12). Moreover, even as tariffs were slashed further in 1988 and 1991, compensatory policies undermined the imperative for reform in a number of industries.

By 1988, Button's position on industrial protection had hardened to the point where he advocated a more comprehensive tariff reduction. The government announced that the nominal tariff rate for industries that enjoyed tariffs above 15 percent would be capped at that rate, and all industries with tariffs between 10 and 15 percent would be capped at 10 percent. The exceptions were TCF—which was to retain the tariff levels set out in the 1986 industry plan (levels that constituted only a slight reduction from 1970s levels)—and PMV—where import quotas were to be eliminated and the nominal tariff reduced to 35 percent by 1992 (Garnaut 1994b, 227–28).

In 1989, a government task force headed by prominent economist Ross Garnaut (1989) called for the elimination of all import protection by the end of the 1990s and spurred the government into a new round of trade liberalization measures. Announced in March 1991, this initiative was designed to eliminate most of the remaining vestiges of nontariff import protection and reduced the general tariff rate to 5 percent by July 1, 1996 (Australia 1991), a significant reduction from the average nominal tariff rate of 23 percent in 1982–1983 and 19 percent as late as 1987–1988 (Garnaut 1994a). In addition, except for the TCF and PMV sectors, there were to be no import barriers on most commodities from Papua New Guinea, New Zealand, Indonesia, Malaysia, Thailand, China, India, and the Philippines. The TCF sector was to see the elimination of quotas, and there would be a maximum tariff of 25 percent by 2000; PMV nominal tariff rates were to fall to a maximum of 15 percent by the end of the century (Australia 1991; Garnaut 1994a). While many of the rent reductions announced in 1991 did come to fruition, follow-through was sporadic. Especially under the government of John Howard (significantly, a cabinet minister under Malcolm Fraser), rent reductions followed the familiar path of least resistance.

Despite the powerful downward trend in import protection, the government attempted to soften the blow through its continuation of industry plans and subsidies. In addition, other compensatory policies continued throughout the era of tariff reduction. Even as the right hand took away state-supplied rents, they were returned in different form by the left. In part this was a function of the vastly differing philosophies that continued to operate within the ALP tent (Dodd and Spiers 1991). Reminiscent of the cleavages under Whitlam, and not surprising given that the free-market initiatives were undertaken by a Labour government, moderate interventionists like Button came into conflict with free marketeers such as Keating.[8]

A good example of compensatory rents is the so-called Tariff Concessions System (TCS) maintained by the Hawke and Keating governments as a means of mitigating the transition costs to a free-market economy. Under the TCS and its predecessor, the Commercial Tariff Concession Scheme, imports for which there were no direct domestic competitors were allowed into Australia duty free.[9] Specifically, importers were eligible for tariff concessions where there were no domestic producers of substitute goods (the so-called substitute test) or, if there were local substitutes, where duty-free imports would have little impact on the domestic market (the so-called market test).[10] With the TCS, factor inputs for domestic production were kept as low as possible. At the same time, however, there was less pressure from importers of these factor inputs to seek reduced import protection—even in the more heavily protected sectors.

It is here that the Hawke and Keating governments made a tactical error—the TCS system constituted a policy of insulating protected industries from pressure to reform. In the absence of the TCS, government would have enjoyed the political support of a natural ally—industries that rely on imported factor inputs for product export—in the fight for trade liberalization. Indeed, according to the logic of the limits of rent seeking model, it is easy to envision exporting industries leading the charge for further reductions in industrial protection, with the government placed in the more politically comfortable position of merely reacting to such pressure. In short, the TCS system thwarted the logic of the nascent divide-and-conquer strategy that would have served as a superior prescription for rent reduction in Australia.

Evidence for this position is found in the proposed changes to the TCS late in 1995. In the last year of the Keating administration, the government announced its intention to eliminate the market test for tariff concessions. In this way, domestic producers seeking to block duty-free imports would be relieved of the need to demonstrate harm. The (National-Liberal) coalition government of John Howard went further in 1996, announcing that it would abolish the TCS altogether, effectively raising the cost of imported factor inputs by as much as 15–28 percent in the textile and automotive sectors (Abernehty 1996). After heavy lobbying by industries concerned about the loss of international competitiveness, however, the government backed down and implemented a compromise 3 percent tariff where duty-free imports had previously been permitted under the TCS; the market test was not reinstated (Deloitte Touche Tohmatsu 1996). Again an opportunity was missed. Rather than acquiesce to pressure from an emerging pro–free-trade coalition, a natural ally of a government seeking to liberalize trade, the government once again sought to compromise to satisfy rent seekers.

Despite the apparent progress made during the Hawke-Keating years, the liberalization initiative has not been taken to its logical conclusion. While it took a leading role in the APEC initiative, the Keating government appeared to lose its zeal for liberalization.[11] Further backsliding has occurred under Howard. The Keating government's White Paper of May 1994 stated that the 5 percent uniform tariff rate would be retained after 1996 and that there would be a review of existing rates of protection for the PMV and TCF sectors (Australia 1994).[12] Indeed, Australia's increased use of nontariff barriers—especially antidumping action—drew criticism from the GATT in 1994 and from the WTO on numerous occasions since (*Australian Financial Review* 1994a; Marshallsea 1998). Moreover, industry assistance plans—especially in the telecommunications and pharmaceuticals sectors—provided generous assistance benefits long into the period of supposed liberalization.

With the election of the Howard government in 1996, the trade liberalization initiative appears to have stalled. The government announced early in its mandate that no new reductions in tariffs were forecast for the rest of the century. Moreover, not only did existing subsidies continue, but investigations into antidumping complaints were speeded up (Moore 1996; see also Porter 1996). The Howard government did announce in late 2002 its desire to pursue a free-trade agreement with the United States. However, other actions belie its commitment to free trade. Worrisome is the apparent reversal of existing commitments to trade liberalization in the most heavily protected sectors. In the automobile sector, for example, under a timetable created by the Keating government, tariffs were set to be reduced to 15 percent by 2000 and to 5 percent by 2004. However, in the face of stiff lobbying by carmakers, who threatened to withhold investments in Australia, Howard announced that the 15 percent tariff would be retained until 2005, at which point it would fall to 10 percent (Agence France Presse 1997; Seneviratne 1997; *REWBN Australian Business News* 1997). In December 2002, the government announced that the 10 percent tariff would be extended until 2010 and that $A4 billion in direct subsidies would be made available to the automotive sector (Grubel, Adam, and Lienert 2002).

While these concessions to the automotive industry appear marginal, the message they send is one that has damaged efforts at trade liberalization since the 1970s—failure of resolve in the face of industry pressure. As one editorial in the *Sydney Morning Herald* put it, "John Howard has blinked. His failure of courage in the face of carmakers' threadbare threats signals the start of a retreat on a wide front of macroeconomic reform" (Seneviratne 1997). Indeed, the predictable effect was to stimulate lobbying on the part of other heavily protected sectors, especially TCF. Three months after his 1997 concession to the PMV sector, Howard granted a similar concession to the TCF industry. Despite strong resistance from members of his own cabinet, as well as the IC, Howard decided that tariff reductions would be frozen from 2000 to 2005 (Bedi 1997).

Fate of the Rent Seekers

Inflexible Rent Seekers

In the aftermath of the rent reductions of 1973 and 1988–1991 a number of inflexible rent seekers exited the marketplace, either voluntarily or involuntarily. A survey of six hundred manufacturers by the Australian Chamber of Manufacturers (ACM) in 1991, for example, found that one in twelve had considered shutting down at least part of their operations in Australia. Twenty-eight thousand manufacturing jobs in the past year had been sent abroad, and as many as forty-eight thousand jobs could be exported in 1992. The New South Wales chief executive of the ACM, Philip Holt, interpreted the data to suggest that "[t]hese tragically high figures underpin the urgent need for government to rethink its industry policy. . . . Restructuring industry by reducing tariffs in a recession is sheer economic masochism" (Colebatch 1991).

Such an interpretation seems a bit self-serving. Indeed, it is always difficult to isolate the effects of rent reductions and recession. On the other hand, using aggregate figures of firms in production across sectors over time in Australia, a picture emerges of the severity with which the combined effects of recession and rent reduction hit the Australian economy. If those data are compared with figures from all other OECD countries for which there is complete information, we can also, in a very proximate way, control for the effects of recession. Table 7.1 and figure 7.1 summarize these data.

Table 7.1 and figure 7.1 indicate quite clearly that fears of wide-scale job loss and plant closures were exaggerated in the Australian case. Indeed, for each of the International Standard Industrial Classifications (ISIC) for which the OECD maintains information, Australia had more firms in production in 1992 than it had in the base year 1984. This contrasts with the

Table 7.1
Establishments in production by industry, Australia and OECD average

	Food, beverages, and tobacco		Textiles, apparel, and leather		Paper, paper products, and printing		Wood, wood products, and furniture		None Chemical products		None Basic metal industries		Nonmetallic mineral products		Fabricated metal products	
	OECD Australia	OECD average	OECD Australia	OECD average	OECD Australia	OECD average	OECD Australia	OECD average	OECD Australia	OECD average	OECD Australia	OECD average	OECD Australia	OECD average	OECD Australia	OECD average
1984	100.00	100.00	100.00	100.00	100.00	100.00	100.00	100.00	100.00	100.00	100.00	100.00	100.00	100.00	100.00	100.00
1985	98.63	72.85	103.37	74.30	102.10	77.49	101.23	74.60	98.70	79.25	99.25	73.80	99.88	76.56	99.96	77.33
1986	72.36	—	74.33	—	78.52	—	73.25	—	80.88	—	70.97	—	76.08	—	77.34	—
1987	103.70	71.53	106.05	72.28	105.67	77.31	108.20	72.41	99.28	78.41	106.38	68.85	105.72	74.08	103.51	76.03
1988	114.68	71.47	118.15	72.92	115.29	79.50	117.97	71.51	108.35	82.16	109.19	69.83	108.76	74.40	114.51	79.13
1989	108.77	70.43	116.04	71.30	116.73	78.37	122.02	71.07	110.08	81.72	111.63	69.24	87.62	76.96	114.50	78.83
1990	105.94	71.90	106.52	71.69	116.73	81.48	120.66	72.66	104.03	84.37	126.45	70.61	83.42	76.46	111.82	82.89
1991	115.67	70.02	135.68	69.36	161.25	79.40	169.22	70.04	132.79	84.21	151.78	69.24	98.48	75.91	115.64	82.27
1992	123.12	68.02	135.53	65.90	168.77	79.28	165.83	67.58	136.25	83.36	166.79	67.08	102.57	74.56	157.54	80.28
1993	—	61.42	—	72.81	—	79.23	—	57.38	—	98.52	—	75.77	—	80.40	—	87.85

Source: Organisation for Economic Co-operation and Development (1997).

Note: Base year 1985 = 100.

OECD average (for countries with complete data), which in each sector had significantly fewer firms in each sector in 1992 than in 1984. While such data, of course, mask numerous business failures, in general Australian rent seekers in this period either were disproportionately flexible or received sufficient compensatory rents to ensure their survival.

Flexible Rent Seekers

Perhaps the most interesting feature of the Australian case is that as of this writing, there is no clear indication of how flexible rent seekers will respond in the long term. While some flexible rent seekers appear to have altered their trade policy demands, other rent seekers persist. As early as the mid-1970s, in the aftermath of the Whitlam tariff cut, "a small but growing number of manufacturers [altered] their corporate strategies and [became] less reliant on tariffs" (Bell 1993, 59). Indeed, Fagan and Webber (1994, 128)

Figure 7.1: Total manufacturing establishments, Australia
compared to OECD average

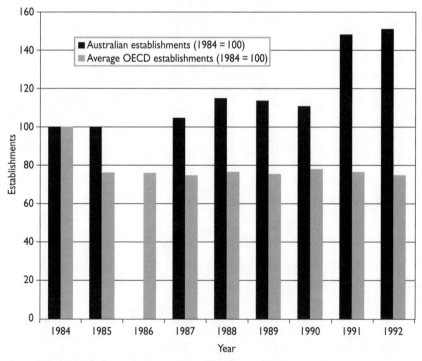

Source: Organisations for Economioc Co-operation and Development (1966).

Table 7.2

Average effective rates of import protection to manufacturing in Australia (by percentage)

Year	Textiles	Clothing and Footwear	Wood, wood products and printing	Paper, paper products and printing	Chemical petroleum and coal products	Non-metallic mineral products	Basic metal products	Fabricated metal products	Transport equipment	Other machinery and equipment	Food beverage, and tobacco	Miscellaneous manufacturing	Total manufacturing
1968–69	43	97	26	52	31	15	31	61	50	43	16	34	36
1973–74	35	64	16	38	25	11	22	44	39	29	18	24	27
1977–78	47	141	18	24	19	5	10	40	48	20	10	30	23
1981–82	54	204	14	25	14	4	11	31	71	21	9	27	25
1984–85	74	>250	17	16	12	4	10	22	66	23	6	24	22
1986–87	66	175	18	16	13	4	9	23	46	23	5	27	19
1988–89	72	171	17	12	12	3	9	20	39	19	3	24	17
1990–91	51	113	14	7	8	4	8	18	34	17	4	19	14
1991–92	46	92	12	7	7	3	8	16	31	15	4	18	13
1992–93	41	73	10	7	7	3	6	15	29	14	4	17	12
1993–94	37	65	9	6	6	3	6	12	26	11	3	14	10

Source: Industries Assistance Commission (1980, 1982); Industries Commission (1991); INDECS Economics (1995, 283).

Note: Figures for 1968–69 and 1973–74 are based on production weights for 1971–72; 1977–78 and 1981–82 figures are based on 1977–78 production weights; 1984–85 figures are based on 1983–84 production weights. These discrepancies marginally affect strict comparability between figures.

cite the increase of firms with global trade ties by the early 1980s as a source of growing pressure for reduction or elimination of the tariff.[13] Even so, the majority of Australian manufacturing remained strongly committed to protectionism throughout the 1970s (Bell 1993, 59). By the late 1980s, further changes in the trade policy demands of flexible rent seekers become clear. The Confederation of Australian Industry (CAI), for example, which in 1982 had been equivocal in its support for any tariff reductions, and which had opposed any reduction below 25 percent (Industries Assistance Commission 1982, 156–57), came out in favor of the 1988 tariff reductions (Capling and Galligan 1992, 150).[14]

However, in general it seems quite clear that Australian manufacturing did not perceive the need to restructure operations until after the Hawke government's rent-reduction initiatives of the late 1980s. Table 7.2 illustrates the downward trend in effective rates of protection from 1968–1969 to 1993–1994 according to industry (ISIC figures).

The dramatic increase in exports of major industrial commodities after 1987 is clear from figure 7.2, which shows constant dollar export figures by commodity (using SITC) and corresponding industry from 1978 to 1992. In the three years ending in 1991–1992, the volume of total manufactured exports grew by 18 percent, compared to just 7 percent between 1980–1981 and 1988–1989. In real terms, manufactured exports were 63 percent higher in 1991–1992 than they were three years previously (Stutchbury 1992a). Even in the small-business sector, traditionally the slowest to embrace trade liberalization, there is evidence of support for trade liberalization. A 1995 BRW Dun and Bradstreet survey found that 43 percent of small businesses expected to benefit from the removal of all tariffs by 2010 under the APEC initiative, while 57 percent expected either to be harmed or for the cuts to have no effect (Gome 1995).

Not surprisingly, Australian business in the 1990s has also taken a more active role in attempting to influence foreign economic policy. As Australian businesses' stakes in offshore investment and exports have grown, business groups have foreseen the need to provide expert policy advice to the Department of Foreign Affairs and Trade (DFAT) in increasingly complex international negotiations. As a consequence, leading business organizations created the Council for International Business Affairs (CIBA). Rather than serving merely as a defensive lobby protecting industry from further cuts to tariffs and subsidies, the CIBA's mandate is to expand trade opportunities for Australian business (Dodson 1992).

Finally, the proposed elimination of the TCS provides evidence of the increased importance of international trade to Australian flexible rent seekers. Business organizations responded decisively in opposition to what amounted to the restoration of a 5 percent tariff on a number of commodities. A number of peak associations—including the Aluminum Development Council, Australian Automobile Association, Australian Chamber of Commerce and Industry, ACM, Australian Electrical and Electronics Manufacturers, Business Council of Australia, Heavy Engineering Manufacturers, Minerals Council, National Association of Forest Industries, National Farmers' Federation, Plastics and Chemicals Industry Association, and Pulp and Paper Manufacturers Federation—applied significant pressure on the government to retain the TCS (*Inside Canberra* 1996).

Figure 7.2: Total manufacturing exports compared to
effective rates of import protection

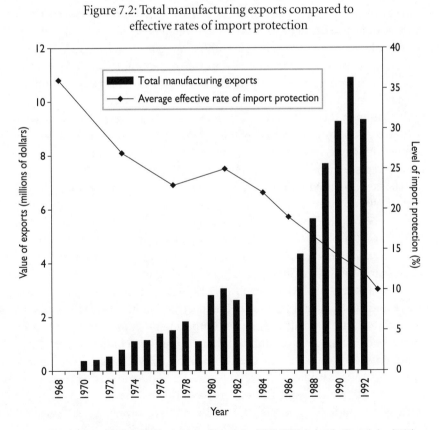

Sources: United Nations (1995); Industries Assistance Commission (1980, 1982); Industries Commission (1991); INDECS Economics (1995, 283).

On the other hand, given the substantial reductions in state-supplied rents in Australia from 1973 to 1991, it is surprising that protectionism is not a spent force. Despite the fact that effective rates of protection for most industries have fallen precipitously since the late 1960s, rent-seeking activity persists in Australia. Even after the general trend toward a greater reliance on exports after 1987, major industrial organizations appeared to hedge their bets by persisting in their quest for state-supplied rents. In 1990, for example, the government's industrial advisory body, the Australian Manufacturing Council (AMC), still remained staunchly opposed to a laissez-faire foreign economic policy for Australia. In response to the Garnaut Report, the AMC responded with its own blueprint for Australia's economic future. The so-called Pappas-Carter Report called for reduced tariffs to be offset by an increase in nontariff barriers. While recognizing the desirability of a more outward-looking and export-oriented economy, the report suggested that such an objective could be realized only through positive government intervention through greater export incentives, more accessible venture capital, and strategic procurement policies—in short, the report called for the replacement of one sort of rent with a less-visible one (Australian Manufacturing Council 1990). Indeed, the 1989 interim report read as though it had been written in the early 1970s. "Our level playing field may have no players left on it. Weak industries may wither as their protection is reduced, while competitive adversity will allow few new traded manufacturing industries to arise to replace them" (Australian Manufacturing Council 1989).

Hawke, disgusted with the unwillingness of businesses to adjust to the new climate of low tariffs, claimed that business leaders were "bloody hopeless" (quoted in Stewart 1994, 54). Keating, more diplomatic, suggested in 1990 that "[t]here just isn't the leadership on the business side in this country that we've seen on the Labour side. It hasn't been a feature of the last seven years" (quoted in Stewart 1994, 54).

Even after the 1991 cuts, the heads of the Australian Chamber of Commerce and Industry and the Heavy Engineering Manufacturers Association decried the fact that tariff reform was outpacing other aspects of microeconomic reform and stronger antidumping legislation (Hooper 1992). These sentiments were echoed by the chief of the Australian Chamber of Manufacturers in 1994: "It would be naive for Australia to pursue further reductions in tariffs until we see gains from microeconomic reform and reciprocal actions by our trade competitors" (Cornell 1994). The problem is summed up best by the *Australian Financial Review* (1994b), which concluded gloomily in mid-1994, "While the 5% tariff level is not high (especially given floating exchange rates), those with it will fight to keep it. . . . Instead of chasing real sales around Asia, senior executives make easier profits by chasing subsidies around Canberra."

Australian exceptionalism is a function of poor policy decisions. One was Whitlam's big bang strategy in 1973. It is easy to criticize this decision in hindsight, but experiences in other countries explored here indicate why the big bang approach could have been predicted to be suboptimal in Australia. There are at least four reasons. First, the big bang approach tends to work best when there is some sort of protective camouflage for the liberalizing government. Carlos Salinas got away with the strategy because of the dire economic crisis in which Mexico was engulfed. Similarly, Canada's Brian Mulroney enacted a free-trade agreement on the tails of a significant reduction of tariffs mandated by the GATT. Whitlam, however, like Sir Robert Peel and Canada's Wilfrid Laurier, enjoyed no political cover for his actions. He made himself a political lightning rod, and, like Peel and Laurier, paid a high political cost for his forcefulness.

Second, like Laurier, Whitlam played into a blind game. Neither had a strong idea about the distribution of flexible versus inflexible rent seekers within his producer population, and neither was very clear on how close to the margin of the critical threshold most producers were situated. Thus, neither was able to gauge how large the rent reduction should be to be most effective.

This lack of information, moreover, cut two ways and is the third reason the big bang approach is problematic. Rent seekers themselves are often unable to gauge their competitiveness in global trade. This is not terribly surprising. Few of us are able, absent concrete evidence, to evaluate our abilities vis-à-vis others. Even where rent reductions are of an optimal size (for example, in hindsight Peel's elimination of the Corn Laws did not doom British agriculture and hence can be considered a success), risk-averse flexible rent seekers may not recognize their own competitiveness and instead adopt a defensive response to swift and radical rent reductions. This happened in Britain in the 1840s and in Australia after 1973.

Finally, the big bang approach is suboptimal if its failure leads to a policy reversal. This is the worst possible outcome for a liberalizing government because it sends the message that trade liberalization initiatives are intrinsically reversible if enough pressure is brought to bear on government. In Australia, the Whitlam government's retrenchment in 1974 created a powerful incentive to mobilize for rent seekers well into the future. Similarly, Laurier's defeat in the election of 1910 doomed free trade in Canada for decades to come.

The second suboptimal policy choice in Australia, following Whitlam's use of the big bang strategy, was Fraser's decision (carried on by successor governments) to mitigate the political costs associated with trade liberalization through the use of selective side payments. Successive Australian governments followed, and continue to follow, the path of least resistance strategy. These side payments had two negative effects.

First, side payments created incentives for flexible rent seekers to lobby for retention and even extension of these new rents. For rent seekers in sectors deemed most robust by the government, these side payments largely took the form of export incentive subsidies (although powerful antidumping legislation also falls into this category). While not large (in 1991, even with rather emaciated rates of import protection, subsidies constituted less than 12 percent of the estimated subsidy equivalent of tariffs and quotas [Industries Commission 1991]), these side payments were important because they conveyed the sense that additional rents were available if a sufficiently strenuous lobbying campaign was mounted. Erstwhile flexible rent seekers, therefore, were provided an incentive to hedge their bets by relying on government subsidy as a substitute, in part, for aggressive pursuit of expanded export markets. Indeed, the knowledge that government was underwriting part of the risk of industrial restructuring enticed many erstwhile flexible rent seekers to dedicate resources that could have been used more productively to the retention and even expansion of this insurance policy.

The second negative effect of side payments, and consistent with the path of least resistance strategy, was to insulate the most vulnerable sectors of the economy through industry plans and differential rates of protection. Industries that were able to demonstrate the least competitiveness actually were granted alternative forms of rent through industry assistance plans and exemptions from the general rate of tariff reductions. Industries were functionally rewarded for their demonstrated inability to compete. Not only did such a policy slow, and perhaps halt, the rationalization of inflexible rent seekers from the market, but it created an incentive for potentially flexible rent seekers to seek special exemptions. This strategy would not have been so ill conceived had it been part of a plan to divide and conquer and hence construct a free-trade coalition among flexible rent seekers. However, with the TCS in place, this opportunity was missed.

Among the virtues of the logic of the limits of rent seeking model is that rent reductions, if skillfully manipulated, allow the government to construct a free-trade coalition among flexible rent seekers, thereby weakening the protectionist coalition and reducing government's role to that of reacting to, rather than seemingly creating, pressure for trade liberalization. In this way, the most difficult rent reductions can be accomplished at minimal cost. However, by continuing the TCS in Australia through the late 1980s and early 1990s, the government missed the opportunity to exploit a wedge issue. It was not until the last months of the Keating administration that the government proposed elimination of the TCS, finally forcing confrontation between exporting interests and persistent rent seekers in Australia.

In sum, unlike in the other cases examined here, the Fraser, Hawke, and Keating governments sought to mitigate the political effects of trade liberalization through the extensive use of side payments. However, rather than building a free-trade-acceptant coalition among the more competitive firms and industries in the economy, as the limits of rent seeking model anticipates, Australian governments now find themselves fighting a rearguard battle with significant portions of the manufacturing sector. Even the most determined effort, in the period 1987–1991, did not convince the most committed rent seekers that increased lobbying would be fruitless.

In hindsight, the reasons seem clear. The logic of the limits of rent seeking model is that former enemies are converted into allies, and, at the same time, the hard core of the protectionist rent-seeker alliance is culled from the population. However, the path of least resistance strategy thwarts the model's logic. While some flexible rent seekers do become free traders, the inflexible core remains protected, and there will continue to be strong political resistance to free trade. Moreover, there will remain a powerful incentive on the part of future governments to retrench. Unlike the case in countries where the protectionist, inflexible core is largely purged, Australia's tentative movement toward free trade remains vulnerable to pressures for policy reversal. It is not surprising, therefore, that the Howard government has put the brakes on further trade liberalization initiatives.

8

Brazil and Chile
Divergent Directions in the Southern Cone

Brazil and Chile represent polar cases in Latin America. They share similar postwar histories. Both adopted policies of ISI during the 1940s, both suffered military coups d'etat between 1964 and 1973, both became nascent democracies in the mid-1980s, and both embraced neoliberal reform as a means of recovering from ISI exhaustion. However, Brazil has seen its commitment to liberalism stall and founder. MERCOSUR, which it helped found in 1989, increasingly serves as a vehicle for Southern Cone economic insularity. Chile, by contrast, appears to have forsaken MERCOSUR in favor of a more liberal foreign economic policy. Rebuffed in its attempts to join NAFTA, Chile is at the forefront of efforts to liberalize hemispheric trade, most prominently through the proposed FTAA and a bilateral free-trade deal with the United States.

The limits of rent seeking model can illustrate why one transition to liberalism has been successful and the other far less so. Like Australia, Brazil used the pernicious path of least resistance approach. Chile opted for the big bang strategy. In Canada (under Mulroney) and Mexico, for example, the big bang approach succeeded structurally imposed rent reductions. Government leaders in both countries had a fairly good read on the production profiles of their producer populations.

Chile's big bang approach was unusual, and while an important objective of this analysis is to provide prescriptions for governments seeking to avoid blame, the brutal and repressive Augusto Pinochet regime is a poor model to champion. The most important reason for the success of the big bang approach in this case is that rent seekers had few options but to take what the government dished out. Successful dictatorships tend to be (albeit not entirely) insensitive to the preferences of their constituents. On the other hand, there clearly are lessons to be learned here. Chile was not the only brutal dictatorship in Latin America. Yet it was the one that experienced success. Finally, while severe repression may have helped quell opposition to the Pinochet reforms, the case can be made that brutality was extraneous to the ultimate success of the Chilean economy. In theory, the Chilean approach, purged of its authoritarianism, can serve as a model for the transition from an authoritarian to a liberal and ultimately democratic regime.

The Historical Context

More than most geographically proximate countries, Latin America has witnessed similar and contemporaneous trends in the history of its political economy. As Green (1995, 15) points out, the larger Latin American economies have had to contend with regular, regime-altering crises that have occurred roughly every second generation. These crises struck during the 1820s, 1870s, 1930s, and 1980s. Moreover, consistent with the argument advanced by Gourevitch (1986), each crisis swept away the previous model of economic development and laid the basis for a new regime that persisted until the subsequent crisis.

After the crises of the 1820s, most Latin American countries were politically unstable and did not pursue economic modernization. This changed by the final quarter of the nineteenth century as many Latin American countries sought to integrate into the global economy through the sale of raw materials to the lucrative North American and European markets. This export-led growth, an acceptance of liberal economic doctrines that saw most countries pursue their comparative advantage in production of primary goods and resources, characterized economic development until World War I. Complementing export-led growth in the larger economies (including Brazil, Chile, and Mexico) was a nascent industrial structure. However, the disruption in trade flows during the war, combined with economic instability in the postwar era, doomed the export-led growth strategy (Bulmer-Thomas 1998).

By the 1930s, the global division of labor, combined with the colonialism that preceded it and the subsequent penetration by multinational corporations from the Northern Hemisphere, ultimately contributed to a sense among left-leaning scholars and politicians that Latin America had been forced into a dependent economic relationship with the more established powers.[1] It was largely the perception that Latin America had been structurally relegated to its dependent position within the global division of labor that stimulated the rise of ISI in Latin America.[2] ISI was a defensive reaction to import penetration in industrial goods by more established economies. While its use was not restricted to Latin America (Canada and New Zealand used the strategy earlier in the twentieth century), ISI and its inherent protectionist ethos epitomized Latin American political economy until the crisis of the 1970s and 1980s.

The most recent crisis was a function of ISI exhaustion, the inability of the domestic market to provide opportunities for economic growth. In truth, ISI exhaustion had hit by the early 1970s or even earlier. However, in most countries—Chile is an obvious exception—governments were able to postpone the structural reforms necessary to recover from declining economic performance. Thus it was not until the 1980s and 1990s that a fourth distinct model of political economy, liberalization, emerged in Latin America, and there have been marked differences in the success and enthusiasm with which the countries of the region have embraced it.

Chile

ISI started early in Chile. In 1928, Chile adopted a system of commodity-specific tariffs that constituted the backbone of Chile's impressive wall of import protection for almost fifty years. The 1928 tariff was revised upward almost on an annual basis throughout the 1930s and early 1940s. In 1943 a more institutionalized tariff structure created a 3 percent tariff on prime necessities, 30 percent for ordinary consumption goods, and 62 percent on luxury items. In addition, Chile adopted a system of import quotas beginning in 1932; import licensing followed in 1939, initially in response to the pernicious and sustained problem of trade and foreign-exchange deficits. In 1956 Chile began to mandate a prior deposit for imported goods. While the structure varied widely over time, deposits for some commodities reached 10,000 percent with a minimum deposit period of ninety days (Behrman 1976, ch. 4).

Chile's experience with ISI was not as successful as that of Mexico or Brazil.[3] The initial results were modest. Between 1937 and 1945, for example, the economy grew by an average of 3.5 percent per year; the period 1946–

1952 saw an average annual expansion of 3.9 percent (Velasco 1994, 384). However, Chile quickly ran into economic difficulties that cannot be explained merely by the ISI life cycle.

A corporatist-clientelist relationship between government officials and business leaders led to a strange hybrid of excessive state regulation for small businesses and arbitrarily assigned monopoly rents for groups with privileged access to the policy-making process. Chile had a large number of semi-autonomous boards that oversaw numerous aspects of the country's economy. Typically these boards comprised equal representation from bureaucrats, technical experts, and private interests. As a result, by the late 1950s, the four largest business organizations in Chile had voting privileges on all major organs of financial policy, including the Central Bank and the Corporacíon de Fomento de la Produccíon (Chilean Development Corporation, CORFO; Valenzuela 1978, 15–16).

CORFO was an important element in the clientelist relationship between business and state in Chile. Created as a quasi-public corporation in 1939, it sought to accelerate industrial development (at the expense of mining and agriculture) through state-led capital accumulation and investment. Its specific mandate was to raise the standard of living and to rectify Chile's balance of international payments. This was to be accomplished by providing loans and equity investment to private and public ventures, while ensuring artificially low rates of interest and generous schedules of amortization.[4] While the agency generated income through its own investments, a substantial share of its assets were provided by the Chilean government, in the form of revenues (derived in part through taxation on foreign corporations largely concentrated in the copper sector) and lines of credit extended by the Central Bank of Chile.[5]

CORFO was not the only instrument of statism in Chile. By the time Salvador Allende came to power in 1970, public funds constituted more than half of all direct investment in Chile. Organs of the state were responsible for more than 50 percent of all credit. In addition, the government generated 14 percent of GNP and employed 13 percent of the workforce (Valenzuela 1978, 13). The result was a remarkably weak economy. Because there was limited access to foreign (and domestic) capital, government finances tended to be secured through expansion of the money supply, creating a persistently elevated rate of inflation.[6] High levels of taxation and a lack of fiscal discipline contributed to the poor performance of the Chilean economy through the 1950s and 1960s.

The first signs of trouble appeared in the mid-1950s. In 1954 and 1955, real per capital GDP declined by 4 percent, real wages fell by 17 percent, and the annual inflation rate peaked at 84 percent in 1955 (Behrman 1976, 27; Edwards and Edwards 1987, 5). The result was a series of lukewarm, albeit partially successful, plans during the administrations of Carlos Ibanez (1952–1958), Jorge Alessandri (1958–1964), and Eduardo Frei (1964–1970) to institute stabilization programs that would cut inflation and stimulate economic growth. While economic performance improved during the 1960s, Chile remained deeply committed to high levels of import protection and regulation of foreign investment, especially in the large mining sector. Indeed, the mean effective rate of protection for manufactured goods increased from 146 percent in 1961 to 177 percent in 1967 (Mierau 1987, 30).

Each plan was ultimately unsuccessful, falling victim to its inability to generate the short-term economic success that might have allowed the sponsoring administration to survive the subsequent election. Each suffered from a perverse political business cycle featuring accelerated government spending and subsidized loans during the early years of the administration, followed by more economically painful attempts to ameliorate the inevitable macroeconomic consequences. As a result, each plan generated considerable political opposition (see Behrman 1976, ch. 13; Edwards and Edwards 1987, ch. 1; de la Cuadra and Hachette 1991, 181–82; Kline 1992, ch. 1; Hojman 1993, ch. 1).

It was the failure of the Frei administration that ultimately set the stage for fundamental reform in Chile. Frei's Partido Demócrata Cristiano (Christian Democratic Party, PDC) had succeeded in the 1964 election largely as a consequence of Alessandri's unpopularity. Fearing that the Marxist Allende might reap the benefits, the Liberal and Conservative parties supported Frei. However, Frei's mandate to govern from the center, bolstered by an absolute majority in the Chamber of Deputies after 1965, ultimately had a destabilizing effect. Heretofore, political stability was achieved in Chile through effective group representation in Congress. While the prevailing system could hardly be described as consociational, both political parties and Congress served as the locus of accommodation, where groups (largely land owners, mining interests, manufacturers, and the middle class) achieved their *reivindicaciones*, or claims for that which they were due (Valenzuela 1978, 18). Goldberg (1975, 102) suggests that "the real stakes of Chilean politics . . . were not broad policy alternatives, but the maintenance and extension of pork-barrel patronage to small groups." Under Frei, however, initiatives such as land reform, prolabor legislation, and trade liberalization threatened the balance of interests traditionally placated by Congress and the traditional party system. In the words of Velasco (1994, 393), the administration was marked by "the arrival of several new guests . . . at the dinner table of the distributive state."

The increased mobilization of underrepresented interests, especially trade unions and newly organized rural workers (courtesy of the 1967 Agrarian Reform Law permitting rural unions to operate across more than one farm) constituted an excellent opportunity for the PDC to challenge the Communist-Socialist alliance by sponsoring mobilization on the political left.[7] In 1964 Chile had 632 industrial unions; by 1970 there were 1,440. In the countryside, mobilization was even more pronounced. While only 2,118 rural workers were organized in 1965, by 1970 that figure had swollen to 136,984 (Valenzuela 1978, ch. 2; Velasco 1994, 393–95; Angell 1972, 202–3). In addition, the Frei administration sponsored creation of roughly twenty thousand grassroots organizations, including neighborhood associations, mothers' associations and sporting clubs (Faundez 1988, 151–52). However, the controlled mobilization envisioned by Frei began to work against the government, giving way to uncontrolled, or what Landsberger and McDaniel (1976) called hypermobilization. Strike activity increased sharply and state-labor relations deteriorated. More importantly, hypermobilization also undermined the accommodationist role of Congress.

Governing as though its congressional majority were a reflection of mass popular support rather than an artifact of partisan politics, the government eschewed the clientelistic practices that had long characterized Chilean politics and, whatever its vices, had maintained political peace in a polarized society. Ultimately, far from succeeding in creating a new monolithic force at the center of Chilean politics, the PDC regime served to energize parties at the extremes at the expense of both its own electoral success and the political stability of the regime (Valenzuela 1978, 33–39; Faundez 1988, ch. 9).

In 1970, the PDC gave way to the ill-fated Popular Unity government led by Allende. Popular Unity was an alliance of left and center parties, consisting in the main of the Socialists, Communists, and Radicals. In the presidential election, Allende won a plurality of the popular vote and carried the presidency on the support of the PDC, which declined to align with the National Party on the right.[8] The new government was far more radical, and hence polarizing, than the previous administration had been. It called for state control of large-scale mining, important industrial monopolies, international trade, banking, insurance, and companies in the energy and transport sectors. The private sector would control small and medium-sized firms. In the high-tech sectors, it was envisioned that the state would form joint ventures with private, largely foreign, capital. Finally, there would be wide-scale land reform in the countryside. Taking their cues from the government, moreover, peasants and workers invaded and occupied factories and rural estates as a form of grassroots income redistribution (Faundez 1988, 191–93; Goldberg 1975, 104–5).[9]

Implementation of the agenda created economic chaos. Despite an early stimulus to economic growth sparked by a generous income and social security policy, the Chilean economy sank into a deep recession. In 1973, GDP shrank by 4.3 percent. Inflation soared to an annual rate of 261 percent in 1972 and 605 percent the next year. Real wages fell by almost one-third between 1972 and 1973. Expropriation of ITT (International Telephone and Telegraph) and the Anaconda and Kennecott copper mines raised the ire of the United States, which vetoed Chile's loan applications to international development banks, thereby exacerbating the economic misery (Velasco 1994, 391; Goldberg 1975, 108–9; Kline 1992, 11–12).

Political instability also ensued. The demise of the stable, clientelist system of congressional accommodation reached crisis proportions during the 1970s. The traditional process of bargaining between government and opposition parties was scaled back, and, when tried, was generally ineffective. Especially contentious was the program of nationalization. By the middle of 1973, the government had taken over more than five hundred businesses, largely without congressional approval. Outside of Congress, mass protests, strikes, producer boycotts, and even acts of sabotage became increasingly common. As the crisis intensified, the military leadership remained loyal to the army's noninterventionist tradition. However, late in 1972, a group of colonels began to plot the overthrow of the Allende government. In September 1973, the plot came to fruition. Allende was killed in the coup d'etat and General Augusto Pinochet became Chile's military dictator (Goldberg 1975, 98–100, 111–13).

Brazil

In 1930, revolution struck Brazil. Deposed was the agrarian oligarchy whose wealth and power had derived from the production of coffee. In its place came a modernizing regime under Getúlio Vargas, supported by a corporatist-clientelist alliance of the urban poor and emerging industrial class (not to mention the military, which in contrast to Chile, long had served as the ultimate source of constitutional authority in Brazilian politics [Busey 1969, esp. 64–66; Schmitter 1973; Erickson 1977]). While industrial development surged during the 1930s, it was not until after the war that Brazil adopted the full range of import protections associated with ISI. A pattern of state-business relations was entrenched with ISI that was to benefit the former through much of the rest of the century (see O'Donnell 1978; Weyland 1996, ch. 3).

The economic stimulus for state-led industrialization was Brazil's desire to maintain an overvalued cruziero as a means of keeping its balance of trade in check. Compensatory import licensing, as well as a system of multiple exchange rates (whereby different classifications of imports were purchased at different rates of exchange) soon followed. The effects were to limit the flow of imports, thereby allowing subsidized domestic firms to emerge for the production of an increasing range of previously imported goods. Tariffs, some higher than 250 percent, were an important part of the import-substitution program. Based on Brazil's traditional Law of Similars, which since the late nineteenth century had protected import-competing goods, high tariffs were granted liberally to firms and sectors seeking relief in the 1950s. In part, the objective was to encourage foreign investors to open branch plants in Brazil to service the local economy. As in Chile, moreover, a state-run development agency, the Banco Nacional de Desenvolvimento Econômico (National Economic Development Bank, BNDE), complemented private investment in strategic sectors such as iron, steel, transport equipment, and heavy machinery (Baer and Kerstenetzky 1964; Baer 1965, ch. 3; Huddle 1969; Bergsman and Candal 1969; Baer 1995, chs. 4, 10).

The effects of ISI during the 1950s were quite spectacular. Between 1947 and 1961, real industrial product increased by 262 percent; industrial production went from roughly one-fifth of the economy in 1947 to about one-third by 1961. The economy's average annual rate of real growth for the years 1948 to 1961 was 6.1 percent (Baer and Kerstenetzky 1964, 415–16).

But cracks were already beginning to show in the system. The inward-looking development scheme created a precarious imbalance in Brazil's export profile. Because industrialization was geared toward production for the internal market, 90 percent of Brazil's exports were in primary commodities; only 2 percent of exports were in industrial goods (Baer 1995, 206). Inflation began to surge in the second half of the 1950s, the balance-of-trade deficit persisted (in part due to decline of international coffee prices), and the economic infrastructure remained obsolete and substandard. The effects were felt in the early 1960s, as the economy slowed dramatically (Bergsman and Candal 1969, 49–54; Bresser Pereira 1984, ch. 5).

It is tempting to cite the economic slowdown of the early 1960s as the cause of the military coup d'etat that overthrew the government of President

João Goulart. Brazil faced large debts, high inflation, and, most importantly, a sclerotic Congress that seemed incapable of dealing with the problem (Kingstone 1999, 32–33). On the other hand, one can argue that the seeds of military intervention already had long been sown in Brazil. Indeed, the period between the end of Vargas's Estado Nôvo (New State), which ended in 1945, and the 1964 coup can be characterized as a mere democratic interlude (Skidmore 1973). The crisis came with the 1961 resignation of President Jânio Quadros and the succession of his vice president, Goulart. Goulart's leftist credentials did not endear him to the business community or the military, which had forced his resignation as minister of labor in 1954. Right-wing opposition to the new president deepened his ties to the Left. The effect was a vicious cycle of declining investor confidence and increasing political polarization that ended with the military seizing power on March 31, 1964 (Cohen 1987; Bresser Pereira 1984, ch. 5; Roett 1984, ch. 4).

The military authoritarian regime that followed remained until 1985. Politically, it retained and further institutionalized the prevailing corporatist-clientelist structure of business-state relations. Economically, the new regime led to a more balanced export profile, although this was not achieved through the rigor of the free market. Instead, the postcoup years witnessed state subsidization of industrial exports through the abolition of export taxes (and indeed creation of tax incentives to export), more streamlined bureaucratic procedures for exporting goods, and export subsidies. At the same time, although import protection remained relatively high during the late 1960s and early 1970s, the nominal tariff rate declined, as did the effective rate of protection (largely as a function of numerous special exemptions on imported goods [Kingstone 1999, 33; Baer 1995, 207; see also Tyler 1976]).

The new military regime sought to correct for the excesses of the previous era. Even as it devalued the cruzeiro through episodic minidevaluations, it succeeded in bringing down inflation through amelioration of the distortions created by "official" and market prices of vital commodities and through the imposition of greater fiscal discipline on the federal budget. As a result, inflation was brought down fivefold to an average of near 20 percent for the period 1968–1974, and the government's operating deficit fell from 4.3 percent of GDP in 1963 to a more modest 0.3 percent by 1971. Finally, GDP grew by an average annual rate of 10.3 percent in the years 1968–1974 (Baer 1976; Fishlow 1973).

Industrial growth was driven, in large part, by direct state ownership. Between 1967 and 1973, 108 new federal enterprises were created. Many of these were important players in the economy. In 1972, for example, of the fifty largest firms in Brazil, just over half were state enterprises. By the early 1980s, Brazil had almost seven hundred publicly owned firms, many of which dominated the domestic economy (Hagopian 1996, 76–77; Graham 1982, 32). Even where the state did not enjoy direct ownership, moreover, it maintained close relations with private firms through the system of *cartorios*, "a dense network of formal and informal links that facilitated unproductive rent-seeking" (Kingstone 2001, 992).

The oil crisis brought an end to Brazil's economic miracle. Faced with the inflationary effect of rising petroleum prices, the new government of Ernesto Geisel boldly engaged in a new round of statist intervention designed to insulate Brazil from the economic instability associated with the oil crisis. Under the auspices of the Second Plano Nacional de Desenvolvimento (National Development Plan, PND II), which began in 1975, the Brazilian government launched a two-pronged offensive. First, import substitution was extended to a broader range of basic capital and industrial goods, the latter including aluminum, copper, fertilizers, petrochemicals, and steel. Second, there was large-scale investment in economic infrastructure, such as communications, power plants (nuclear and hydroelectric), and transportation. While a number of initiatives were undertaken by the private sector (albeit with generous funding from the BNDE), state-owned enterprises (which could more easily borrow abroad) took the lead in sectors such as communications, energy, steel, and transportation (Baer 1995, 90–91; Fishlow 1986, 63–65).

As was the case with Mexico, the oil crisis also brought with it the incentive to take on high levels of foreign debt. Easy access to credit, combined with the imperative to finance the PND II, led to a net debt increase at an average annual rate of 38.7 percent between 1973 and 1978; net medium- and long-term foreign debt increased by a factor of five, from $6.2 billion to $31.6 billion. Even so—and the parallel with Mexico is evident—by the late 1970s, the Brazilian economy appeared to have stabilized, achieving growth rates of roughly 7 percent. But the heavy debt load, in conjunction with the spike in interest rates following the second oil shock of 1979, proved too great a burden for the Brazilian economy to withstand (Baer 1995, 92-100; Bacha and Malan 1989).

The problem, as with so many Latin American economies at the time, was the twin evils of public debt and inflation. By 1980, the annual inflation rate, spurred by a sharp currency devaluation aimed at ameliorating the trade deficit and rapidly dwindling reserves, had risen to 110 percent. By 1981, Brazil was forced to rely on short-term foreign borrowing, even as the prime rate peaked at 20.2 percent, merely to keep its finances afloat.[10] With the fall in oil prices in 1982, petrodollars dried up, and short-term loans began to be called. In the aftermath of Mexico's August announcement that it was unable to meet its debt commitments, a banking panic ensued and Brazil teetered on the brink of economic collapse. Such a fate was avoided only by virtue of a bailout by the U.S. Federal Reserve and the IMF (see Bresser Pereira 1984, ch. 8).

Meanwhile, the economic problems of the 1970s provided a suboptimal backdrop for the *Abertura*, or political liberalization through the electoral process. Progress was neither swift nor linear. In 1974, for example, Geisel initiated the *Abertura* in state and federal elections, permitting for the first time in over a decade a contest that was—on its face—fair, between the government party, Aliança Renovadora Nacional (National Alliance for Renewal, ARENA) and the state-sanctioned opposition Movimento Democrático Brasileiro (Movement for a Democratic Brazil, MDB). By 1977, however, opposition party successes obligated Geisel temporarily to close Congress and to decree the *pacote de abril* (April Package), providing legal sanction to ARENA's legislative dominance.[11]

Acceleration of the *Abertura* continued under Geisel's successor, General João Figueiredo in 1979. That year witnessed party reform, allowing for a multiparty system and an increasingly powerful role for opposition forces both inside and outside of Congress. In the elections of 1982, ten state governorships went to opposition candidates, and the government party (reborn under the unlikely moniker Partido Democrático Social [Social Democratic Party, PDS] lost its majority in the Chamber of Deputies as well as functional control of the reform process. Indeed, the old regime's last stronghold, control of the Electoral College that elected the president, fell in the face of popular pressure for reform. In 1985, for the first time in twenty-one years, Brazil elected a civilian administration under President Tancredo Neves (Selcher 1986; Martínez-Lara 1996, ch. 1).

Trade Liberalization

Regime shifts in Chile and (to a lesser extent) Brazil served as catalysts to economic reform on the heels of ISI exhaustion. In Brazil, import substitution was unsustainable in the face of the oil shocks and attendant debt crisis. By the early 1990s, Brazil had begun to adopt a more outward orientation in its economic policy. In Chile, ISI exhaustion occurred earlier and more dramatically.

Crisis as Catalyst in Chile

Chile's transition to free-market orthodoxy in the 1970s was neither subtle nor difficult to explain. The same economic crisis that helped stimulate the military coup in September 1973 also mandated the radical economic transformation undertaken by the Pinochet dictatorship. The 1973 coup was not proactive in the sense that it was based on a well-developed sense of what path Chile should take toward economic development. Rather, its purpose was to rid the country of a regime that threatened to impose socialism, wreak economic havoc, and provoke even greater political discord. By early in 1974, however, the military government had settled on the neoliberal approach that was to inform the course of Chile's economic future.

By 1975, the government embraced radical reform. Following a visit from eminent neoliberal scholars Milton Friedman and Arnold Harberger in March, the Pinochet government brought in a new cadre of advisers to accelerate the reform process. Largely educated in economics at the University of Chicago through a scholarship program for Chilean postgraduates that had been in place for two decades, these new advisers were known as the Chicago Boys. The most prominent Chicago Boys taught in the economics departments at the Catholic University and the University of Chile, or were prominent private-sector economists. The influence of the Chicago Boys was broad: roughly one hundred students were educated at the University of Chicago alone between 1957 and 1970. In addition, core members of the group achieved positions of prominence in the government, with several serving in cabinet or holding key positions in the central bank, budget office, and various planning ministries.[12]

The Chicago Boys made their presence felt quickly. By 1976 most NTBs had been eliminated or marginalized. Import quotas were completely eliminated. The government also repealed the mandate (which had applied to more than half of all tariff positions) for official approval prior to importation of goods into the country. In addition, of the 187 tariff positions that prohibited importation, only 6 remained by 1976. Finally, the 10,000 percent import deposits that had been required for more than 50 percent of tariff positions were eliminated (Corbo 1985, 113–14; Hachette 1991, 42).

Tariff reforms were almost as radical and nearly as fast. By the middle of 1975, the maximum tariff rate had fallen from 750 to 120 percent, the average nominal rate had gone from 105 to 57 percent, and the modal nominal tariff fell from 90 to 55 percent. By mid-1977, tariffs were compressed to range from a high of 35 percent to a low of 10 percent, with the modal rate of 15 percent at the lower end of the range. Finally, by June 1979, tariffs for almost all industrial goods was set at 10 percent (Corbo 1985, 114–15; Hachette 1991, 43).

Orthodoxy followed in matters other than trade policy. By 1980 almost all government control of retail pricing was eliminated. Banking and movement of international capital regulations were relaxed significantly between 1975 and 1981. Fiscal policy was brought under control with a decrease in public spending of roughly 25 percent from the high-water mark in the late 1960s. Similarly, in the six years that followed the coup, public investment fell by roughly one-half, as the number of publicly owned companies in Chile fell from more than five hundred to forty-three. Critically, this included privatization of banking and investment. After 1975, CORFO transferred 86 percent of its bank stock (as well as its stock in 110 other firms) to the private sector. Fiscal restraint was followed up (especially after 1976) by a tight-money policy that saw inflation fall to 10 percent by 1982 from a high of 750 percent in 1973 (Balassa 1985; Hachette 1991, 43; Velasco 1994, 398–99; Valdés 1985, 23; Saez and Ffrench-Davis 1996, 5.3).

By the middle of 1979, Chile's was one of the most open markets in the world. All NTBs (including antidumping laws and countervails) had been eliminated. Export subsidies were a thing of the past, and save for the automotive sector, all imports faced only the uniform 10 percent tariff.[13] The next stage in the reform process, announced in 1979, was the introduction of a fixed exchange rate to replace the crawling peg system that had allowed the currency to fluctuate within set parameters. The overvalued peso kept inflation under control while reducing the cost of the dollar, which the petrodollar phenomenon had made readily available. It also had disastrous economic consequences. Differential inflation rates in Chile and the rest of the world led to a deterioration of the real exchange rate. The effect was to flood the Chilean markets with imports (which were not held back by the modest tariff) as Chilean exports became more costly abroad. By 1981, the trade deficit was at the historic (and unsustainable) level of $2.7 billion (Silva 1996, 305–6; Dornbusch and Edwards 1994, 85–90; Hachette 1991, 47–48; Griffith-Jones 1991, 22–23).

The deep recession that resulted forced some revision of the full-throttle pace of economic reform. Even before the government freed the exchange rate in mid-1982, it announced that it would begin to impose countervailing surcharges on imports that were unfairly subsidized. These surcharges were limited to a nominal value of 25 percent that would be imposed on top of the uniform tariff. These surcharges had modest effect, with only a handful of requests for relief being granted (de la Cuadra and Hachette 1991, 268). More significant were increases to the uniform tariff rate. With the persistence of the recession, the uniform tariff was doubled to 20 percent in June 1983. While the change was intended to last only thirty months, the government announced in December that the increase would persist indefinitely. Indeed, in September 1984 the uniform tariff once again was raised, this time to 35 percent (de la Cuadra and Hachette 1991, 268–70).

From this high-water mark of postcoup protectionism, however, Chile returned to its internationalist orientation. The nominal universal tariff rate fell twice in 1985, to 30 and later 20 percent. In January 1988, it was reduced to 15 percent. In addition, to stimulate exports after 1986, Chile reformed its export incentive structure to offset the harm to exports created by tariffs on imported factor inputs. Under the so-called simplified reimbursement program, exporters received payment of a fixed percentage of exports, regardless of the extent to which production costs were inflated by import tariffs (Saez and Ffrench-Davis 1996, 5.11–5.12).

In 1990, following the terms of the 1981 constitution, Chile's military regime ceded power to civilian authorities. The transition came about as a result of a 1988 plebiscite in which Chileans were asked to vote on Pinochet's petition for an eight-year extension on his rule. Given the dictator's abysmal human rights record, it is not surprising that the referendum failed. Elections in 1989 returned Patricio Aylwin, whose Concertación de Partidos por la Democracia (Alliance of Democratic Parties) emerged from under the persistent shadow cast by Pinochet (who remained at the head of the armed forces) to dominate Chilean politics through the 1990s.

The transition to democracy did not come at the expense of the prevailing economic development plan. In the middle of 1991, the uniform tariff rate was reduced to 11 percent. From 1998 until 2003, Chile continued to lower the uniform tariff rate for goods not covered by specific free-trade agreements by 1 percent per year. In addition, the government abandoned unilateralism, seeking to secure concessions from trading partners abroad. Chile entered into bilateral trade deals with Mexico (1991 and 1998), Venezuela and Colombia (both in 1993), Ecuador (1994), Canada (1996), and Peru (1998). In addition, negotiations for a free-trade deal with the European Union are under way, and a pact with the United States was finalized in 2003. On the multilateral front, Chile actively sought membership in NAFTA. It also enjoys associate status in MERCOSUR, although it has expressed frustration over the glacial pace of economic reform in Brazil and Argentina.

Chile's Big Bang Strategy

Chile represents a deviant case because it is the only country discussed here in which, strictly speaking, the government required no electoral calculus to factor into its trade policy reform. However, although a military dictatorship, the Pinochet regime was not wholly insulated from the effects of popular dissatisfaction; the resources of even repressive governments to forestall popular agitation are not limitless. Within the government itself, there were calls for a return to the ISI status quo ante (Soto 1995, 239). Similarly, as Chile's experience in the early 1980s suggests, macroeconomic shocks can confound the ability of even strongly committed authoritarian regimes to realize their policy objectives. Too much reform too quickly can redound with a force capable of capsizing the ship of even the most repressive state.

Chile's big bang strategy, then, while facilitated by the advantage of dictatorship, was fraught with some risk. As was the case with Whitlam in Australia, Laurier in Canada, and Peel in Great Britain, Chile's use of the big bang strategy illustrates just how difficult it is to gauge the optimal pace of reform. Certainly dictatorship is all that can explain why Pinochet's government lived to press on with its policies while Whitlam, Laurier, and Peel were dispatched to political obscurity.

In one sense, Pinochet's reasons for taking the risk were not so different than those of other political entrepreneurs. His immediate political objective was maintenance of power. But his longer-term goal was to institutionalize his (and the Chicago Boys') vision of the political good life. In democratic regimes, political entrepreneurs attempt to do this through electoral realignment and alterations to the institutional structure of the state. (Excellent examples include Peel in Great Britain, Roosevelt in the United States, Mulroney in Canada, and Salinas in Mexico.) In Chile, the stakes were higher. The last quarter of the twentieth century in Chile represented quite literally an armed struggle over the future of the regime that pitted communism against a system based on free enterprise. This had been the raison d'etre of the 1973 coup, and, while Pinochet will be remembered as an odd standard bearer for liberalism, it informed the economic philosophy of the Pinochet regime.

The logic of the limits of rent seeking model explains the Pinochet strategy. Given the high stakes associated with failure or success, the government sought to institutionalize an economy based on liberal principles as quickly as possible. Critical to the success of the strategy were three factors. First, the iterative nature of the reforms were clearly articulated. Rent-seeking producer groups may not have liked the economic shock treatment they received, but they were adequately forewarned through the course of the 1970s. Second, and most critically, reforms were comprehensive. The idea of a uniform tariff that applied equally to all goods (with the sole exception of the automotive sector) underscored the inflexibility in the government's position. Productive resources were not wasted in an attempt to lobby for more favorable rents, and political resources were not squandered in an attempt to identify and satisfy core rent-seeking constituents. Finally, the government kept a fairly firm whip hand. The minireversal of 1981–1985 was followed by a renewed (albeit less frenetic) commitment to neoliberal reform. Indeed, the ultimate success of the big bang strategy is clear from the fact that after 1985, it was industrial producers themselves who advocated further liberalization of the country's tariff structure.

Crisis as Catalyst in Brazil

As in Chile, ISI exhaustion was the proximate cause of neoliberal economic change in Brazil. That shift, however, came more slowly. Popular mobilization during the *Abertura*, as well as severe economic problems, made the shift to civilian government somewhat chaotic. An important distinction between the military governments in Chile and Brazil was that the military undertook the heavy lifting of economic change in the former. In the latter, the painful reform process was bequeathed to the civilian government (see Lamounier 1996). The result was a series of economic and political crises that led to an incomplete neoliberal economic revolution in Brazil.

By the time the military government agreed to return power to the civilian authorities, inflation was running above 300 percent per year and per capita income growth was virtually stagnant (Fishlow 1997, 47). The transition was not aided by the fact that president-elect Neves died in early 1985. His successor, a late defector from the military regime named José Sarney, proved a weak and ineffective leader. The result was a deepening of the economic crisis in the latter half of the 1980s. The centerpiece of the Sarney administration's economic program was a heterodox anti-inflation initiative known as the Cruzado Plan. At its core, the plan was a dual initiative, consisting of wage and price controls and the creation of a new currency, the cruzado. The plan was problematic from the start. To appease workers, the wage freeze was accompanied by two anomalous features. First, real wages were given an initial boost of 8 percent across the board, with the minimum wage being increased by 15 percent. Second, the "freeze" included a wage escalator that was triggered by an annual increase of 20 percent or more in the consumer price index. On the other hand, there were no price adjustments. As a result, and fueled by an expansionary monetary policy, the economy witnessed an explosion on the demand side with limited long-term incentive to increase supply. Moreover, because of heavy state involvement in the economy, price deficits in publicly owned firms put pressure on the federal treasury. For 1986, the total (federal, state, and municipal) budget deficit rose to 3.7 percent of GDP (2.3 percent of which was generated by state-owned enterprises) (Baer 1995, 162). Finally, it was difficult to maintain the value of the cruzado. Export markets dried up as the currency became increasingly overvalued. The result was a growing and unsustainable trade deficit. While the Cruzado Plan initially was successful in coupling high growth with low inflation, the effect was illusionary. Inflationary pressures resisted merely by force of legislative fiat created an untenable equilibrium.[14]

By late 1986 it was clear that the Cruzado Plan had failed. Despite three further attempts at stabilization, most notably the 1987 Bresser Plan,[15] Brazil's economy continued to suffer from near hyperinflation and escalating debt. In February 1987, Sarney was forced to impose a moratorium on interest payments to private banks. Although a settlement package was reached the following year, the Brazilian government resisted a supervisory role for the IMF in controlling new disbursements and, in the process, imposing greater fiscal discipline (see Lehman 1993, 133–55). Constitutional reform in 1988 also had negative economic consequences. The new constitution increased the already large transfer payments from the federal government to the states without imposing on the latter meaningful mechanisms for fiscal restraint.[16] In 1990 Sarney was replaced by Fernando Collor, whose presidency ended thirty-three months later under a cloud of scandal and the threat of impeachment.

Meanwhile, tentative steps toward trade liberalization were being taken. Beginning in 1986, Brazil and Argentina entered into a limited trade agreement known as the Programa de Integración y Cooperación Económica (Program of Integration and Cooperation, PICE). Two years later, they signed the Treaty on Integration, Cooperation and Development, which constituted an agreement in principle to eliminate all tariffs and NTBs between the two nations over a ten-year period (see Manzetti 1990). While hardly a liberalizing revolution, the bilateral negotiations paved the way for more significant reforms during the brief Collor administration.

Collor came to power facing the same inflationary problems that had undermined the Sarney presidency. Ironically, while this lowered the prestige of the office, Sarney's failures also lowered expectations and facilitated policy maneuverability (see Schneider 1991). Like his predecessor, Collor embarked on a radical stabilization program that included wage and price controls as well as a freeze (essentially a confiscation) of much of the country's liquid assets.[17] However, in contrast to the previous regime, Collor also sought to limit the role of clientelist special interests and increase the policy autonomy of the state (see Weyland 1997). The means to this entailed a massive retrenchment of the state. A large number of state agencies were closed; 360,000 of the state's 1.5 million public servants were let go. In their stead, Collor sought to put trusted allies into important leadership positions within the state administration. The overall objective was not to limit the role of the state in the same fashion as the Pinochet reforms in Chile. Rather, it was to create a strong state to replace the weak, fragmented state that was beholden to the point of sclerosis to special societal interests, largely in the business community (Weyland 1997; Schneider 1991). While Collor's stabilization initiative was bedeviled by the same rebound inflationary problems as its predecessors had been, administrative reform had a slightly more salutary effect.

Part of the deregulation initiative entailed reorientation of the nation's foreign economic policy. For example, Collor disbanded the foreign trade department of the Banco do Brasil, the notorious Carteira de Comércio Exterior (Foreign Trade Agency, CACEX), which was almost proverbial for its commitment to market protection. Intricately associated with protectionist interests that had flourished during the long decades of ISI protection, CACEX had control over dispersion of import licenses. In addition, under the auspices of the Law of Similars, CACEX was in a position to prohibit importation of goods that competed with established industries (Kingstone 1999, 50, 162).

In place of CACEX, Collor created the Departmento de Comércio Exterior (Foreign Trade Department, DECEX). Staffed with bureaucrats not nearly so wedded to the corporatist, ISI development model, DECEX also enjoyed relatively little policy autonomy. In contrast to the previous practice, import and export licenses, for example, were granted to anyone who could establish a line of credit. Even more significantly, DECEX no longer maintained administrative control over the roughly fifteen hundred items that had been prohibited from importation into Brazil. That list, known as Annex C, fell into desuetude in the face of the liberalizing reforms. Finally, the role of DECEX was reduced with the functional elimination of the Law of Similars (Kingstone 1999, 163).

Collor attacked Brazil's tariff structure as well. The tariff was unilaterally eliminated on a number of items. The government also undertook a program of tariffication (shifting NTBs to more transparent tariffs) and pledged to reduce tariff levels over time. Collor's successor, Itamar Franco, sustained this initiative, with the result that the average nominal tariff fell from 32 percent in 1990 to 14 percent by 1993. On the multilateral front, Brazil took steps to institutionalize reforms through the auspices of MERCOSUR (Bresser Pereira 1996, 192–93; da Motta Veiga 1997, 199; Kingstone 1999, 163–64).

MERCOSUR came into force with the 1991 Treaty of Asunción. The objective was to create a common market among Argentina, Brazil, Paraguay, and Uruguay. The four countries would maintain a common external tariff but would liberalize trade within the union. Intraregional tariffs would be reduced regularly in six-month increments until full free trade was achieved by the end of 1994 (1995 for the two smaller countries, whose tariff-reduction schedules were slightly more generous). Pertinently (and perniciously) each country was permitted to exempt certain sensitive commodities from the liberalization schedule. Other ambitious goals of MERCOSUR, such as macroeconomic policy coordination and the size of the common external tariff would be negotiated through multilateral institutions created under the Treaty of Asunción.[18]

Brazil's liberalizing initiative under Collor came to a sudden end with the corruption and impeachment scandal of 1992. In part, Collor was undone by two factors: the enormity of his task and his unwillingness to accommodate the entrenched interests (both congressional and societal) in the still-clientelist state. There were few friends available to support Collor in his darkest political hour. Collor came to power as a political outsider intent on changing the process of Brazilian politics. The fact that his party held less than 3 percent of the seats in Congress afforded him little choice but to impose his reforms by executive decree; thus, he sought to govern outside of the corporatist-clientelist alliance of state and business community interests. Indeed, he made the unprecedented move of failing to consult with the most prominent business confederation in the nation, the Federação das Indústrias do Estado de São Paulo (Industrial Federation of São Paulo), when embarking on his reform initiatives of 1990, and his relations with the business community remained strained (see Weyland 1997; Schneider 1991; Payne 1995; Bresser Pereira 1996, ch. 10; de Sousa 1999, esp. 52).

Collor's strategy, unsuccessful as it was, probably represented his best course of action. While the failure of his stabilization initiative undoubtedly weakened him, it was the corruption scandal that brought down his presidency. The brevity of Collor's term in office makes it impossible to say if his trade strategy would have succeeded over the long run. However, there is evidence that some of the behavioral change anticipated by the limits of rent seeking model was already under way by the early 1990s (Kingstone 2001).

Brazil's Path of Least Resistance Strategy

As Collor's successor, Franco was unremarkable save for his choice of Fernando Henrique Cardoso as finance minister in 1993. Cardoso, who became president in 1995, has been largely responsible for the recovery of the Brazilian economy. However, his path of least resistance strategy has retarded Brazil's adoption of a truly liberal foreign economic policy.

Cardoso's masterstroke was his own stabilization initiative, known as the Real Plan. Launched under the Franco administration, the Real Plan fought inflation from the supply rather than the demand side. The plan was grounded in fundamental fiscal reforms stemming from the imperative for a balanced budget in 1994. As a result, the government embarked on a (rather unsuccessful) commitment to reform the social security system, the federal bureaucracy, and the tax code. It also sought to privatize much of the state-owned industrial sector and to eliminate deficit spending at all levels of government.[19] In addition, the plan called for a new currency, the real, which was introduced in mid-1994 and was fixed at a one-to-one ratio with the U.S. dollar. A stable exchange rate, it was reasoned, would serve to anchor prices and control inflation. While the tight-money policy ultimately proved recessionary (and necessitated a U.S./IMF bailout in 1999), the result was the long-desired price stabilization that Brazil had been seeking since the birth of the New Republic in 1985 (see Sachs and Zini 1996; Fishlow 1997).

However, with respect to fundamental economic and trade policy reform, Cardoso has moved at a more leisurely pace. He was hampered in his first presidential term by the fact that his Social Democratic Party and its core partisan allies (which included the Brazilian Labor Party) held just over one-third of the seats in Congress. Because the Brazilian constitution played a ubiquitous role in the system of spending commitments, Cardoso was obliged to rely on pork barreling and economic side payments to construct legislative coalitions large enough (a two-thirds majority) to secure vital constitutional amendments.

A number of other factors have conspired to make Cardoso's task even trickier than most attempts at neoliberal reform. Trade liberalization was but one of many reform initiatives on the agenda of both business and political leaders during the 1990s. Indeed, business leaders' attention was focused on reversing the constitutional entrenchment of policies that undermined competitiveness. It is difficult to dissociate this objective from the adjustment process required for competing in a global environment. Similarly, President Cardoso's suboptimal strategy in liberalizing trade has to be considered in light of the fact that trade reform was not his highest priority. All reforms (including trade and constitutional liberalization) were subordinated to the goal of sustaining the Real Plan and containing inflation. Finally, the events of the 1990s must be understood in the context of the implicit (and by 1998, explicit) economic crisis. No government action could be undertaken absent consideration of the potential to tip the economy into either a recessionary or a hyperinflationary spiral.

Despite the logistical problems, though, Cardoso enjoyed a good deal of initial success. Through 1995 he was able to pass constitutional amendments that prohibited discriminatory treatment of foreign capital and that eliminated monopolies (state or national) in energy, internal transport (roads and railroads), mining, oil, shipping, and telecommunications (de Sousa 1999, 54; Levitsky 1998, 56). However, by 1996 the progress of reform had slowed, as Congress became more resistant to reform of tricky issues such as taxes, social security, and administrative structure. Meanwhile, generally positive economic numbers meant that Cardoso remained sufficiently popular to secure a 1997 constitutional amendment that allowed him to run for another term as president. Economic strategy turned to consolidating the gains of the previous four years and to ensuring that the economy remained stable in the run-up to the 1998 election (de Sousa 1999, 56–57). This objective mandated stronger relations with the nation's producers.

According to Kingstone, the deep recession of the 1990s served to anesthetize many producers from the effects of the tariff cuts introduced by Collor. Although prevailing economic conditions created plenty of pain on their own, the recession served as its own barrier to imports. With the revitalization of the economy in the middle of the decade, however, a resurgence of domestic demand stimulated imports. Meanwhile, the graduated tariff-reduction schedule had been completed. For sectors that had failed to adjust, the effect was a devastating flood of imports. In the textile sector, for example, imports increased from U.S.$500 million in 1992 to U.S.$3 billion by 1996 at the cost of roughly one million jobs (Kingstone 1999, 221).

It was partly for this reason that in early 1995 Brazilian policy makers decided that rather than follow up on the liberalizing initiative of the early 1990s (and reinforced through MERCOSUR) that Brazilian producers needed time to "digest" the adjustment costs that had been imposed on them (da Motta Veiga 1999, 28). There was some justification for this position. By 1996 there was a growing consensus that the real was overvalued. While this helped control inflation, it undermined the ability of firms to adjust through expansion of export markets. Similarly, Cardoso's insistence prior to 1997 on constitutional reform of the taxation system rather than piecemeal legislative remedies meant the persistence of glaring problems such as taxes that penalized exports while simultaneously increasing the price of imported factor inputs (Kingstone 1999, 218–22).

Faced with deep structural problems, high levels of debt, the persistent threat of inflation, and a presidential system that forced him to deal with a Congress still steeped in clientelist practices, it is easy to sympathize with Cardoso's cautious approach to reform. Still, it is clear that in the face of mounting pressure from Brazilian rent seekers, the president flinched. Indeed, given his other priorities (especially stabilization and reelection) Cardoso was unwilling to move too far in advance of what business would tolerate. While business leaders praised Cardoso for his willingness to listen to their concerns, many of these concerns extended beyond the elimination of structural disadvantages in the taxation system and into the realm of insulation from the effects of global competition (see Kingstone 2000, 200–2). As da Motta Veiga explains it, "Brazilian policy-makers view Brazilian industry as non-competitive vis-à-vis most developed economies. This perception shapes a trade policy dominated by the interests of the import-competing industries" (2000, 2).

In March 1996, the staff of the office investigating unfair trade practices was increased from four to forty. While there can be no doubt that some countries engage in predatory trade practices, it is equally clear that antidumping practices often represent the thin end of the protectionist wedge. Sure enough, two months later, tariffs on textiles and toys were raised to 40 percent as a hedge against uncompetitive trade practices abroad. Over the summer of 1996, the government proposed tariff protection and state-subsidized credit for a series of sectors that had been found to be victims of dumping. Protectionist interests were gratified once again in November 1997, when Brazil imposed a 3 percent tariff increase against goods from non-MERCOSUR nations (da Motta Veiga 1997, 200; Kingstone 1999, 221; Jenkins 1999, 48). Brazil also increased its use of NTBs in the second half of the 1990s. For example, the percentage of imported goods (based on the standard two-digit harmonized system product codes) subjected to Core Non-Tariff Measures[20] rose from 16.5 percent for the period 1989–1994 to 21.6 percent in 1995–1998 (Michalopoulos 1999).

A similar pattern of placating the least competitive sectors of the economy characterized bargaining over the deepening of MERCOSUR. Schneider argues that in both Brazil and Argentina "businesses, especially narrow sectoral associations geared up to push states to protect hard hit sectors, slow integration, and/or compensate losers. Politically the government's strategy seems to have been less one of building a strong pro-Mercosur coalition . . . and more one of undercutting the formation of an anti-Mercosur coalition by granting exceptions and concessions" (Schneider 2001, 177; see also Jenkins 1999, esp. 35, 54; Kaltenthaler and Mora 2002).

MERCOSUR also imposes limited discipline with respect to external trade. The Common External Tariff (CET), which continues to impose tariffs as high as 20 percent on some positions, is sufficiently high to have dissuaded Chile from choosing to abandon its associate status and become a full member of MERCOSUR (Weintraub 2000, 23; Wheatley 2001). It is also high enough, apparently, to have limited MERCOSUR nations' integration into the world economy. Between 1990 and 1996, for example, Brazil's exports to non-MERCOSUR countries grew annually by only 5.0 percent, as compared to 33.3 percent per year to other member states (da Motta Veiga 1999, 30; see also Markwald and Machado 1999). If we consider global integration as a function of exports to GDP ratio, Brazil and Argentina are the most insular economies in Latin America (Hakim 2002, 150). Finally, even within MERCOSUR, Brazil stands out as the country most committed to protectionism. It has fought hard to retain a high CET as a means of protecting its own industries and creating a unified set of interests to resist American influence in the Southern Cone.[21]

Reinforcing the high external tariff rate, until 2001 each member state was permitted to exclude up to three hundred items from the CET. In addition, MERCOSUR contains institutionalized exceptions, including the maintenance of an automobile agreement between Brazil and Argentina, and continued special protection against textile imports from non-MERCOSUR countries for both Brazil and Argentina. MERCOSUR also provides for accords in the petrochemical, chemical, shoe, paper, electronics, and agroindustry sectors (Nofal 1995, 212; Bernier and Roy 1999, 77–78, 85; Jenkins 1999, 37–38). Finally, MERCOSUR has suffered from numerous "process relaunches" that have served to postpone member states' commitments to further liberalization of trade (Ffrench-Davis 2001). While no free-trade deal is wholly free from exceptions, MERCOSUR stands out as particularly hospitable to inefficient special interests. One leaked World Bank report noted that MERCOSUR is a "fool's paradise" that actually represents a threat to free trade in the region (quoted in Jenkins 1999, 42).

The weakness of Brazil's commitment to free trade under MERCOSUR is most strikingly underscored in its opposition to further trade liberalization under the proposed FTAA. Brazil has emerged as the primary obstacle to the institutionalization of market reforms in the hemisphere that such an agreement would represent. Brazil's intransigence has created tension both within the Southern Cone (including other MERCOSUR members) and with the United States. While there is no doubt that Brazil's foreign policy vision of serving as a regional hegemon is threatened by the increased U.S. presence that a true hemispheric trade regime would engender, it seems equally clear that Brazil is hostage to "the predominance of the interests of the import competing sectors over the export-oriented sectors in determining industrial policy and foreign trade policy" (da Motta Veiga 1999, 26).[22] Or in the remarkably frank words of the president of the Confederação Nacional de Indústria (National Industrial Confederation, CNI), "The United States wants to accelerate integration so that it begins in 2005. For our part, we want to slow it down" (quoted in Cason 2000, 36; see also da Motta Veiga 1997; Hakim 2002; Soares de Lima 1999).

Fate of the Rent Seekers

Chile

The reaction of the Chilean business class to the rent reductions undertaken by the Pinochet administration conforms to the expectations of the limits of rent seeking model. Flexible industrial rent seekers who survived the radical tariff reductions of the 1970s and economic turbulence of the early 1980s are strong advocates of consolidating and extending the benefits of free trade.

An important reason, of course, is that the hard core of Chilean protectionism failed to survive the first round of rent reductions during the 1970s. Clearly this was a calculated move on the part of the Pinochet regime. Temporary deindustrialization, it was felt, would break the strength of organized labor. As for the business sector, Silva (1997, 163) notes that by 1975 "organized business was effectively shut out of the policy formulation stage of the policy-making process and was relegated to polite, after-the-fact meetings with ministers and undersecretaries in fruitless attempts to influence policy implementation." Between 1975 and 1982, 2,748 manufacturing enterprises filed for bankruptcy; manufacturing's share of GDP fell from 29.5 percent in 1974 to 18.9 percent eight years later.

Inflexible rent seekers in Chile were unable to mount much opposition in the face of the wave of neoliberal reform. Small and medium-sized businesses, as well as agricultural interests, engaged in public protests during the mid-1970s and during the recession of 1982–1983. However, the government held firm in the face of this popular agitation.[23] (A partial exception was the decision to grant price supports and other concessions to farmers during the early 1980s.) As a result, producers in the industrial sector went under or adjusted (Velasco 1994, 401, 404–5; see also Gatica Barros 1989, esp. 32–39). The decision to allow so many firms to go to the wall paved the way for the deepening of neoliberal reforms in the industrial sector. Predictably, the concessions granted to farmers had the opposite effect. As in the United States, agricultural producers sheltered from the deepest rent reductions have emerged as the sector least receptive to further liberalization of trade (see Schneider 2001).

Reformed flexible rent seekers and new entrants into the marketplace are far more prevalent in Chile, however. In 1975, roughly two hundred firms were engaged in the export of goods worth roughly $1.5 billion; by 1998, the value of exports had increased roughly tenfold, with almost six thousand firms exporting goods (*International Trade Forum* 1999). Table 8.1 indicates that Chile's export profile represents a positive trend in global competitiveness, while table 8.2 demonstrates that, especially through the 1990s, exports of manufactured goods have outpaced traditional staples copper and fruits.

As might be expected, given the depth of the rent reductions through the

Table 8.1
Growth of Chilean exports, 1960–2000

Years	Annual average growth rate (%)
1960–65	4.2
1965–70	3.0
1970–75	5.6
1975–80	15.3
1980–85	1.8
1985–90	10.8
1990–94	9.1
1990–2000	9.4

Sources: Meller (1997); World Bank (n.d.).

early 1980s, the entrepreneurial class in Chile is attitudinally distinct from the provincial rent-seeking elite that sheltered so long behind the protectionism afforded by ISI. Bartell's study of Chilean business leaders found (1995, 61) that by the late 1980s "a new generation of Chilean entrepreneurs was emerging, competitively professional and self-confident and committed ideologically or pragmatically to a liberal economic model." In part, this new confidence was both born of, and contributed to, active business participation in the deepening of neoliberal reform in Chile during the 1990s. This participation is facilitated by the fact that business interests are represented largely through a single dominant peak organization, the Confederación de la Producción y Comercio (Confederation for Production and Commerce, CPC). While the CPC cannot be said to speak with a single voice (again, farmers represent a significant challenge to a neoliberal consensus), it has worked to ensure that there has been no backsliding on neoliberal reform under the postmilitary governments (Silva 1997; Schneider 2001). Indeed, a major obstacle to Chile's membership in MERCOSUR is the opposition of many in the business community to that agreement's high CET and the poor prospects of lowering the tariff in the face of Brazil's intransigence. Similarly, in terms of unilateral trade policy, it was the business community that represented a major catalyst in the Chilean government's ongoing commitment to lower the domestic tariff through 2003 (Corbo 1997; Agosin 2000; Kingstone 1999, 8).

Brazil

It would be inaccurate to characterize Brazil's neoliberal reforms as a complete failure. Between 1985 and 1995, the average nominal tariff rate fell

Table 8.2
Total Chilean exports, 1980–2000 (in $U.S. billions)

	1980	1990	Change, 1980–90 (%)	2000	Change, 1990–2000 (%)
Total exports (fob)	4.706	8.373	178	18.158	217
Copper	2.125	3.810	179	7.347	193
Fruits	0.340	0.757	223	1.122	148
Manufactures	1.751	2.739	156	8.172	298

Source: World Bank (n.d.).

Note: fob = free on board.

from almost 50 percent to a low of just under 12 percent (Hakim 2002, 149). Moreover, Brazil appears to have recovered from the crisis of 1998–1999. Inflation for 2000 was only 6.0 percent while GDP grew by 4.4 percent (Werneck 2001). MERCOSUR established an ambitious, if often breached, timetable for regional trade liberalization, and intraregional trade has increased in the decade of the bloc's existence (see Markwald and Machado 1999). It would be equally inaccurate to maintain that neoliberal reforms have had no impact on the behavior of rent-seeking activity in Brazil. Many inflexible rent seekers were unable to survive the turbulent 1990s. Bankruptcy rates in 1995, for example, were 40 percent higher than during the previous year. In 1996, bankruptcy requests increased by 300 percent (Kingstone 1999, 210, 220). Moreover, as the limits of rent seeking model predicts, many "free-trade 'losers' support free trade" (Kingstone 2001). However, in contrast to Chile's experience and to other more successful examples of transitions to freer trade, Brazil's trade policy reforms have been insufficient to trigger behavioral change in a large portion of the rent-seeking population (Soares de Lima 1999, 141–43); the result has been only partial liberalization.

While Brazil's manufactured exports have increased at an impressive rate through the 1990s (total exports of manufactured goods increased in that decade by a total of roughly 209 percent [World Bank n.d.]), this figure is somewhat illusory. As noted, much of the expansion of Brazil's external trade has been with its MERCOSUR partners and has taken place under the shelter of the common external tariff.[24] The disadvantages are fairly clear. The growth potential of the MERCOSUR market is limited, and as the 2002 crisis in Argentina suggests, MERCOSUR does not represent a terribly stable market for exports.

As might have been expected, the wave of liberalization that ended in 1994 appears to have met with differential support within the business community. Certainly a 1995 CNI survey of 814 Brazilian industrialists across a wide range of industrial sectors found that roughly two-thirds had positive feelings about commercial liberalization.[25] Of course, commercial liberalization cannot be equated with trade liberalization. The former represented an omnibus reform initiative that included privatization of state-owned firms, liberalization of investment and financial markets, restraint on public spending, tax reform, and less state intervention in the economy. On the other hand, by 1995 a portion of the industrial producer population was receptive to a set of policies in which trade liberalization featured prominently (Kingstone 1999, 224–26). Rather than signal its commitment to staying the course, however, the Cardoso administration indicated its willingness to trade off trade policy concessions for short-term political support among the most committed rent seekers.

Brazil's glacial progress on deepening of MERCOSUR and widening trade through the auspices of the FTAA is largely attributable to two factors: many rent-seeking producers will not adjust to global competition merely as a matter of preference, and the Brazilian government did not force such adjustment during the critical crisis years of the mid-1990s. Despite Collor's deep cuts to the tariff rates, most of which occurred between 1990 and 1994, there was remarkably little follow-through on the part of the Cardoso administration. Those firms that adjusted in response to neoliberal reforms became advocates of freer trade. While many firms that did not adjust were rationalized from the market, other indicators suggest that neoliberal reform has not done much to reorient the structure of the upper echelons of Brazilian business. Among the largest three hundred business groups (firms or conglomerates) in 1990, only eleven suffered what might be called catastrophic failure, defined as having all member firms cease operations, by 1997. Seven of these catastrophic failures occurred by 1994. Similarly, of groups that were in the top one hundred in 1990, only twenty-seven had fallen out of the top three hundred by 1997. There was also very little movement into the top one hundred enterprises. By 1994, only nine distinctly new groups had broken into the top one hundred; by 1997, that figure had increased to ten (Kingstone 2001, 999). Such stability suggests that the elite producers that were in place at the end of the ISI era were still disproportionately in place by 1997 (Soares de Lima 1999, esp. 146–47). This does not necessarily preclude the possibility that most of these firms had adjusted to the realities of the new global economy. However, given Brazil's tepid pace of trade policy reform, stability at the pinnacle of the Brazilian business elite suggests that reform has been marginal or superficial.

The mid-1990s represented a turning point for the Brazilian economy. While deepening the reforms would have increased economic disruption, there is evidence that a proto–free-trade coalition was in place. Had the government demonstrated resolve and moved steadily (if only incrementally) to expose Brazilian business to more market competition through liberalization under MERCOSUR and the FTAA, a liberal revolution could have succeeded. Instead, ameliorative actions such as unilaterally raising tariffs and NTBs, engaging in only marginal reforms through MERCOSUR, and shunning the imperative for more meaningful reform through the market discipline that would be imposed under an FTAA were the hallmark of Brazil's strategy to follow the path of least resistance. As a result, the pace of Brazil's sclerotic trade liberalization initiative appears to be controlled by the large remaining cadre of inflexible rent seekers.

As late as the mid-1980s, the situations in Brazil and Chile were reasonably comparable. Both had democratization in their immediate futures, both had serious economic worries born of the difficult transition from a managed to a more market-based economy. Of the two, it might have been predicted that Brazil's massive and more diversified economy would have been the more likely to become the economic model for Southern Cone economic development. The Chilean economy was able to weather economic turbulence in the 1990s without a return to either capital flight or debilitating inflation. By contrast, while Brazil has survived the crisis of the late 1990s, it is still protecting its inefficient producers.

While the brutal Pinochet regime serves as a poor model for political and economic development, it demonstrates that successful reform does not require full-bore neoliberal reform. However, as in other countries, the big bang strategy adopted during the 1970s in Chile was suboptimal because reformers were not able to gauge the optimal size of the initial rent reduction. By the early 1980s, the economy was pitched into a dreadful recession. It seems quite safe to say that no democratically elected government would have survived such a blunder. On the other hand, the decision to embark on a second wave of liberalization after the initial one certainly explains, consistent with the logic of the limits of rent seeking model, the broad support of the business community for further liberalization of trade in Chile. In fact, the neoliberal consensus, while not universal, appears well entrenched. In the three-man democratic presidential elections of 1989, for example, both the winner, Aylwin, and the runner-up campaigned in favor of maintaining free-market open economic policies (Hojman 1994, 211). The hegemony of neoliberalism has remained immune from challenge, even under the current Social Democratic president, Ricardo Lagos.

By contrast, while it is easy to sympathize with the plight in which the Cardoso government found itself in Brazil, it is equally clear that seeking to build a coalition by satisfying protectionist rent seekers dooms, or at least seriously undermines, the prospects for successful neoliberal reform. While it is not inconceivable that future reforms could build in iterative fashion on the rent reductions of the early 1990s, the path of least resistance strategy undertaken by Cardoso will make such a job more difficult. Indeed, Cardoso's successor as president is the leader of the Worker's Party, Luis Inacio Lula da Silva, a trade union activist and opponent of neoliberal reform.

The path of least resistance strategy did not insulate Brazil from the economic crisis of 1998–1999. What it did was in part to extend the old ISI logic to a new quasi-protectionist trade zone, MERCOSUR. In turn, MERCO-SUR's intransigence, led by Brazil, has not helped the progress of the FTAA. Such a hemispheric trade zone, however, would be an excellent way to complement neoliberal reform in Brazil. Subsequent rent reductions mandated by the regime would serve to provide a degree of political insulation to Brazilian policy makers. Finally, as a counterfactual argument it is worth considering that although it is unlikely that a more dynamic MERCOSUR could have prevented Argentina's own economic crisis of 2002, it is possible that it could have moderated the effects.

Counterfactual musings are fraught with risk, but they also can be illustrative. Krueger challenges us to consider what might have happened had Chile done as Brazil did under Cardoso, privileging stabilization at the expense of trade policy reform. The result, she suggests (1994, 69), is that "it is relatively straightforward to imagine the entire reform process foundering on balance of payments difficulties." While the Mexican experience of 1994–1995 suggests that trade reform is not a panacea against balance-of-payments crises, it is worth noting that Chile avoided the destabilizing effects of forced currency devaluations experienced in recent years by MERCOSUR members Brazil and Argentina.

9

Lessons
Economic Gain without Political Pain?

Governments can achieve more open markets and can do so without suffering sustained or severe political backlash. Trade liberalization, though risky, tends to remain institutionalized once it has been achieved. As the limits of rent seeking model shows, liberalizing governments have at their disposal the means to alter the behavior of protectionists—compelling them to exit the market or creating incentives for them to join a pro–free-trade coalition. In either case, if handled appropriately, a country's protectionist lobby can be greatly emaciated. Once established, free trade enjoys a political constituency that lobbies for its retention and even expansion (see Milner 1988).

Although the evidence demonstrates that trade liberalization can be achieved without devastating political backlash, it is not my contention that successful conversion to free trade is merely a matter of political entrepreneurs' creativity and political will. The case studies show that circumstances dictate opportunities and condition chances for success. While one of my objectives is to offer a prescription, its applicability is not universal.

The limits of the rent-seeking model and the cases studied here illustrate the circumstances under which protectionist producers can be expected to shift their trade policy preferences from protectionism to freer trade, thus helping to institutionalize trade liberalization. Government leaders who wish to liberalize trade while suffering limited political backlash can choose from the prescriptive menu of options analyzed here. The data from ten attempts at trade liberalization are summarized in table 9.1. The fact that some strategies worked better than others, and worked better with certain opportunities, provides some additional lessons.

Catalysts

The limits of rent seeking model poses three catalysts for trade liberalization. The first two, structural in nature, are crisis and regime-mandated change. The third is strategic and is motivated by the private or political objectives of the government leaders. While ten cases are hardly sufficient to draw meaningful conclusions about the relative costs and benefits posed by these three types of opportunity, they can provide tentative insights.

All cases of trade liberalization require an element of strategic calculation on the part of sponsoring politicians. Thus, in isolating the catalyst for trade liberalization in the cases examined here, I base my decision on the circumstance that precipitated the first iteration in rent reductions. For example, even though Mexico's big bang strategy was undertaken for strategic reasons, the first rent reductions in the 1980s were precipitated by crisis and regime-mandated change. Similarly, even though Roosevelt's conversion to free trade in the 1930s took place in the context of crisis, it seems clear that

Table 9.1
The cases

STRATEGY	CRISIS	MANDATED CHANGE	STRATEGIC
Big Bang	Mexico (S)	Canada (S)	Great Britain (F)
	Chile (S)	Mexico (S)	Canada [Laurier] (F)
			Australia [Whitlam] (F)
Divide and Conquer	New Zealand (S)		
Iteration	New Zealand (S)		United States (S)
Least Resistance	Australia (M)		
	Brazil (M)		

Note: S = success: significant liberalization of trade without meaningful political backlash; F = failure: sufficient political backlash to unseat liberalizing government; M = mixed: insignificant liberalization of trade, but no meaningful political backlash.

he simply took advantage of the ambient economic upheaval to advance his electoral objectives.

Crisis played a dominant role in five of the cases studied here (Mexico, New Zealand, Australia [under Hawke], Chile, and Brazil). Crises take the form of depressions, severe and sustained recessions, or discrete events that disrupt commerce in a particular sector or industry for a sustained period. Interestingly, in none of these cases did the government that sponsored trade liberalization suffer meaningful political backlash. (The Australian and Brazilian cases are nonetheless classified as failures because neither country can be said to have abandoned protectionism—in both a committed cadre of protectionist producers exercise decisive influence over trade policy.)

Crisis has the effect of forcing rent seekers to reveal their true profiles. Most manifestly, crisis serves to eliminate the weakest strata of the producer population, thereby culling the hardest core of the protectionist lobby. Moreover, crisis tends to reduce the flow of state subsidies to producers. As the case studies in this book show, the effect of crisis is typically to force flexible rent seekers to demonstrate their capacity to compete in the context of reduced levels of state-supplied rents. In the aftermath of crisis, governments are better able to gauge the extent to which flexible rent seekers are distributed among the producer population, while at the same time being confident that the least efficient producers have been eliminated.

Prescriptively, of course, crisis is not recommended. While governments that liberalize trade in the aftermath of crisis tend to be successful, there is no guarantee that the government will survive the crisis. Indeed, in each of the cases in which crisis played a significant role, the government that liberalized trade manifestly was not the one perceived to be responsible for the crisis. While we have only two illustrations (Mexico and Canada under Mulroney) here, regime-mandated change offers the political advantages of crisis without the obvious attendant negative consequences. Like crisis, regime-mandated change forces flexible rent seekers to reveal their true colors while forcing the least competitive producers from the market. As with crisis, moreover, the sponsoring government can avoid much of the political blame. In both Mexico and Canada, for example, liberalization mandated by the GATT (and in Mexico, the World Bank and IMF) could be perceived as externally imposed.[1] Governments can use this external mandate to promote an "us against them" sense of national spirit, almost a diversionary theory of free trade, to borrow a well-known concept from the literature on conflict studies.[2]

Far and away the riskiest catalyst is strategic considerations. Four of the cases discussed here were precipitated by strategic factors. Only the U.S. case was successful. Significantly, that took place in the context of a prevailing crisis, and that crisis was used as justification for trade liberalization. Even though the evidence suggests that President Roosevelt was motivated by strategic considerations, his administration was at great pains to make it appear that trade liberalization was undertaken in response to crisis. Ironically, British prime minister Peel's strategic calculus was that Corn Law repeal was necessary to avoid a political crisis. Indeed, while he perceived a looming, possibly revolutionary, crisis on the horizon, he could not articulate its presence for fear of precipitating the very event he wished to avoid. Trade liberalization, then, was strategic in that it was the means to a higher-order objective, but it was electorally catastrophic. Two more ordinary cases of trade liberalization motivated by strategic calculations ended in disaster, for reasons clearly articulated in public choice theory—all things being equal, free trade is politically problematic. Canada's prime minister Laurier was simply blindsided. His party had always stood for free trade, and he merely underestimated the intensity with which established rent seekers preferred the status quo ante. By contrast, Australian prime minister Whitlam acted on economic principle, hoping to weather the political storm by sheer force of will.

In the aggregate, the lesson that emerges seems quite clear. In the absence of some sort of political camouflage created by structural conditions—crisis or regime-mandated change—trade liberalization is a risky course of action. Politicians who liberalize trade because it is the right thing to do meet the fate predicted by the public choice literature. Instead, it is a virtual imperative that politicians who seek to liberalize trade do so under the pretext of some event to which they can point as an unavoidable circumstance against which they must react. Once this imperative is met, the logic of the limits of rent seeking model and the menu of options presented in chapter 1 become operative.

Execution

Although a small number of cases are presented here, and in most of them, government leaders chose to employ the big bang strategy, some interesting insights can still be gleaned.

The one manifestly suboptimal strategy is the path of least resistance. There is no mystery as to why this is the case; nor is it difficult to understand why governments employ the strategy. In some cases—Australia and Brazil are fine examples—it behooves the government to appear as if it is solving the country's economic problems while in reality it seeks to ensure that no important economic interests are harmed. The strategy may prolong the life of the government, but it can hardly be expected to address the underlying economic pathologies that made reform desirable in the first place. Because the strategy thwarts the logic of the limits of rent seeking model, it is not surprising that cases in which the strategy is used do not yield the outcome predicted by the model.

The other three strategies are more successful. Taken together, the similar (in that both are incremental) divide-and-conquer and iteration strategies generated two successes—the United States and New Zealand. Both can be considered hard cases, in the sense that free trade was implemented in countries that had had no recent history of accepting economic internationalism. In the United States, President Roosevelt succeeded in laying what Haggard (1988) called the "institutional foundations of hegemony" in the climate of a crumbling (First New Deal) electoral coalition and an entrenched cultural antipathy to international encumbrances. In New Zealand, the reforming government was social democratic, a party whose core constituency typically does not favor weakening the control of the state in favor of the rigor of the market. In both cases, the shift in foreign economic policy was remarkable not only for its starkness but also for its robustness. In both cases, the skill with which government leaders engineered their respective trade policy revolutions is clear from the fact that both governments enjoyed enormous popularity even as they systematically slashed state-supplied rents.

Two other hard cases, which technically used the big bang approach, relied on a logic that was similar to divide-and-conquer/iteration. In both Mexico and Canada the big bang strategy was used in the wake of a structurally imposed rent reduction. In other words, while government leaders did not set out to employ an incrementalist approach to rent reductions, they followed up a significant regime-mandated rent reduction with a comprehensive (big bang) free-trade agreement. This subset of the big bang approach, then, relies on the same logic as the two incremental strategies. Government leaders take advantage of an earlier rent reduction (1) to gauge the profile of the rent-seeker population and (2) to construct a pro–free-trade coalition among those producers whose response to the initial reduction was to adjust for global competition.

By contrast, three of the four remaining big bang cases ended in political disaster. These failures were cases in which the big bang strategy was employed without the benefit of either a structurally imposed rent reduction or an incremental approach. In each of the failed cases, the government leader played into a blind game. In Britain, Peel made a half-hearted attempt to play an iterative strategy, but for reasons of state security failed to signal his government's resolve to reduce agricultural rents further. Laurier and Whitlam played their cards boldly and paid the political price. Indeed, the fate of these three "naked big bang" cases suggests that Roger Douglas's advice (1993, 222) that "[s]peed is essential[,] it is almost impossible to go too fast" is subject to significant qualification.

Anything Else?

The prescriptive logic of the limits of rent seeking model can be extended to countries that seek to influence trade politics within their trading partners. This is especially germane to hegemonic powers, such as the United States. An area ripe for further exploration, moreover, is the United States' burgeoning relationship with its hemispheric trading partners in Latin America.

Since the Monroe Doctrine, the United States has sought to guarantee its influence in Latin America. A fairly consistent, albeit unsuccessful, U.S. objective has been to institutionalize capitalism and democracy in the notoriously unstable Iberian New World. Coincident with the era of ISI exhaustion, and the inherent economic crisis, the 1980s and 1990s witnessed a greater acceptance of free-market economics and nascent liberal democracy in Latin America. The process climaxed with the 1994 Summit of the Americas in Miami, which produced an agreement in principle to establish a hemispheric free-trade zone by 2005. This proposed FTAA has been hampered, however, by economic (and democratic) backsliding in Latin America, as well as the inability (at least until 2002) of Presidents Bill Clinton and George W. Bush to secure Trade Promotion Authority (TPA).[3]

The FTAA is a fundamental component of U.S. foreign policy. While most Latin American markets are too small or too distant to have the stimulant effect that NAFTA potentially will have on the U.S. economy, there remain two demonstrable reasons for the imperative to pursue the hemispheric trade deal. The first is inherent in the limits of rent seeking model. While an FTAA may have only marginal direct benefits to many Latin American economies, it can serve to impose market rigor on countries that have a tradition of shrinking away from the discipline of market forces when times turn tough. (Excellent examples are the experience in Brazil and the recent crisis in Argentina.) In this sense, then, trade liberalization can promote political stability. As Sandholtz (1993) points out, one reason countries commit themselves to economic regimes is, like Ulysses' attempt to resist the Sirens' song, to ensure that they avoid the temptation to take the easy political decision in favor of the tougher economic choice. By extension, once governments are mandated to stick to the tough choices, the limits of rent seeking model suggests that the natural mortality or conversion of former protectionists mitigates the political costs. In other words, the very existence of a trade regime provides a reforming government with the political camouflage to facilitate deeper, more meaningful rent reductions.

The second basis for the claim that an FTAA is vital to U.S. foreign policy interests is that it is likely to institutionalize liberal, and ultimately liberal democratic, values. On the one hand, it is no great trick to create a democracy. If we employ the standard of elite selection by popular vote, much of Latin America has been democratic for decades. More difficult is the construction of a liberal democracy, which can be defined as a government structure that preserves the rights and the autonomy of all individuals, where state authority is limited and grounded in the protection of the rights of the individual, and where government elites are selected by merit. This selection mechanism, moreover, must ensure responsiveness of elites to the civil society and must entail selection of representatives through popular elections with (near) universal voting rights.

Liberal democracies cannot be imposed. They must be nurtured. While an institutional structure that limits the powers of officeholders is a necessary condition for liberal democracies, this condition is insufficient. To be fully operational, liberal democracy requires the active support of the electorate. The ultimate backstop for a system of institutional checks and balances is a citizenry with a stake in the political system and an unwillingness to allow elites to take liberties with the limits of their constitutional authority. This citizenry, moreover, must be united in certain core values, including belief in limited government and respect for individual liberty. As modernization theorists noted many years ago, democracy mandates a citizenry that feels sufficiently powerful to enforce the parameters of state authority and that is imbued with sufficient social capital—society's stock of shared values[4]—to retain a stake in the political system.[5] Social capital is akin to what Almond and Verba (1963) call interpersonal trust, which in turn is fundamental to democracy in the Schumpeterian sense of democratic self-control, or willingness to follow the rules of the democratic process (Schumpeter 1950, 294–95). It also should be taken to require legitimacy, which Lipset

(1959, 86) defines as "the capacity of a political system to engender and maintain the belief that existing political institutions are the most appropriate or proper ones for the society." Succinctly, a large part of the democratic transition entails "growing the political culture"; that is, to create social capital where it has not existed in the past. Evidence of social capital is seen in high levels of interpersonal trust and high levels of perception that the prevailing regime is legitimate.

Political culture is the lens through which members of society acquire and maintain an understanding about politics. Like other forms of culture, political culture is acquired through socialization—that is, it is transmitted through learning rather than through biological instinct. The dominant agents of socialization (family, church, school, media, and so on) are what we might call the keepers of the culture. They are responsible for perpetuating the culture, for maintaining its robust quality. However, it is this robust quality that makes democratic transitions so difficult.

Two things quickly become obvious about political culture: it changes, and it changes slowly. The robust quality of political culture provides a sense of continuity with the past. Thus, every society maintains its folklore, its myths, and its essential truths. These are passed from generation to generation and help define the essence of that society. Political culture is not frozen in time. There is a dynamic element to it. Many of the political values of previous generations are strikingly anachronistic today.

Cultural change is largely generational, and it is largely incremental. As a rule, culture changes at the margins. New generations import new ideas into the political culture, but the effect is generally to modify the culture. As a result, cultural change is slow and all but imperceptible. For reasons of comparison, we might call such incrementalism microcultural change. On occasion, however, cultural change can occur more dramatically. There are instances where wholesale attitudinal changes happen quite quickly, within the space of one or two generations. The widespread acceptance of liberal democratic values in West Germany after World War II is a good example. Such cultural revolutions can be thought of as macrocultural change. Successful liberal democratic transitions require macrocultural change.

One final distinction between micro- and macrocultural change is that the latter requires a catalyst. Macrocultural change must be precipitated by a seminal event. An example is crisis. Crisis weakens attachment to the status quo and creates a receptive market for innovation on the part of interests that previously had been resistant to change. For macrocultural change, the seminal event need not take the form of crisis. Social upheavals associated with changing technology, for example, also can constitute a seminal event (see Piore and Sabel 1984; Fukuyama 1999; Putnam 2000). Similarly, major policy shifts can be the catalyst. The reorientation of British politics in the early twentieth century was precipitated by a seminal event: the Third Reform Act (1884). The successful transition to liberal democracy in West Germany followed World War II. Finally, the "postmaterial revolution" was a function of the postwar construction of the welfare state in advanced industrial societies (Inglehart 1971).

An important example of a seminal event is the emergence of a powerful, independent bourgeoisie, which can be stimulated in the developing world through the institutionalization of a free-trade regime (Mexico is an excellent example). It is for this reason that the Industrial Revolution is so critical to understanding sociopolitical change in nineteenth-century Europe and the United States. Although it occurred at different times in different countries, industrialization has tended to produce a powerful middle class, imbued with the desire to be free to make its own economic decisions free of state supervision and control. This demand for economic liberty extends to a demand for political liberty as well, that is, for a political system that promotes liberty and equality over social hierarchy and regulation.[6] It extends, in other words, to a demand for liberal democracy. This is the logic, inherent in Marx's notion of historical determinism, behind Barrington Moore's famous blunt contention "no bourgeois, no democracy" (1967, 418).[7]

The role played by a powerful, independent middle class has been well documented in the literature on modernization. Dominguez (1998, 73) is exceptionally blunt: "No democratic regime has ever survived in the absence of a market economy." Lipset (1959) explains that economic development creates a sense of inclusion on the part of the lower social strata. Specifically, increased income and economic security, as well as the higher levels of education that a wealthier economy provides, give members of the lower strata both a greater stake in the existing system and a longer-term, more gradualist approach to politics. It precludes radicalism and antisystem politics. At the same time, the upper classes feel less political threat and, correspondingly, less need to create oppressive institutions that reinforce social hierarchy. If political power shifts are not revolutionary, but rather take the form of peaceful alternations, the upper classes have a lesser stake in the political status quo. In short, Lipset (1959, 83) argues, economic development changes the "shape of the stratification structure so that it shifts from an elongated pyramid, with a large lower class base, to a diamond, with a growing middle class. A large middle class plays a mitigating role in moderating conflict since it is able to reward moderate and democratic parties and penalize extremist groups." The bourgeoisie plays two critical roles. It serves as a buffer between an otherwise excluded lower class and an otherwise repressive upper class. Also, it creates a sense of political legitimacy. It helps to ensure that democratic transitions are accompanied by sufficient political legitimacy to preserve necessary levels of social capital.

The existence of a middle class is a necessary condition for a successful democratic transition, although not a sufficient one. Free trade, by virtue of its injection of liberal values and its expansion of the middle class, constitutes a seminal event sufficient to trigger macrocultural change. The recent example of Mexico, where the introduction of NAFTA appears to have precipitated a groundswell of support and demand for democratic values (Drury and Lusztig n.d.), is suggestive of the effect that an FTAA could have on the rest of Latin America.

Free trade is not a risk-free option for the countries of the Western Hemisphere. Even in the United States in recent years the quest for TPA has proven politically tricky. The ameliorative effects, however, especially on economies on the verge of democratic transition, are enormous. The lesson of this analysis is that free trade is not an accident of circumstance; it must be made to happen. Under normal circumstances it involves significant risk of political backlash. Managed properly, however, government leaders can overcome the logistical advantages enjoyed by rent seekers. Indeed, the limits of rent seeking model demonstrates that, in a form of political jujitsu, government leaders can turn the political momentum of rent seekers to their own advantage. When the strategy is executed properly, the result is economic gain without political pain.

Notes

1. November 9, 1993.

2. Rent seeking entails the attempt to use the power of the state to transfer, rather than create, wealth (Conybeare 1983).

3. The logic is similar to that of why governments are loath to undertake retrenchment of the welfare state. See Pierson (1996).

4. The logic of the theory of comparative advantage is that specialization of production is economically beneficial to all countries, independent of size or circumstance. See Ricardo (1960).

5. Bhagwati (1982) defines DUP as activities that "yield pecuniary returns but do not produce goods or services that enter a utility function directly or indirectly via increased production or availability to the economy of goods that enter a utility function."

6. There are qualifications to this argument, however. See Hillman and Katz (1984).

7. Suppliers of rents can range from minor officials with the opportunity to demand, for example, personal kickbacks for state-supplied goods such as import licenses to governments at large that generate utility from political support associated with enacting socially inefficient policies. See Krueger (1974).

8. Even in developed economies, a case can be made for protecting industries that depend on new technologies. See, for example, Murtha, Lenway, and Hart (2001).

9. Of course, not all domestic producers in countries with high tariff walls are protectionist. Sectors that export efficiently—and thus have geared production to compete internationally—will seek reduction of tariffs to lower the costs of factor inputs and to encourage tariff reduction abroad. Where firms have developed effective multinational operations (including integrated global production and intrafirm trade flows) there will be even greater resistance to protectionism (Milner 1993).

10. Obviously a third option is implicit, in which producers exit the marketplace as a means of cutting their losses because neither production option is viable.

11. For more on firms' options in restructuring operations, see Kingstone (1999, xx–xxii) and Bollard and Savage (1990).

12. For inflexible rent seekers, the critical level of rents is the minimum required for the survival of the firm or industry.

13. To use the American example, such industries include consumer electronics, steel, and automobiles. See Schiller (2000).

14. There are a number of factor-based models of trade. They turn on the assumption that

trade policy is a function of the interaction among owners of critical factors of production—land, labor, and capital. Among the most prominent factor-based models is the Stolper-Samuelson theorem. In its briefest form, Stolper-Samuelson predicts that free trade will empower politically owners of factors with which a country is abundantly endowed (and hence in which it presumably enjoys comparative advantage) and weakens scarce factor owners. Protectionism has the opposite effect. Changes in the trade policy status quo have the potential to alter the structure of prevailing political alliances, and in extreme cases change the structure of the regime (for a fuller articulation, see Rogowski 1989). Some factor-based models assume limited mobility among productive factors—wealth from land cannot easily be translated into wealth from capital. Others suggest that technology and institutions such as stock markets have rendered productive factors more mobile. In either case, factor-based models suggest that political behavior is a function of economic interests. Where factors are deemed less mobile, coalitions are expected to form along industry or sectoral lines; where they are more mobile, class-based coalitions are predicted to emerge (for more on factor-based models see, for example, Brawley 1998).

15. For more on how international regimes and agreements can constrain governments, see Sandholtz (1993) and Milner (1997). Compare Nelson (1989).

16. Obviously this term is a bit misleading—it is reasonable to assume that any action undertaken by self-interested politicians will be strategic in nature. I employ this concept more narrowly, restricting its application to circumstances where the liberalization process is not forced on reluctant politicians by circumstance (crisis or mandated change) but instead is pursued proactively as the means to a larger end.

17. For empirical applications, see Lusztig (1996).

18. For more on costly signals, see Schelling (1960) and Spence (1973).

19. Again, if we wish to impose the qualification that rent seekers may be uncertain as to their status, a time lag will be necessary to observe meaningful results.

20. Moreover, at least in Canada, studies have shown that the advantages of free trade with the United States were probably greater in the 1960s than in later decades. See Wonnacott and Wonnacott (1967) and Watson (1987). In spite of this, Canadian business remained protectionist until the 1980s (Canada 1978a; Cameron 1986; Doern and Tomlin 1991).

21. As Milner (1993, 147) notes, "While it is commonly believed that protectionism grew substantially in the 1970s and early 1980s, U.S. trade policy actually had mixed currents."

22. These include those sensitive to the inherent dynamism in the world political economy and that thus constitute explanations relevant to cases across a fairly broad range in time. See, inter alia, Gourevitch (1986), Rogowski (1989), and Kindleberger (1996).

23. In this sense, the model goes beyond the existing literature more generally. Explanations based on the American case, like those of Ferguson (1984) and Frieden (1988) for example, which hold that the increased competitiveness of U.S. industry in the 1920s and 1930s led to the push for internationalism, are able to show only why government changed its trade policy. See also Goldstein (1988). They provide no explanation of why the protectionist industrial bloc, still politically powerful in the mid-1930s, was virtually a spent force by the end of the decade.

Notes to Chapter 2

1. There is not general agreement as to when the depression actually began. Its effects were not universally felt across economic sectors or geographic locations. Most analysts date it to 1873, but many suggest that its impact was not felt until as late as 1876, or even 1879.

2. In discussing the United States in the 1930s, Goldstein (1988) suggests that free trade tends to become institutionalized where it is popularly perceived to contribute to increased prosperity.

3. For a comprehensive history of the English Corn Laws, see Nicholson (1904), Gras (1915), Fay (1932), and Barnes (1965).

4. A partial exception was granted to cereals imported from the North American colonies. A significantly lower pivot price was used to qualify these commodities for sale in the domestic market (Chambers and Mingay 1966, 123; Williamson 1990, 124-125; Stratton 1969, 97).

5. Between 1815 and repeal, the price of wheat reached the pivot price only three times, 1817, 1818, and 1821 (Stratton 1969, 98–100). A related problem was that the Corn Law of 1815 tended to contribute to price fluctuations. The culprit was the lag time between the realization of a certain price and the logistics associated with importation of grain. For example, while poor harvests in 1817 and 1818 sent wheat prices above the pivot price, slowly arriving imports did not quickly suppress prices. By the time that imports had arrived and been warehoused, they served only to depress wheat prices in years when the price of wheat had already fallen below the pivot (Chambers and Mingay 1966, 124–25).

6. The actual economic effect of the 1815 Corn Law is controversial. Fay (1932, 110) claims that given the virtual prohibition of imported cereals between 1815 and 1828, "it is impossible to calculate the indirect effects of a non-existent tax." Certainly this issue confounded British economists in the 1820s (Gambles 1999, ch. 2). Fay thus contends that the principal effect of the nineteenth century Corn Laws was symbolic—a bulwark against a flood of foreign cereals that in reality did not exist. See also Kitson Clark (1951). By contrast, Fairlie (1965, 562) argues that between 1819 and 1826, "there really was a glut of corn in Europe, which the Corn Laws kept back." See also Wordie (2000). This position is supported by the fact that cereal imports increased in the aftermath of the relaxation of import protection after 1828 (Chambers and Mingay 1966, 148–49). In any event, the economic consequences of the Corn Laws were politically subordinate to popular perception, which quite clearly was that the Corn Laws mattered. As Barnes (1965, 189) notes of the mid-1820s, "The price of wheat was not especially high, but to the labourer who was out of work, it offered a tangible explanation for his distress." See also Unwin (1904).

7. The new pivot price was set at 52s., below which imports were prohibited. See Chambers and Mingay (1966, 148) and Barnes (1965, 200).

8. See also his speeches to the House of Commons, March 21 and December 17, 1831 (reprinted in Peel 1843, 379, 384–85).

9. Anti–Corn Law League leader Richard Cobden made this point explicitly during the Corn Law debates of 1845. On March 13 his speech in the House of Commons constituted a clear warning to the aristocracy: "[Y]ou cannot have the advantages of commercial rents and retain your feudal privileges too. If you identify yourselves with the spirit of the age, you may yet do well . . . but your power was never got, and you will not keep it by obstructing that progressive spirit." (Cobden 1870, 2:282–83). See also Peel's implicit concurrence in his speech to the House May 15, 1846 (Peel 1853, 695).

10. For more on Peel's philosophy on reform, and hence his decision to repeal the Corn Laws, see Lusztig (1995).

11. Ireland became controversial in the Conservative ranks again in 1845 when the party divided over whether to continue to fund the Roman Catholic Maynooth College. In a precursor to the 1846 Corn Law, the bill passed over the opposition of Ultra-Tories and only with the support of the opposition Whigs.

12. Lord Malmesbury, for example, predicted that total repeal was not far off. His diary of February 7, 1842, states of Peel, "It is clear that he has thrown over the landed interest, as my father always said he would" (Malmesbury 1884, 139).

13. For complete details, see Peel (1857, 2:app.).

14. Peel also saw trade liberalization as a means of increasing imports and revenues generated by import duties and hence ameliorating the government's finances.

15. Peel himself appeared to recognize this in the debates following the introduction of the Corn Law of 1842. Replying to a Whig critic he noted, "It's easy enough to say apply great principles, but I find that mighty interests have grown up under this present law, and in full dependence on its faith" (quoted in Trumbull 1892, 68).

16. It was generally conceded that the only man capable of securing passage of a repeal bill through the House of Lords was the Duke of Wellington. It was equally well understood that while the Duke deferred to Peel on policy matters, no one else enjoyed such powers of persuasion with Wellington. Leaders of the Anti–Corn Law League were quite clear on this point. A.W. Paulton wrote to Cobden in November 1845: "There are *few* difficulties [sic] in the way of Peel doing it now, but we ought not to blind ourselves to the immense obstacles the Whigs would encounter, should Peel refuse to stir—These would be a strong party in the Commons, and the *whole* of the House of Lords *dead* against it" (emphasis in original). Quoted from the unpublished Cobden papers in McCord (1968, 196). Similarly, Greville's diary (1885, 52) suggests that in December 1845, the Whigs were of the opinion that they would be unable to get repeal through the House of Lords.

17. For more on the political implications of the November 22 announcement, see Greville (1885, esp. 96), Russell (1925, esp. 85), Peel (1857, vol. 2), Barnes (1965, 275–76), Morley (1905, 338), Dreyer (1965), Gash (1972, ch. 16), Read (1987, ch. 4), and Adelman (1989, 66–69).

18. The best histories of the Anti–Corn Law League are Prentice (1853) and McCord (1968).

19. In a June 18 speech he noted, "They are going to repeal it, as I told you—mark my words—at a season of distress. That distress may come; ay, three weeks of showery weather when the wheat is in bloom or ripening would repeal these Corn-laws" (Cobden 1870, 1:299). See also his letter to J. B. Smith, May 29, 1845, cited in McCord (1968, 197).

20. He was quite explicit in his speech of March 2, 1846: "I cannot help thinking that whatever may be the menaces of continued agitation, that agitation would be of a very different character than that which would prevail if no attempt were made to adjust this question" (Peel 1853, 636).

21. Indeed, an exasperated Peel confessed to a supporter, Sir Henry Bunbury, that repeal was undertaken in the interests of his landed critics "whom I verily believe I am protecting from Evils and dangers of which they seem little aware" (quoted in Read 1987, 170).

22. In total there were 312 "landed" Tory MPs and 41 businessmen (Aydelotte 1967, 54).

23. Briggs (1959, 322) suggests that by the mid-1840s, the most active supporters of protection were tenant farmers in the so-called Anti-League.

24. See also Peel's speech to the House of Commons on May 15, 1846 (Peel 1853, 690; Kitson Clark 1951).

25. Under the terms of the Cobden-Chevalier Treaty, privileges granted to France were extended to Britain's other trading partners. Thus, Cobden-Chevalier was a forerunner of the unconditional most-favored-nation principle that underscored the GATT and later, WTO. Duties

that were retained in 1860 were for revenue purposes only; none sheltered import-competing industries (Irwin 1993).

26. Caird later authored a pioneering study of the state of British agriculture in the early 1850s. This quote is from an 1848 pamphlet entitled *High Farming under Liberal Covenants the Best Substitute for Protection*; the pamphlet is excerpted from Mingay (1977, 269–72).

27. Grain prices did dip from their mid-1840s prices. However, mid-1840s prices themselves represented a spike in the context of prices of the 1830s and 1850s (Prothero 1912, 371; Olson and Harris 1959; Turner 1971, 19–20).

28. The Netherlands, Belgium, and New South Wales also maintained open markets (Bowley 1905, 41–46; Gourevitch 1986, ch. 3).

29. While the commission also suggested that there were burdens on farmers that the government might relieve, it is interesting to note that commission was "led by the landowning aristocracy and gentry," and that its farmer witnesses "overwhelming reflect[ed] the interests of corn growers . . . with almost all concerned sharing a similar set of assumptions as to the nature of English agriculture" (Fletcher 1961, 426–27). In other words, despite a composition that might be thought most likely to reflect the interests of neoprotectionists, the Royal Commission found the primary cause of the farmers' plight to be less a function of the invisible hand than of the celestial finger.

30. During the 1880s, calls for a return to protection were more widespread; the National Fair Trade League was founded in 1881. Fair traders were a coalition of free traders who wanted to force open markets abroad and advocates of a league of Imperial preferences (Armitage-Smith 1898, ch. 10; Eichengreen 1992, 167–68; Howe 1997, 213–18). This incongruous agenda found voice in the Conservative Party, although that party's commitment to protectionism in the 1880s remained ambivalent. The fair-trade movement did provoke controversy and debate within the Conservative Party. Delegates to the 1887 party conference voted overwhelmingly in favor of tariff reform; the party leadership, however, sidestepped the controversy (Turner 1971, 21). Brown suggests that the Tory strategy in the 1880s was to "damn without defining" an alternative to the trade policy status quo (Brown 1943, 61; see also ch. 3).

31. Some caveats must be noted. First, the sample is small. Van Vugt's sample consisted of roughly 10 percent of emigrants in 1851. While this yielded an n of 2224, the number of farmers in the sample was just 475. Second, farmer is a fairly general category and almost certainly included agricultural laborers who would have used the more generic term for emigration purposes. Third, and related, the census likely would have employed a more rigorous standard of occupational classification. Indeed, agricultural laborers were underrepresented on passenger lists when compared to census data. Van Vugt himself acknowledged some of these limitations.

32. I emphasize the word *rough*. The data set is small; fewer than one in six emigrating farmers provided information on their county of residence.

33. The remainder were from counties not defined by Caird. Of the two intermediate classifications, 20 percent formerly resided in moderately distressed counties, 13.2 percent in minimally distressed (Van Vugt 1988, 422).

34. The objective of the English (later Royal) Agricultural Society was "To encourage men of science in their attention to the improvement of agricultural implements, the construction of farm buildings and cottages, the application of chemistry to the general purposes of agriculture, the destruction of insects injurious to vegetable life, and the eradication of weeds." See Russell (1966, 110–11, ch. 4).

35. Loans were provided at 1.5 to 3.5 percent below the normal rate, and accounted for roughly one-sixth of the total estimated expenditure on drainage between 1846 and 1876 (Heuckel 1981, 194).

36. It is not clear, however, that investment in drainage generated an optimal return (Murphy 1973, 606–7).

37. For more on mixed farming, see Jones (1974) and Grigg (1989, ch. 14).

38. Milk consumption trebled between 1860 and 1900, while consumption of meat doubled (Thompson 1981, 112). For more income and population growth patterns, see Feinstein (1972, 42).

Notes to Chapter 3

1. This is the primary motivation behind Alexander Hamilton's famous report to Congress in 1791. See Hamilton (1893).

2. The substance of Clay's philosophy is evident in his speech in the House of Representatives during the tariff debates of 1824 (Clay 1893).

3. For more on the Tariff of Abominations, see Stanwood (1903, 1:ch. 8) and Ashley (1926, 149–55).

4. Obviously such regional characterizations obscure internal deviations. More detail is provided in Taussig (1923, ch. 2).

5. The South-West alliance of the early 1830s was based on western support for a lower tariff in exchange for the South's support for a proposal that the federal government dedicate budgetary surplus to price reductions for public lands in the West. See Van Deusen (1959, 40) and Wellington (1914, ch. 2). The 1840s alliance was a response to new opportunities for western exports upon Corn Law repeal. See James and Lake (1989).

6. In the period 1837–1861, tariffs constituted roughly 90 percent of federal revenues (Pastor 1980, 73).

7. In fact, almost every session during the war saw the passage of some incremental protectionist legislation. For more on the Civil War tariffs, see Stanwood (1903, 2:ch. 13) and Taussig (1923, pt. II, ch. 1).

8. Indeed, the war tariffs survived long after the repeal of most of the internal revenue statutes (Stern 1971, 2). See also Gideonse (1944, 560–61) and Taussig (1923, esp. 165–70).

9. With Democratic Party gains in the elections of 1892, Congress passed the mildly liberalizing Wilson-Gorman Tariff in 1894, but both its effects and duration were limited.

10. For more on reciprocity policy in the United States, see United States Tariff Commission (1919, 18–20, 39–42).

11. The System of '96 was the formalization of the alliance among the Republican Party and high-tariff/tight-money industrialists and bankers. For more on the tariff acts of the 1890s, see Taussig (1923, pt. II, chs. 5–7), Stanwood (1903, 2:chs. 16–18), Ashley (1926, pt. II, chs. 6–8), Stern (1971), Terrill (1973, ch. 7), Becker (1982, ch. 4), and Lake (1988a, chs. 3–4; 1988b).

12. In part this was a function of the split within the Republican Party between traditional Republicans and the progressive, or Bull Moose, faction under Theodore Roosevelt, which broke away from the party in 1912.

13. For more on the Underwood Tariff, see Taussig (1923, pt. II, ch. 9) and Lake (1988a, ch. 5).

14. It must be noted, however, that a large number of noncompeting imports were allowed to enter the U.S. market on the duty-free list. As a result, the average rate of duty as applied

against total imports was actually a fair bit more liberal than the average post–Civil War tariff (see Lake 1988a, 194; O'Halloran 1994, 4).

15. The best discussion of the Smoot-Hawley bargaining process remains Schattschneider (1935). See also Larkin (1940, ch. 5) and Brenner (1978, ch. 5).

16. As America's trading partners retaliated, world exports fell by roughly one-half between 1928 and 1932, and U.S. exports declined by two-thirds (Yoffie 1985, 106).

17. For more on the AAA, see Wallace (1944), Schlesinger (1958, esp. chs. 2–5), and Dallek (1979).

18. For more on the NIRA, see Johnson (1935), Schlesinger (1958, esp. chs. 6–10), Hawley (1966), and Finegold and Skocpol (1984).

19. In the 1920s, for example, the domestic market absorbed 90 percent of output by U.S. manufacturers (Smith 1990).

20. For more on growing business opposition to the First New Deal, see Burns (1956, 202–8), Hawley (1975, 64–65), and Skocpol (1980).

21. For more on the decline of the First New Deal coalition, see Lusztig (1996, ch. 3).

22. For more on the American Liberty League, see Rudolph (1950), Wolfskill (1962), and Berkowitz and McQuaid (1980).

23. For more on the divisions between nationalist and internationalist business, see Ferguson (1984), Frieden (1988), and Dallek (1979).

24. The 1945 renewal of the RTAA allowed the president to reduce tariffs by as much as 50 percent from their January 1, 1945, levels.

25. For more on the RTAA, see Tasca (1938), Sayre (1939), United States Tariff Commission (1948), Hull (1948, chs. 26–27), Brenner (1978), Haggard (1988), and Gilligan (1997).

26. It is important to note that while the RTAA did lower some agricultural tariffs, its impact was restricted largely to the industrial sector. As a result of the continued support for the New Deal of the agricultural sector, severe restrictions were placed on the State Department's ability to negotiate reciprocal agreements in agricultural goods (Verdier 1994, esp. 188). Moreover, rents lost to tariff reductions were offset by generous farm subsidies and by the fact that agricultural products were often covered by quotas in reciprocal trade deals. See, for example, Roosevelt's speech to the American Farm Bureau Convention, December 9, 1935, in Nixon (1969, 3:115–16).

27. For more on the TMA, see Cleveland (1976) and Dallek (1979).

28. For more on the Wagner Act and the effects of the Second New Deal on organized labor, see Derber (1975), Finegold and Skocpol (1984), and Skocpol and Finegold (1990).

29. For more on the Social Security Act, see Altmeyer (1966) and Berkowitz and McQuaid (1980).

30. As Bailey, Goldstein, and Weingast (1997, esp. 318) suggest, the construction of a support coalition for trade liberalization in Congress is facilitated when tariff reductions are bundled with increased access to foreign markets.

31. Obviously certain problems were inherent in the chief-supplier principle. Small countries, for example, were less likely to be principal suppliers of any commodities. Moreover, some suppliers were roughly equivalent in their supply of a particular commodity. Finally some commodities for which a country was a chief supplier were fairly marginal to that country's export profile (Hody 1996, 127–28).

32. See also Roosevelt's letter to Representative William Fiesinger of Ohio, July 9, 1935, in Nixon (1969, 2:551–52).

33. As one internal State Department memo suggested, "A reciprocity program which hurt

no one could not go very far in improving the general economic welfare" (quoted in Eckes 1995, 145).

34. See, for example, his press conference of July 17, 1935, in Nixon (1969, 2:566–68); see also his letters to Frederic Coudert and Elliot Wadsworth, November 23 and 25, 1935, respectively, in Nixon (1969, 3:90, 91).

35. Data are drawn from 1939 import statistics, average ad valorem equivalent rates are drawn from the United States Tariff Commission's sample of 80 percent of the total dutiable imports in 1939. See also Letiche (1948, 24–35).

36. For a comprehensive discussion of the escape clause, see Leddy and Norwood (1962).

37. For more on postwar protectionism associated with the no-injury concept, see Bidwell (1956, ch. 10), Leddy and Norwood (1962), and Hody (1996, ch. 6).

38. This point is supported by the event study analysis of the RTAA undertaken by Schnietz (2003).

39. Gilligan's analysis (1997) generates similar findings. While space does not allow for a full articulation of his argument, Gilligan constructs a model to measure the demand for liberalization in each congressional district, for eight pieces of U.S. trade legislation, including the RTAA and subsequent renewals. This demand is a function of the economic (and hence political) importance of industries lobbying for and against liberalization in each district. Gilligan concludes, using logic similar to that of the limits of rent seeking model, that the reciprocal trade agreements created an incentive for exporters to lobby for market access abroad. As a result, he finds that "demand for liberalization did rise substantially with the advent of the reciprocal trade agreements program and that the increase in the demand for liberalization had a great deal to do with the liberalization of American trade policy in the 1930s" (118).

40. Testimony of Frederick E. Hasler, President of the Chamber of Commerce of the State of New York (United States 1943a, 925).

41. Testimony of Gerald Le Vino, Chairman of the New York City Committee on Foreign Trade, Commerce and Industry (United States 1943a, 777–78).

42. While the NAM's membership during this period consisted overwhelmingly of companies employing fewer than five hundred workers, much of the organization's leadership came from big business (Cleveland 1948; *Fortune* 1948, 166). For more on the NAM, see Burch (1973).

43. Large manufacturers were those whose annual production of goods totaled $50 million or more. Small manufacturers produced less than $1 million worth of goods per annum, while small retailers sold less than $30,000 per year (*Fortune* 1939).

44. The poll consisted of 903 executives from both large and small firms (*Fortune* 1955). See also the study on which the *Fortune* article was based: Bauer, Keller, and de la Sola Pool (1955).

Notes to Chapter 4

1. Díaz was in power between 1876 and 1910, save for a brief interregnum in 1881–1884.

2. For more on the role of technocrats in the modernization of economies, see Williamson (1994a).

3. This is an error that the new modernizers did not commit. Salinas was careful to combine trade liberalization with the construction of the welfare system, under the rubric of the Program for National Solidarity (PRONASOL) and reform of the communal land-holding system in the countryside.

4. For more on the revolutionary and prerevolutionary period in Mexico, see inter alia Tweedie (1917), Vernon (1963), Reynolds (1970), Wilkie and Michaels (1969), Cockcroft (1972), Hansen (1974), and Hamilton (1982, ch. 2).

5. CANACINTRA was organized as a member of CONCAMIN. However, its size and importance justifies its classification as one of the prominent confederations in its own right.

6. For more on business-state relations during the formative years of the PRI, see Bensabat (1995, 53), Purcell and Purcell (1977, 1980), Newell and Rubio (1984), Mena (1987), Heredia (1992), Ten Kate and Wallace (1980), and Schneider (2002).

7. Specifically, the other allied organizations are the Consejo Mexicano de Hombres de Negocios (Mexican Businessmen's Council, CMNH), Asociación de Banqueros de México (Association of Mexican Bankers, ABM), Asociación Mexicana de Instituciones de Seguros (Association of Mexican Insurance Institutions, AMIS), Asociación Mexicana de Intermediarios Bursátiles (Mexican Securities Industry Association, AMIB), and Consejo Nacional Agropecuario (National Agriculture and Livestock Council, CNA) (Tirado 1998, 188–91; Bensabat 1995, 94–95; Heredia 1992, 295). CANACINTRA's representation within the CCE has been mediated through its parent chamber, CONCAMIN.

8. For more on the CCE, see Tirado (1998) and Schneider (2002).

9. For more on ISI, see Hirschman (1968). For a discussion of the intellectual origins of ISI in Latin America, see Love (1980). For a specific application to Mexico, see Izquierdo (1964), King (1970), Bueno (1971), and Story (1986).

10. The most famous articulation of this argument is Hamilton's 1791 report to Congress (Hamilton 1893).

11. In Mexico the dominant institution of public financing was Nacional Financiera (Financial National), created in 1934.

12. Story cautions that inconsistencies in census taking during the years discussed may create some distortions. However, the figures are useful for broad illustration of the trend.

13. Obviously, some export growth is required to avoid a chronic negative trade balance. To this end, foreign investors in Mexico were obliged to meet "performance requirements." In other words, a certain proportion of locally produced goods by foreign manufacturers had to be exported (Weintraub 1988, 6–7).

14. Put differently, total federal government expenditure and investment in 1970 was 13.1 percent of GNP. By 1976, that figure had risen to 39.6 percent of GNP (Newell and Rubio 1984, 126).

15. As Lustig notes, this optimism was not completely unfounded. She cites the 1981 *World Development Report*'s prediction of 3 percent real growth in the price of oil throughout the 1980s, which would have seen the price of oil in 1980 dollars rise from approximately $32 to $42 per barrel by 1990 (Lustig 1992, 21; Newell and Rubio 1984, 251).

16. For details of the protocol of accession, see Story (1982, 773).

17. The most thorough analyst of Mexico's 1980 GATT decision is Story (1982, 1986). See also Escobar Toledo (1987), Camp (1989), and Davis (1992).

18. Between late 1979 and late 1981, Mexico took on roughly $26 billion in new debts to foreign banks (an increase of nearly 100 percent). Of this new debt, about $17 billion was in short-term loans (Kuczynski 1988, 79).

19. The logic of this institutional shift corresponds with Goldstein's (1988) thesis that institutional innovation in the realm of trade policy is facilitated by crisis and the perceived failure of the existing institutional structure to deal with the crisis.

20. The price of oil fell precipitously in 1986, to $12 per barrel from $25.50 the previous year (Lustig 1992, 39).

21. For more on the intellectual antecedents of PRONASOL, see Salinas de Gortari (1982), Dresser (1992), and Needler (1993).

22. This argument is spelled out in more detail in Lusztig (1996, ch. 5).

23. The logic is consistent with welfare economics, whereby surplus profits from market reforms are redistributed to those who do not directly benefit from the initiative. See Kaldor (1939) and Scitovszky (1941).

24. This sentiment is captured in the oft-quoted line from Lázaro Cárdenas, architect of Mexico's corporatist system: "Poor Mexico, so far from God and so close to the United States." For more on the nationalist element of Mexican corporatism, see Stevens (1977).

25. Between 1987 and 1994, the Bolsa Mexicana de Valores was among the fastest growing stock markets in the world. By the end of 1993, capitalization was at U.S. $200.6 billion. In 1993 alone, capitalization increased by 43.9 percent (Mexican Investment Board 1994).

26. CCE president Francisco Calderon stated early in 1980 that it would not be in Mexico's interest to join the GATT with the peso as overvalued as it was (Escobar Toledo 1987, 70). Such a weak justification suggests that the CCE was internally divided and unwilling to take a firm stance.

27. See also Bensabat (1995, 211–12), Schneider (2002), and Thacker (1998).

28. Smaller organizations such as the Confederacion National de la Pequena Propiedad (National Confederation of Small Business Owners) also opposed NAFTA (Bensabat 1995, 212).

29. COECE represented 114 sectors of the Mexican economy as well as sixteen business associations including CANACINTRA (Poitras and Robinson 1994, 17).

30. On the other hand, given these inefficiencies, CANACINTRA has opposed plans to accelerate the tariff reduction schedule under NAFTA (*Economic News and Analysis on Mexico* 1994).

Notes to Chapter 5

1. The Corn Laws of 1815, 1822, and 1828, for example, all granted special preferences for Canadian flour and wheat. Even more important was the Canada Corn Act, which permitted free entry of American wheat provided it was ground in Canadian mills (Easterbrook and Aitken 1967, 352).

2. As the president of the Toronto Board of Trade lamented upon repeal, "We are in the same condition as a man suddenly precipitated from a lofty eminence. We are labouring under concussion of the brain" (quoted in Porritt 1908, 55). The effects were almost immediate. Wheat and flour exports fell from 3,883,000 bushels to 2,248,000 from 1847 to 1848; square timber exports from New Brunswick alone went from 290,000 tons in 1846 to 150,000 tons the following year (Cross 1971, 6).

3. For more on the Elgin-Marcy Treaty, see Haynes (1892).

4. Confederation united Canada (which was divided into Quebec and Ontario) with New Brunswick and Nova Scotia. In part, the logic was to create an internal market among the British North American colonies denied free access to the U.S. market. Manitoba joined in 1870, British Columbia the following year, and Prince Edward Island in 1873. The remaining British North American colony, Newfoundland, did not enter Confederation until 1949. Canada was a "self-governing dominion"—essentially a state within an imperial federation— prior to receiving full independence in 1931. For more on Confederation, see Waite (1962).

5. The incompatibility between the fur trade and agriculture helps to explain the late settlement of the Canadian West, which had been controlled by the Hudson's Bay Company until the transfer of Rupert's Land to Canada in 1868. As a means of preventing the expansion of agricultural production on its land, the Hudson's Bay Company had restricted white settlement through the first seven decades of the nineteenth century (Conway 1994, 15–16).

6. A brief Liberal interregnum in the early 1870s witnessed another Canadian attempt to establish free trade. A draft treaty was negotiated in 1874. The treaty was notable in that it marked Canada's willingness to liberalize trade in industrial goods. However, the Reconstruction era was inopportune for such an agreement and it went down to defeat in the U.S. Senate. This ended the last real chance for reciprocity in the nineteenth century. Although all Canadian tariff bills until 1894 offered at least some form of reciprocal free trade in nonmanufactured goods, and the Liberals fought the 1891 election on an "unrestricted reciprocity" platform, the increasingly protectionist United States evinced little interest in pursuing free trade. The one exception came during the Harrison administration, but the United States demanded reciprocity in the form of a customs union, a condition that Canada was unwilling to meet (Ellis 1939, ch. 1).

7. See chapter 3.

8. For more on the National Policy, see Porritt (1908), Fowke (1952), Canada (1954, ch. 3), Easterbrook and Aitken (1967, ch. 17), and Williams (1994, 26–33).

9. French Canadian nationalists objected on the grounds that a larger military was more likely to draw Canada into Britain's military obligations.

10. The proposed treaty consisted of three parts. Most primary products, as well as a very few manufactured items, were to enjoy duty-free access across the border; secondary food products, agricultural implements, and a few other specified commodities were to receive identical, lower tariff rates; finally, both countries made concessions on certain goods in exchange for consideration on other items (Brown and Cook 1974, 180).

11. In the early 1920s, the Liberal government of Mackenzie King advocated a "measure of reciprocity" between Canada and the United States, and King suggested that "it is well we should try again" (McDiarmid 1946, 274). As noted below, King's government ultimately did negotiate a free trade deal with the United States immediately following World War II, but King decided not to risk pursuing it.

12. For more on the emergence of the branch plant economy in Canada, see Laxer (1989, ch. 5).

13. The average nominal tariff rate on dutiable imports fell from 22 percent in 1941 to slightly over 16 percent by 1960. However, this relatively low rate masks the fact that tariffs were unevenly distributed across industries and were prohibitive in certain sectors (Finlayson and Bertasi 1992, 23).

14. Other, minor bilateral accords were reached during this time, most notably on taxes, air travel, antitrust measures, and nuclear energy (Canada 1985a, 1:227–28).

15. The escape clause, which provides temporary import relief for industries demonstrably harmed by trade liberalization, has long been a mainstay of U.S. trade policy. During the Kennedy Administration, the escape clause had been strengthened, limiting relief to industries that could prove serious injury, the "major cause" of which was import penetration that resulted from U.S. tariff concessions. The operational definition of "major cause," moreover, was the demonstration that the injury caused by import penetration was greater than all other factors combined. Under the Trade Act of 1974, the threshold for escape-clause relief was relaxed; industries were subsequently eligible for relief if they could demonstrate that imports were a

"substantial cause of serious injury, or the threat thereof." In addition, industries were no longer obliged to demonstrate a causal link between injury and specific tariff concessions (Destler 1995, 142–43).

16. Under the fast-track procedure, congressional oversight is limited to approval or rejection of an agreement as negotiated—no amendments are permitted as part of the ratification process. A similar process had been instituted under the 1934 RTAA. Under the RTAA, however, while the president enjoyed slightly more autonomy from Congress, his authority did not extend to NTBs.

17. For example, in addition to numerous individual corporations, the following industry associations sent written briefs to the Trade and Tariffs Committee (submission dates are in parentheses): Canadian Chemical Producers' Association (February 1974), Canadian Paint Manufacturers' Association (May 1974), Rubber Association of Canada (June 1974), Machinery and Equipment Manufacturers' Association (June 1974), Society of the Plastics Industry of Canada (June 1974), Canadian Particle Board Association (July 1974), Canadian Council of Furniture Manufacturers (August 1974), Canadian Manufacturers' Association (August 1974), Canadian Battery Manufacturers' Association (September 1974), Tanners' Association of Canada (December 1974), Canadian Printing Ink Manufacturers' Association (December 1974), Canadian Truck Trailer Manufacturers' Association (December 1974), Canadian Hardwood Bureau (January 1975), Canadian Grocery Bag Manufacturers' Association (March 1975), Canadian Cast Iron Soil Pipe Association (April 1975), Society of the Button Industry (April 1975), Boxboard Manufacturers' Association (April 1975), Canadian Toy Manufacturers' Association (June 1975), and Canadian Chamber of Commerce (June 1978). While these briefs have not been published, they are accessible under the Freedom of Information Act. Submissions to the Senate Standing Committee on Foreign Affairs also suggest a strong bias in favor of protectionism in Canada (Canada 1978b).

18. Few were as candid in their pursuit of monopoly/oligopoly rents as were the officers of Union Trunk and Luggage: "We are the only manufacturer in Canada. We supply the entire Canadian market. Any tariff negotiation that might be done should be very careful not to allow trunks from other lands to be sold in Canada. We must have the entire volume of Canada to maintain minimum production runs and continue to increase our productivity." Submission from Union Trunk and Luggage to the Canadian Tariffs and Trade Committee, Department of External Affairs, August 30, 1974.

19. The recommendations were in the third report, issued in 1982 and bearing the same title as the previous reports, of the Standing Committee's investigation (Canada 1982).

20. Other aspects of Canada's foreign policy also sought to signal independence from the United States. The most obvious was Canada's defiance of the U.S. embargo of Cuba.

21. The two-tiered pricing scheme was a carry over from the National Oil Policy of 1973, which, unlike the NEP, had featured negotiation between the federal and provincial governments with respect to the domestic price of oil. Under the National Oil Policy and the NEP, exported oil and natural gas were subject to an export tax that captured the differential between domestic and market prices. These taxes then were used to subsidize the cost of imported energy. By 1980, the domestic price had fallen to less than 45 percent of the market price of petroleum (Norrie 1988, 177–80).

22. Under the terms of the NEP, the federal government increased its share of petroleum revenues from 10 to 24 percent (Norrie 1988, 181). For more on the NEP, see James (1990).

23. The view is not unreasonable. The term NEP is somewhat of a misnomer insofar as the energy component was restricted to petroleum products, almost exclusively produced in west-

ern Canada. Left unregulated was hydroelectric energy, which is produced primarily in Quebec and Ontario.

24. Prior to 1984, the Liberals had been in power in 1896–1911, 1921–1926, 1926–1930, 1935–1957, 1962–1979, and 1979–1984.

25. These elections took place in 1968, 1972, 1974, 1979, and 1980. The 1979 election saw the Conservatives win a plurality of the seats and form a short-lived minority government.

26. The Quiet Revolution characterized the 1960s in Quebec. It saw the secularization of that largely Catholic province and hence the economic and political modernization of the French Canadian nation.

27. Specifically, these reforms entailed an indigenous constitutional amending formula and a Charter of Rights and Freedoms. The former corrected an anomaly born of Canada's gradual independence from Britain. Until 1982, Canada's constitution was an act of the British Parliament and hence could only be amended by that body. Several previous attempts to forge unanimous provincial approval on a domestic amending formula had failed.

28. The constitutional crisis of 1980–1982 is far more complicated than can be described here. For excellent comprehensive insight into the issues, see Romanow, Whyte, and Leeson (1984) and Russell (1993, esp. ch. 8).

29. For a fuller account, see Lusztig (1996, ch. 4).

30. Some clarification may be necessary for those not familiar with Canada's byzantine constitutional politics. Canada's post-1982 constitutional amending formula is extremely complex. However, for the Meech Lake Accord, constitutional entrenchment would have required ratification by all ten provincial legislatures and by both houses of the federal Parliament, within three years of the date that the first legislature ratified the accord. For more on the Meech Lake Accord, see Hogg (1988) and Swinton and Rogerson (1988).

31. Space does not permit a full articulation of the logroll. For a comprehensive discussion, see Lusztig (1996, ch. 4). For an excellent discussion of the genesis of the free-trade decision from within the bureaucracy, see Doern and Tomlin (1991) and Hart (1994).

32. This seemingly unlikely alliance was motivated by a mutual antipathy toward the weakening of the redistributive role of the state at the expense of the market.

33. Speech to the Conference Board of Canada, Toronto, February 6, 1985 (quoted in Hart 1994, 77).

34. For more on the BCNI, see Langille (1987) and Coleman (1988, esp. 83–87).

35. The classic study of the CMA remains Clark (1938); see also Coleman (1988, 195–98). Forster (1986, ch. 10) provides an excellent discussion of the role of manufacturers' associations in the National Policy campaign.

36. CMA, Submission to the Canadian Trade and Tariff Committee, August 1974. See also the testimony of Laurent Thibault, later president of the CMA, to the Senate Standing Committee on Foreign Affairs, November 18, 1976. By contrast, Thibault's testimony to the House of Commons Standing Committee on External Affairs and International Trade, November 18, 1987, suggested a far different consensus on the part of his organization's members: "I think it is important for the committee to know that we find the manufacturing community very supportive of this [proposed Canada-U.S. Free Trade Agreement] right across the country. We find it quite ironic that despite statements by a number of people in politics who are against the agreement, they certainly do not reflect the views of the manufacturing community in our forums across the country." (See Canada, Parliament, 1987, *Minutes of Proceedings*, Ottawa: Minister of Supply and Services, for the appropriate committees.)

37. See Canada, Parliament, 1987, *Minutes of Proceedings*, Ottawa: Minister of Supply and Services.

38. See Canada, Parliament, November 3, 1987, *Minutes of Proceedings*, Ottawa: Minister of Supply and Services. The CFIB conducted 42,027 face-to-face interviews with its members. Thirty-four percent favored free trade, 13 percent opposed it, and 53 percent had no position. Another internal survey by the Canadian Organization of Small Business (COSB) found that more than two-thirds of its members supported free trade in principle. See the testimony of Geoffrey Hale, vice president of the COSB, House Committee on External Affairs and International Trade, *Minutes of Proceedings*, November 3, 1987.

39. Submission to the Canadian Trade and Tariff Committee, July 20, 1978, and Canada, Parliament, House Committee on External Affairs and International Trade, November 4, 1987, *Minutes of Proceedings*, Ottawa: Minister of Supply and Services.

40. Submission to the Canadian Trade and Tariff Committee, June 1975, and correspondence with the author regarding the organization's position on CUFTA and NAFTA, April 6, 1994.

41. Submission to the Canadian Trade and Tariff Committee, February 14, 1974; and Canada, Parliament, House Committee on External Affairs and International Trade, November 5, 1987, *Minutes of Proceedings*, Ottawa: Minister of Supply and Services.

42. Submission to the Canadian Trade and Tariff Committee, June 26, 1974, and correspondence with the author regarding the organization's position on CUFTA and NAFTA, April 5, 1994.

43. Submission to the Canadian Trade and Tariff Committee, June 1974, and correspondence with the author regarding the organization's position on CUFTA and NAFTA, April 11, 1994.

44. Submission from the Canadian Steel Institute to the Canadian Trade and Tariff Committee, May 27, 1975, and testimony of the Canadian Steel Producers' Association, Canada, Parliament, House Committee on External Affairs and International Trade, November 3, 1987, *Minutes of Proceedings*, Ottawa: Minister of Supply and Services.

45. The Mulroney government made two fundamental errors in its constitutional strategy. First, Mulroney neglected to consider the implications of the fact that the ratification deadline for the Meech Lake Accord extended well beyond that for the Free Trade Agreement. Indeed, the three-year window for ratification in every provincial legislature allowed too much opportunity for defection. Second, and more damaging, upon the failure of the Meech Lake Accord, the Mulroney government sought to throw good money after bad. It brokered a second constitutional amendment package—the 1992 Charlottetown Accord. This accord, which was to be ratified in ten discrete provincial referenda, was a far more inclusive package than the Meech Lake Accord had been. Featuring an unprecedented sixty constitutional amendments, it sought to make the constitution all things to all voting constituents. The result was widespread dissatisfaction. Referenda failed in every western province; even worse, the referendum failed in Quebec, where alienated voters felt Quebec had given up too much to receive too little. The result sealed the electoral fate of the Conservative Party. For more on the constitutional debacle, 1987–1992, see Simeon (1990), Cairns (1990), Russell (1993), and Lusztig (1994).

Notes to Chapter 6

1. For more on the politics of the shift to neoliberalism by parties of the left, see Schwartz (1994) and Wilson (1994).

2. For more on the early economic history of New Zealand, see Thornton (1982) and Hawke (1985).

3. For a good discussion of NAFTA, see Holmes (1966), Burtt (1977), and Hoadley (1995).

4. For more on licensing reforms in the 1979 budget, see Lattimore and Wooding (1996, 326–29).

5. See also Douglas (1993, 29).

6. The Manfed maintained this position into 1982 as well. According to then-president Bill Christie, "The Federation stands by its opposition to the Government's objective of a full trade agreement covering all goods. We do not consider it appropriate that New Zealand should enter into this type of commitment at this stage" (*Manufacturer* 1982b).

7. See also the statement of then-president Bill Christie (*Manufacturer* 1982c).

8. Hand binding, or precommitment, is a common tactic used by reformers uncertain as to their abilities to withstand countervailing demands by domestic constituents. See Elster (1979).

9. For more on the specifics of the CER, see Thakur and Gold (1983), Bollard (1986), Wooding (1987), and Alchin (1990).

10. Sandrey and Scobie (1994) put the pastoral assistance rate slightly higher, at 3 percent by 1994.

11. For a comprehensive list of reforms during the period 1984–1990, see Wooding (1987), Savage and Bollard (1990), Rayner and Lattimore (1991), Bollard (1992, 14–27; 1994), and Hoadley (1995).

12. For more on this proposed accord, see Dwyer (1995).

13. The Business Roundtable consists of the chief executive officers of roughly sixty of New Zealand's largest businesses. See Cullinane (1995).

14. This is not to say that all sectoral federations also shifted their positions by 1994. Some, especially those that had benefited from higher rates of protection under the industry assistance plans, continued to resist reduction of state-supplied rents. However, these industries were increasingly isolated in the 1990s. See the 1994 trade policy submissions to the New Zealand Ministry of Commerce by the textile, apparel, and footwear industries (New Zealand 1994, 54–55, 93). On the other hand, even such traditionally protectionist sectors as the motor vehicle industry showed signs of moderating their positions (New Zealand 1994, 50–52).

15. Roger Kerr, the executive director of the New Zealand Business Roundtable, a pro–free-trade big-business lobby (the New Zealand equivalent to the U.S. Business Roundtable) favorably contrasts the actions of the Lange and Bolger governments with the path of least resistance strategy followed by Robert Muldoon, who "repeatedly backed down when the going got tough." Indeed, Kerr suggests that the "timid gradualism" pursued by Muldoon served to increase the hardships for New Zealand producers and to militate against a rapid recovery (Kerr 1995). As Roger Douglas himself put it (1993, 217–18), "When governments compromise, the result is mediocre policies and an increasingly dissatisfied public."

16. Labour, of course, was defeated in the election of 1990. However, it is important to note three things. First, Labour won a majority government in 1987, at a time when the effects of rent reductions were more likely to have pinched. Second, Labour was afflicted with a number of internal conflicts, including a falling out with Roger Douglas. Third, and most importantly, the National Party government that succeeded Labour carried on the policies of its predecessor.

17. It was the Labour government's unwillingness to move with the alacrity he thought necessary that led to Douglas's departure in 1988.

18. See especially the analysis of the Australian case (chapter 7).

NOTES TO CHAPTER 7

1. Import licenses were converted to tariffs after 1960, but tariff rates were sufficiently high that tariffication did not constitute a reduction in state-supplied rents. See Lloyd (1973).

2. For more on early Australian import protection, see Carmody (1952), Crawford (1968), Glezer (1982), Anderson (1987), Dyster and Meredith (1990), and Ravenhill (1994).

3. See also (federal director of ACMA) Anderson (1967), Associated Chambers of Manufacturers of Australia (1968), and Bell (1989).

4. See also Noble and Nettle (1972); for a comprehensive discussion of rent-seeking activity during this period, see Rattigan (1986, chs. 3–4).

5. For more on increased protectionism in Australia after 1974, see Warhurst (1982), esp. ch. 3.

6. For the non-PMV and -TCF sectors, aggregate levels of effective import protection fell from 23 percent to 14 percent between these years (Anderson 1987, 178).

7. For more on industry plans, see Stewart (1990, 1994) and Capling and Galligan (1992).

8. Significantly, Keating's commitment to trade liberalization weakened after he became prime minister.

9. In addition, the government maintained the Duty Drawback and TEXCO schemes, in which goods are imported duty free if they have value added and are then exported, as well as the Policy By-Law System, which permits duty-free import of certain capital equipment for companies engaged in production for export (Australia 1995).

10. For more on the TCS, see Senator Chris Schacht (1995), minister for small business, customs, and construction.

11. Indeed, the APEC initiative appears to provide the opportunity for the appearance of action on the trade liberalization front while requiring few politically difficult decisions. See Ravenhill (1996).

12. The Keating government first adopted this position as early as the spring of 1992. See Stutchbury (1992b).

13. This logic is similar to Milner's (1988) argument on how globalization of industry facilitates freer trade.

14. This point must be qualified, however, as key players within the CAI lobbied Hawke to abandon plans to proceed with the 1988 tariff reductions.

NOTES TO CHAPTER 8

1. This is the basis for world system and dependency theories, which describe the global division of labor in Marxian terms, suggesting that the southern (or peripheral) economies are exploited by the northern (core) ones in terms analogous to the relationship between proletariat and bourgeoisie. See, for example, Baran and Sweezy (1966), Wallerstein (1974), Chase-Dunn (1975), and Valenzuela and Valenzuela (1978).

2. For a fuller discussion of ISI, see chapter 5.

3. Between 1960 and 1979, for example, Mexico and Brazil attracted more than 70 percent of foreign direct investment and produced over 60 percent of Latin America's industrial output (Green 1995, 17–18).

4. By 1953 interest rates were negative in real terms insofar as they were lower than the annual rate of inflation. See Davis (1963).

5. For more on CORFO, see Mamalakis (1976, ch. 12) and Faundez (1988, 43–50).

6. The problem was both large and sustained. Between 1940 and 1970, the money supply

grew by an annual average of almost 31 percent. Between 1965 and 1970, the expansion rate was 42.7 percent (Velasco 1994, 388); see also Davis (1963).

7. For more on agrarian reforms under Frei, see Loveman (1976).

8. Because no presidential candidate had secured an absolute majority, the Chilean constitution mandated that Congress was to select the president.

9. For more on the philosophy of the Popular Unity Party, see Allende (1973).

10. To give some idea of the problem involved, Brazil's gross foreign debt requirement for 1982 alone was roughly $20 billion (Bacha and Malan 1989, 132).

11. For more on the *Abertura*, see Lamounier (1989) and Martínez-Lara (1996, ch. 1).

12. Key names include Sergio de Castro, Pablo Baraona, Alvaro Bardón, Rolf Luders, Miguel Kast, and Sergio de la Cuadra. A superb history of the influence of the Chicago Boys in the "second" Chilean revolution of the 1970s is Valdés (1985).

13. In fact, even the 10 percent tariff was breached for certain commodities from member states of the Latin American Integration Association.

14. For more on the Cruzado Plan, see Baer (1995, ch. 8) and Cardoso and Dornbusch (1987, 288–92).

15. The Bresser Plan also was a wage and price control, but with a more flexible mandate. Wages and prices were to be evaluated every ninety days. The exchange rate also was subject to periodic reevaluation. Like its predecessor, however, the Bresser Plan was successful in the short term, but double-digit monthly inflation quickly returned (Baer 1995, 180–81).

16. For more on the effects of the 1988 constitution, see Montero (2000).

17. All savings account assets higher than roughly $1,300 were frozen (and ravished by inflation) for eighteen months.

18. For more on MERCOSUR, see Roett (1999) and Kaltenthaler and Mora (2002).

19. To this end, state governments were prohibited from borrowing from their own banks. In addition, a (temporary) clawback was instituted from money earmarked for the states. This clawback was constitutionally entrenched in 1993 under the auspices of the Social Emergency Fund, which permitted the federal government to withhold 20 percent of transfer payments to the states to counter social emergencies. See de Sousa (1999, 52) and Kingstone (1999, 192–93).

20. Specifically, this refers to import licensing, quotas, administered pricing, and outright prohibitions.

21. This was especially evident following the 2001 MERCOSUR summit in Asunción. See Masi (2001).

22. See also Hakim (2002, esp. 158). Perhaps the best illustration of Brazil's intransigence came at the 2001 Economic Summit in Quebec City. See Smith (2001) and the *Economist* (2001).

23. The Chicago Boys' famous response to protesting farmers, reminiscent of Marie-Antoinette, was "let them eat their cows" (Silva 1997, 164).

24. It bears mentioning, however, that although MERCOSUR has accounted for much of the growth of Brazil's exports, its total trade is still quite diversified, with the European Union and the United States collectively accounting for roughly one-half of its export market (Brazil n.d.).

25. Respondents were asked to rate their feelings toward commercial liberalization on a scale from 1 (very negative) to 6 (very positive). Scores of 4–6 are classified as positive. Reported in Kingstone (2001, 993–94); for the original study, see Confederação Nacional de Indústria (1995).

Notes to Chapter 9

1. The Canadian government used this tactic in the aftermath of the Uruguay Round of the GATT, in which agricultural rents were decreased in defiance of the preferences of Canadian farmers (see Reguly 1993). The symbolic autonomy of international regimes is clear from the protests against globalization that have occurred at almost every major economic summit since the abortive attempt to launch a new round of the WTO in Seattle in 1999. Significantly, protestors do not seek to sanction their own governments, concentrating instead on the regime as the source of the problem.

2. The logic of the diversionary theory of war is that domestic political turmoil often evaporates in the presence of a common national enemy. International military incidents tend to provoke a rally-round-the-flag effect that serves the political interest of the government. An excellent example is the change in Margaret Thatcher's political popularity in the aftermath of Argentina's invasion of the Falkland Islands in 1982. For more, see Levy (1989).

3. TPA is the modern incarnation of fast-track authority. First introduced with the Trade Act of 1974, TPA allows the president to negotiate free-trade deals, subject to certain congressionally mandated parameters, in the absence of strict congressional oversight. Such oversight is limited to acceptance or rejection of the negotiated agreement, with no legislative amendments permitted. For more on TPA/fast track, see Destler (1995, 71–77).

4. This definition comes from Fukuyama (1999, 14).

5. The most important pioneering work on the relationship between mass attitudes and democratic stability is Almond and Verba (1963). See also Almond (1956).

6. Obviously this is an oversimplification of a complex and controversial issue. Space does not permit a full discussion of the point, but see Dominguez (1998). Among the most controversial elements is the direction of the causal arrow between economic growth and democracy. See, for example, Heo and Tan (2001). Regarding political culture, the direction of the causal arrow is less important. Instead, we are concerned with the extent to which growth-associated economic change has the potential to institutionalize liberal democratic attitudes.

7. It must be noted, however, that industrialization need not produce an independent powerful bourgeoisie. Since Bismarck, authoritarian governments have managed to control the liberalizing effects of industrialization. Bismarck, of course, accomplished this through his notorious marriage of iron and rye. Fascism, by its very definition, is a form of authoritarian capitalism. Finally, ISI was a common means for Latin American governments to enjoy the fruits of industrial development while still controlling the bourgeoisie through the narcotic of import protection.

References

Abernethy, Mark. 1996. "Australia: Good News and Bad News in New Tariff Concessions—Small." *Australian Financial Review*, May 21.

Adams, Leonard P. 1932. *Agricultural Depression and Farm Relief in England, 1813–1852*. London: P. S. King and Son.

Adelman, Paul. 1989. *Peel and the Conservative Party, 1830–1850*. London: Longman.

Agence France Presse. 1997. "Australian Car Tariffs Plan Condemned as a Retreat from Free Trade," June 6.

Agosin, Manuel R. 2000. "Chile's Trade Strategy—A Problem of Focus." *America's Insights*, May.

Albinski, Henry S. 1986. "Australia and New Zealand in the 1980's." *Current History* 85:144–54.

Alchin, Terry Maxwell. 1990. "The Role of the CER in Improving Australian–New Zealand Relations." *Australian Quarterly* 62:21–35.

Allen, William R. 1953. "The International Trade Philosophy of Cordell Hull, 1907–1933." *American Economic Review* 43:101–16.

Allende, Salvador. 1973. *Chile's Road to Socialism*, trans. J. Darling, ed. Joan E. Graces. Hammondsworth, UK: Penguin.

Almond, Gabriel. 1956. "Comparative Political Systems." *Journal of Politics* 18:391–409.

Almond, Gabriel, and Sidney Verba. 1963. *The Civic Culture: Political Attitudes and Democracy in Five Nations*. Princeton, NJ: Princeton University Press.

Altmeyer, Arthur. 1966. *The Formative Years of Social Security*. Madison: University of Wisconsin Press.

Alvarez Bejar, Alejandro, and Gabriel Mendoza Pichardo. 1993. "Mexico 1988–1991: A Successful Adjustment Program?" *Latin American Perspectives* 20:32–45.

Anderson, Kym. 1987. "Tariffs and the Manufacturing Sector." In *The Australian Economy in the Long Run*, ed. Rodney Maddock and Ian W. McLean. Cambridge: Cambridge University Press.

Anderson, Kym, and Ross Garnaut. 1986. "The Political Economy of Manufacturing Protection in Australia." In *The Political Economy of Protection: Experiences of ASEAN and Australia*, ed. Christopher Findlay and Ross Garnaut. Sydney: Allen and Unwin.

———. 1987. *Australian Protectionism: Extent, Causes and Effects*. Sydney: Allen and Unwin.

Anderson, R. W. C. 1967. "Tariff Policy and the Present Controversy." *Canberra Letter* 953, May 23.

Angell, Alan. 1972. *Politics and the Labour Movement in Chile*. Oxford: Oxford University Press.

Armitage-Smith, G. 1898. *The Free Trade Movement and Its Results*. Chicago: Herbert S. Store.

Arnold, R. Douglas. 1990. *The Logic of Congressional Action*. New Haven, CT: Yale University Press.

Ashley, Percy. 1926. *Modern Tariff History: Germany, United States, France*. New York: E. P. Dutton.

Associated Chambers of Manufacturers of Australia. 1968. "Does the Government Know Where the Tariff Board is Going?" *Canberra Letter* 958, January 22.

Atkinson, Paul E. 1997. "New Zealand's Radical Reforms." *OECD Observer* 205:43–48.

Australia. 1977. *White Paper on Manufacturing Industry*. Canberra: Australian Government Publishing Service.

———. 1991. *Building a Competitive Australia*. Canberra: Australian Government Publishing Service.

———. 1994. *The Working Nation*. Canberra: Australian Government Publishing Service.

———. Ministry for Small Business, Customs and Construction. 1995. "Changes to the Tariff Concession System & Policy By-Laws." http://www.dist.gov.au/events/innovate/r29/html, accessed December 6, 1995.

Australian Financial Review. 1994a. "Australia: GATT's Warning on Dumping," February 7.

———. 1994b. "Chasing Subsidies Not Sales," May 6.

Australian Labour Party. 1982. "New Directions for Australian Industry: ALP Policy for Manufacturing Industry." Position paper.

Australian Manufacturing Council. 1989. *What Part Will Manufacturing Play in Australia's Future?* Melbourne: Australian Manufacturing Council.

———. 1990. *The Global Challenge: Australian Manufacturing in the 1990s*. Melbourne: Australian Manufacturing Council.

Axelrod, Robert. 1984. *The Evolution of Cooperation*. New York: Basic Books.

Aydelotte, William O. 1967. "The Country Gentlemen and the Repeal of the Corn Laws." *English History Review* 82:47–60.

Bacha, Edmar L., and Pedro S. Malan. 1989. "Brazil's Debt: From the Miracle to the Fund." In *Democratizing Brazil: Problems of Transition and Consolidation*, ed. Alfred Stepan. New York: Oxford University Press.

Baer, M. Delal. 1991. "North American Free Trade." *Foreign Affairs* 70:132–49.

———. 1993. "Mexico's Second Revolution: Pathways to Liberalization." In *Political and Economic Liberalization in Mexico: At a Critical Juncture?* ed. Riordan Roett. Boulder, CO: Lynne Reinner.

Baer, Werner. 1965. *Industrialization and Economic Development in Brazil*. Homewood, IL: Richard D. Irwin.

———. 1976. "The Brazilian Growth and Development Experience: 1964–1975." In *Brazil in the Seventies*, ed. Riordan Roett. Washington, DC: American Enterprise Institute for Public Policy Research.

———. 1995. *The Brazilian Economy: Growth and Development*. 4th ed. Westport, CT: Praeger.

Baer, Werner, and Issac Kerstenetzky. 1964. "Import Substitution and Industrialization in Brazil." *American Economic Review* 54:411–25.

Bailey, John. 1986. "The Impact of Major Groups on Policy-Making Trends in Government-Business Relations in Mexico." In *Mexico's Political Stability: The Next Five Years*, ed. Roderic Ai Camp.Boulder, CO: Westview.

Bailey, Michael A., Judith Goldstein, and Barry R. Weingast. 1997. "The Institutional Roots of American Trade Policy: Politics, Coalitions and International Trade." *World Politics* 49:309–39.

Balassa, Bela. 1985. "Policy Experiments in Chile, 1973–1983." In *The National Economic Policies of Chile*, ed. Gary M. Walton. Greenwich, CT: JAI.

Baldwin, Robert E. 1989. "The Political Economy of Trade Policy." *Journal of Economic Perspectives* 3:119–35.

Baran, Paul A., and Paul M. Sweezy. 1966. *Monopoly Capital: An Essay on the American Economic and Social Order.* New York: Monthly Review Press.

Barber, David. 1997. "New Zealand: Manufacturers Up Pressure to Ease Tasman Trade Rules." *National Business Review*, April 24.

Barnes, Donald Grove. 1965. *A History of the English Corn Laws, from 1660–1846.* New York: Augustus M. Kelley.

Barry, Donald. 1987. "Eisenhower, St. Laurent and Free Trade, 1953." *International Perspectives* 16:8–10.

Bartell, Ernest. 1995. "Perceptions by Business Leaders and the Transition to Democracy in Chile." In *Business and Democracy in Latin America*, ed. Ernest Bartell and Leigh A. Payne. Pittsburgh: University of Pittsburgh Press.

Basanez, Miguel. 1993. "Is Mexico Headed Toward its Fifth Crisis?" In *Political and Economic Liberalization in Mexico: At a Critical Juncture?* ed. Riordan Roett. Boulder, CO: Lynne Reinner.

Bassett, Michael. 1993. "Interview." *Canadian Parliamentary Review* 16 (Summer):22–23.

Bates, Robert H., and Anne O. Krueger. 1993. *Political and Economic Interactions in Economic Policy Reform.* Oxford: Blackwell.

Bauer, Raymond A., Ithiel de la Sola Pool, and Lewis Anthony Dexter. 1972. *American Business and Public Policy.* 2nd ed. Chicago: Aldine-Atherton.

Bauer, Raymond A., Suzanne Keller, and Ithiel de la Sola Pool. 1955. "What Foreign Trade Policy Does American Business Want?" Working paper, Center for International Studies, Massachusetts Institute of Technology, February 16.

Becker, Gary. 1983. "A Theory of Competition Among Pressure Groups for Political Influence." *Quarterly Journal of Economics* 98:371–400.

Becker, William H. 1982. *The Dynamics of Business-Government Relations: Industry and Exports 1893–1921.* Chicago: University of Chicago Press.

Bedi, Bishen. 1997. "Howard Backs Down Again on Tariff Reform." *New Straits Times Press*, September 13.

Behrman, Jere R. 1976. *Foreign Trade Regimes and Economic Development: Chile.* New York: Columbia University Press.

Bell, Stephen. 1989. "State Strength and Capitalist Weakness: Manufacturing Capital and the Tariff Board's Attack on McEwenism, 1967–74." *Politics* 24:23–38.

———. 1992a. "Policy Responses to Manufacturing Decline: The Limits of State Economic Intervention, 1974–83." *Australian Journal of Politics and History* 38:41–61.

———. 1992b. "Structural Power in the Manufacturing Sector: The Political Economy of Competitiveness and Investment." In *Business-Government Relations in Australia*, ed. Stephen Bell and John Wanna. Sydney: Harcourt, Brace, Jovanovich.

———. 1993. *Australian Manufacturing and the State.* Cambridge: Cambridge University Press.

———. 1995. "Between the Market and the State: The Role of Australian Business Associations in Public Policy." *Comparative Politics* 28:25–53.

Bensabat, Remonda R. 1995. "The Mexican Private Sector's Role in the North American Free Trade Negotiations: Implications for Business-State Relations." PhD dissertation, University of Toronto.

Bergsman, Joel, and Arthur Candal. 1969. "Industrialization: Past Success and Future Problems." In *The Economy of Brazil*, ed. Howard S. Ellis. Berkeley: University of California Press.

Berkowitz, Edward, and Kim McQuaid. 1980. *Creating the Welfare State*. New York: Praeger.

Bernhardt, Joshua. 1922. *The Tariff Commission: Its History, Activities and Organization*. New York: D. Appleton.

Bernier, Ivan, and Martin Roy. 1999. "NAFTA and MERCOSUR: Two Competing Models?" In *The Americas in Transition: The Contours of Regionalism*, ed. Gordon Mace and Louis Bélanger. Boulder, CO: Lynne Rienner.

Berry, Albert. 1996. "Small and Medium Enterprise (SME) Under Trade and Foreign Exchange Liberalization: Latin American and Canadian Experiences and Concerns." *Canadian Journal of Development Studies* 27:53–74.

Bertram, Geoff. 1993. "Keynesianism, Neoclassicism, and the State." In *State and Economy in New Zealand*, ed. Brian Roper and Chris Rudd. Auckland, NZ: Oxford University Press.

Bhagwati, Jagdish N. 1989. "Is Free Trade Passé After All?" *Weltwirtschaftliches Archiv* 125:17–44.

———. 1982. "Directly Unproductive, Profit-Seeking (DUP) Activities." *Journal of Political Economy* 90:988–1002.

Bidwell, Percy W. 1956. *What the Tariff Means to American Industries*. New York: Harper & Brothers.

Birks, Stuart. 1992. "Policies for the Manufacturing Sector." In *The New Zealand Economy: Issues and Policies*, ed. Stuart Birks and Srikanta Chatterjee. Palmerston North, NZ: Dunmore.

Bollard, Alan. 1986. "The Economic Relations Agreement Between Australia and New Zealand: A Tentative Appraisal." *Journal of Common Market Studies* 25:89–105.

———. 1992. *New Zealand: Economic Reforms, 1984–1991*. San Francisco: ICS.

———. 1994. "New Zealand." In *The Political Economy of Policy Reform*, ed. John Williamson. Washington, DC: Institute for International Economics.

Bollard, Alan, and John Savage. 1990. "How Firms Rationalize." In *Turning it Around: Closure and Revitalization in New Zealand Industry*, ed. John Savage, Alan Bollard, Douglas Greer, Timothy Hazeldine, and Richard Miller. Auckland, NZ: Oxford University Press.

Bowley, Arthur L. 1905. *A Short Account of England's Foreign Trade in the Nineteenth Century: Its Economic and Social Results*. London: Swan Sonnenschein.

Brady, David W. 1988. *Critical Elections and Congressional Policy Making*. Stanford, CA: Stanford University Press.

Brandenburg, Frank R. 1969. "Causes of the Revolution." In *Revolution in Mexico: Years of Upheaval, 1910–1940*, ed. James W. Wilkie and Albert L. Michaels. New York: Alfred A. Knopf.

Brash, Donald. 1996. Governor of the Reserve Bank of New Zealand. Address to the Institute of Economic Affairs, London 4 June. http://www.rbnz.gov...eeches/sp960604.htm.

Brawley, Mark R. 1998. *Turning Points: Decisions Shaping the Evolution of the International Political Economy*. Peterborough, ON: Broadview.

Brazil. National Economic Development Bank. n.d. "Brazilian Trade Balance." http://www.bndes.gov.br/english/brtab4a.htm.

Brenner, Steven Robert. 1978. "Economic Interests and the Trade Agreements Program, 1937–1940: A Study of Institutions and Political Influence." PhD dissertation, Stanford University.

Bresser Pereira, Luiz Carlos. 1984. *Development and Crisis in Brazil, 1930–1983*, trans. Marcia Van Dyke. Boulder, CO: Westview.

————. 1996. *Economic Crisis and State Reform in Brazil: Toward a New Interpretation of Latin America*. Boulder, CO: Lynne Rienner.

Briggs, Asa. 1959. *The Age of Improvement, 1783–1867*. New York: David McKay.

Brock, Michael. 1973. *The Great Reform Act*. London: Hutchison.

Brock, William A., and Stephen P. Magee. 1978. "The Economics of Special Interest Politics: The Case of the Tariff." *American Economic Review* 68:246–50.

Brooks, Michael A., and Ben J. Heijdra. 1988. "In Search of Rent-Seeking." In *The Political Economy of Rent-Seeking*, ed. Charles K. Rowley, Robert D. Tollison, and Gordon Tullock. Boston: Kluwer Academic.

Brooks, Stephen, and Andrew Stritch. 1991. *Business and Government in Canada*. Scarborough, ON: Prentice-Hall.

Broughton, Lord. 1911. *Recollections of a Long Life*. Vol. 6. Ed. Lady Dorchester. London: John Murray.

Brown, Benjamin H. 1943. *The Tariff Reform Movement in Great Britain, 1881–1895*. New York: Columbia University Press.

Brown, Jonathan. 1987. *Agriculture in England: A Survey of Farming, 1870–1947*. Manchester, UK: Manchester University Press.

Brown, Robert Craig, and Ramsay Cook. 1974. *Canada, 1896–1921*. Toronto: McClelland and Stewart.

Bueno, Gerardo. 1971. "The Structure of Protection in Mexico." In *The Structure of Protection in Developing Countries*, ed. Bela Balassa and associates. Baltimore: Johns Hopkins University Press.

Bulmer-Thomas, Victor. 1998. "The Latin American Economies, 1929–1939." In *Latin American Economy and Society Since 1930*, ed. Leslie Bethell. Cambridge: Cambridge University Press.

Burch, Philip. 1973. "The NAM as an Interest Group." *Politics and Society* 4:97–130.

Burnett, Alan, and Robin Burnett. 1978. *The Australian and New Zealand Nexus*. Canberra: Australian Institute of International Affairs.

Burnham, Walter Dean. 1970. *Critical Elections and the Mainsprings of American Politics*. New York: Norton.

Burns, James MacGregor. 1956. *Roosevelt: The Lion and the Fox*. New York: Harcourt Brace.

Burtt, D. J. 1977. *Trans-Tasman Development and Trade*. Wellington: New Zealand Institute of Economic Research.

Busey, James L. 1969. "The Old and the New in the Politics of Modern Brazil." In *The Shaping of Modern Brazil*, ed. Eric N. Baklanoff. Baton Rouge: Louisiana State University Press.

Business Line. 1997. "Reforms and Transparency: Lessons from New Zealand," 14 July.

Button, John. 1985. "Australia's New Industry Policy—Now and the Future." In *Poor Nation of the Pacific: Australia's Future?* ed. Jocelynne A. Scutt. Sydney: Allen and Unwin.

Caird, James. 1878. "General View of British Agriculture." *Journal of the Royal Agricultural Society of England*, second series, 14:277–332.

————. 1967 [1852]. *English Agriculture in 1850–51*. 2nd ed. New York: Augustus M. Kelley.

Cairns, Alan C. 1990. "Constitutional Minoritarianism in Canada." In *Canada: State of the Federation 1990*, ed. Ronald L. Watts and Douglas M. Brown. Kingston, Canada: Queen's University Institute of Intergovernmental Relations.

Cámara Nacional de la Industria de Transformación. 1992. "Recomendaciones de CANACINTRA en la Etapa Actual de las Negociones T.L.C." Mexico City: CANACINTRA, February 11.

Cameron, Duncan. 1986. "Introduction." In *The Free Trade Papers*, ed. Duncan Cameron. Toronto: James Lorimer.

Camp, Roderic Ai. 1989. *Entrepreneurs and Politics in Twentieth Century Mexico*. New York: Oxford University Press.

———. 1993. "Political Liberalization: The Last Key to Economic Modernization in Mexico." In *Political and Economic Liberalization in Mexico: At a Critical Juncture?* ed. Riordan Roett. Boulder, CO: Lynne Reinner.

Canada. Department of External Affairs. 1983a. *Canadian Trade Policy for the 1980s*. Ottawa: Minister of Supply and Services.

———. Department of External Affairs. 1983b. *A Review of Canadian Trade Policy*. Ottawa: Minister of Supply and Services.

———. Department of External Affairs. 1986a. *Canadian Trade Negotiations*. Ottawa: Minister of Supply and Services.

———. Economic Council. 1975. *Looking Outward: An Outline of a New Trade Strategy for Canada*. Ottawa: Minister of Supply and Services.

———. Parliament. Senate Standing Committee on Foreign Affairs. 1978a. *Canada–United States Relations*. Vol. 2. Ottawa: Minister of Supply and Services.

———. Prime Minister's Office. 1986b. "Communications Strategy for Canada-US Bilateral Trade Initiative." In *The Free Trade Papers*, ed. Duncan Cameron. Toronto: James Lorimer.

———. Royal Commission on Dominion-Provincial Relations. 1954. *Report*. Book 1. Ottawa: Queen's Printer.

———. Royal Commission on the Economic Union and Development Prospects for Canada. 1985a. *Report*. Vols. 1 and 2. Ottawa: Minister of Supply and Services.

———. Senate Standing Committee on Foreign Affairs. 1978b. *Canada–United States Relations: Canada's Trade Relations with the United States*. Ottawa: Minister of Supply and Services.

———. Senate Standing Committee on Foreign Affairs. 1982. *Canada–United States Relations: Canada's Trade Relations with the United States*. Ottawa: Minister of Supply and Services.

———. Statistics Canada. 1985b. *Canada Yearbook 1985*. Ottawa: Minister of Supply and Services.

———. Statistics Canada. 1987. *Canada Yearbook 1988*. Ottawa: Minister of Supply and Services.

Capling, Ann, and Brian Galligan. 1992. *Beyond the Protective State*. Cambridge: Cambridge University Press.

Cardoso, Eliana A., and Rudiger Dornbusch. 1987. "Brazil's Tropical Plan." *American Economic Review* 77:288–92.

Carmody, A. T. 1952. "The Level of the Australian Tariff: A Study in Method." *Yorkshire Bulletin of Economic and Social Research* 4:51–65.

Cason, Jeffrey. 2000. "On the Road to Southern Cone Economic Integration." *Journal of Interamerican Studies and World Affairs* 42:23–42.

Centeno, Miguel Angel, and Sylvia Maxfield. 1992. "The Marriage of Finance and Order: Changes in the Mexican Political Elite." *Journal of Latin American Studies* 24:57–85.

Chambers, J. D., and G. E. Mingay. 1966. *The Agricultural Revolution, 1750–1880*. London: B. T. Batsford.

Chase-Dunn, Christopher. 1975. "The Effects of International Economic Dependence and Inequality: A Cross-National Study." *American Sociological Review* 40:720–38.

Christie, O. F. 1928. *The Transition from Aristocracy, 1832–1867.* London: Seeley, Service.

Clapham, J. H. 1930. *An Economic History of Modern Britain.* Cambridge: Cambridge University Press.

Clark, S. D. 1938. *The Canadian Manufacturers' Association: A Study in Collective Bargaining and Political Pressure.* Toronto: University of Toronto Press.

Clay, Henry. 1893. "Speech in the U.S. House of Representatives, March 30 and 31, 1824." In *State Papers and Speeches on the Tariff,* ed. Frank W. Taussig. Cambridge, MA: Harvard University Press.

Cleaves, Peter S., and Charles J. Stephens. 1991. "Businessmen and Economic Policy in Mexico." *Latin American Research Review* 26:187–202.

Cleveland, Alfred S. 1948. "NAM: Spokesman for Industry?" *Harvard Business Review* 26:353–71.

Cleveland, Harold Van B. 1976. "The International Monetary System in the Interwar Period." In *Balance of Power or Hegemony,* ed. Benjamin M. Rowland. New York: New York University Press.

Cobden, Richard. 1870. *Speeches by Richard Cobden, MP.* Vols. 1 and 2. Ed. John Bright and Thorold Rogers. London: Macmillan.

Cockcroft, James D. 1972. "Social and Economic Structure of the Porfiriato: Mexico 1877–1911." In *Dependence and Underdevelopment: Latin America's Political Economy.* ed. James D. Cockcroft, André Gunder Frank, and Dale L. Johnson. Garden City, NY: Anchor.

Coddington, Deborah. 1993. *Turning Pain into Gain: The Plain Person's Guide to the Transformation of New Zealand, 1984–1993.* Auckland: Alister Taylor.

Cohen, Stephen D., Joel R. Paul, and Robert A. Blecker. 1996. *Fundamentals of U.S. Foreign Trade Policy: Economics, Politics, Laws and Issues.* Boulder, CO: Westview.

Cohen, Youssef. 1987. "Democracy from Above: The Political Origins of Military Dictatorship in Brazil." *World Politics* 40:30–54.

Colebatch, Tim. 1991. "Australia: Production Jobs Going Overseas, Survey Finds." *The Age,* December 19.

Coleman, William D. 1988. *Business and Politics: A Study of Collective Action.* Montreal: McGill-Queen's University Press.

Confederação Nacional de Indústria. 1995. *Abertura Comercial e Estratégia Tecnológica: A Visão de Líderes Industrias Brasileiros.* Rio de Janeiro: CNI.

Connors, T. 1981. "NCP Blasted on Australia's High Tariffs." *Australian Financial Review,* July 3.

Conway, J. F. 1994. *The Canadian West: The History of a Region in Confederation.* 2nd ed. Toronto: James Lorimer.

Conybeare, John A. C. 1983. "Tariff Protection in Developed and Developing Countries: A Case Sectoral and Longitudinal Analysis." *International Organization* 37:441–67.

Corbo, Vittorio. 1985. "Chilean Economic Policy and International Economic Relations Since 1970." In *The National Economic Policies of Chile,* ed. Gary M. Walton. Greenwich, CT: JAI.

———. 1997. "Trade Reform and Uniform Import Tariffs: The Chilean Experience." *American Economic Review* 87:73–77.

Cordoba, José. 1994. "Mexico." In *The Political Economy of Policy Reform,* ed. John Williamson. Washington, DC: Institute for International Economics.

Cornelius, Wayne A. 1986. *The Political Economy of Mexico Under de la Madrid: The Crisis Deepens, 1985–1986.* La Jolla: Center for U.S.-Mexican Studies, University of California, San Diego.

Cornell, Andrew. 1994. "Australia: Business Groups Warn Government on Tariff Slashing—the GATT—The Reform of the Australian Economy." *Australian Financial Review*, February 7.

Crawford, J. G. 1968. *Australian Trade Policy, 1942–1966*. Canberra: Australian National University Press.

Croker, John Wilson. 1884. *The Correspondence and Diaries of the Late Right Honourable John Wilson Croker*. Vol. 2. Ed. Louis J. Jennings. New York: Charles Scribner's Sons.

Crosby, Travis L. 1977. *English Farmers and the Politics of Protection, 1815–1852*. Hassocks, UK: Harverster.

Cross, Michael S. 1971. *Free Trade, Annexation and Reciprocity*. Toronto: Holt, Rinehart and Winston.

Cullinane, Tim. 1995. Chief Executive, Forestry Corporation of New Zealand. "The Business Roundtable in 1995." Speech to the Spectrum Club, Rotorua, June 12. http://speeches. com/cullin1.htm.

Curtiss, George B. 1896. *Protection and Prosperity: An Account of Tariff Legislation and its Effects in Europe and America*. New York: Pan-American.

Cypher, James. 1990. *The State and Capital in Mexico*. Boulder, CO: Westview.

da Motta Veiga, Pedro. 1997. "Brazil's Strategy for Trade Liberalization and Economic Integration in the Western Hemisphere." In *Integrating the Hemisphere: Perspectives from Latin America and the Caribbean*, ed. Ana Julia Jatar and Sidney Weintraub. Washington, DC: Inter-American Dialogue.

———. 1999. "Brazil in Mercosur: Reciprocal Influence." In *MERCOSUR: Regional Integration, World Markets*, ed. Riordan Roett. Boulder, CO: Lynne Rienner.

———. 2000. "Brazil's Cautious and Selective Trade Strategy." *America's Insight*, May.

Dallek, Robert. 1979. *Franklin D. Roosevelt and American Foreign Policy, 1932–1945*. New York: Oxford University Press.

Davis, Diane E. 1992. "Mexico's New Politics: Changing Perspectives on Free Trade." *World Policy Journal* 9:655–71.

Davis, Tom E. 1963. "Eight Decades of Inflation in Chile, 1879–1959: A Political Interpretation." *Journal of Political Economy* 71:389–97.

de la Cuadra, Sergio, and Dominique Hachette. 1991. "Chile." In *Liberalizing Foreign Trade*, ed. Demetrius Papageorgiou, Michael Michaely, and Armeane M. Choksi. Vol. 1. Oxford, UK: Basil Blackwell.

de Maria y Campos, Maurico. 1987. "Mexico's New Industrial Development Strategy." In *The United States and Mexico: Face to Face with New Technology*, ed. Cathryn L. Thorup. New Brunswick, NJ: Transaction Books.

de Sousa, Amaury. 1999. "Cardoso and the Struggle for Reform in Brazil." *Journal of Democracy* 10:48–49.

Deloitte Touche Tohmatsu. 1996. "Temporary Relief With Government Backdown," http://www.deloitte.com.au/taxnews/gct/press10.htm, accessed December 3, 1996.

Derber, Milton. 1975. "The New Deal and Labor." In *The New Deal: The National Level*, ed. John Braeman, Robert H. Bremner, and David Brody. Columbus: Ohio State University Press.

Destler, I. M. 1995. *American Trade Politics*. 3rd ed. Washington, DC: Institute for International Economics.

Dodd, Tim, and Rowley Spiers. 1991. "Australia: Dawkins Challenges Tariff Cuts, Calls for Intervention." *Australian Financial Review*, April 8.

Dodson, Louise. 1992. "Australia: Business Talks Tough on Trade." *Australian Financial Review*, September 17.

Doern, G. Bruce, and Brian W. Tomlin. 1991. *Faith and Fear: The Free Trade Story*. Toronto: Stoddard.

Dominguez, Jorge I. 1998. "Free Politics and Free Markets in Latin America." *Journal of Democracy* 9:70–84.

Dornbusch, Rudiger, and Sebastian Edwards. 1994. "Exchange Rate Policy and Trade Strategy." In *The Chilean Economy: Policy Lessons and Challenges*, ed. Barry P. Bosworth, Rudiger Dornbusch and Raúl Labán. Washington, DC: The Brookings Institution.

Doubleday, Thomas. 1856. *The Political Life of the Right Honourable Sir Robert Peel*. Vol. 1. London: Smith, Elder.

Douglas, Roger. 1993. *Unfinished Business*. Auckland, NZ: Random House.

Downs, Anthony. 1957. *An Economic Theory of Democracy*. New York: Harper and Row.

Drake, P. J., and J. P. Nieuwenhuysen. 1988. *Economic Growth for Australia: Agenda for Action*. Melbourne: Oxford University Press.

Dresser, Denise. 1992. "Bringing the Poor Back In: Poverty Alleviation and Regime Legitimacy in Mexico." Paper presented at the Congress of the Latin American Studies Association, Los Angeles.

Dreyer, F. A. 1965. "The Whigs and the Political Crisis of 1845." *English Historical Review* 80:514–37.

Drury, A. Cooper, and Michael Lusztig. n.d. "Economic Change and Democracy in Mexico."

Dun's Review and Modern Industry. 1962. "Business and the Common Market," March.

Durham, Arthur Lewis. 1930. *The Anglo-French Treaty of Commerce of 1860*. Ann Arbor: University of Michigan Press.

Dwyer, Michael. 1995. "Treaty to Promote Trans-Tasman Trade—Trade and Exporting." *Australian Financial Review*, April 19.

Dyster, Barrie, and David Meredith. 1990. *Australia in the International Economy in the Twentieth Century*. Cambridge: Cambridge University Press.

Easterbrook, W. T., and Hugh G. J. Aitken. 1967. *Canadian Economic History*. Toronto: Macmillan.

Eckes, Alfred E., Jr. 1995. *Opening America's Market: U.S. Foreign Trade Policy Since 1776*. Chapel Hill: University of North Carolina Press.

Economic News and Analysis on Mexico. 1994. "Mexican Manufacturing and Agriculture Groups Criticize Proposal for Faster Tariff Phase-Out Under NAFTA," June 22.

Economist. 1983. "Mexico Under the IMF," August 20.

———. 1991. "Sell Them Sunny Meadows," February 23.

———. 1992a. "Don't Wait Until the Cows Come Home," December 12.

———. 1992b. "It's Happening in Monterrey," June 27.

———. 2001. "All in the Familia," April 21.

Edwards, Sebastian, and Alejandra Cox Edwards. 1987. *Monetarism and Liberalization: The Chilean Experiment*. Cambridge, MA: Ballinger Publishing.

Eichengreen, Barry. 1992. "The Eternal Fiscal Question: Free Trade and Protection in Britain, 1860–1929." In *Protectionism in the World Economy*, ed. Forrest H. Capie. Aldershot, UK: Edward Elgar.

Ellis, L. Ethan. 1939. *Reciprocity 1911: A Case Study in Canadian-American Relations*. New Haven, CT: Yale University Press.

Elster, Jon. 1979. *Ulysses and the Sirens: Studies in Rationality and Irrationality*. New York: Cambridge University Press.

Erickson, Kenneth Paul. 1977. *The Brazilian Corporative State and Working Class Politics*. Berkeley: University of California Press.

Escobar Toledo, Saúl David. 1987. "Rifts in the Mexican Power Elite, 1976–1986." In *Government and Private Sector in Contemporary Mexico*, ed. Sylvia Maxfield and Ricardo Anzaldua M. San Diego: Center for U.S.-Mexican Studies.

Fagan, Robert H., and Michael Webber. 1994. *Global Restructuring: The Australian Experience*. Melbourne: Oxford University Press.

Fairlie, Susan. 1965. "The Nineteenth-Century Corn Law Reconsidered." *Economic History Review*, second series 18:544–61.

Faundez, Julio. 1988. *Marxism and Democracy in Chile: From 1932 to the Fall of Allende*. New Haven, CT: Yale University Press.

Fay, C. R. 1932. *The Corn Laws and Social England*. Cambridge: Cambridge University Press.

Feinstein, C. H. 1972. *National Income, Expenditure and Output of the United Kingdom, 1855–1965*. Cambridge: Cambridge University Press.

Ferguson, Thomas. 1984. "From Normalcy to New Deal: Industrial Structure, Party Competition, and American Public Policy in the Great Depression." *International Organization* 38:41–94.

Ffrench-Davis, Ricardo. 2001. "Is MERCOSUR in a Crisis?" *America's Insight*, October.

Finegold, Kenneth, and Theda Skocpol. 1984. "State, Party, and Industry, From Business Recovery to the Wagner Act in America's New Deal." In *Statemaking and Social Movements*, ed. Charles Bright and Susan Harding. Ann Arbor: University of Michigan Press.

Finger, J. Michael. 1991. "The GATT as an International Discipline Over Trade Restrictions: A Public Choice Approach." In *The Political Economy of International Organizations: A Public Choice Approach*, ed. Roland Vaubel and Thomas D. Willet. Boulder, CO: Westview.

Finlayson, Jock A. 1985. "Canadian International Economic Policy: Context, Issues and a Review of Some Recent Economic Literature." In *Canada and the International Political/Economic Environment*, ed. Denis Stairs and Gilbert R. Winham. Toronto: University of Toronto Press.

Finlayson, Jock A., and Stefano Bertasi. 1992. "Evolution of Canadian Postwar International Trade Policy." In *Canadian Foreign Policy and International Economic Regimes*, ed. A. Claire Cutler and Mark W. Zacher. Vancouver: University of British Columbia Press.

Fishlow, Albert. 1997. "Is the *Real* Plan for Real?" In *Brazil Under Cardoso*, ed. Susan Kaufman Purcell and Riordan Roett. Boulder, CO: Lynne Rienner.

———. 1973. "Some Reflections on Post-1964 Brazilian Economic Policy." In *Authoritarian Brazil*, ed. Alfred Stepan. New Haven, CT: Yale University Press.

———. 1986. "Latin American Adjustment to the Oil Shocks of 1973 and 1979." In *Latin American Political Economy: Financial Crisis and Political Change*, ed. Jonathan Hartlyn and Samuel A. Morley. Boulder, CO: Westview.

Fletcher, T. W. 1961. "The Great Depression of English Agriculture, 1873–1896." *Economic History Review* 13:417–32.

Forster, Ben. 1986. *A Conjunction of Interests: Business, Politics, and Tariffs, 1825–1879*. Toronto: University of Toronto Press.

Fortune. 1939. "Survey of Public Opinion," October.

———. 1948. ""Renovation in the NAM," July.

———. 1955. "The Shift in Business Opinion on the Tariff," April.

Fowke, V. C. 1952. "The National Policy—Old and New." *Canadian Journal of Economics and Political Science* 18:271–86.

Fox, Jonathan. 1994. "The Difficult Transition from Clientelism to Citizenship: Lessons from Mexico." *World Politics* 46:151–84.

Frey, Bruno S. 1984. *International Political Economics*. Oxford, UK: Basil Blackwell.

Frieden, Jeff. 1988. "Sectoral Conflict and Foreign Economic Policy, 1914–1940." *International Organization* 42:59–90.

Fukuyama, Francis. 1999. *The Great Disruption: Human Nature and the Reconstitution of Social Order*. New York: Free Press.

Gambles, Anna. 1999. *Protection and Politics: Conservative Economic Discourse, 1815–1852*. Woodbridge, UK: Royal Historical Society.

Gardner, Lloyd C. 1964. *Economic Aspects of New Deal Diplomacy*. Madison: University of Wisconsin Press.

Garnaut, Ross. 1989. *Australia and the Northeast Asian Ascendency*. Canberra: Australian Government Publishing Service.

———. 1994a. "Australia." In *The Political Economy of Policy Reform*, ed. John Williamson. Washington, DC: Institute for International Economics.

———. 1994b. "Trade and Tariffs and Australian Business." In *Government and Business Relations in Australia*, ed. Randal G. Stewart. St. Leonards: Allen and Unwin.

Gash, Norman. 1972. *Sir Robert Peel: The Life of Sir Robert Peel After 1830*. New York: Longman.

Gatica Barros, Jaime. 1989. *Deindustrialization in Chile*. Boulder, CO: Westview.

Gherson, Giles. 1985. "Freer Trade with the US: Ready to Take on the Americans." *Financial Post*, May 4.

Gibbins, Roger, Howard Palmer, Brian Rusted, and David Taras, eds. 1988. *Meech Lake and Canada: Perspectives from the West*. Edmonton, AB: Academic Printing and Publishing.

Gideonse, Max. 1944. "Foreign Trade and Commercial Policy Since 1860." In *The Growth of the American Economy*, ed. Harold F. Williamson. New York: Prentice Hall.

Gilligan, Michael J. 1997. *Empowering Exporters: Reciprocity, Delegation and Collective Action in American Trade Policy*. Ann Arbor: University of Michigan Press.

Glezer, Leon. 1982. *Tariff Politics: Australian Policy-Making, 1960–1980*. Melbourne: Melbourne University Press.

Gold, Hyam, and Ramesh Thakur. 1981. "Looking for the Yellow Brick Road." *New Zealand International Review* 6:9–11.

Goldberg, Peter A. 1975. "The Politics of the Allende Overthrow in Chile." *Political Science Quarterly* 90:93–116.

Goldstein, Judith. 1988. "Ideas, Institutions, and American Trade Policy." *International Organization* 42:179–217.

———. 1993a. "Creating the GATT Rules: Politics, Institutions, and American Policy." In *Multilateralism Matters: The Theory and Praxis of an International Form*, ed. John Gerard Ruggie. New York: Columbia University Press.

———. 1993b. *Ideas, Institutions and American Trade Policy*. Ithaca, NY: Cornell University Press.

Goldthorpe, ed., John H. 1984. *Order and Conflict in Contemporary Capitalism: Studies in the Political Economy of Western European Nations*. Oxford, UK: Clarendon.

Gome, Amanda. 1995. "Australia: Tariff Target Splits Opinion—The BRW Dun and Bradstreet Poll." *Business Review Weekly*, January 30.

Gould, David M. 1996. "Mexico's Crisis: Looking Back to Assess the Future." In *Changing Struc-*

ture of Mexico: Political, Social, and Economic Prospects, ed. Laura Randall. Armonk, NY: M. E. Sharpe.

Gould, John. 1982. *The Rake's Progress? The New Zealand Economy Since 1945.* Auckland: Hodder and Stoughton.

Gourevitch, Peter A. 1986. *Politics in Hard Times: Comparative Responses to International Economic Crises.* Ithaca, NY: Cornell University Press.

Graham, Douglas H. 1982. "Mexican and Brazilian Economic Development: Legacies, Patterns, and Performance." In *Brazil and Mexico: Patterns in Late Development*, ed. Sylvia Ann Hewlett and Richard S. Weinert. Philadelphia: Institute for the Study of Human Issues.

Graham, Pamela. 1994. "New Zealand: NZ Unveils Next Stage of Tariff Reducing Programme." Reuter News Services—Australia and New Zealand, December 16.

Gras, Norman. 1915. *The Evolution of the English Corn Law Market.* Cambridge, MA: Harvard University Press.

Great Britain. Ministry of Agriculture, Fisheries and Food, Department of Agriculture and Fisheries for Scotland. 1968. *A Century of Agricultural Statistics: Great Britain, 1866–1966.* London: Her Majesty's Stationery Office.

Green, Duncan. 1995. *Silent Revolution: The Rise of Market Economics in Latin America.* London: Cassell.

Greville, Charles. 1885. *The Greville Memoirs: A Journal of the Reign of Queen Victoria, 1837–1852.* Vol. 2. Ed. Henry Reeve. New York: Appleton.

Griffith-Jones, Stephany. 1991. *Chile to 1991: The End of an Era.* London: Economist Intelligence Unit.

Grigg, David. 1989. *English Agriculture: An Historical Perspective.* Oxford, UK: Basil Blackwell.

Grindle, Merilee S., and John W. Thomas. 1991. *Public Choices and Policy Change: The Political Economy of Reform in Developing Countries.* Baltimore: Johns Hopkins University Press.

Grossman, Gene M., and Elhanan Helpman. 1994. "Protection for Sale." *American Economic Review* 84:833–50.

Grubel, James, Barbara Adam, and Sam Lienert. 2002. "Car Industry Wins Tariff Extension." *AAP Newsfeed*, December 13.

Gruen, F. H. 1975. "The 25% Tariff Cut: Was it a Mistake?" *Australian Quarterly* 47:7–20.

Hachette, Dominique. 1991. "Chile: Trade Liberalization Since 1974." In *Trade Reform: Lessons From Eight Countries*, ed. Geoffrey Sheperd and Carlos Geraldo Langoni. San Francisco: ICS.

Haggard, Stephan. 1988. "The Institutional Foundations of Hegemony: Explaining the Reciprocal Trade Agreements Act of 1934." In *The State and American Foreign Economic Policy*. ed. G. John Ikenberry, David A. Lake, and Michael Mastanduno. Ithaca, NY: Cornell University Press.

Hagopian, Frances. 1996. *Traditional Politics and Regime Change in Brazil.* Cambridge: Cambridge University Press.

Hakim, Peter. 2002. "Two Ways to Go Global." *Foreign Affairs* 81:148–55.

Hamilton, Alexander. 1893. "Report on Manufactures." In *State Papers and Speeches on the Tariff*, ed. Frank W. Taussig. Cambridge, MA: Harvard University Press.

Hamilton, Colleen, and John Whalley. 1985. "The GATT and Canadian Interests: Summary of the Proceedings of a Research Symposium." In *Canada and the Multilateral Trading System*, ed. John Whalley. Toronto: University of Toronto Press.

Hamilton, Nora. 1982. *The Limits of State Autonomy: Post-Revolutionary Mexico.* Princeton, NJ: Princeton University Press.

Hansen, Marcus Lee. 1961. *The Atlantic Migration, 1607–1860.* New York: Harper.

Hansen, Roger D. 1974. *The Politics of Mexican Development.* Baltimore: Johns Hopkins University Press.

Hart, Michael M. 1985. *Canadian Economic Development and the International Trading System.* Toronto: University of Toronto Press.

———. 1994. *Decision at Midnight: Inside the Canada-US Free Trade Negotiations.* Vancouver: University of British Columbia Press.

Hathaway, Oona A. 1998. "Positive Feedback: The Impact of Trade Liberalization on Industry Demands for Protection." *International Organization* 52:575–612.

Hawke, G. R. 1985. *The Making of New Zealand.* Cambridge: Cambridge University Press.

Hawley, Ellis W. 1966. *The New Deal and the Problem of Monopoly.* Princeton, NJ: Princeton University Press.

———. 1975. "The New Deal and Business." In *The New Deal: The National Level*, ed. John Braeman, Robert H. Bremner, and David Brody. Columbus: Ohio State University.

Haynes, F. E. 1892. "The Reciprocity Treaty with Canada of 1854." *Publications of the American Economic Association* 7:417–86.

Hazeldine, Tim. 1993. "New Zealand Trade Policy and Patterns." *Australian Economic Review* 104:23–27.

Heo, Uk, and Alexander C. Tan. 2001. "Democracy and Economic Growth: A Causal Analysis." *Comparative Politics* 33:463–73.

Heredia, Blanca. 1992. "Profits, Politics and Size: The Political Transformation of Mexican Business." In *The Right and Democracy in Latin America*, ed. Douglas A. Chalmers, Maria do Carmo Campello de Souza, and Atilio A. Boron. New York: Praeger.

Heuckel, G. 1981. "Agriculture During Industrialization." In *The Economic History of Britain Since 1700*, ed. Roderick Floud and Donald McCloskey. Vol. 1. Cambridge: Cambridge University Press.

Higgins, Winton. 1991. "Missing the Boat: Labor and Industry in the Eighties." In *Business and Government Under Labor*, ed. Brian Galligan and Gwyneth Singleton. Melbourne, Australia: Longman, Cheshire.

Hillman, Arye L., and Eliakim Katz. 1984. "Risk-Averse Rent Seekers and the Social Cost of Monopoly Power." *Economic Journal* 94:104–10.

Hirschman, Albert O. 1968. "The Political Economy of Import-Substituting Industrialization in Latin America." *Quarterly Journal of Economics* 82:2–32.

Hiscox, Michael. 2002. *International Trade and Political Conflict: Commerce, Coalitions and Mobility* Princeton, NJ: Princeton University Press.

Hoadley, Steve. 1995. *New Zealand and Australia: Negotiating Closer Economic Relations.* Wellington: New Zealand Institute of International Affairs.

Hody, Cynthia A. 1996. *The Politics of Trade: American Political Development and Foreign Economic Policy.* Hanover, NH: University Press of New England.

Hogg, Peter W. 1988. *Meech Lake Constitutional Accord Annotated.* Toronto: Carswell.

Hojman, David E. 1993. *Chile: The Political Economy of Development and Democracy in the 1990s.* Pittsburgh: University of Pittsburgh Press.

———. 1994. "The Political Economy of Recent Conversions to Market Economics in Latin America." *Journal of Latin American Studies* 26:191–220.

Holmes, Sir Frank. 1966. *Freer Trade with Australia*. Wellington: New Zealand Institute of Economic Research.

Hooper, Narelle. 1992. "Australia: Tariff Victory Sits Uneasily with Labor." *Business Review Weekly*, September 25.

Howe, Anthony. 1997. *Free Trade and Liberal England, 1846–1946*. Oxford, UK: Clarendon.

Huddle, Don. 1969. "Postwar Brazilian Growth Patterns, Inflation and Sources of Stagnation." In *The Shaping of Modern Brazil*, ed. Eric N. Baklanoff. Baton Rouge: Louisiana State University Press.

Hufbauer, Gary Clyde, Diane T. Berliner, and Kimberly Ann Elliott. 1986. *Trade Protection in the United States: 31 Case Studies*. Washington, DC: Institute for International Economics.

Hull, Cordell. 1948. *The Memoirs of Cordell Hull*. Vol. 1. New York: Macmillan.

Humphrey, Don D. 1955. *American Imports*. New York: Twentieth Century Fund.

Ikenberry, G. John, David A. Lake, and Michael Mastanduno. 1988. "Introduction: Approaches to Explaining American Foreign Economic Policy." *International Organization* 42:1–14.

Imlah, Albert H. 1958. *Economic Elements in the Pax Britannica: Studies in British Foreign Trade in the Nineteenth Century*. Cambridge, MA: Harvard University Press.

INDECS Economics. 1995. *State of Play 8*. St. Leonards, Australia: Allen and Unwin.

Industries Assistance Commission. 1980. *Annual Report 1979–80*. Canberra: Australian Government Publishing Service.

———. 1982. *Approaches to General Reductions in Protection*. Canberra: Australian Government Publishing Service.

Industries Commission. 1991. *Annual Report 1990–91*. Canberra: Australian Government Publishing Service.

Inglehart, Ronald. 1971. "The Silent Revolution in Europe: Intergenerational Change in Post-Industrial Societies." *American Political Science Review* 65:991–1017.

Innis, Harold A. 1962. *The Fur Trade in Canada*. New Haven, CT: Yale University Press.

Inside Canberra. 1996. "Business Anger on Tariff Scheme," February 27.

International Trade Forum. 1999. "Chile," October–December.

Irwin, Douglas A. 1993. "Free Trade and Protection in Nineteenth Century Britain and France Revisited: A Comment on Nye." *Journal of Economic History* 53:146–52.

Izquierdo, Rafael. 1964. "Protectionism in Mexico." In *Public Policy and Private Enterprise in Mexico*, ed. Raymond Vernon. Cambridge, MA: Harvard University Press.

James, Patrick. 1990. "The Canadian National Energy Program and its Aftermath." *Canadian Public Policy* 16:174–90.

James, Scott C., and David A. Lake. 1989. "The Second Face of Hegemony: Britain's Repeal of the Corn Laws and the American Walker Tariff of 1846." *International Organization* 43:1–29.

Jenkins, Barbara. 1999. "Assessing the 'New' Integration: The Mercosur Trade Agreement." In *Racing to Regionalize: Democracy, Capitalism, and Regional Political Economy*, ed. Kenneth P. Thomas and Mary Ann Tétreault. Boulder, CO: Lynne Rienner.

Johnson, Hugh S. 1935. *The Blue Eagle from Egg to Earth*. Garden City, NJ: Doubleday.

Johnston, Warren E., and Gerald A. G. Frengley. 1994. "Economic Adjustments and Changes in Financial Viability of the Farming Sector: The New Zealand Experience." *American Journal of Agricultural Economics* 76:1034–41.

Jones, E. L. 1968. *The Development of English Agriculture, 1815–1873*. London: Macmillan.

———. 1974. "The Changing Basis of English Agricultural Prosperity, 1853–73." In *Agriculture and the Industrial Revolution*, ed. E. L. Jones. Oxford, UK: Basil Blackwell.

Jones, Joseph. 1934. *Tariff Retaliation: Repercussions of the Smoot-Hawley Bill*. Philadelphia: University of Pennsylvania Press.

Kaldor, Nicholas. 1939. "Welfare Propositions of Economics and Interpersonal Comparisons of Utility." *Economic Journal* 49:549–52.

Kaltenthaler, Karl, and Frank O. Mora. 2002. "Explaining Latin American Economic Integration: The Case of Mercosur." *Review of International Political Economy* 9:72–97.

Keeler, John. 1993. "Opening the Window for Reform: Mandates, Crises, and Extraordinary Policy-Making." *Comparative Political Studies* 25:433–86.

Kelly, William B., Jr. 1963. "Antecedents of Present Commercial Policy, 1922–34." In *Studies in United States Commercial Policy*, ed. William B. Kelly, Jr. Chapel Hill: University of North Carolina Press.

Kemp, Betty. 1962. "Reflections on the Repeal of the Corn Laws." *Victorian Studies* 5:189–204.

Kerr, Roger. 1995. "High Achievers or Timid Gradualists?" Speech to the Australian Stock Exchange Annual Dinner, Melbourne, June 26. <http://speeches.com/kerr2.htm>.

Key, V. O. 1955. "A Theory of Critical Elections." *Journal of Politics* 17:3–13.

Kindleberger, Charles P. 1964. *Economic Growth in France and Britain, 1851–1950*. Cambridge, MA: Harvard University Press.

———. 1973. *The World in Depression, 1929–1939*. Berkeley: University of California Press.

———. 1996. *World Economic Primacy: 1500–1990*. New York: Oxford University Press.

King, Timothy. 1970. *Mexico: Industrialization and Trade Policies Since 1940*. London: Oxford University Press.

Kingstone, Peter R. 1999. *Crafting Coalitions for Reform: Business Preferences, Political Institutions, and Neoliberal Reform in Brazil*. University Park: Pennsylvania State University Press.

———. 2000. "Muddling Through Gridlock: Economic Policy Performance, Business Responses, and Democratic Sustainability." In *Democratic Brazil: Actors, Institutions, and Processes*, ed. Peter R. Kingstone and Timothy J. Power. Pittsburgh: University of Pittsburgh Press.

———. 2001. "Why Free Trade 'Losers' Support Free Trade: Industrialists and the Surprising Politics of Trade Reform in Brazil." *Comparative Political Studies* 34:986–1010.

Kitson Clark, G. 1951. "The Repeal of the Corn Laws and the Politics of the Forties." *Economic History Review*, second series, 4:1–13.

———. 1964. *Peel and the Conservative Party*. London: Frank Cass.

Klesner, Joseph L. 1993. "Modernization, Economic Crisis, and Electoral Alignment in Mexico." *Mexican Studies* 9:187–223.

Kline, John M. 1992. *Foreign Investment Strategies in Restructuring Economies: Learning From Corporate Experiences in Chile*. Westport, CT: Quorum Books.

Krasner, Stephen. 1984. "Approaches to the State." *Comparative Politics* 16:223–46.

Krueger, Anne O. 1974. "The Political Economy of the Rent-Seeking Society." *American Economic Review* 64:291–303.

———. 1994. "Comment." In *The Chilean Economy: Policy Lessons and Challenges*, ed. Barry P. Bosworth, Rudiger Dornbusch, and Raúl Labán. Washington, DC: The Brookings Institution.

Kuczynski, Pedro-Pablo. 1988. *Latin American Debt*. Baltimore: Johns Hopkins University Press.

Lake, David A. 1988a. *Power, Protection and Free Trade: International Sources of U.S. Commercial Strategy, 1887–1939*. Ithaca, NY: Cornell University Press.

———. 1988b. "The State and American Trade Strategy in the Pre-Hegemonic Era." *International Organization* 42:33–58.

Lamounier, Bolívar. 1989. "*Authoritarian Brazil* Revisited: The Impact of Elections on the *Abertura*." In *Democratizing Brazil: Problems of Transition and Consolidation*, ed. Alfred Stepan. New York: Oxford University Press.

———. 1996. "Brazil: The Hyperactive Paralysis Syndrome." In *Constructing Democratic Governance: Latin America and the Caribbean in the 1990s*, ed. Jorge I. Domínguez and Abraham F. Lowenthal. Baltimore: Johns Hopkins University Press.

Landsberger, Henry, and Tim McDaniel. 1976. "Hypermobilization in Chile, 1970–1973." *World Politics* 28:502–41.

Langille, David. 1987. "The Business Council on National Issues and the Canadian State." *Studies in Political Economy* 24:41–85.

Larkin, John Day. 1940. *Trade Agreements: A Study in Democratic Methods*. New York: Columbia University Press.

Lattimore, Ralph. 1987. "Economic Adjustment in New Zealand: A Developed Country Case Study of Policies and Problems." In *Economic Adjustment: Policies and Problems*, ed. Sir Frank Holmes. Washington, DC: International Monetary Fund.

Lattimore, Ralph, and Paul Wooding. 1996. "International Trade." In *A Study of Economic Reform: The Case of New Zealand*, ed. Brian Silverstone, Alan Bollard, and Ralph Lattimore. Amsterdam: Elsevier.

Lavergne, Real. 1983. *The Political Economy of U.S. Tariffs: An Empirical Analysis*. Toronto: Academic Press.

Laxer, Gordon. 1989. *Open for Business: The Roots of Foreign Ownership in Canada*. Toronto: Oxford University Press.

Leddy, John M., and Janet L. Norwood. 1962. "The Escape Clause and Peril Points Under the Trade Agreements Program." In *Studies in United States Commercial Policy*, ed. William B. Kelly, Jr. Chapel Hill: University of North Carolina Press.

Lehman, Howard P. 1993. "Strategic Bargaining in Brazil's Debt Negotiations." *Political Science Quarterly* 108:133–55.

Leigh, Andrew. 2002. "Trade Liberalisation and the Australian Labor Party." *Australian Journal of Politics and History* 48: 487–509.

Letiche, J. M. 1948. *Reciprocal Trade Agreements in the World Economy*. Morningside Heights, NY: King's Crown.

Levitsky, Melvyn. 1998. "The New Brazil: A Viable Partner for the United States." *SAIS Review* 18:51–71.

Levy, Jack. 1989. "The Diversionary Theory of War: A Critique." In *The Handbook of War Studies*, ed. Manus Midlarsky. Boston: Unwin Hyman.

Lewis, Charles, and Margaret Ebrahim. 1993. "Can Mexico and Big Business USA Buy NAFTA?" *The Nation*, June 14.

Lindblom, Charles. 1977. *Politics and Markets: The World's Political-Economic Systems*. New York: Basic Books.

Lipset, Seymour Martin. 1959. "Some Social Requisites of Democracy: Economic Development and Political Legitimacy." *American Political Science Review* 53:69–105.

Lloyd, P. J. 1973. *Non-Tariff Distortions of Australian Trade*. Canberra: Australian National University Press.

Lougheed, Peter. 1988. "The Rape of the National Energy Program Will Never Happen Again." In *Free Trade, Free Canada*, ed. Earle Grey. Woodville, ON: Canadian Speeches.

Love, Joseph L. 1980. "Raúl Prebisch and the Origins of the Doctrine of Unequal Exchange." *Latin American Research Review* 15:45–72.

Loveman, Brian. 1976. "The Transformation of the Chilean Countryside." In *Chile: Politics and Society*, ed. Arturo Valenzuela and J. Samuel Valenzuela. New Brunswick, NJ: Transaction Books.

Lower, A. R. M. 1933. "The Trade in Square Timber." *Contributions to Canadian Economics* 6:40–61.

Luna, Matilde. 1995. "Entrepreneurial Interests and Political Action in Mexico: Facing the Demands of Economic Modernization." In *The Challenge of Institutional Reform in Mexico*, ed. Riordan Roett. Boulder, CO: Lynne Rienner.

Luna, Matilde, Ricardo Tirado, and Francisco Valdes. 1987. "Businessmen and Politics in Mexico, 1982–86." In *Government and Private Sector in Contemporary Mexico*, ed. Sylvia Maxfield and Ricardo Anzaldua M. San Diego: Center for U.S.-Mexican Studies.

Lustig, Nora. 1992. *Mexico: The Remaking of an Economy*. Washington, DC: The Brookings Institution.

Lusztig, Michael. 1994. "Constitutional Paralysis: Why Canadian Constitutional Initiatives Are Doomed to Fail." *Canadian Journal of Political Science* 27:747–71.

———. 1995. "Solving Peel's Puzzle: Repeal of the Corn Laws and Institutional Preservation." *Comparative Politics* 27:393–408.

———. 1996. *Risking Free Trade: The Politics of Trade in Britain, Canada, Mexico and the United States*. Pittsburgh: University of Pittsburgh Press.

———. 1998. "The Limits of Rent-Seeking: Why Protectionists Become Free Traders." *Review of International Political Economy* 5:38–63.

Lusztig, Michael, Patrick James, and HeeMin Kim. 2003. "Signaling and Tariff Policy: The Strategic Multi-Stage Rent Reduction Game." *Canadian Journal of Political Science* 36:765–89.

Maitra, Priyatosh. 1997. "The Globalisation of Capitalism and Economic Transition in New Zealand." In *The Political Economy of New Zealand*, ed. Chris Rudd and Brian Roper. Auckland: Oxford University Press.

Malmesbury, Lord. 1884. *Memoirs of an Ex-Minister*. Vol.1. London: Longman, Green.

Mamalakis, Markos J. 1976. *The Growth and Structure of the Chilean Economy: From Independence to Allende*. New Haven, CT: Yale University Press.

Manufacturer: The Newsletter of the New Zealand Manufacturers Association. 1981. July 27.

———. 1982a. February 10.

———. 1982b. February 24.

———. 1982c. March 24.

———. 1982d. July 14.

Manzetti, Luigi. 1990. "Argentine-Brazilian Economic Integration." *Latin American Research Review* 25:109–40.

Markwald, Ricardo, and João Bosco Machado. 1999. "Establishing an Industrial Policy for Mercosur." In *MERCOSUR: Regional Integration, World Markets*. ed. Riordan Roett. Boulder, CO: Lynne Rienner.

Marshallsea, Trevor. 1998. "WTO Takes Australia to Task Over Trade Practices." *AAP Newsfeed*, July 3.

Martínez-Lara, Javier. 1996. *Building Democracy in Brazil: The Politics of Constitutional Change, 1985–95*. New York: St. Martin's.

Masi, Fernando. 2001. "MERCOSUR: The Difficult Path Toward Integration." *North-South Center Update* 45. http://www.miami.edu/nsc/pages/newsupdates/Update45.html.

Matthew, Bob. 1997. "Retreat from Reform: Are Australia and New Zealand Becoming Laggards Again?" *Australian Financial Review*, April 29.

May, Trevor. 1987. *An Economic History of Great Britain, 1760–1970*. New York: Longman.

McCord, Norman. 1968. *The Anti-Corn Law League, 1838–1846*. 2nd ed. London: Unwin.

McDiarmid, O. J. 1946. *Commercial Policy in the Canadian Economy*. Cambridge, MA: Harvard University Press.

McInnis, Edgar. 1947. *Canada: A Political and Social History*. New York: Rinehart.

Meller, Patricio. 1997. "An Overview of Chilean Trade Strategy," in *Integrating the Hemisphere: Perspectives from Latin America and the Caribbean*, ed. Ana Julia Jatar and Sidney Weintraub. Washington, DC: Inter-American Dialogue.

Mena, Luis Felipe Bravo. 1987. "COPARMEX and Mexican Politics." In *Government and Private Sector in Contemporary Mexico*, ed. Sylvia Maxfield and Ricardo Anzaldua M. San Diego: Center for U.S.-Mexican Studies.

Mexican Investment Board. 1994. *Mexico Investment Update*, 1st quarter. New York: Mexican Investment Board.

Mexico. Secretariat of Commerce and Industrial Development. 1993. *Mexique-Canada: Une Nouvelle Ere de Relations*. Ottawa: Mexican Embassy.

Michalopoulos, Constantine. 1999. "Trade Policy and Market Access Issues for Developing Countries." *World Bank PRWP* 2214, October.

Mierau, Barbara H. 1987. "The Impact of Trade Policies on Productivity Performance in the Chilean Manufacturing Sector, 1960–1981." PhD dissertation, Georgetown University.

Milner, Helen V. 1988. *Resisting Protectionism: Global Industries and the Politics of International Trade*. Princeton, NJ: Princeton University Press.

———. 1993. "Trading Places: Industries for Free Trade." In *International Trade Policies: Gains from Exchange between Economic and Political Science*, ed. John S. Odell and Thomas D. Willet. Ann Arbor: University of Michigan Press.

———. 1997. *Interests, Institutions, and Information: Domestic Politics and International Relations*. Princeton, NJ: Princeton University Press.

Mingay, G. E., ed. 1977. *Documents in Economic History: The Agricultural Revolution: Changes in Agriculture, 1650–1880*. London: Adam and Charles Black.

Moley, Raymond. 1966. *The First New Deal*. New York: Harcourt Brace and World.

Montero, Alfred P. 2000. "Devolving Democracy? Political Decentralization and the New Brazilian Federalism." In *Democratic Brazil: Actors, Institutions, and Processes*, ed. Peter R. Kingstone and Timothy J. Power. Pittsburgh: University of Pittsburgh Press.

Moore, Barrington. 1967. *Social Origins of Dictatorship and Democracy: Lord and Peasant in the Making of the Modern World*. Boston: Beacon.

Moore, D. C. 1965. "The Corn Laws and High Farming." *Economic History Review*, second series, 18:544–61.

Moore, Hon. John. 1996. Shadow Minister for Industry, Commerce and Public Administration. "Federal Liberal/National Coalition Industry and Commerce Policy," February. http://www.liberal.org.au/POLICY/INDUSTRY/industry.htm.

More, Charles. 1989. *The Industrial Age: Economy and Society in Britain, 1750–1985*. London: Longman.

Morici, Peter. 1993. "Grasping the Benefits of NAFTA." *Current History* 92:49–55.

Morley, John. 1905. *The Life of Richard Cobden*. Vol. 1. London: T. Fisher Unwin.

———. 1909. *The Life of William Ewart Gladstone*. Vol. 1. New York: Macmillan.

Morris, Stephen D. 1992. "Political Reformism in Mexico: Salinas at the Brink." *Journal of Interamerican Studies and World Affairs* 34:27–57.

Morton, W. L. 1963. *The Kingdom of Canada: A General History from Earliest Times*. Indianapolis: Bobbs-Merrill.

Mosk, Sanford A. 1950. *Industrial Revolution in Mexico*. Berkeley: University of California Press.

Mulroney, Brian. 1980. Speech to the Annual Conference of the Canadian Institute of Chartered Accountants, Montreal, September 25.

———. 1984. Speech at Sept Iles, Quebec, August 6.

Murphy, Brian. 1973. *A History of the British Economy, 1086–1970*. London: Longman.

Murtha, Thomas P., Stefanie Ann Lenway, and Jeffrey A. Hart. 2001. *Managing New Industry Creation: Global Knowledge Formation and Entrepreneurship in High Technology*. Stanford, CA: Stanford University Press.

Musson, A. E. 1972. "The 'Manchester School' and Exportation of Machinery." *Business History* 14:17–50.

National Business Review. 1990. "New Zealand: Industry to Fight Further Tariff Cuts," February 23.

Needler, Martin. 1993. "Economic Policy and Political Survival." *Mexican Studies* 9:139–43.

Nelson, Joan M. 1989. "Overview: The Politics of Long-Haul Economic Reform." In *Fragile Coalitions: The Politics of Economic Adjustment*, ed. Joan M. Nelson. New Brunswick, NJ: Transaction Books.

Newell G., Roberto, and Luis Rubio F. 1984. *Mexico's Dilemma: The Political Origins of the Economic Crisis*. Boulder, CO: Westview.

Newman, Peter C. 1998. *Titans: How the New Canadian Establishment Seized Power*. Toronto: Viking.

New York Times. 1952. "NAM Hears Plea for Wise Guidance in Free Enterprise," December 4.

New Zealand. Ministry of Commerce. 1994. *Review of Post-1996 Tariff Policy*. Wellington: Ministry of Commerce.

New Zealand Herald. 1990a. "New Zealand: Days of Subsidies Gone, Palmer Says," March 1.

———. 1990b. "New Zealand: Plastics Firms Imperilled by Tariff Reductions," April 27.

Nicholson, J. S. 1904. *The History of the English Corn Laws*. London: Swan Sonnenschein.

Nieuwenhuysen, John. 1989. "Towards Freer Trade for Australia." In *Towards Freer Trade Between Nations*, ed. John Nieuwenhuysen. Melbourne: Oxford University Press.

Nixon, Edgar B., ed. 1969. *Franklin D. Roosevelt and Foreign Affairs*. Vols. 2 and 3. Cambridge, MA: Belknap.

Noble, C. E., and R. W. Nettle. 1972. *Case Studies in Australian Economic Policy*. Melbourne: Cheshire Publishing.

Nofal, María Beatriz. 1995. "The Economic Integration of Argentina and Brazil, MERCOSUR, and the Regionalization of the Southern Cone Market." In *NAFTA and Trade Liberalization in the Americas*, ed. Elsie Echeverri-Carroll. Austin: Bureau of Business Research, University of Texas at Austin.

Norrie, Kenneth H. 1988. "Energy, Canadian Federalism and the West." In *Canadian Federalism: From Crisis to Constitution*, ed. Harold Waller, Filippo Sabetti, and Daniel J. Elazar. Lanham, MD: University Press of America.

Nutt, Rodney. 1992. "Totally Free Trade Across Tasman Sea Boon to N.Z." *Vancouver Sun*, July 24.

Ó Gráda, Cormac. 1994. "British Agriculture, 1860–1914." In *The Economic History of Britain Since 1700*, ed. Roderick Floud and Donald McCloskey. Vol. 2, 2nd ed. Cambridge: Cambridge University Press.

O'Brien, Robert. 1995. "North American Integration and International Relations Theory." *Canadian Journal of Political Science* 28:693–725.

O'Donnell, Guillermo A. 1978. "Reflections on the Pattern of Change in the Bureaucratic-Authoritarian State." *Latin American Research Review* 13:3–38.

Offe, Claus. 1984. *Contradictions of the Welfare State*. ed. John Keane. Cambridge, MA: MIT Press.

O'Halloran, Sharyn. 1994. *Politics, Process, and American Tariff Policy*. Ann Arbor: University of Michigan Press.

Olson, Mancur. 1965. *The Logic of Collective Action: Public Goods and the Theory of Groups*. Cambridge, MA: Harvard University Press.

———. 1982. *The Rise and Decline of Nations: Economic Growth, Stagflation, and Social Rigidities*. New Haven, CT: Yale University Press.

Olson, Mancur, Jr., and Curtis C. Harris, Jr. 1959. "Free Trade in 'Corn': A Statistical Study of the Prices and Production of Wheat in Great Britain from 1873 to 1914." *Quarterly Journal of Economics* 73:145–68.

Organisation for Economic Co-operation and Development. 1984. *Main Economic Indicators: Historical Statistics, 1964–1983*. Paris: OECD.

———. 1996. *Industrial Structure Statistics*. Paris: OECD.

———. 1997. *Industrial Structure Statistics*. Paris: OECD.

———. 1998. *New Zealand*. Paris: OECD.

Ortiz, M. H., and Yvonne Stinson. 2000. "Mexican Trade Policy." *America's Insights*, June.

Orwin, Christabel S., and Edith H. Whetham. 1964. *History of British Agriculture, 1846–1914*. London: Longmans.

Pagan, Adrian. 1987. "The End of the Long Boom." In *The Australian Economy in the Long Run*, ed. Rodney Maddock and Ian W. McLean. Cambridge: Cambridge University Press.

Pastor, Manuel, Jr., and Carol Wise. 1994. "The Origins and Sustainability of Mexico's Free Trade Policy." *International Organization* 48:459–89.

Pastor, Robert A. 1980. *Congress and the Politics of US Foreign Economic Policy, 1929–1976*. Berkeley: University of California Press.

———. 1990. "Post-Revolutionary Mexico: The Salinas Opening." *Journal of Interamerican Studies and World Affairs* 32:1–22.

Payne, Leigh A. 1995. "Brazilian Business and the Democratic Transition: New Attitudes and Influence." In *Business and Democracy in Latin America*, ed. Ernest Bartell and Leigh A. Payne. Pittsburgh: University of Pittsburgh Press.

Peel, Sir Robert. 1843. *The Opinions of Sir Robert Peel*. ed. W. T. Haley. London: Whittaker.

———. 1853. *Speeches of the Late Right Honourable Sir Robert Peel, Bart*. Vol. 4. London: George Routledge.

———. 1857. *Memoirs*. Vols. 1 and 2. Ed. Lord Mahon and Edward Cardwell. London: John Murray.

———. 1970. *From His Private Papers*. Vol. 2. Ed. Charles Stuart Parker. New York: Kraus.

Peltzman, Sam. 1976. "Toward a More General Theory of Regulation." *Journal of Law and Economics* 15:211–40.

Perren, Richard. 1973. "The Landlord and Agricultural Transformation." In *British Agriculture, 1875–1914*, ed. P. J. Perry. London: Methuen.

———. 1995. *Agriculture in Depression, 1870–1940*. Cambridge: Cambridge University Press.

Pew Research Center for the People and the Press. 1997. *America's Place in the World II*. Washington, DC: Pew Research Center.

Pierson, Paul. 1996. "The New Politics of the Welfare State." *World Politics* 48:143–79.

Pincus, Jonathan J. 1977. *Pressure Groups and Politics in Antebellum Tariffs*. New York: Columbia University Press.

Piore, Michael J., and Charles F. Sabel. 1984. *The Second Industrial Divide: Possibilities for Prosperity*. New York: Basic Books.

Poitras, Guy, and Raymond Robinson. 1994. "The Politics of NAFTA in Mexico." *Journal of Interamerican Studies and World Affairs* 36:1–35.

Porritt, Edward. 1908. *Sixty Years of Protection in Canada, 1846–1907*. London: Macmillan.

Porter, Ian. 1996. "Australia: Tariff Program May be Moving Too Fast." *ABIX: Australasian Business Intelligence*, June 17.

Prentice, Archibald. 1853. *History of the Anti-Corn Law League*. London: W. & F. G. Cash.

Prothero (Lord Ernle), Rowland E. 1912. *English Farming, Past and Present*. London: Longmans, Green.

Pugel, Thomas A., and Ingo Walter. 1985. "U.S. Corporate Interests and the Political Economy of Trade Policy." *Review of Economics and Statistics* 67:465–74.

Purcell, John F. H., and Susan Kaufman Purcell. 1977. "Mexican Business and Public Policy." In *Authoritarianism and Corporatism in Latin America*, ed. James M. Malloy. Pittsburgh: University of Pittsburgh Press.

Purcell, Susan Kaufman, and John F. H. Purcell. 1980. "State and Society in Mexico: Must a Stable Polity be Institutionalized?" *World Politics* 32:194–227.

Pusey, Philip. 1842. "On the Progress of Agricultural Knowledge During the Last Four Years." *Journal of the Royal Agricultural Society of England* 3:169–217.

Putnam, 1988. "Diplomacy and Domestic Politics: The Logic of Two-Level Games." *International Organization* 42:427–60.

———. Robert D. 2000. *Bowling Alone: The Collapse and Revival of American Community*. New York: Simon and Schuster.

Ramirez, Miguel D. 1993. "Stabilization and Trade Reform in Mexico: 1983–1989." *Journal of Developing Areas* 27:173–90.

Ramirez de la O, Rogelio. 1991. "A Mexican Vision of North American Economic Integration." In *Continental Accord: North American Economic Integration*, ed. Steven Globerman. Vancouver, BC: Fraser Institute.

Rattigan, Alf. 1986. *Industry Assistance: The Inside Story*. Melbourne: Melbourne University Press.

Ravenhill, John. 1994. "Australia and the Global Economy." In *State, Economy and Public Policy in Australia*, ed. Stephen Bell and Brian Head. Melbourne: Oxford University Press.

———. 1996. "Trade Policy Options Beyond APEC." *Australian Quarterly* 68:1–15.

Rayner, Anthony C., and Ralph Lattimore. 1991. "New Zealand." In *Liberalizing Foreign Trade*, ed. Demetris Papageorgiou, Michael Michaely, and Armeane M. Choksi. Vol. 6. Oxford, UK: Basil Blackwell.

Read, Donald. 1987. *Peel and the Victorians*. Oxford, UK: Basil Blackwell.

Reforma. 1997. "CANACINTRA Accuses Sugar Producers of Damaging Industrial Development in Mexico," September 1.

Reguly, Eric. 1993. "Canada Admits Farm Board Defeat." *Financial Post*, December 14.

Reisman, Simon S. 1984. "The Issue of Free Trade." In *US-Canada Economic Relations: Next Steps?* ed. Edward R. Fried and Philip H. Tresize. Washington, DC: The Brookings Institution.

Reuters News Service—Australia and New Zealand. 1990a. "New Zealand: NZ Govt to Announce More Tariff Reforms—Caygill," February 27.

———. 1990b. "New Zealand: NZ Govt to Cut Import Tariffs to 10 Pct by 1996," March 20.

———. 1996a. "New Zealand: NZ Manfed Urges No Compromise on Key Economic Policies," October 12.

———. 1996b. "New Zealand: NZ's Birch Slams Alliance Tariffs Plan," October 7.

REWBN Australian Business News. 1997. "PM Howard Warned Tariff Protection Won't Save Jobs," July 1.

Reynolds, Clark W. 1970. *The Mexican Economy: Twentieth Century Structure and Growth*. New Haven, CT: Yale University Press.

———. 1993. "Power, Value, and Distribution in the NAFTA." In *Political and Economic Liberalization in Mexico: At a Critical Juncture?* ed. Riordan Roett. Boulder, CO: Lynne Reinner.

Rhodes, Carolyn. 1993. *Reciprocity, US Trade Policy, and the GATT Regime*. Ithaca, NY: Cornell University Press.

Ricardo, David. 1960. *The Principles of Political Economy and Taxation*. New York: E. P. Dutton.

Richardson, Jack R. 1992. "Free Trade: Why Did it Happen?" *Canadian Review of Sociology and Anthropology* 29:307–28.

Ritchie, Gordon. 1997. *Wrestling with the Elephant: The Inside Story of the Canada-US Trade Wars*. Toronto: Macfarlane, Walter and Ross.

Rocher, François. 1991. "Canadian Business, Free Trade and the Rhetoric of Economic Continentalization." *Studies in Political Economy* 35:135–54.

Roddick, Jackie. 1988. *The Dance of the Millions: Latin America and the Debt Crisis*. London: Latin America Bureau.

Rodrik, Dani. 1992. "The Rush to Free Trade in the Developing World: Why So Late? Why Now? Will it Last?" National Bureau of Economic Research, Working Paper No. 3947.

———. 1996. "Understanding Economic Policy Reform." *Journal of Economic Literature* 34:9–41.

Roett, Riordan. 1984. *Brazil: Politics in a Patrimonial Society*. 3rd ed. New York: Praeger.

———. 1993. "At the Crossroads: Liberalization in Mexico." In *Political and Economic Liberalization in Mexico: At a Critical Juncture?* ed. Riordan Roett. Boulder, CO: Lynne Reinner.

———, ed. 1999. *MERCOSUR: Regional Integration, World Markets*. Boulder, CO: Lynne Reinner.

Rogowski, Ronald. 1989. *Commerce and Coalitions: How Trade Affects Domestic Political Alignments*. Princeton, NJ: Princeton University Press.

Romanow, Roy, John Whyte, and Howard Leeson. 1984. *Canada Notwithstanding: The Making of the Constitution, 1976–1982*. Toronto: Carswell.

Roosevelt, Franklin D. 1967. *Roosevelt and Frankfurter: Their Correspondence, 1928–1945*. ed. Max Freeman. Boston: Little, Brown.

Roper, Brian. 1990. "The Dynamics of Capitalism in Crisis." PhD dissertation, Griffiths University.

———. 1992. "Business Political Activism and the Emergence of the New Right in New Zealand, 1975 to 1987." *Political Science* 44:1–23.

———. 1993. "A Level Playing Field? Business Political Activism and State Policy Formation." In *State and Economy in New Zealand*, ed. Brian Roper and Chris Rudd. Auckland: Oxford University Press.

Rowley, Charles K., and Robert D. Tollison. 1988. "Rent-Seeking and Trade Protection." In *The Political Economy of Rent-Seeking*, ed. Charles K. Rowley, Robert D. Tollison, and Gordon Tullock. Boston: Kluwer Academic.

Rubio, Luis. 1993. "Economic Reform and Political Change in Mexico." In *Political and Economic Liberalization in Mexico: At a Critical Juncture?* ed. Riordan Roett. Boulder, CO: Lynne Reinner.

———. 1998. "Coping with Political Change." In *Mexico Under Zedillo*, ed. Sarah Kaufman Purcell and Luis Rubio. Boulder, CO: Lynne Reinner.

Rudolph, Frederick. 1950. "The American Liberty League, 1934–1940." *American History Review* 56:19–33.

Russell, Sir E. John. 1966. *A History of Agricultural Science in Great Britain, 1620–1954*. London: George Allen and Unwin, 1966.

Russell, Lord John. 1925. *The Later Correspondence of Lord John Russell, 1840–1878*. Vol. 1. ed. G. P. Gooch. London: Longmans, Green.

Russell, Peter H. 1993. *Constitutional Odyssey: Can Canadians Become a Sovereign People?* 2nd ed. Toronto: University of Toronto Press.

Russell, Philip L. 1994. *Mexico Under Salinas*. Austin, TX: Mexico Resource Center.

Sachs, Jeffrey, and Álvaro Zini, Jr. 1996. "Brazilian Inflation and the *Plano Real*." *World Economy* 19:13–38.

Saez, Raul, and Ricardo Ffrench-Davis. 1996. "Trade and Industrial Development in Chile." In *Trade and Industrialization Policies in Mexico and Chile*, Working Paper 208, ed. Montague J. Lord. Washington, DC: Inter-American Development Bank.

Salembier, G. E., Andrew R. Moroz, and Frank Stone. 1987. *The Canadian Import File: Trade, Protection and Adjustment*. Montreal: The Institute for Research on Public Policy.

Salinas de Gortari, Carlos. 1982. *Political Participation, Public Investment, and Support for the System: A Comparative Study of Rural Communities in Mexico*. La Jolla: Center for U.S.-Mexican Studies, University of California, San Diego.

———. 1991. "A New Hope for the Hemisphere?" *New Perspective Quarterly* 8:7–8.

Sampson, Anthony. 1982. *The Money Lenders: Bankers and a World in Turmoil*. New York: Viking.

Sandholtz, Wayne. 1993. "Choosing Union: Monetary Politics and Maastricht." *International Organization* 47:1–39.

Sandrey, Ron A., and Grant M. Scobie. 1994. "Changing International Competitiveness and Trade: Recent Experience in New Zealand Agriculture." *American Journal of Agricultural Economics* 76:1041–46.

Saturday Review. 1954. "Free Trade," January 23.

Savage, John, and Alan Bollard. 1990. "Rationalization in New Zealand: An Overview." In *Turning it Around: Closure and Revitalization in New Zealand Industry*, ed. John Savage, Alan Bollard, Douglas Greer, Timothy Hazeldine, and Richard Miller. Auckland: Oxford University Press.

Sayre, Francis. 1939. *The Way Forward: The American Trade Agreements Program*. New York: Macmillan.

Schacht, Senator Chris. 1995. Minister for Small Business, Customs and Construction.

"Changes to the Tariff Concession System and Policy By-Laws." http://www.dist.gov.au/events/innovate/r29.html, accessed December 6, 1995.

Schattschneider, E. E. 1935. *Politics, Pressures and the Tariff: A Study of Private Enterprise in Pressure Politics, as Shown in the 1929–1930 Revision of the Tariff.* New York: Prentice-Hall.

Schelling, Thomas.1960. *The Strategy of Conflict.* New York: Oxford University Press.

Schiller, Wendy J. 2000. "Has Free Trade Won the War in Congress or is the Battle Still Raging? A Study of the Influences of Industry Coalition Building on Congressional Trade Politics." *NAFTA: Business and Law Review of the Americas* 6:363–88.

Schlesinger, Jr., Arthur M. 1958. *The Coming of the New Deal.* Boston: Houghton Mifflin.

Schmitter, Philippe C. 1973. "The 'Portugalization' of Brazil?" In *Authoritarian Brazil*, ed. Alfred Stepan. New Haven, CT: Yale University Press.

Schneider, Ben Ross. 1991. "Brazil Under Collor: Anatomy of a Crisis." *World Policy Journal* 8:321–47.

———. 2001. "Business Politics and Regional Integration: The Advantages of Organization in NAFTA and MERCOSUR." In *Regional Integration in Latin America and the Caribbean*, ed. Victor Bulmer-Thomas. London: Institute of Latin American Studies.

———. 2002. "Why Is Mexican Business so Organized?" *Latin American Research Review* 37:77–120.

Schnietz, Karen E. 2003. "The Reaction of Private Interests to the 1934 Reciprocal Trade Agreements Act." *International Organization* 57:213–33.

Schonhardt-Bailey, Cheryl. 1991. "Specific Factors, Capital Markets, Portfolio Diversification, and Free Trade: Domestic Determinants of Repeal of the Corn Laws." *World Politics* 43:545–69.

Schumpeter, Joseph A. 1950. *Capitalism, Socialism and Democracy.* 3rd ed. New York: Harper.

Schwartz, Herman. 1994. "Small States in Big Trouble: State Reorganization in Australia, Denmark, New Zealand and Sweden in the 1980s." *World Politics* 46:527–55.

Scitovszky, T. 1941. "A Note on Welfare Propositions in Economics." *Review of Economic Studies* 8:77–88.

Selcher, Wayne A. 1986. "Contradictions, Dilemmas, and Actors in Brazil's *Abertura*, 1979–1985." In *Political Liberalization in Brazil: Dynamics, Dilemmas, and Future Prospects*, ed. Wayne A. Selcher. Boulder, CO: Westview.

Seneviratne, Kalinga. 1997. "Reversal on Car Tariffs Dents Free Trade Policy." *Inter Press Service*, June 18.

Silva, Eduardo. 1996. "From Dictatorship to Democracy: The Business-State Nexus in Chile's Economic Transformation, 1975–1994." *Comparative Politics* 28:299–320.

———. 1997. "Business Elites, the State and Economic Change in Chile." In *Business and the State in Developing Countries*, ed. Sylvia Maxfield and Ben Ross Schneider. Ithaca, NY: Cornell University Press.

Simeon, Richard. 1990. "Why Did the Meech Lake Accord Fail?" In *Canada: State of the Federation 1990*, ed. Ronald L. Watts and Douglas M. Brown. Kingston: Queen's University Institute of Intergovernmental Relations.

Skelton, Oscar D. 1916. *The Day of Sir Wilfrid Laurier.* Toronto: Glasgow, Brook.

Skidmore, Thomas. 1973. "Politics and Economic Policy Making in Authoritarian Brazil, 1937–71." In *Authoritarian Brazil*, ed. Alfred Stepan. New Haven, CT: Yale University Press.

Skocpol, Theda. 1980. "Political Response to Capitalist Crisis: Neo-Marxist Theories of the State and the Case of the New Deal." *Politics and Society* 10:155–201.

Skocpol, Theda, and Kenneth Finegold. 1990. "Explaining New Deal Labor Policy." *American Political Science Review* 84:1297–304.

Skowronek, Stephen. 1982. *Building a New American State: The Expansion of National Administrative Capacities, 1877–1920*. Cambridge: Cambridge University Press.

Sloan, Judith. 1994. "New Zealand: Kiwi Economic Reform Going Like a Bomb." *Australian Financial Review*, September 22.

Smith, Daniel Bennett. 1990. *Toward Internationalism*. New York: Garland.

Smith, Geri. 2001. "Betting on Free Trade." *Business Week*, April 23.

Smith, Peter H. 1992. "The Political Impact of Free Trade on Mexico." *Journal of Interamerican Studies and World Affairs* 3:1–25.

Snape, R. H. 1994. "Australia's Relations with GATT." *Economic Record* 60:23–26.

Soares de Lima, Maria Regina. 1999. "Brazil's Alternative Vision." In *The Americas in Transition: The Contours of Regionalism*, ed. Gordan Mace and Louis Bélanger. Boulder, CO: Lynne Reinner.

Soto, Raimundo. 1995. "Trade Liberalization in Chile: Lessons for Hemispheric Integration." In *NAFTA and Trade Liberalization in the Americas*, ed. Elsie Echeverri-Carroll. Austin: University of Texas Bureau of Business Research.

Spence, Michael. 1973. "Job Market Signalling." *Quarterly Journal of Economics* 87:355–74.

Spencer, Stephen. 1998. "Australian Government Assistance for Industry Cut to Five Year Low." *AAP Newsfeed*, November 4.

Staiger, Robert W. 1995. "A Theory of Gradual Trade Liberalization." In *New Directions in Trade Theory*, ed. Jim Levinsohn, Alan V. Deardorf, and Robert M. Stern. Ann Arbor: University of Michigan Press.

Stanwood, Edward. 1903. *American Tariff Controversies in the Nineteenth Century*. Vols. 1 and 2. Boston: Houghton Mifflin.

Stein, Arthur. 1984. "The Hegemon's Dilemma: Great Britain, the United States, and the International Economic Order." *International Organization* 38:355–86.

Stern, C. A. 1971. *Protectionist Republicanism: Republican Tariff Policy in the McKinley Period*. Ann Arbor, MI: Edwards Brothers.

Stevens, Evelyn P. 1977. "Mexico's PRI: The Institutionalization of Corporatism." In *Authoritarianism and Corporatism*, ed. James M. Molloy. Pittsburgh: University of Pittsburgh Press.

Stewart, Randall G. 1990. "Industrial Policy." In *Hawke and Australian Public Policy*, ed. Christine Jennett and Randall G. Stewart. South Melbourne: Macmillan.

———. 1994. "Federal Government and Australian Business." In *Government and Business Relations in Australia*, ed. Randall G. Stewart. St. Leonard's: Allen and Unwin.

Stewart, Robert. 1971. *The Politics of Protection: Lord Derby and the Protectionist Party, 1841–1852*. Cambridge: Cambridge University Press.

Stigler, George J. 1971. "The Theory of Economic Regulation." *Bell Journal of Economics and Management Science* 2:3–21.

Stone, Frank. 1984. *Canada, the GATT and the International Trade System*. Montreal: The Institute for Research on Public Policy.

Story, Dale. 1982. "Trade Politics in the Third World: A Case Study of the Mexican GATT Decision." *International Organization* 36:767–94.

———. 1986. *Industry, the State, and Public Policy in Mexico*. Austin: University of Texas Press.

Stratton, J. M. 1969. *Agricultural Records, A.D. 220–1968*. Ed. Ralph Whitlock. New York: Augustus M. Kelley.

Sturgess, R. W. 1966. "The Agricultural Revolution on the English Clays." *Agricultural History Review* 14:104–21.

Stutchbury, Michael. 1992a. "Australia: Factory Sector Starts to Pay Own Way." *Australian Financial Review*, September 25.

———. 1992b. "Australia: Keating's Sleight-of-Hand on Protectionism." *Australian Financial Review*, April 1.

Swinton, Katherine E., and Carol J. Rogerson, eds. 1988. *Competing Constitutional Visions: The Meech Lake Accord*. Toronto: Carswell.

Tariff Board. 1968. *Annual Report 1967–68*. Canberra: Australian Government Publishing Service.

———. 1970. *Annual Report 1969–70*. Canberra: Australian Government Publishing Service.

Tasca, Henry J. 1938. "The Reciprocal Trade Policy of the United States." PhD dissertation, University of Pennsylvania.

Taussig, Frank. 1923. *The Tariff History of the United States*, 7th ed. New York: G. P. Putnam and Sons.

Ten Kate, Adriaan. 1992. "Trade Liberalization and Economic Stabilization in Mexico: Lessons of Experience." *World Development* 20:659–72.

Ten Kate, Adriaan, and Robert Bruce Wallace. 1980. *Protection and Economic Development in Mexico*. New York: St. Martin's.

Terrill, Tom E. 1973. *The Tariff, Politics, and American Foreign Policy 1874–1901*. Westport, CT: Greenwood.

Thacker, Strom C. 1998. "Big Business, the State, and Free Trade in Mexico: Interests, Structure and Political Access." Paper presented at the annual meeting of the Latin American Studies Association, Chicago, IL.

Thakur, Ramesh, and Hyam Gold. 1983. "The Politics of a New Economic Relationship: Negotiating Free Trade Between Australia and New Zealand." *Australian Outlook* 37:82–87.

Thompson, F. M. L. 1981. "Free Trade and the Land." In *The Victorian Countryside*, vol. 1, ed. G. E. Mingay. London: Routledge.

Thornton, G. G. 1982. *New Zealand's Industrial Heritage*. Wellington: Reed.

Tirado, Ricardo. 1998. "Mexico: From the Political Call for Collective Action to a Proposal for Free Market Economic Reform." In *Organized Business, Economic Change, and Democracy in Latin America*, ed. Francisco Durand and Eduardo Silva. Miami, FL: University of Miami North-South Center Press.

Trevelyan, George Macaulay. 1913. *The Life of John Bright*. London: Constable.

Truell, Peter. 1990. "U.S. and Mexico Agree to Seek Free Trade Pact." *Wall Street Journal*, March 27.

Trumbull, M. M. 1892. *The Free Trade Struggle in England*, 2nd ed. Chicago: Open Court.

Tullock, Gordon. 1967. "Welfare Costs of Tariffs, Monopolies and Theft." *Western Economic Journal* 5:224–32.

———. 1988. "Future Directions for Rent-Seeking Research." In *The Political Economy of Rent-Seeking*, ed. Charles K. Rowley, Robert D. Tollison, and Gordon Tullock. Boston: Kluwer Academic.

Turner, Barry. 1971. *Free Trade and Protection*. London: Longman.

Tweedie, Mrs. Alec (Ethel Brilliana). 1917. *Mexico from Díaz to the Kaiser*. London: Hutchinson.

Tyler, William G. 1976. *Manufactured Export Expansion and Industrialization in Brazil*. Tübingen, Germany: J. C. B. Mohr.

United Nations. Department of Economic and Social Affairs. 1995. *Yearbook of International Trade Statistics.* New York: United Nations.

U.S. Bureau of the Census. 1975. *Historical Statistics of the United States, Colonial Times to 1970, Part 2.* Washington, DC: U.S. Bureau of the Census.

U.S. Congress. House. Committee on Ways and Means. 1934a. *Hearings, on H.R. 8430, Reciprocal Trade Agreements.* Washington, DC: Government Printing Office.

———. 1937a. *Hearings, on H.J. Res. 96, Extension of Reciprocal Trade Agreements Act.* Washington, DC: Government Printing Office.

———. 1940a. *Hearings, on H.J. Res. 407, Extension of Reciprocal Trade Agreements Act.* Washington, DC: Government Printing Office.

———. 1943a. *Hearings, on H.J. Res. 111, Extension of Reciprocal Trade Agreements Act.* Washington, DC: Government Printing Office.

U.S. Congress. Senate. Committee on Finance. 1934b. *Hearings, on H.R. 8687, Reciprocal Trade Agreements.* Washington, DC: Government Printing Office.

———. 1937b. *Hearings, on H.J. Res. 96, Extension of Reciprocal Trade Agreements Act.* Washington, DC: Government Printing Office.

———. 1940b. *Hearings, on H.J. Res. 407, Extension of Reciprocal Trade Agreements Act.* Washington, DC: Government Printing Office.

———. 1943b. *Extension of Reciprocal Trade Agreements Act.* Washington, DC: Government Printing Office.

U.S. Tariff Commission. 1919. *Reciprocity and Commercial Treaties.* Washington, DC: Government Printing Office.

———. 1948. *Operation of the Trade Agreements Program, June 1934 to April 1948.* Vol. 1. Washington, DC: Government Printing Office.

———. 1955. *Trade Agreements Manual.* Washington, DC: Government Printing Office.

Unwin, Mrs. Cobden, ed. 1904. *The Hungry Forties: Life Under the Bread Tax, Descriptive Letters and Other Testimonies From Contemporary Witnesses.* London: T. Fisher Unwin.

Uslaner, Eric M. 1992. "Political Parties, Ideas, Interests, and Free Trade in the United States." Paper presented at the Conference on Party and Trade: Political Perspective on External Trade, Washington, DC.

———. 1994. "Political Parties and Free Trade in the United States." In *The NAFTA Puzzle: Political Parties and Trade in North America,* ed. Charles F. Doran and Gregory P. Marchildon. Boulder, CO: Westview.

Valdés, Juan Gabriel. 1985. *Pinochet's Economists: The Chicago School in Chile.* Cambridge: Cambridge University Press.

Valenzuela, Arturo. 1978. "Chile." In *The Breakdown of Democratic Regimes,* ed. Juan J. Linz and Alfred Stepan. Baltimore: Johns Hopkins University Press.

Valenzuela, J. Samuel, and Arturo Valenzuela. 1978. "Modernization and Dependency: Alternative Perspectives in the Study of Latin American Underdevelopment." *Comparative Politics* 10:535–57.

Vamplew, Wray. 1980. "The Protection of English Cereal Producers: The Corn Laws Reassessed." *Economic History Review,* second series, 33:382–95.

Van Deusen, Glyndon G. 1959. *The Jacksonian Era, 1828–1848.* New York: Harper Brothers.

Van Vugt, William E. 1988. "Running from Ruin? The Emigration of British Farmers to the U.S.A. in the Wake of the Repeal of the Corn Laws." *Economic History Review,* second series, 41:411–28.

Vega-Canovas, Gustavo. 1994. "The Free Trade Policy 'Revolution' and Party Politics in Mexico." In *The NAFTA Puzzle: Political Parties and Trade in North America*, ed. Charles F. Doran and Gregory P. Marchildon. Boulder, CO: Westview.

Velasco, Andrés. 1994. "The State and Economic Policy: Chile 1952–1992." In *The Chilean Economy: Policy Lessons and Challenges*, ed. Barry P. Bosworth, Rudiger Dornbusch, and Raúl Labán. Washington, DC: The Brookings Institution.

Verdier, Daniel. 1994. *Democracy and International Trade: Britain, France, and the United States, 1860–1990.* Princeton, NJ: Princeton University Press.

Vernon, Raymond. 1963. *The Dilemma of Mexico's Development: The Roles of Private and Public Sectors.* Cambridge, MA: Harvard University Press.

Wagner, R. Harrison. 1989. "Uncertainty, Rational Learning, and Bargaining in the Cuban Missile Crisis." In *Models of Strategic Choice in Politics*, ed. Peter C. Ordeshook. Ann Arbor: University of Michigan Press.

Waite, P. B. 1962. *The Life and Times of Confederation: Politics, Newspapers and the Union of British North America.* Toronto: University of Toronto Press.

Wallace, Henry A. 1944. *Democracy Reborn.* ed. Russell Lord. New York: Reynal and Hitchcock.

Wallerstein, Immanuel. 1974. *The Modern World System.* New York: Academic Press.

Warhurst, John. 1982. *Jobs or Dogma? The IAC and Australian Politics.* St. Lucia: University of Queensland Press.

Watson, Richard A. 1956. "The Tariff Revolution: A Study of Shifting Party Attitudes." *Journal of Politics* 18:678–701.

Watson, William G. 1987. "Canada-U.S. Free Trade: Why Now?" *Canadian Public Policy* 13:337–49.

Weintraub, Sidney. 1988. *Mexican Trade Policy and the North American Community.* Washington, DC: Center for Strategic and International Studies.

———. 1993. "The Economy on the Eve of Free Trade." *Current History* 92:67–72.

———. 2000. *Development and Democracy in the Southern Cone: Imperatives for U.S. Policy in South America.* Washington, DC: Center for Strategic and International Studies.

Weintraub, Sidney, and M. Delal Baer. 1992. "The Interplay Between Economic and Political Opening: The Sequence in Mexico." *Washington Quarterly* 15:187–201.

Wellington, Raynor G. 1914. *The Political and Sectional Influence of the Public Lands, 1828–42.* Cambridge, MA: Riverside.

Werneck, Rogério L. F. 2001. "Brazil's Rough Passage." *America's Insight*, November.

Weyland, Kurt. 1996. *Democracy Without Equity: Failures of Reform in Brazil.* Pittsburgh: University of Pittsburgh Press.

———. 1997. "The Brazilian State in the New Democracy." *Journal of Interamerican Studies and World Affairs* 39:63–95.

Wheatley, Jonathan. 2001. "The MERCOSUR Marriage is in Trouble." *Business Week*, January 29.

White, Randall. 1989. *Fur Trade to Free Trade: Putting the Canada-US Free Trade Agreement in Historical Perspective.* 2nd ed. Toronto: Dundurn.

Whitlam, Gough. 1973. Speech to the annual dinner of the New South Wales Chamber of Manufacturers, August 30.

Wilkie, James W., and Albert L. Michaels, eds. 1969. *Revolution in Mexico: Years of Upheaval, 1910–1940.* New York: Alfred A. Knopf.

Williams, Glen. 1994. *Not for Export*, 3rd ed. Toronto: McClelland and Stewart.

Williamson, Jeffrey G. 1990. "The Impact of the Corn Laws Just Prior to Repeal." *Explorations in Economic History* 27:123–56.

Williamson, John. 1994a. "In Search of a Manual for Technopols." In *The Political Economy of Policy Reform*, ed. John Williamson. Washington, DC: Institute for International Economics.

———, ed. 1994b. *The Political Economy of Policy Reform*. Washington, DC: Institute for International Economics

Wilson, Bruce M. 1994. "When Social Democrats Choose Neoliberal Economic Policies: The Case of Costa Rica." *Comparative Politics* 26:149–68.

Wilson, Joan Hoff. 1971. *American Business and Foreign Policy 1920–1933*. Lexington: University Press of Kentucky.

Winham, Gilbert R. 1986. *International Trade and the Tokyo Round Negotiations*. Princeton, NJ: Princeton University Press.

———. 1988. *Trading With Canada: The Canada-US Free Trade Agreement*. New York: Priority.

Wolfskill, George. 1962. *The Revolt of the Conservatives: A History of the American Liberty League, 1934–1940*. Boston: Houghton Mifflin.

Wonnacott, Paul, and Ronald J. Wonnacott. 1967. *Free Trade Between the U.S. and Canada*. Cambridge, MA: Harvard University Press.

Wooding, Paul. 1987. "Liberalizing the International Trade Regime." In *Economic Liberalization in New Zealand*, ed. Alan Bollard and Robert Buckles. Wellington: Allen and Unwin.

Wordie, J. R. 2000. "Perceptions and Reality: The Effects of the Corn Laws and Their Repeal in England, 1815–1906." In *Agriculture and Politics in England, 1815–1939*, ed. J. R. Wordie. London: Macmillan.

World Bank. 2001. *World Bank Development Indicators*. CD-ROM. Washington, DC: World Bank.

World Bank. (n.d.) "Brazil at a Glance."
http://www.worldbank.org/data/countrydata/aag/bra_aag.pdf.

Wright, Gerald. 1985. "Bureaucratic Politics and Canada's Foreign Economic Policy." In *Selected Problems in Formulating Foreign Economic Policy*, ed. Denis Stairs and Gilbert R. Winham. Toronto: University of Toronto Press.

Wyman, Donald L. 1983. "The Mexican Economy: Problems and Prospects." In *Mexico's Economic Crisis: Challenges and Opportunities*, ed. Donald L. Wyman. La Jolla: Center for U.S.-Mexican Studies, University of California, San Diego.

Yoffie, David B. 1985. "American Trade Policy: An Obsolete Bargain?" In *Can the Government Govern?* ed. John E. Chubb and Paul E. Peterson. Washington, DC: Brookings Institution.

Zedillo Ponce de León, Ernesto. 1985. "The Mexican External Debt: The Last Decade." In *Politics and Economics of External Debt Crisis: The Latin American Experience*, ed. Miguel S. Wionczek and Luciano Tomassini. Boulder, CO: Westview.

Index